TEACHER'S EDITION

F

Spelling Workout

Phillip K. Trocki

Modern Curriculum Press
is an imprint of

SAVVAS
LEARNING COMPANY

COVER DESIGN: Pronk & Associates

ILLUSTRATIONS: Eric Larsen. 187: Jim Steck.

PHOTOGRAPHS: Cover: *l.* Maxim Petrichuk/Fotolia, *r.* Artbase Inc.
5: © BlooD2oo1/Fotolia.com. 8: © Jaak/Fotolia.com. 9: © Tomislav/Fotolia.com. 12: © Vladimir Popovic/Fotolia.com. 13: © Ryan Dunfee/Fotolia.com. 15: © hotshotsworldwide/Fotolia.com. 16: © Getty Images. 17: © Susan Stevenson/Fotolia.com. 20: © mkm3/Fotolia.com. 21: © gwimages/Fotolia.com. 24: © Comstock. 29: © Dmitry Knorre/Fotolia.com. 32: © Tyler Boyes/Fotolia.com. 33: NASA Ames Research Center. 36: © Madera/Fotolia.com. 37: © AbsentAnna/Fotolia.com. 40: © Maxim Petrichuk/Fotolia.com. 41: © Dreef/Fotolia.com. 44: © Monkey Business/Fotolia.com. 45: © Medioimages/PhotoDisc, Inc. 48: © ussatlantis/Fotolia.com. 53: © siloto/Fotolia.com. 56: © Dmytro Tkachuk/Fotolia.com. 57: © Anyka/Fotolia.com. 60: © Elenathewise/Fotolia.com. 61: © Wimbledon/Fotolia.com. 64: © Kurt De Bruyn/Fotolia.com. 65: Lindsley, H. B./Library of Congress Prints and Photographs Division Washington, D.C./LC-USZ62-7816. 68: © PhotoDisc, Inc. 69: © Ryan McVay/PhotoDisc, Inc. 72: Library of Congress Prints and Photographs Division. 77: © willtu/Fotolia.com. 80: © Arnie/Fotolia.com. 81: © Getty Images/Photos.com. 85: © blindfire/Fotolia.com. 88: © Thomas Perkins/Fotolia.com. 89: © Kenton/Fotolia.com. 92: © fuxart/Fotolia.com. 93: *t.* © Rob/Fotolia.com. *b.* © Andy Crawford/Dorling Kindersley. 96: © Rob/Fotolia.com. 101: © Darcy Finley/Fotolia.com. 104: © Thinkstock. 105: © Dorling Kindersley Ltd., Courtesy of St. Bride Printing. 108: © Igor Dutina/Fotolia.com. 112: © Hunta/Fotolia.com. 113: © Maria Teijeiro/Digital Vision. 117: © Thinkstock. 120: © Comstock. 125: Library Of Congress Prints and Photographs Division. 128: *t.* © Stockbyte. *b.* © klikk/Fotolia.com. 129: © Getty Images. 132: © Holger Mette/Fotolia.com. 133: © Getty Images. 136: © Jacek Chabraszewski/Fotolia.com. 137: © Getty Images/Hemera Technologies. 140: © JaM/Fotolia.com. 141: © Sean Prior/Fotolia.com.

Acknowledgments

ZB Font Method Copyright © 1996 Zaner-Bloser.

Some content in this product is based upon WEBSTER'S NEW WORLD DICTIONARY, 4/E. Copyright ©2013 by Houghton Mifflin Harcourt Publishing Company. Reprinted by permission of Houghton Mifflin Harcourt Publishing Company. All rights reserved.

The Tournament of Roses is a registered trademark of Pasadena Tournament of Roses Association, Inc. Use of this trademark implies no relationship, sponsorship, endorsement, sale, or promotion on the part of Modern Curriculum Press.

Modern Curriculum Press
is an imprint of

SAVVAS
LEARNING COMPANY

ISBN-13: 978-0-7652-2493-4
ISBN-10:   0-7652-2493-3
34 21

Table of Contents

5

6

Spelling Workout—Our Philosophy

Integration of Spelling with Reading and Writing

In each core lesson for *Spelling Workout*, students read spelling words in context in a variety of fiction and nonfiction selections. The reading selections provide opportunities for reading across the curriculum, focusing on the subject areas of science, social studies, health, language arts, music, and art.

After students read the selection and practice writing their spelling words, they use list words to help them write about a related topic in a variety of forms such as descriptive paragraphs, stories, news articles, poems, letters, advertisements, and posters. A proofreading exercise is also provided for each lesson to help students apply the writing process to their own writing and reinforce the use of spelling words in context.

The study of spelling should not be limited to a specific time in the school day. Use opportunities throughout the day to reinforce and maintain spelling skills by integrating spelling with other curriculum areas. Point out spelling words in books, texts, and the student's own writing. Encourage students to write, as they practice spelling through writing. Provide opportunities for writing with a purpose.

Phonics-Based Instructional Design

Spelling Workout takes a solid phonic and structural analysis approach to encoding. The close tie between spelling and phonics allows each to reinforce the other. *Spelling Workout* correlates closely to *MCP Phonics*, although both programs are complete within themselves and can be used independently.

Research-Based Teaching Strategies

Spelling Workout utilizes a test-study-test method of teaching spelling. The student first takes a pretest of words that have not yet been introduced. Under the direction of the teacher, the student then self-corrects the test, rewriting correctly any word that has been missed. This approach not only provides an opportunity to determine how many words a student can already spell but also allows students to analyze spelling mistakes. In the process students also discover patterns that make it easier to spell list words. Students study the words as they work through practice exercises, and then reassess their spelling by taking a final test.

High-Utility List Words

The words used in *Spelling Workout* have been chosen for their frequency in students' written and oral vocabularies, their relationships to subject areas, and for structural as well as phonetic generalizations. Each list word has been cross-referenced with one or more of the following:

Carroll, Davies, and Richman. *The American Heritage Word Frequency Book*

Dale and O'Rourke. *The Living Word Vocabulary*

Dolch. *220 Basic Sight Words*

Fry, Polk, and Fountoukidis. *Spelling Demons—197 Words Frequently Misspelled by Elementary Students*

Green and Loomer. *The New Iowa Spelling Scale*

Hanna. *Phoneme Grapheme Correspondences as Cues to Spelling Improvement*

Harris and Jacobson. *Basic Elementary Reading Vocabularies*

Hillerich. *A Written Vocabulary of Elementary Children*

Kucera and Francis. *Computational Analysis of Present-Day American English*

Rinsland. *A Basic Vocabulary of Elementary Children*

Sakiey and Fry. *3000 Instant Words*

Thomas. *3000 Words Most Frequently Written*

Thomas. *200 Words Most Frequently Misspelled*

A Format That Results in Success

Spelling Workout treats spelling as a developmental process. Students progress in stages, much as they learn to speak and read. In *Spelling Workout*, they move gradually from simple sound/letter relationships to strategies involving more complex word-structure patterns.

Sample Core Lesson

- **Spelling Words in Action** presents an engaging and informative reading selection in each lesson that illustrates the spelling words in context.

- The activity in the box at the end of the reading selection helps students focus on the spelling patterns of the list words presented in the lesson.

- The **Tip** explains the spelling patterns, providing a focus for the lesson.

- The **List Words** box contains the spelling words for each lesson.

- **Spelling Practice** exercises give students an opportunity to practice new words while reinforcing the spelling patterns.

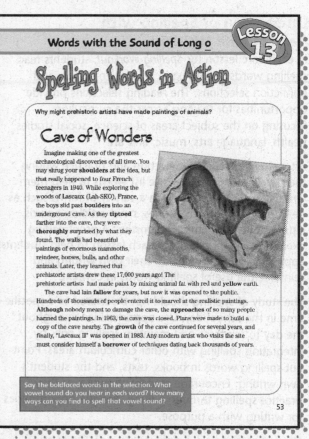

Words with the Sound of Long o — Lesson 13

Spelling Words in Action

Why might prehistoric artists have made paintings of animals?

Cave of Wonders

Imagine making one of the greatest archaeological discoveries of all time. You may shrug your **shoulders** at the idea, but that really happened to four French teenagers in 1940. While exploring the woods of Lascaux (Lah-SKO), France, the boys slid past **boulders** into an underground cave. As they **tiptoed** farther into the cave, they were **thoroughly** surprised by what they found. The walls had beautiful paintings of enormous mammoths, reindeer, horses, bulls, and other animals. Later, they learned that prehistoric artists drew these 17,000 years ago! The prehistoric artists had made paint by mixing animal fat with red and **yellow** earth.

The cave had lain **fallow** for years, but now it was opened to the public. Hundreds of thousands of people entered it to marvel at the realistic paintings. **Although** nobody meant to damage the cave, the **approaches** of so many people harmed the paintings. In 1963, the cave was closed. Plans were made to build a copy of the cave nearby. The **growth** of the cave continued for several years, and finally, "Lascaux II" was opened in 1983. Any modern artist who visits the site must consider himself a **borrower** of techniques dating back thousands of years.

Say the boldfaced words in the selection. What vowel sound do you hear in each word? How many ways can you find to spell that vowel sound?

53

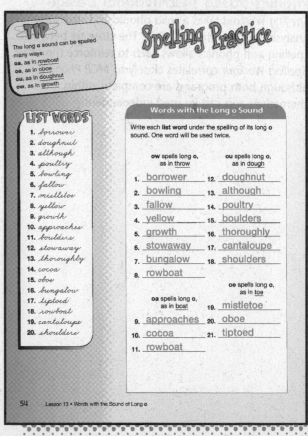

Spelling Practice

TIP
The long o sound can be spelled many ways:
oa, as in rowboat
oe, as in oboe
ou, as in doughnut
ow, as in growth

LIST WORDS

1. borrower
2. doughnut
3. although
4. poultry
5. bowling
6. fallow
7. mistletoe
8. yellow
9. growth
10. approaches
11. boulders
12. stowaway
13. thoroughly
14. cocoa
15. oboe
16. bungalow
17. tiptoed
18. rowboat
19. cantaloupe
20. shoulders

Words with the Long o Sound

Write each **list** word under the spelling of its long o sound. One word will be used twice.

ow spells long o, as in throw
1. borrower
2. bowling
3. fallow
4. yellow
5. growth
6. stowaway
7. bungalow
8. rowboat

ou spells long o, as in dough
12. doughnut
13. although
14. poultry
15. boulders
16. thoroughly
17. cantaloupe
18. shoulders

oa spells long o, as in boat
9. approaches
10. cocoa
11. rowboat

oe spells long o, as in toe
19. mistletoe
20. oboe
21. tiptoed

54   Lesson 13 • Words with the Sound of Long o

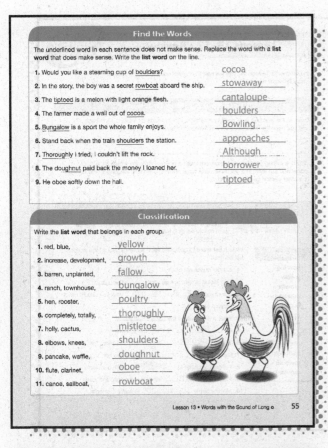

Find the Words

The underlined word in each sentence does not make sense. Replace the word with a **list word** that does make sense. Write the **list word** on the line.

1. Would you like a steaming cup of <u>boulders</u>? ____cocoa____

2. In the story, the boy was a secret <u>rowboat</u> aboard the ship. ____stowaway____

3. The <u>tiptoed</u> is a melon with light orange flesh. ____cantaloupe____

4. The farmer made a wall out of <u>cocoa</u>. ____boulders____

5. <u>Bungalow</u> is a sport the whole family enjoys. ____Bowling____

6. Stand back when the train <u>shoulders</u> the station. ____approaches____

7. <u>Thoroughly</u> I tried, I couldn't lift the rock. ____Although____

8. The doughnut paid back the money I loaned her. ____borrower____

9. He oboe softly down the hall. ____tiptoed____

Classification

Write the **list word** that belongs in each group.

1. red, blue, ____yellow____
2. increase, development, ____growth____
3. barren, unplanted, ____fallow____
4. ranch, townhouse, ____bungalow____
5. hen, rooster, ____poultry____
6. completely, totally, ____thoroughly____
7. holly, cactus, ____mistletoe____
8. elbows, knees, ____shoulders____
9. pancake, waffle, ____doughnut____
10. flute, clarinet, ____oboe____
11. canoe, sailboat, ____rowboat____

Lesson 13 • Words with the Sound of Long o   55

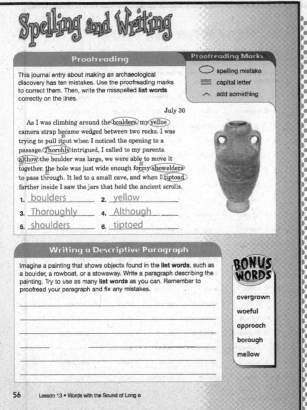

Spelling and Writing

Proofreading

This journal entry about making an archaeological discovery has ten mistakes. Use the proofreading marks to correct them. Then, write the misspelled **list words** correctly on the lines.

Proofreading Marks

◯ spelling mistake
≡ capital letter
∧ add something

July 30

As I was climbing around the boulders, my yelloe camera strap became wedged between two rocks. I was trying to pull it out when I noticed the opening to a passage. Thorohly intrigued, I called to my parents. althow the boulder was large, we were able to move it together. the hole was just wide enough for my showelders to pass through. It led to a small cave, and when I tiptoad farther inside I saw the jars that held the ancient scrolls.

1. ____boulders____   2. ____yellow____
3. ____Thoroughly____   4. ____Although____
5. ____shoulders____   6. ____tiptoed____

Writing a Descriptive Paragraph

Imagine a painting that shows objects found in the **list words**, such as a boulder, a rowboat, or a stowaway. Write a paragraph describing the painting. Try to use as many **list words** as you can. Remember to proofread your paragraph and fix any mistakes.

_____
_____
_____
_____
_____

BONUS WORDS

overgrown
woeful
approach
borough
mellow

56   Lesson 13 • Words with the Sound of Long o

• Word meaning activities provide opportunities to practice list words while helping students develop their vocabularies.

• Activities such as crossword puzzles, riddles, and games help motivate students by making learning fun.

• **Spelling and Writing** reinforces the connection between spelling and everyday writing, and encourages students to apply the list words in different contexts.

• **Proofreading** practice builds proofreading proficiency and encourages students to check their own writing.

• **Writing** activities provide opportunities for students to write their spelling words in a variety of writing forms and genres. Write-on lines are provided. Students also may wish to use a separate piece of paper.

• **Bonus Words** offer more challenging words with similar spelling patterns. Activities in the Teacher's Edition give students the opportunity to practice the words with a partner.

Sample Review Lesson

- The **Review** lesson allows students to practice what they've learned.

- The spelling patterns used in the previous five lessons are reviewed at the beginning of the lesson.

- **Check Your Spelling Notebook** suggests that students evaluate words they are having trouble with by reviewing the words they've written in their spelling notebooks. A partner activity provides practice for those words in a variety of learning modalities—kinesthetic, visual, and auditory.

- A variety of activities provide practice and review of selected list words from the previous lessons.

- **Show What You Know** is a cumulative review of the words in the five previous lessons using a standardized-test format.

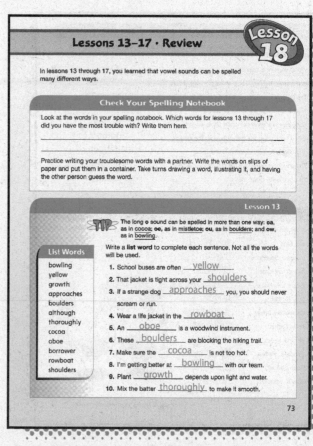

Spelling Workout in the Classroom

Classroom Management

Spelling Workout is designed as a flexible instructional program. The following plans are two ways the program can be taught.

The 5-day Plan
Day 1 – Spelling Words in Action and Warm-Up Test
Days 2 and 3 – Spelling Practice
Day 4 – Spelling and Writing
Day 5 – Final Test

The 3-day Plan
Day 1 – Spelling Words in Action and Warm-Up Test/Spelling Practice
Day 2 – Spelling Practice/Spelling and Writing
Day 3 – Final Test

Testing

Testing is accomplished in several ways. A **Warm-Up Test** is administered after reading the **Spelling Words in Action** selection and a **Final Test** is given at the end of each lesson. Dictation sentences for each **Warm-Up Test** and **Final Test** are provided.

Research suggests that students benefit from correcting their own pretests. After the **Warm-Up Test** has been administered, have students self-correct their tests by checking the words against the list words. You may also want to guide students by reading each letter of the word, asking students to point to each letter and circle any incorrect letters. Then, have students rewrite each word correctly.

Tests for review lessons are provided in the *Teacher's Edition* as reproducibles following each lesson. These tests provide not only an evaluation tool for teachers, but also added practice in taking standardized tests for students.

Individualizing Instruction

Bonus Words are included in every core lesson as a challenge for better spellers and to provide extension and enrichment for all students.

Review lessons reinforce correct spelling of difficult words from previous lessons.

Spelling Notebook allows each student to analyze spelling errors and practice writing troublesome words independently. Notebook pages appear as reproducibles in the *Teacher's Edition* and as pages at the back of the student book.

A reproducible individual **Student Record Chart** provided in the *Teacher's Edition* allows students to record their test scores.

Ideas for meeting the needs of ESL students are provided.

Dictionary

In the back of each student book is a comprehensive dictionary with definitions of all list words and bonus words. Students will have this resource at their fingertips for any assignment.

The Teacher's Edition —Everything You Need!

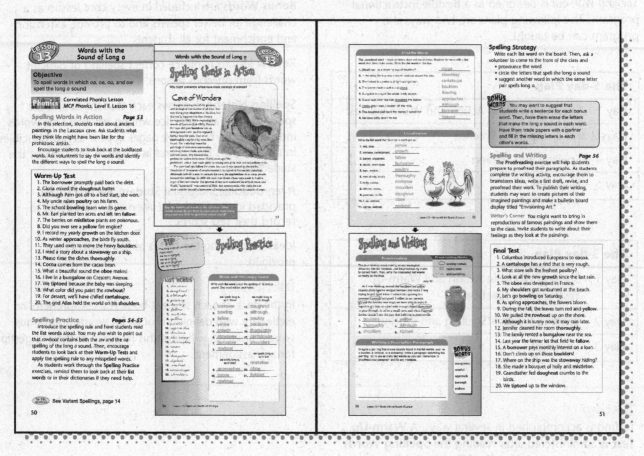

- The **Objective** clearly states the goals of each core lesson.

- Spelling lessons are correlated to *MCP Phonics*.

- Ideas for introducing and setting a purpose for reading are given for each reading selection.

- A **Warm-Up Test**, or pretest, is administered before the start of each lesson. Dictation sentences are provided.

- Concise teaching notes give guidance for working through the lesson.

- Ideas for meeting the needs of ESL students are highlighted.

- **Spelling Strategy** activities provide additional support for reinforcing and analyzing spelling patterns.

- Activities for using the **Bonus Words** listed in the student books are provided.

- **Spelling and Writing** includes suggestions for helping students use proofreading marks to correct their work. Suggestions for using the writing process to complete the writing activity are also offered.

- **Writer's Corner** extends the content of each reading selection by suggesting ways in which students can explore real-world writing.

- A **Final Test** is administered at the end of the lesson. Dictation sentences are provided.

Review Test (Side A)

Lesson 18

Read each sentence and set of words. Fill in the circle next to the word that is spelled correctly to complete the sentence.

1. This applicant is seeking _____ in the engineering department.
   - ⓐ emploiment
   - ⓒ employement
   - ⓑ employmint
   - ⓓ employment

2. Autumn foliage is an _____ sight in Vermont.
   - ⓐ ausome
   - ⓒ awsome
   - ⓑ awesome
   - ⓓ auesoma

3. The _____ of modern skyscrapers is amazing.
   - ⓐ hight
   - ⓒ height
   - ⓑ haight
   - ⓓ helt

4. Hot _____ is a popular beverage in the wintertime.
   - ⓐ coacoe
   - ⓒ cocoa
   - ⓑ cocoe
   - ⓓ coaco

5. A damp cellar provides favorable conditions for _____ growth.
   - ⓐ mildew
   - ⓒ mildue
   - ⓑ milldew
   - ⓓ milldue

6. Athletes must train _____ to participate in the Olympics.
   - ⓐ fiersely
   - ⓒ fircely
   - ⓑ fiercely
   - ⓓ feircely

7. When the basement for our house was excavated, huge _____ were uncovered.
   - ⓐ boalders
   - ⓒ bolders
   - ⓑ boulders
   - ⓓ boleders

8. The bride wore a beautiful white _____.
   - ⓐ veil
   - ⓒ vaile
   - ⓑ vayl
   - ⓓ viel

62　Lesson 18 • Review　　© Pearson Education, I...

Take It Home 3

Your child has learned to spell many new words and would like to share them with you and your family. Here are some ideas that will make reviewing the words in lessons 13–17 fun for everyone.

Secrets of Spelling
Every day this week, try to guess the secret spelling word that your child has chosen and is using in conversations. After you guess each word, don't keep its spelling to yourself—spell it aloud together!

Lesson 13
1. although
2. approaches
3. borrower
4. boulders
5. bowling
6. bungalow
7. cantaloupe
8. cocoa
9. doughnut
10. fallow
11. growth
12. mistletoe
13. oboe
14. poultry
15. rowboat
16. shoulders
17. stowaway
18. thoroughly
19. tiptoed
20. yellow

Lesson 14
1. ancient
2. briefly
3. conceit
4. diesel
5. fiercely
6. height
7. mischief
8. neighborly
9. perceived
10. pierced
11. protein
12. reindeer
13. relieved
14. retrieve
15. seized
16. sleigh
17. unbelievable
18. veil
19. weird
20. yields

Lesson 15
1. applause
2. astronauts
3. authentic
4. automatically
5. autumn
6. awesome
7. awning
8. brawny
9. dinosaur
10. drawback
11. exhausted
12. launched
13. laundry
14. paused
15. precautions
16. saucepan
17. squawking
18. taught
19. thesaurus
20. withdrawal

Lesson 16
1. biscuit
2. bruised
3. building
4. circuit
5. cruise
6. curfew
7. fruitful
8. gloomy
9. guilty
10. guitar
11. juicy
12. mildew
13. nuisance
14. pewter
15. pursued
16. quilted
17. shampoo
18. smoother
19. soothing
20. suitable

Lesson 17
1. acquaintance
2. maintenance

64　Take It Home Master • Lessons 13–17　　© Pearson Educatio...

Spelling Enrichment

Bulletin Board Suggestion
Overcome the Hurdles Make large frame-like race barriers out of colored poster board and display them on a bulletin board. On separate strips of tagboard, write commonly misspelled words such as "receive" or "beautiful." Arrange these words on the bulletin board. Change the words periodically with other words students are finding difficult to spell. These words could come from other subject areas, such as science and social studies.

Encourage students to work with partners to test each other on these challenging spelling words. Extra credit might be given for these words when they are included at the end of regular tests.

Group Practice
Fill-In Write spelling words on the board. Omit some of the letters and replace them with dashes. Have the first student in Row One come to the board to fill in one of the missing letters in any of the words. Then, have the first student in Row Two continue the procedure. Continue having students in each row take turns coming up to the board to fill in letters until all the words are completed. Any student who is able to correctly fill in a word earns a point for his or her row. The row with the most points at the end of the game wins.

Erase Write list words on the board. Then, ask the class to put their heads down while you call on a student to come to the board and erase one of the words. This student then calls on a class member to identify the erased word. The identified word is then restored and the student who correctly identified the erasure can be the person who erases next.

Crossword Relay First draw a large grid on the board. Then, divide the class into several teams. Teams compete against each other to form separate crossword puzzles on the board. Individuals on each team take turns racing against members of the other teams to join list words until all possibilities have been exhausted. A list word may appear on each crossword puzzle only once. The winning team is the team whose crossword puzzle contains the greatest number of correctly spelled list words or the team who finishes first.

Scramble Prepare letter cards sufficient to spell all the list words. Distribute letter cards to all students. Some students may be given more than one letter card. The

teacher then calls out a list word. Students holding the letters contained in the word race to the front of the class to form the word by standing in the appropriate sequence with their letter cards.

Proofreading Relay Write two columns of misspelled list words on the board. Although the errors can differ, be sure that each list has the same number of errors. Divide the class into two teams and assign each team to a different column. Teams then compete against each other to correct their assigned lists by team members taking turns erasing and replacing an appropriate letter. Each member may correct only one letter per turn. The team that corrects its entire word list first wins.

Detective Call on a student to be a detective. The detective must choose a spelling word from the list and think of a structural clue, definition, or synonym that will help classmates identify it. The detective then states the clue using the format, "I spy a word that..." Students are called on to guess and spell the mystery word. Whoever answers correctly gets to take a turn being the detective.

Spelling Tic-Tac-Toe Draw a tic-tac-toe square on the board. Divide the class into X and O teams. Take turns dictating spelling words to members of each team. If the word is spelled correctly, allow the team member to place an X or O on the square. The first team to place three X's or O's in a row wins.

Words of Fortune Have students put their heads down while you write a spelling word on the board in large letters. Then, cover each letter with a sheet of sturdy paper. The paper can be fastened to the board with magnets. Call on a student to guess any letter of the alphabet they think may be hidden. If that particular letter is hidden, then reveal the letter in every place where it appears in the word by removing the paper.

The student continues to guess letters until an incorrect guess is made or the word is revealed. In the event that an incorrect guess is made, a different student continues the game. Continue the game until every list word has been hidden and then revealed.

Dictionary Activities
Around the World Designate the first person in the first row to be the traveler. The traveler must stand next to the student seated behind him or her. Then, dictate any letter of the alphabet at random. Instruct the two

158

• **Review** lessons review spelling objectives, give guidance for further practice of list words, and provide dictation sentences for a **Final Test**. Reproducible two-page standardized tests to help prepare students for test-taking are supplied for assessment purposes after each **Review** lesson.

• Reproducible **Take It Home Masters** that also follow each **Review** lesson strengthen the school–home connection by providing ideas for parents and students for additional practice at home. In addition, they provide the complete set of spelling words for that group of lessons.

• Suggested games and group activities make spelling more fun.

Meeting the Needs of Your ESL Students

Spelling Strategies for Your ESL Students

You may want to try some of these suggestions to help you promote successful language learning for ESL students.

- Prompt use of spelling words by showing pictures or objects that relate to the topic of each selection. Invite students to discuss the picture or object.

- Demonstrate actions or act out words. Encourage students to do the same.

- Read each selection aloud before asking students to read it independently.

- Define words in context and allow students to offer their own meanings of words.

- Make the meanings of words concrete by naming objects or pictures, role-playing, or pantomiming.

Spelling is the relationship between sounds and letters. Learning to spell words in English is an interesting challenge for English First Language speakers as well as English as a Second Language speakers. You may want to adapt some of the following activities to accommodate the needs of your students—both native and non-English speakers.

Rhymes and Songs

Use rhymes, songs, poems, or chants to introduce new letter sounds and spelling words. Repeat the rhyme or song several times during the day or week, having students listen to you first, then repeat back to you line by line. To enhance learning for visual learners in your classroom and provide opportunities for pointing out letter combinations and their sounds, you may want to write the rhyme, song, poem, or chant on the board. As you examine the words, students can easily see similarities and differences among them. Encourage volunteers to select and recite a rhyme or sing a song for the class. Students may enjoy some of the selections in *Miss Mary Mack and Other Children's Street Rhymes* by Joanna Cole and Stephanie Calmenson or *And the Green Grass Grew All Around* by Alvin Schwartz.

Student Dictation

To take advantage of individual students' known vocabulary, suggest that students build their own sentences incorporating the list words. For example:

Mary ran.

Mary ran away.

Mary ran away quickly.

Sentence building can expand students' knowledge of how to spell words and of how to notice language patterns, learn descriptive words, and so on.

Words in Context

Using words in context sentences will aid students' mastery of new vocabulary.

- Say several sentences using the list words in context and have students repeat after you. Encourage more proficient students to make up sentences using list words that you suggest.

- Write cloze sentences on the board and have students help you complete them with the list words.

Point out the spelling patterns in the words, using colored chalk to underline or circle the elements.

Oral Drills

Use oral drills to help students make associations among sounds and the letters that represent them. You might use oral drills at listening stations to reinforce the language, allowing ESL students to listen to the drills at their own pace.

Spelling Aloud Say each list word and have students repeat the word. Next, write it on the board as you name each letter, then say the word again as you track the letters and sound by sweeping your hand under the word. Call attention to spelling changes for words to which endings or suffixes were added. For words with more than one syllable, emphasize each syllable as you write, encouraging students to clap out the syllables. Ask volunteers to repeat the procedure.

Variant Spellings For a group of words that contain the same vowel sound, but variant spellings, write an example on the board, say the word, and then present other words in that word family (*cake: rake, bake, lake*). Point out the sound and the letter(s) that stand for the sound. Then, add words to the list that have the same vowel sound (*play, say, day*). Say pairs of words (*cake, play*) as you point to them, and identify the vowel sound and the different letters that represent the sound (long *a*: *a_e, ay*). Ask volunteers to select a different pair of words and repeat the procedure.

Vary this activity by drawing a chart on the board that shows the variant spellings for a sound. Invite students to add words under the correct spelling pattern. Provide a list of words for students to choose from to help those ESL students with limited vocabularies.

Categorizing To help students discriminate among consonant sounds and spellings, have them help you categorize words with single consonant sounds and consonant blends or digraphs. For example, ask students to close their eyes so that they may focus solely on the sounds in the words, and then pronounce *smart*, *smile*, *spend*, and *special*. Next, pronounce the words as you write them on the board. After spelling each word, create two columns—one for *sm*, one for *sp*. Have volunteers pronounce each word, decide which column it fits under, and then write the word in the correct column. Encourage students to add to the columns any other words they know that have those consonant blends.

To focus on initial, medial, or final consonant sounds, point out the position of the consonant blends or digraphs in the list words. Have students find and list the words under columns labeled *Beginning*, *Middle*, and *End*.

Tape Recording Encourage students to work with a partner or their group to practice their spelling words. If a tape recorder is available, students can practice at their own pace by taking turns recording the words, playing back the tape, and writing each word they hear. Students can then help each other check their spelling against their *Spelling Workout* books. Observe as needed to be sure students are spelling the words correctly.

Comparing/Contrasting To help students focus on word parts, write list words with prefixes or suffixes on the board and have volunteers circle, underline, or draw a line between the prefix or suffix and its base word. Review the meaning of each base word, then invite students to work with their group to write two sentences: one using just the base word; the other using the base word with its prefix or suffix. For example: *My favorite mystery was due at the library Monday afternoon. By Tuesday afternoon the book was overdue!* Or, *You can depend on Jen to arrive for softball practice on time. She is dependable.* Have students contrast the two sentences, encouraging them to tell how the prefix or suffix changed the meaning of the base word.

Questions/Answers Write list words on the board and ask pairs of students to brainstorm questions or answers about the words, such as "Which word names more than one? How do you know?" (*foxes*, an *es* was added at the end) or, "Which word tells that something belongs to the children? How do you know?" (*children's* is spelled with an *'s*)

Games
You may want to invite students to participate in these activities.

Picture Clues Students can work with a partner to draw pictures or cut pictures out of magazines that represent the list words, then trade papers and label each other's pictures. Encourage students to check each other's spelling against their *Spelling Workout* books.

Or, you can present magazine cutouts or items that picture the list words. As you display each picture or item, say the word clearly and then write it on the board as you spell it aloud. Non-English speakers may wish to know the translation of the word in their native language so that they can mentally connect the new word with a familiar one. Students may also find similarities in the spellings of the words.

Letter Cards Have students create letter cards for vowels, vowel digraphs, consonants, consonant blends and digraphs, and so on. Then, say a list word and have students show the card that has the letters representing the sound for the vowels or consonants in that word as they repeat and spell the word after you. You may wish to have students use their cards independently as they work with their group.

Charades/Pantomime Students can use gestures and actions to act out the list words. To receive credit for a correctly guessed word, players must spell the word correctly. Such activities can be played in pairs so that beginning English speakers will not feel pressured. If necessary, translate the words into students' native languages so that they understand the meanings of the words before attempting to act them out.

Change or No Change Have students make flash cards for base words and endings. One student holds up a base word; another holds up an ending. The class says "Change" or "No Change" to describe what happens when the base word and ending are combined. Encourage students to spell the word with its ending added.

Scope and Sequence for MCP Spelling Workout

Skills	Level A	Level B	Level C	Level D	Level E	Level F	Level G	Level H
Consonants	1–12	1	1–2	1	1	1, 7, 9	RC	3
Short Vowels	14–18	3–5	3	2	RC	RC	RC	RC
Long Vowels	20–23	7–11, 15	4–5, 7–8	3	RC	RC	RC	RC
Consonant Blends/Clusters	26–28	13–14	9–10, 17	5, 7	RC	RC	RC	RC
y as a Vowel	30	16	11, 13	RC	RC	RC	27	RC
Consonant Digraphs—th, ch, sh, wh, ck	32–33	19–21	14–16	9	RC	RC	RC	RC
Vowel Digraphs		33	6–7, 9	19–21, 23	8–10	11, 14–17	25	RC
Vowel Pairs	29		26	20, 22	7–8, 10	14	25	
r-Controlled Vowels		22, 25	19–20	8	RC	RC	RC	4
Diphthongs	24	32	31	22–23	11	17	RC	RC
Silent Consonants			28	11	4	8–9	RC	RC
Hard and Soft c and g		21	2	4	2	2	RC	
Plurals			21–22	25–27, 29	33–34	33	RC	RC
Prefixes		34	32–33	31–32	13–17	20–23, 25	7–8, 33	7–11, 19–20
Suffixes/Endings	34–35	26–28	21–23, 25, 33	13–17	25–29, 31–32	26–29, 31–32	5, 9, 13–14, 16, 26	5, 25–27
Contractions		23	34	28	20	RC	RC	RC
Possessives				28–29	20	RC	RC	RC
Compound Words				33	19	RC	34	RC
Synonyms/Antonyms				34	RC	RC	RC	RC
Homonyms		35	35	35	RC	34	RC	RC
Spellings of /f/: f, ff, ph, gh				10	3	3	RC	RC
Syllables					21–23	RC	RC	1
Commonly Misspelled Words					35	34	17, 35	17, 29, 35
Abbreviations						35	RC	RC
Latin Roots							11, 15, 31	13–16

Skills	Level A	Level B	Level C	Level D	Level E	Level F	Level G	Level H
Words with French or Spanish Derivations							10, 29	RC 28
Words of Latin/ French/Greek Origin								21–23, 28
List Words Related to Specific Curriculum Areas							19–23, 28, 32	
Vocabulary Development	•	•	•	•	•	•	•	•
Dictionary	•	•	•	•	•	•	•	•
Writing	•	•	•	•	•	•	•	•
Proofreading	•	•	•	•	•	•	•	•
Reading Selections	•	•	•	•	•	•	•	•
Bonus Words	•	•	•	•	•	•	•	•
Review Tests in Standardized Format	•	•	•	•	•	•	•	•
Spelling Through Writing								
Poetry	•	•	•	•	•		•	
Narrative Writings	•	•	•	•	•	•	•	•
Descriptive Writings	•	•	•	•	•	•	•	•
Expository Writings	•	•	•		•	•	•	•
Persuasive Writings					•	•	•	•
Notes/Letters	•	•	•		•	•	•	•
Riddles/Jokes	•	•	•					
Recipes/Menus	•	•	•					
News Stories		•	•	•	•	•	•	•
Conversations/Dialogues	•	•		•	•	•	•	•
Stories	•	•	•	•	•		•	•
Interviews/Surveys		•			•	•	•	•
Logs/Journals	•	•	•		•	•	•	•
Ads/Brochures		•	•	•	•	•	•	•
Reports					•	•	•	•
Literary Devices							•	•
Scripts		•					•	•
Speeches					•		•	•
Directions/Instructions	•	•		•				

Numbers in chart indicate lesson numbers

RC = reinforced in other contexts

• = found throughout

Lesson 1
Words with the Sound of k, kw, and n

Objective
To spell words in which *k*, *ck*, *que*, and *ch* spell the *k* sound, *qu* spells the *kw* sound, and *kn* spells the *n* sound

 Correlated Phonics Lesson
MCP Phonics, Level F, Lesson 1

Spelling Words in Action   Page 5

In this selection, students discover how some superstars in the movies are created. After reading, encourage students to describe man-made characters they have seen in films.

Ask volunteers to say the boldfaced words and name the letters that stand for the sound of *k*, *kw*, and *n*.

Warm-Up Test

1. We heard the **echoes** of our voices in the cave.
2. The school **chorus** sang songs by Irving Berlin.
3. My brother Carlos studied **chemistry**.
4. Miko passed a test to **qualify** as a lifeguard.
5. He smiled to **acknowledge** my presence.
6. What a **remarkable** performance!
7. Dad called the **locksmith** when he lost his keys.
8. I made a large **quantity** of applesauce.
9. Christina read a **technical** book on computers.
10. Did you receive an award at the **banquet**?
11. By reading books, we increase our **knowledge**.
12. Alanna has the skills **required** to do the job.
13. Max sat at the **keyboard** and began to type.
14. The bumpers on the car are made of **chrome**.
15. Jim owns a valuable **antique** table.
16. Roger **knelt** in the garden and pulled weeds.
17. My **headache** disappeared after I napped.
18. Each person's fingerprints are **unique**.
19. Did the plane arrive on **schedule**?
20. The coach helped me improve my **technique**.

Spelling Practice   Pages 6–7

Introduce the spelling rule and have students read the **list words** aloud. Point out that *acknowledge* contains a combination of *ck* and *kn*, and *technique* has two of the spellings for the *k* sound. Then, encourage students to look back at their **Warm-Up Tests** and apply the spelling rule to any misspelled words.

As students work through the **Spelling Practice** exercises, remind them to look back at their **list words** or in their dictionaries if they need help.

 See Categorizing, page 15
for ESL students

18

Words with the Sound of k, kw, and n   Lesson 1

Spelling Words in Action

What does it take to make a superstar?

Shaping a Superstar

You are the producer of a space adventure movie. Your script calls for a **unique** character. You must find an actor who will **qualify** for the part. Masks, make-up, and costumes can turn the actor into a truly **remarkable** character from space. Applying the make-up for an alien character is a highly **technical** job that can take hours. If you're working on a tight **schedule**, you may not have time. What do you do? You can build your own character!

First, artists make a great **quantity** of sketches. Then the sketches are brought to life in one of two ways. The design can be part of a computer program. Then, the character exists only on the computer and on the film. Or, the character can be built as a model. This **technique** uses materials such as foam rubber, fiberglass, plastic, and **chrome**. Complex systems control the model's actions. Three or four people might be **required** to operate the controls.

Knowledge and technology have joined hands to shape superstars that can do almost anything but sign autographs!

Say each boldfaced word in the selection. Listen for the sounds of k, kw, and n. What do you notice about the spellings for each sound?

5

Spelling Practice

TIP
The k sound can be spelled several different ways:
k, as in keyboard;
ck, as in locksmith;
que, as in technique;
ch, as in chorus.
The kw sound is spelled qu, as in quantity and banquet. The n sound is sometimes spelled kn, as in knowledge and knelt.

LIST WORDS
1. echoes
2. chorus
3. chemistry
4. qualify
5. acknowledge
6. remarkable
7. locksmith
8. quantity
9. technical
10. banquet
11. knowledge
12. required
13. keyboard
14. chrome
15. antique
16. knelt
17. headache
18. unique
19. schedule
20. technique

Words with the Sound of k, kw, and n

Write the **list words** that contain the sound given. You will write two words twice.

k spells the sound of k, as in king
1. remarkable   2. keyboard

ch spells the sound of k, as in chord
3. echoes   4. chorus
5. chemistry   6. technical
7. chrome   8. headache
9. schedule   10. technique

ck spells the sound of k, as in deck
11. acknowledge   12. locksmith

que spells the sound of k, as in boutique
13. antique   14. unique
15. technique

kn spells the sound of n, as in knife
16. acknowledge   17. knowledge
18. knelt

qu spells the sound of kw, as in quite
19. qualify   20. quantity
21. banquet   22. required

6   Lesson 1 • Words with the Sound of k, kw, and n

Missing Words

Write the **list word** that completes each sentence.

1. The cat tiptoed along the __keyboard__, making a little song.
2. We had to call a __locksmith__ after Sam lost the key.
3. I received this trophy at the awards __banquet__ last night.
4. Are you singing in the school __chorus__ this year?
5. Dad polished the __chrome__ on his car until it was shiny.
6. Karen __knelt__ to play with the little puppy.
7. The loud music gave me a __headache__.
8. By studying computer science, he gained __technical__ knowledge.
9. Before she became a scientist, she received her degree in __chemistry__.
10. Mom has a busy __schedule__ at her new job.

Mixed-Up Words

Parts of these **list words** have become mixed up: qualify, antique, required, unique, acknowledge, remarkable, quantity, technique, echoes, knowledge. Put the word parts back where they belong and write the two correct words on the lines.

1. acknoulique	technedge	__acknowledge__	__technique__
2. remarkoes	echable	__remarkable__	__echoes__
3. quallred	requify	__qualify__	__required__
4. antity	quantique	__antique__	__quantity__
5. unedge	knowlique	__unique__	__knowledge__

Lesson 1 • Words with the Sound of **k, kw,** and **n**   7

Spelling and Writing

Proofreading

This dialogue from the movie "My Friend Is a Robot" has ten mistakes. Use the proofreading marks to correct them. Then, write the misspelled **list words** correctly on the lines.

ROBOT (in a panicky voice): I'm having tecnicle difficulties. I'm losing all of my knowlege Now I know what a headake feels like! you must skeduel time to make the requred repairs

IRMA (rolling her eyes in amusement): Don't panic! All you need is to have your batteries recharged

ROBOT (more frantic): Hurry up and recharge them! I'm quickly becoming a useless pile of krome

Proofreading Marks

◯ spelling mistake
≡ capital letter
⊙ add period

1. __technical__   2. __knowledge__   3. __headache__
4. __schedule__   5. __required__   6. __chrome__

Writing a Dialogue

Put yourself into a movie about a space adventure with a remarkable robot. Write the dialogue for the scene that takes place when you first meet this unique character. If you like, add descriptions that go with the actions. Use any **list words** that you can. Remember to proofread your dialogue and fix any mistakes.

_____

_____

_____

_____

_____

BONUS WORDS

knothole

mechanic

plaque

quiz

kindling

8   Lesson 1 • Words with the Sound of **k, kw,** and **n**

Spelling Strategy

Make three columns on the board, labeled *k, kw,* and *n*. Say each **list word** and ask a volunteer to come to the board and write the word in the appropriate column (or columns, if the word contains more than one of the sounds). Ask a second volunteer to circle the letter or letters that stand for the *k, kw,* or *n* sound.

BONUS WORDS You may want to suggest that students draw a simple sketch that gives a clue to the meaning of each bonus word. Then, have them trade picture clues with a partner and try to write the bonus word that fits each sketch.

Spelling and Writing   *Page 8*

The **Proofreading** exercise will help students prepare to proofread their dialogues. As students complete the writing activity, encourage them to brainstorm ideas, write a first draft, revise, and proofread their work. To publish their writing, students may want to get together with a partner to perform their scenes for the class.

Writer's Corner You may want to bring in reviews of movies, TV shows, or plays from your local newspaper. Encourage students to write responses to the reviews, telling whether or not they agree with them.

Final Test

1. The **chemistry** teacher is Mrs Ryan.
2. These woven patterns are **unique**.
3. The pianist's fingers flew over the **keyboard**.
4. A swimming pool holds a large **quantity** of water.
5. What a terrific speech she gave at the **banquet**!
6. Pitchers practice to improve their **technique**.
7. My father gave me this **antique** spoon.
8. I want to **acknowledge** your valuable help.
9. The goalie's speed was **remarkable**.
10. The **echoes** of happy voices rang out clearly.
11. I **knelt** down to pat Tina's pet rabbit.
12. Her **knowledge** of music is amazing.
13. What a relief to finally see the **locksmith**!
14. Did the school **chorus** perform at graduation?
15. A glass of water might soothe your **headache**.
16. The school **required** everyone to take gym.
17. Many electricians attend **technical** schools.
18. To **qualify** for this job, I must take a test.
19. Is this bus **schedule** up-to-date?
20. Becky polished the **chrome** on her car.

Hard and Soft c and g; dge

Objective
To spell words with hard and soft c and g, with dge

 Phonics **Correlated Phonics Lesson**
MCP Phonics, Level F, Lesson 2

Spelling Words in Action   **Page 9**

In "Hard Rock," students learn about the hardest substance on Earth—a diamond. Ask students which information they found the most interesting, and invite them to share other facts they may know about diamonds or other jewels.

Call on volunteers to say the boldfaced words and identify the sounds spelled with c and g.

Warm-Up Test
1. That **crystal** chandelier is really beautiful!
2. The corners of the frame form a right **angle**.
3. Gloria and Jamal are **engaged** to be married.
4. Tall people have an **advantage** in basketball.
5. John **pledges** to do his homework every night.
6. The pencil's graphite is made from **carbon**.
7. Cheese spread is made from **processed** cheese.
8. Was that **medicine** prescribed by a doctor?
9. Lisa planned a birthday **celebration** for Tim.
10. The heat caused the **icicles** to melt.
11. Our **language** changes as new words are added.
12. Ali must **budget** his time.
13. After two wrong **guesses**, I got the answer.
14. Milk must be kept in the **refrigerator**.
15. We're learning to **conjugate** verbs.
16. Clare dreamed about a **magical** journey.
17. The porpoise is an **intelligent** animal.
18. Kathy put a new **cartridge** in the printer.
19. I hope the vase I bought is a **genuine** antique.
20. Do you have a **recipe** for lasagna?

Spelling Practice   **Pages 10–11**

Introduce the spelling rule and have students read the **list words** aloud, telling which sound the c or g stands for in each word. Then, encourage students to look back at their **Warm-Up Tests** and apply the spelling rule to any misspelled words.

As students work through the **Spelling Practice** exercises, remind them to look back at their **list words** or in their dictionaries if they need help.

for ESL students **See Rhymes and Songs, page 14**

Spelling Words in Action

What can you do with a diamond?

Hard Rock

Have you ever heard the expression "Diamonds are forever"? Diamonds can last as long as they take to make. They are made of **carbon**. That's the same substance as the graphite in your pencil. Diamonds become **processed** over millions of years, far below the earth's surface. For a miner, finding a **genuine** diamond is cause for **celebration**.

A diamond is the hardest substance found on the earth. To turn a rough diamond into a gem, flat surfaces called *facets* are carefully carved out of the stone. To increase the sparkle, each facet is ground at a certain **angle**.

Ancient people thought this type of **crystal** had **magical** powers. They were thought to bring luck, power, good health, and long life. It has long been a custom for men to give diamond rings to women as **pledges** of their love when they become **engaged** to be married. They also have less romantic uses. The space program used diamonds in a window of a spacecraft that went to Venus. This window had a big **advantage**. The diamond surface was not destroyed by the heat and atmospheric pressure of the far-off planet.

Look back at the boldfaced words in the selection. What do you notice about the sounds made with the letters c and g?

9

TIP
The letter **g** makes a hard sound, as in angle, and a soft sound, as in magical. The letters **dge** often spell the soft g sound, as in cartridge. The letter **c** makes a hard sound, as in carbon, and a soft sound, as in recipe. Be careful when spelling words with c or g, because their sounds can easily be confused with s or j.

Spelling Practice

Words with Hard and Soft c and g and dge

Write each **list word** under the correct heading. Some words are used more than once.

LIST WORDS
1. crystal
2. angle
3. engaged
4. advantage
5. pledges
6. carbon
7. processed
8. medicine
9. celebration
10. icicles
11. language
12. budget
13. guesses
14. refrigerator
15. conjugate
16. magical
17. intelligent
18. cartridge
19. genuine
20. recipe

g, as in giant or edge
1. engaged
2. advantage
3. pledges
4. language
5. budget
6. refrigerator
7. magical
8. intelligent
9. cartridge
10. genuine

c, as in card
16. crystal
17. carbon
18. icicles
19. conjugate
20. magical
21. cartridge

g, as in gate
11. angle
12. engaged
13. language
14. guesses
15. conjugate

c, as in cinema
22. processed
23. medicine
24. celebration
25. icicles
26. recipe

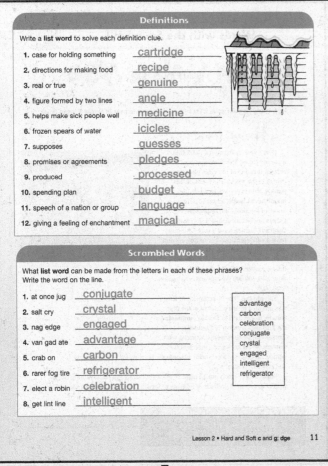

Definitions

Write a **list word** to solve each definition clue.

1. case for holding something   cartridge
2. directions for making food   recipe
3. real or true   genuine
4. figure formed by two lines   angle
5. helps make sick people well   medicine
6. frozen spears of water   icicles
7. supposes   guesses
8. promises or agreements   pledges
9. produced   processed
10. spending plan   budget
11. speech of a nation or group   language
12. giving a feeling of enchantment   magical

Scrambled Words

What **list word** can be made from the letters in each of these phrases? Write the word on the line.

1. at once jug   conjugate
2. salt cry   crystal
3. nag edge   engaged
4. van gad ate   advantage
5. crab on   carbon
6. rarer fog tire   refrigerator
7. elect a robin   celebration
8. get lint line   intelligent

advantage
carbon
celebration
conjugate
crystal
engaged
intelligent
refrigerator

Lesson 2 • Hard and Soft c and g; dge   11

Spelling and Writing

Proofreading

This advertisement has ten mistakes. Use the proofreading marks to correct them. Then, write the misspelled **list words** correctly on the lines.

Proofreading Marks
- ◯ spelling mistake
- ≡ capital letter
- ⌄ add apostrophe

Its time that you bought a genuin diamond! visit the Sparkle Bright diamond store nearest you and take advantidge of our week-long sale selebrasson We have prices that fit every budjit Keep in mind that each Sparkle bright store pledjes to give you the best. Remember our motto: Buy diamonds, youll be making an intellijant investment.

1. genuine   2. advantage
3. celebration   4. budget
5. pledges   6. intelligent

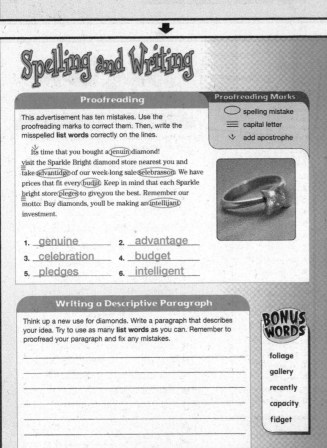

Writing a Descriptive Paragraph

Think up a new use for diamonds. Write a paragraph that describes your idea. Try to use as many **list words** as you can. Remember to proofread your paragraph and fix any mistakes.

_____
_____
_____
_____
_____
_____

BONUS WORDS

foliage

gallery

recently

capacity

fidget

Spelling Strategy

Write each **list word** containing c on the board and invite the class to identify the letter that follows the c, then say the word and tell whether the c is hard or soft.

Follow the same procedure with **list words** that contain g. Point out to students that when they see c or g followed by e or i, they should try the soft sound when pronouncing it. Help them conclude that c and g are usually soft before e or i.

BONUS WORDS You may want to suggest that students create a crossword puzzle that contains the bonus words. Have them write clues and draw a blank grid. Then, have them trade puzzles with a partner and try to solve each other's clues.

Spelling and Writing   *Page 12*

The **Proofreading** exercise will help students prepare to proofread their descriptive paragraphs. As students complete the writing activity, encourage them to brainstorm ideas, write a first draft, revise, and proofread their work. To publish their writing, students may want to illustrate their paragraphs and create a bulletin board called "What Can You Do With a Diamond?"

Writer's Corner Invite the class to formulate their own questions and answers about subjects from nature, such as: What is the fastest land animal? or What is the world's tallest mountain? Students can search for answers in reference books.

Final Test

1. **Carbon** is a very common chemical.
2. Look how clear that **crystal** is!
3. Are you surprised that pigs are **intelligent**?
4. Here's my **recipe** for cheese bread.
5. The accountant helped me **budget** my money.
6. Make sure you take the **medicine** each day.
7. The two lines meet at a sharp **angle**.
8. The film was about a **magical** land.
9. Can you find a **cartridge** for this pen?
10. Endurance is an **advantage** in a marathon.
11. The machine **processed** the food in seconds.
12. The silver is **genuine**, but the stone is fake.
13. How many verbs can you **conjugate** in Latin?
14. The **icicles** on my house finally melted!
15. After winning, the team had a **celebration**.
16. Mary **pledges** to clean her room once a week.
17. The ring shows that they are **engaged**.
18. Will you learn French as a second **language**?
19. You can make three **guesses**.
20. Our **refrigerator** is not keeping the food cold.

Lesson 3 — Words with the Sound of f

Objective
To spell words in which *f*, *ff*, *ph*, and *gh* spell the sound of *f*

 Correlated Phonics Lesson
MCP Phonics, Level F, Lesson 3

Spelling Words in Action   Page 13

In this selection, students learn about a unique parade in which floats are covered with flowers. Ask students if they have ever seen the Tournament of Roses Parade and invite them to talk about their own experiences with parades.

Call on volunteers to say each boldfaced word and name the letter or letters that stand for the *f* sound.

Warm-Up Test
1. Rosa **photographed** her family.
2. A police **officer** directed traffic on the street.
3. The winner flashed a **triumphant** smile.
4. I'll save my money until I can **afford** a bike.
5. Athletes exercise to **toughen** their muscles.
6. **Fifteen** students received awards.
7. Alice likes plums, but I **prefer** peaches.
8. Aunt Miranda is a **physician** at City Hospital.
9. This bouquet of roses is so **fragrant**!
10. He wrote a **pamphlet** on bicycle safety.
11. Chato plays the **saxophone** in the band.
12. The scientists searched for an **effective** cure.
13. What country grows the most **coffee**?
14. A **phrase** is a group of words or musical notes.
15. Should I **hyphenate** this word?
16. What a **magnificent** view this is!
17. Do you have **sufficient** supplies for your hike?
18. Our coaches **emphasize** regular exercise.
19. Canada is in the Northern **Hemisphere**.
20. My first attempt to skateboard was **laughable**.

Spelling Practice   Pages 14–15

Introduce the spelling rule and have students read the **list words** aloud. Discuss the spelling of the *f* sound in each word, and point out that *photographed* contains two instances of the *f* sound. Then, encourage students to look back at their **Warm-Up Tests** and apply the spelling rule to any misspelled words.

As students work through the **Spelling Practice** exercises, remind them to look back at their **list words** or in their dictionaries if they need help.

 See Variant Spellings, page 14

22

Spelling Words in Action

How many flowers does it take to cover a Tournament of Roses Parade float?

Flower Power

Every year in Pasadena, California, a parade called The Tournament of Roses is held. It is one of the most **photographed** events in the world. The focus of this parade, held every January 1, is the **magnificent** floats, all made of flowers. Some of the floats are **laughable**. Others are beautiful, like a ship made of **fragrant** carnations and roses. All must have a **sufficient** number of flowers and other natural materials, such as leaves or fruit, to cover every inch of the float. It isn't easy to **afford** a float. The average float uses 100,000 flowers and costs around $250,000!

The **phrase** "The Tournament of Roses" was invented by the president of the first parade. It was held in 1890 to **emphasize** the beautiful weather in Pasadena. Horses and buggies were decorated with flowers. Today horses still march in the parade. So do lively bands with **saxophone** players, flutes, bass drums, and other instruments.

Some people camp out all night to get a spot along the parade route. Others **prefer** to join the hundreds of millions of viewers who watch the parade on TV!

Look back at the boldfaced words in the selection. How many different ways is the sound of f spelled?

13

TIP
The f sound can be spelled four different ways:
f, as in fifteen;
ff, as in coffee;
ph, as in photographed;
gh, as in laughable.

Spelling Practice

LIST WORDS
1. photographed
2. officer
3. triumphant
4. afford
5. toughen
6. fifteen
7. prefer
8. physician
9. fragrant
10. pamphlet
11. saxophone
12. effective
13. coffee
14. phrase
15. hyphenate
16. magnificent
17. sufficient
18. emphasize
19. hemisphere
20. laughable

Words with the Sound of f

Write each **list word** in the correct category to show how the f sound is spelled.

f as in final
1. fifteen
2. prefer
3. fragrant
4. magnificent

ff as in sheriff
5. officer
6. afford
7. effective
8. coffee
9. sufficient

ph as in photo
10. photographed
11. triumphant
12. physician
13. pamphlet
14. saxophone
15. phrase
16. hyphenate
17. emphasize
18. hemisphere

gh as in enough
19. toughen
20. laughable

Complete the Paragraph

Write the **list word** that completes each blank in the paragraph.

Costa Rica, in Central America, is located in the Northern __Hemisphere__. My parents saved money for a long time so we could __afford__ our trip to Costa Rica. Much of the __coffee__ that people drink grows in this country. Its rair forests, teeming with tropical trees, plants, and wildlife, were absolutely __magnificent__! You can smell the __fragrant__ flowers as you walk through the rain forests. Visitors from around the world have __photographed__ the flora and fauna found in rain forests in Costa Rica. If you don't bring __sufficient__ film, you will not be able to capture all the great photos. Now my family can't __emphasize__ enough the importance of protecting the rain forests. We brought back a __pamphlet__ with more information on how we can do our part. We think countries everywhere should __toughen__ their laws that help save the rain forests!

Move the Words

Each underlined **list word** in the sentences below must be moved to a different **sentence** to make sense. Write the correct word in the blanks at the end of the sentence.

1. I have started taking <u>officer</u> lessons. __saxophone__
2. If you don't feel well, you should see your <u>laughable</u>. __physician__
3. Can you show me where to <u>effective</u> this two-syllable word? __hyphenate__
4. My favorite saying is the <u>prefer</u> "Never give up." __phrase__
5. My feeble attempt to play the clarinet was truly <u>saxophone</u>. __laughable__
6. <u>Physician</u>, where should I turn in this lost wallet? __officer__
7. The winner made a <u>hyphenate</u> lap around the racecourse. __triumphant__
8. I drink tomato juice, but I really <u>fifteen</u> orange juice. __prefer__
9. My big sister is <u>triumphant</u> years old. __fifteen__
10. The new law has been very <u>phrase</u> in stopping speeding. __effective__

Lesson 3 • Words with the Sound of f   15

Proofreading

Mayor Green's speech, to be given at a parade, has ten mistakes. Use the proofreading marks to fix each mistake. Then, write the misspelled **list words** correctly on the lines.

Proofreading Marks
- ⃝ spelling mistake
- ≡ capital letter
- ∧ add something

good day to all of my fellow citizens! Have you ever seen such a magnificent parade? I'm told that there are fifteen more floats this year than at last year's parade. I can't enfasize enough how much this parade means to our town. That's why I'm surprised that my opponent thinks that we can't aforde a parade every year. what a laughabel idea! I say that we can't afford not to hold a parade. our town needs to celebrate its triumfant history. Thank you.

1. __magnificent__   2. __fifteen__
3. __emphasize__   4. __afford__
5. __laughable__   6. __triumphant__

Writing a News Story

Write a newspaper story about a parade. Were the floats <u>effective</u> or <u>laughable</u>? Describe the sights, smells, and sounds. Try to use as many **list words** as you can. Remember to proofread your story and fix any mistakes.

_____
_____
_____
_____
_____

BONUS WORDS

affection
fender
phenomenon
roughen
orphanage

Spelling Strategy

Write each **list word** on the board, but use an incorrect spelling for the *f* sound (*ophicer* for *officer*). Then, call on volunteers to point to the incorrect spelling, rewrite the word correctly, and circle the correct spelling.

BONUS WORDS   You may want to suggest that students pair up with partners and divide the bonus words between them. Have them write both a real and a fake definition for their words. Then, have them trade papers and see if they can match the bonus words with their correct meanings.

Spelling and Writing   *Page 16*

The **Proofreading** exercise will help students prepare to proofread their news stories. Before they begin the exercise, remind students that the proofreading mark ∧ is used to add something. It could be a space, a comma, a question mark, or an exclamation mark. As students complete the writing activity, encourage them to brainstorm ideas, write a first draft, revise, and proofread their work. To publish their writing, students may want to pretend they are commentators and read their articles aloud.

Writer's Corner Students might enjoy looking through *Chase's Calendar of Events*. Suggest that students select an event that occurs on their birthday and write a paragraph telling why they would or would not like to attend.

Final Test

1. Barbara practices her **saxophone** every day.
2. Bob's paintings are **magnificent**!
3. In Wales, Kathy **photographed** many castles.
4. My big sister is **fifteen**.
5. Did we have **sufficient** rainfall this season?
6. I would **prefer** to stay home.
7. My father is an **officer** in the Marine Corps.
8. Let's look for **effective** solutions.
9. Can she **afford** a new car?
10. Don't forget to use the **phrase** "thank you."
11. Brazil is in the Southern **Hemisphere**.
12. A skunk is certainly not a **fragrant** animal.
13. The dentist gave me a **pamphlet** to read.
14. The sun can **toughen** and damage your skin.
15. **Hyphenate** words between their syllables.
16. Our silly skit was **laughable**.
17. My **physician** is named Dr. Novak.
18. The **coffee** plant has bright red berries.
19. Ian felt **triumphant** when he won the race.
20. Did you **emphasize** the important points?

Words with the Sound of s, z, and zh

Objective
To spell words in which s sounds like s, z, and zh

 Phonics Correlated Phonics Lesson
MCP Phonics, Level F, Lesson 4

Spelling Words in Action **Page 17**

In this selection, students learn what it takes to join a jazz band. After reading, invite students to discuss whether they would be interested in playing in a jazz band.

Encourage students to look back at the boldfaced words. Ask volunteers to say the words and identify the different sounds that s stands for.

Warm-Up Test
1. The **purpose** of the meeting is to elect officers.
2. Tien maintained his **composure**.
3. A healthy lifestyle can prevent many **diseases**.
4. Everyone at the party wore **casual** clothes.
5. Are farmworkers hired on a **seasonal** basis?
6. Identical twins **resemble** each other closely.
7. Use the map scale when **measuring** distance.
8. Marie and her **husband** jog every day.
9. The sled dogs are in **position** to begin.
10. Lucy is both a **visual** and an auditory learner.
11. Nick ironed his **trousers** before the dance.
12. Do you play any musical **instruments**?
13. We got the most **desirable** seats in the hall!
14. The swimming **instructor** also teaches diving.
15. Lawanda took a **leisurely** stroll.
16. The students are **deserving** of a reward.
17. The aerobics class is held in the **gymnasium**.
18. Carl's **version** of what happened is inaccurate.
19. How much money is in the club's **treasury**?
20. Colorado **usually** has great skiing in February.

Spelling Practice **Pages 18–19**

Introduce the spelling rule and have students read the **list words** aloud. Discuss the meanings of unfamiliar words, such as *leisurely* and *composure*. Then, encourage students to look back at their **Warm-Up Tests** and apply the spelling rule to any misspelled words.

As students work through the **Spelling Practice** exercises, remind them to look back at their **list words** or in their dictionaries if they need help.

for ESL students **See Charades/Pantomime, page 15**

24

Spelling Words in Action

Would you enjoy being in a jazz band? Why or why not?

All That Jazz

Do you play one of the brass or percussion **instruments**? If you do, consider joining a jazz band! Most jazz bands include trumpets, saxophones, trombones, drums, and piano. Some jazz bands have a **position** for a guitar player. Others include flutes. The band might **resemble** a concert band. A jazz band, though, usually has a smaller number of instruments.

A jazz band's **purpose** is to play music in the jazz, swing, and rock styles. There is a great **treasury** of songs to play. Some are new and some are old. A jazz band can play a new jazzy **version** of an old classic, too.

Most school jazz bands are led by a music **instructor**. They play before a **casual** crowd in a **gymnasium** or for special events. Some even cut their own CDs. They practice before or after school. It takes dedication to make a 7:20 A.M. rehearsal once or twice a week, but members **usually** don't mind the early practice times. Whether they're practicing or performing, they have a good time!

Say the boldfaced words in the selection. Notice the sound that the letter s makes in each word. How many different sounds for s do you hear?

17

Spelling Practice

TIP
The letter s can stand for different sounds. For example, in the word purpose, the letter s spells the s sound. In the word resemble, the letter s spells the z sound. In the word usually, the letter s spells the zh sound.

LIST WORDS
1. purpose
2. composure
3. diseases
4. casual
5. seasonal
6. resemble
7. measuring
8. husband
9. position
10. visual
11. trousers
12. instruments
13. desirable
14. instructor
15. leisurely
16. deserving
17. gymnasium
18. version
19. treasury
20. usually

Words With the Sound of s, z, and zh

Write each **list word** under the sound that s stands for. One word will be written twice.

s spells the sound of **s**, as in secure
1. purpose   2. seasonal
3. instruments   4. instructor

s spells the sound of **z**, as in music
5. diseases   6. seasonal
7. resemble   8. husband
9. position   10. trousers
11. desirable   12. deserving
13. gymnasium

s spells the sound of **zh**, as in pleasure
14. composure   15. casual
16. measuring   17. visual
18. leisurely   19. version
20. treasury   21. usually

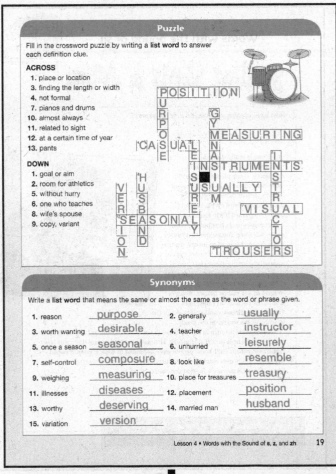

Puzzle

Fill in the crossword puzzle by writing a **list word** to answer each definition clue.

ACROSS
1. place or location
3. finding the length or width
4. not formal
7. pianos and drums
10. almost always
11. related to sight
12. at a certain time of year
13. pants

DOWN
1. goal or aim
2. room for athletics
5. without hurry
6. one who teaches
8. wife's spouse
9. copy, variant

Crossword answers: POSITION, PURPOSE, GYMNASIUM, MEASURING, CASUAL, INSTRUMENTS, INSTRUCTOR, USUALLY, HUSBAND, VERSION, VISUAL, SEASONAL, TROUSERS

Synonyms

Write a **list word** that means the same or almost the same as the word or phrase given.

1. reason — purpose
2. generally — usually
3. worth wanting — desirable
4. teacher — instructor
5. once a season — seasonal
6. unhurried — leisurely
7. self-control — composure
8. look like — resemble
9. weighing — measuring
10. place for treasures — treasury
11. illnesses — diseases
12. placement — position
13. worthy — deserving
14. married man — husband
15. variation — version

Lesson 4 • Words with the Sound of s, z, and zh   19

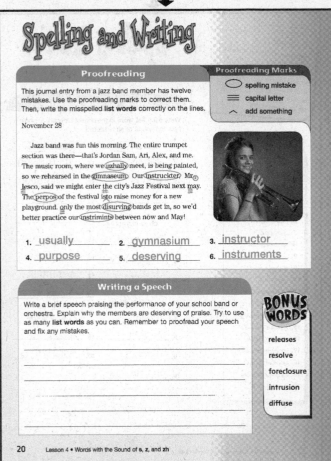

Spelling and Writing

Proofreading

This journal entry from a jazz band member has twelve mistakes. Use the proofreading marks to correct them. Then, write the misspelled **list words** correctly on the lines.

Proofreading Marks
◯ spelling mistake
≡ capital letter
∧ add something

November 28

Jazz band was fun this morning. The entire trumpet section was there—that's Jordan Sam, Ari, Alex, and me. The music room, where we uzhally meet, is being painted, so we rehearsed in the gimnaseum. Our instruckter, Mr. lesco, said we might enter the city's Jazz Festival next may. The perpos of the festival is to raise money for a new playground. only the most disurving bands get in, so we'd better practice our instrimints between now and May!

1. usually
2. gymnasium
3. instructor
4. purpose
5. deserving
6. instruments

Writing a Speech

Write a brief speech praising the performance of your school band or orchestra. Explain why the members are deserving of praise. Try to use as many **list words** as you can. Remember to proofread your speech and fix any mistakes.

_____
_____
_____
_____
_____
_____

BONUS WORDS
releases
resolve
foreclosure
intrusion
diffuse

20   Lesson 4 • Words with the Sound of s, z, and zh

Spelling Strategy

Write each of these headings at the top of a column on the board: s sounds like s; s sounds like z; s sounds like zh.

Call on volunteers to come to the board, write a **list word** in the appropriate column, and circle the s or s's. Then, invite the class to pronounce the word, stressing the sound or sounds that s stands for. Ask students which word can be written in more than one column (*seasonal*).

BONUS WORDS You may want to suggest that students write a newspaper headline for each bonus word. Then, have them erase the bonus word. Ask them to trade headlines with a partner and complete each other's headlines by writing the missing words.

Spelling and Writing   Page 20

The **Proofreading** exercise will help students prepare to proofread their speeches. As students complete the writing activity, encourage them to brainstorm ideas, write a first draft, revise, and proofread their work. To publish their writing, students may want to give their speeches to the class.

Writer's Corner The class might want to write to a local musical group to invite a guest speaker to tell about the work of a musician. Have students compile a list of questions to ask.

Final Test

1. Was the game in the new **gymnasium**?
2. Modern medicines can cure many **diseases**.
3. First, the stringed **instruments** could be heard.
4. He made a **leisurely** survey of the view.
5. What is the **purpose** of the meeting?
6. The car that uses less gas is more **desirable**.
7. The money in the **treasury** is counted daily.
8. The tailor hemmed the pleated **trousers**.
9. The workers are **measuring** the size of the roof.
10. Please hold your **position** while I'm drawing!
11. What is your **version** of the accident?
12. We ate a **casual** meal on the balcony.
13. Is the bus **usually** on time?
14. The joke was **visual**, so it's hard to explain.
15. That bird is a **seasonal** visitor, not a native.
16. The most **deserving** workers received bonuses.
17. I kept my **composure** the entire time.
18. You and Jo **resemble** each other.
19. My dad knows the teacher's **husband**.
20. The diving **instructor** stood near the pool.

Words with the Sound of <u>sh</u>

Objective
To spell words in which *sh, su, ti, cl,* and *ch* spell the sound of *sh*

 Correlated Phonics Lesson
MCP Phonics, Level F, Lesson 5

Spelling Words in Action   *Page 21*
In "Hocus Focus," students read about the history of eyeglasses and discover why frames weren't comfortable in the past. After reading, invite students to share their own experiences with selecting and wearing eyeglasses.

Encourage students to look back at the boldfaced words. Ask volunteers to say the words and identify the different spellings of the *sh* sound.

Warm-Up Test
1. Shouldn't you **insure** that valuable ring?
2. Janelle sent away for **information** about China.
3. Astronauts are pioneers in space **exploration**.
4. Dan was not **ashamed** to express his opinion.
5. When is the next **partial** eclipse of the sun?
6. We will **nourish** the plants with fertilizer.
7. Ms. Ames joined a **social** club to make friends.
8. The store sent a **brochure** about the project.
9. The **invention** of the computer changed our lives.
10. Arriving early will **assure** you of a good seat.
11. His **facial** expression showed great surprise.
12. The doctors' **convention** was held in Tulsa.
13. The maple leaf is the **official** symbol of Canada.
14. What kinds of **machinery** are made here?
15. The sky diver snapped on his **parachute**.
16. We met to **negotiate** a new contract.
17. You will **accomplish** great deeds in your life.
18. Miriam has the **potential** to be a good actress.
19. I truly **appreciate** all your help!
20. When you divide 100 by 4, the **quotient** is 25.

Spelling Practice   *Pages 22–23*
Introduce the spelling rule and have students read the **list words** aloud. Encourage students to look back at their **Warm-Up Tests** and apply the spelling rule to any misspelled words.

As students work through the **Spelling Practice** exercises, remind them to look back at their **list words** or in their dictionaries if they need help.

 See Letter Cards, page 15

Spelling Words in Action

How have eyeglasses changed over the years?

Hocus Focus

No one is really sure who is responsible for the **invention** of eyeglasses. Using pieces of glass to make printed words look bigger goes back to ancient times. Written **information** about eyeglasses goes back to the year 1268 in England.

Eyeglasses were first put in frames made of leather. The wearer tied leather strips around his head to **insure** that the glasses stayed in place. Wearers did not **appreciate** having glasses so close to their eyes. The Chinese found a **partial** solution to **assure** comfort. They added weights to silk ribbon frames. Wearers draped the ribbons over their ears. This held the glasses comfortably—until the weights hit the wearer in the head!

The big breakthrough in frames came in London, England, in 1730. An optician attached the lenses to stiff side pieces. The glasses stayed on and there was less **facial** discomfort. Still, some people were **ashamed** to wear glasses in **social** situations. Then, new **machinery** produced lightweight, attractive frames and lenses. Now, glasses are a fashion statement!

Say the boldfaced words in the selection. How many ways do you find to spell the sound of *sh*?

21

Spelling Practice

 TIP
The **sh** sound can be spelled in several ways:
sh, as in shoe
su, as in insure
ti, as in convention and partial
ci, as in facial
ch, as in machinery

LIST WORDS
1. insure
2. information
3. exploration
4. ashamed
5. partial
6. nourish
7. social
8. brochure
9. invention
10. assure
11. facial
12. convention
13. official
14. machinery
15. parachute
16. negotiate
17. accomplish
18. potential
19. appreciate
20. quotient

Words with the sh Sound
Write each **list word** in the correct category to show how the sound of *sh* is spelled.

sh as in <u>shoe</u>
1. ashamed
2. nourish
3. accomplish

ch as in <u>machine</u>
4. brochure
5. machinery
6. parachute

ci as in <u>glacial</u>
7. social
8. facial
9. official
10. appreciate

ti as in <u>motion</u>
11. information
12. exploration
13. partial
14. invention
15. convention
16. negotiate
17. potential
18. quotient

su as in <u>sure</u>
19. insure
20. assure

Comparing Words

Study the relationship between the first two underlined words. Then, write a **list word** that has the same relationship with the third underlined word.

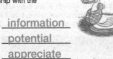

1. movie is to entertainment as newspaper is to **information**
2. wrong is to incorrect as possible is to **potential**
3. dislike is to criticize as enjoy is to **appreciate**
4. find is to seek as discovery is to **exploration**
5. happy is to cheerful as friendly is to **social**
6. swimming is to life preserver as jumping is to **parachute**
7. determine is to decide as bargain is to **negotiate**
8. water is to quench as food is to **nourish**
9. whole is to half as completed is to **partial**
10. innocent is to guilty as proud is to **ashamed**

Word Building

Add and subtract letters to form **list words**.

1. in + surely – ly = **insure**
2. broad – ad + chin – in + sure – s = **brochure**
3. inventory – ory + lion – l = **invention**
4. has – h + surge – g = **assure**
5. fact – t + vial – v = **facial**
6. convene – e + action – ac = **convention**
7. of – fish – sh + special – spe = **official**
8. stomach – sto + dine – d + ry = **machinery**
9. accompany – any + list – t + h = **accomplish**
10. quota – a + patient – pat = **quotient**

Spelling and Writing

Proofreading

This letter to Benjamin Franklin has ten mistakes. Use the proofreading marks to correct them. Then, write the misspelled **list words** correctly on the lines.

August 15, 1789

Dear benjamin,
   I'm so grateful to you for inventing bifocal lenses. I appreciate the the pair you sent to me. I can accomplish so much more work with your invention. I'm ashamed that I haven't written sooner, but I have so many official duties. I assure you that George and I think of you often.
best regards,

Martha Washington

Proofreading Marks
⬭ spelling mistake
≡ capital letter
℘ take out something

1. **appreciate**   2. **accomplish**   3. **invention**
4. **ashamed**   5. **official**   6. **assure**

Writing a Letter

You have a great idea for an invention. Write a letter to a friend naming and describing your invention and its benefits. Try to use as many **list words** as you can. Remember to proofread your letter and fix any mistakes.

_____
_____
_____
_____
_____
_____

BONUS WORDS

flourish
ensure
gracious
chagrin
regulation

Spelling Strategy

To help students recognize the different ways to spell the *sh* sound, write *sh*, *su*, *ti*, *ci*, and *ch* on the board as separate column headings. Invite the class to tell you which column each **list word** belongs in, then write the word in that column. Call on a volunteer to come to the board, point to the letters that spell the *sh* sound, and say the word aloud.

BONUS WORDS   You may want to suggest that students work with a partner to write one definition for each bonus word. Ask them to check their work with a dictionary and see if their definitions are correct. Then, have them put a star next to any words that have more than one meaning.

Spelling and Writing   Page 24

The **Proofreading** exercise will help students prepare to proofread their letters. As students complete the writing activity, encourage them to brainstorm ideas, write a first draft, revise, and proofread their work. To publish their writing, students may want to make drawings or diagrams to accompany their letters and create a bulletin-board display titled "What's New?"

Writer's Corner You may want to bring in ads for eyeglasses from newspapers or catalogs. Invite students to create their own fashionable frames and to write an ad for them.

Final Test

1. I'm not **ashamed** to admit the truth.
2. The factory installed new **machinery**.
3. Bjorn and Sue **appreciate** the gift you sent.
4. Was the lightbulb Edison's greatest **invention**?
5. I took my first **parachute** jump last April.
6. Ms. Hall is **partial** owner of a large shoe store.
7. The **quotient** is the answer in a division problem.
8. I **assure** all my customers of satisfaction.
9. Carlos has a **brochure** sent by Camp Longacre.
10. The chickadee is Maine's **official** state bird.
11. We made an **exploration** of the site.
12. I see **potential** in your idea.
13. We'll **negotiate** a contract that is fair.
14. She removed her makeup with **facial** tissues.
15. Robins catch worms to **nourish** their young.
16. Where will the next **convention** be held?
17. An atlas is a good source of **information**.
18. What a hard task that was to **accomplish**!
19. I'll **insure** my new car against damage or loss.
20. Many people play golf for **social** reasons.

Objectives

To review spelling words with the sounds of *k, kw,* and *n;* hard and soft *c* and *g, dge, f; s, z,* and *zh;* and *sh*

Check Your
Spelling Notebook   **Pages 25–28**

Based on your observations, note which words are giving students the most difficulty and offer assistance for spelling them correctly. Here are some frequently misspelled words to watch for: *knowledge, schedule, icicles, genuine, physician, emphasize, desirable, leisurely, official,* and *appreciate.*

To give students extra help and practice in taking standardized tests, you may want to have them take the **Review Test** for this lesson on pages 30–31. After scoring the tests, return them to students so that they can record their misspelled words in their spelling notebooks.

After practicing their troublesome words, students can work through the exercises for lessons 1–5 and the cumulative review, **Show What You Know.** Before they begin each exercise, you may want to go over the spelling rule.

Take It Home

Invite students to collect the **list words** in lessons 1–5 at home. Suggest that they look for words in books, magazines, and newspapers, and listen for them on the radio and TV. Students can also use **Take It Home** Master 1 on pages 32–33 to help them do the activity. (A complete list of the spelling words is included on page 32 of the **Take It Home** Master.) Invite them to compare their lists at school and to discuss which words they located most frequently.

In lessons 1 through 5, you have learned how to spell words with different consonant sounds. Some sounds, like **k, f,** and **sh,** are spelled more than one way. The letters **g** and **c** have a hard and a soft sound. The letter **s** can stand for more than one sound.

Check Your Spelling Notebook

Look at the words in your spelling notebook. Which words for lessons 1 through 5 did you have the most trouble with? Write them here.

_____

_____

Practice writing your troublesome words with a partner. Say the words and point out to your partner what part of the word is spelled differently than you expected.

Lesson 1

 TIP Consonant sounds can be spelled in different ways. Keyboard, acknowledge, echoes, and antique all have the k sound. Qualify has the kw sound. Knelt has the n sound.

List Words

chorus
schedule
echoes
keyboard
quantity
banquet
required
chrome
knowledge
antique
knelt
unique

Write a **list word** that means the same or almost the same as the word given. Not all the words will be used.

1. piano — keyboard
2. necessary — required
3. timetable — schedule
4. amount — quantity
5. singers — chorus
6. feast — banquet
7. old — antique
8. unequaled — unique
9. bowed — knelt
10. understanding — knowledge

25

↓

Lesson 2

TIP The letter g makes a hard sound, as in guesses, and a soft sound, as in budget. The letter c makes a hard sound, as in magical, and a soft sound, as in celebration.

List Words

crystal
engaged
processed
medicine
icicles
language
guesses
intelligent
budget
cartridge
genuine
recipe

Write a **list word** to complete each sentence. Not all the words will be used.

1. I like the way that __language__ sounds when it is spoken.
2. Anna was __engaged__ two years before she got married.
3. My doctor told me to take this __medicine__.
4. The __recipe__ requires two cups of flour.
5. So far, all your __guesses__ have been wrong.
6. An __intelligent__ dog learns tricks easily.
7. Is that a __genuine__ ruby or a fake?
8. Many fine drinking glasses are made from __crystal__.
9. This __cartridge__ does not fit my tape player.
10. Every winter, long __icicles__ form.

Lesson 3

 TIP The sound of f can be spelled with f, ff, ph, and gh, as in prefer, afford, phrase, and toughen.

List Words

officer
afford
toughen
magnificent
fifteen
prefer
physician
fragrant
hyphenate
pamphlet
phrase
hemisphere

Write the **list word** that belongs in each group. Not all the words will be used.

1. catalog, booklet, — pamphlet
2. five, ten, — fifteen
3. sergeant, captain, — officer
4. globe, planet, — hemisphere
5. word, sentence, — phrase
6. scented, perfumed, — fragrant
7. save, spend, — afford
8. like, favor, — prefer
9. strengthen, stiffen, — toughen
10. nurse, medic, — physician

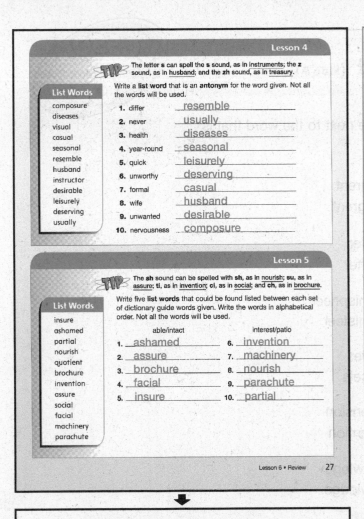

Lesson 4

TIP The letter **s** can spell the **s** sound, as in instruments; the **z** sound, as in husband; and the **zh** sound, as in treasury.

Write a **list word** that is an **antonym** for the word given. Not all the words will be used.

List Words

composure
diseases
visual
casual
seasonal
resemble
husband
instructor
desirable
leisurely
deserving
usually

1. differ — resemble
2. never — usually
3. health — diseases
4. year-round — seasonal
5. quick — leisurely
6. unworthy — deserving
7. formal — casual
8. wife — husband
9. unwanted — desirable
10. nervousness — composure

Lesson 5

TIP The **sh** sound can be spelled with **sh**, as in nourish; **su**, as in assure; **ti**, as in invention; **ci**, as in social; and **ch**, as in brochure.

List Words

insure
ashamed
partial
nourish
quotient
brochure
invention
assure
social
facial
machinery
parachute

Write five **list words** that could be found listed between each set of dictionary guide words given. Write the words in alphabetical order. Not all the words will be used.

able/intact
1. ashamed
2. assure
3. brochure
4. facial
5. insure

interest/patio
6. invention
7. machinery
8. nourish
9. parachute
10. partial

Show What You Know

Lessons 1–5 Review

One word is misspelled in each set of **list words.** Fill in the circle next to the **list word** that is spelled incorrectly.

1. ○ remarkable ○ genuine ○ fragrant ● inventshon ○ schedule
2. ○ deserving ○ information ○ echoes ○ crystal ● efective
3. ○ facial ○ pledges ● refridgerator ○ measuring ○ social
4. ● triumfant ○ qualify ○ instructor ○ fifteen ○ laughable
5. ● bankuet ○ parachute ○ angle ○ carbon ○ purpose
6. ○ usually ○ appreciate ○ hyphenate ○ keyboard ● negochiate
7. ● intellijint ○ officer ○ icicles ○ medicine ○ knelt
8. ● krome ○ quantity ○ resemble ○ assure ○ casual
9. ○ insure ● dizeases ○ guesses ○ phrase ○ recipe
10. ○ unique ○ official ● techniqe ○ husband ○ exploration
11. ● trowsers ○ conjugate ○ chorus ○ saxophone ○ magical
12. ● acomplesh ○ afford ○ knowledge ○ treasury ○ headache
13. ○ photographed ○ chemistry ○ nourish ● qotient ○ sufficient
14. ○ magnificent ○ desirable ● potenchal ○ engaged ○ toughen
15. ○ gymnasium ○ ashamed ○ processed ● aknowledge ○ version
16. ○ partial ○ emphasize ● compochure ○ prefer ○ brochure
17. ○ celebration ○ locksmith ○ position ● convencian ○ machinery
18. ○ physician ● tecknical ○ cartridge ○ leisurely ○ coffee
19. ○ antique ○ budget ○ visual ● seasanol ○ pamphlet
20. ● langwij ○ instruments ○ hemisphere ○ required ○ advantage

Final Test

1. The **invention** of computers changed the world.
2. We **assure** you that there are seats left.
3. Fine **crystal** shines more brightly than glass.
4. My sister is **engaged** to be married.
5. A police **officer** guarded the payroll.
6. I can finally **afford** the bike I want!
7. Uncle Max is Aunt Mollie's **husband**.
8. This style of car is **desirable** in snowy climates.
9. How many members does the **chorus** have?
10. A piano **keyboard** has eighty-eight keys.
11. An actor's **facial** expressions are important.
12. Be very careful around this **machinery**.
13. Luckily this **medicine** is paid for by insurance.
14. Those falling **icicles** might hurt someone.
15. Raking will **toughen** your hands.
16. My aunt lived in that house for **fifteen** years.
17. Let's take a **leisurely** walk through the garden.
18. Both contestants are **deserving** of a prize.
19. The **quantity** of water is not enough to run a mill.
20. The **banquet** was given in honor of the mayor.
21. The soldier learned how to fold a **parachute**.
22. Did you **insure** your belongings yet?
23. German is the **language** spoken in my home.
24. I made several bad **guesses** on the test.
25. Some people **prefer** to take winter vacations.
26. Only a **physician** can prescribe those pills.
27. Doesn't Elena **usually** walk home with you?
28. Some **diseases** are mainly found in the tropics.
29. The guard has no **knowledge** of any visitors.
30. Isn't a lifeguard **required** at the lake?
31. He was **ashamed** to admit the error.
32. I need **partial** payment now and the rest later.
33. An **intelligent** person thinks before acting.
34. The pen has an ink **cartridge**.
35. Your garden is so **fragrant**!
36. This **pamphlet** names the birds in this area.
37. We are having a **casual** get-together.
38. These cabins are rented on a **seasonal** basis.
39. Katy needs the latest train **schedule**.
40. That **antique** store has a suit of armor for sale.
41. This plant food will **nourish** your flowers.
42. This **brochure** explains how to use the appliance.
43. Do you think their affection for us is **genuine**?
44. Does the **recipe** call for noodles or rice?
45. That is a **phrase**, not a complete sentence.
46. Australia is in the Southern **Hemisphere**.
47. Yes, your dog does **resemble** the one on TV.
48. Don't lose your **composure** over one mistake.
49. As the queen entered, everyone **knelt**.
50. That artist has a **unique** style.

Review Test (Side A)

Read each set of words. Fill in the circle next to the word that is spelled correctly.

1. ⓐ fraigrant   ⓒ fragrent
   ⓑ fragrant   ⓓ fraigrent

2. ⓐ perfer   ⓒ prefer
   ⓑ perferr   ⓓ preffer

3. ⓐ hemisphere   ⓒ hemispheer
   ⓑ hemisfere   ⓓ hemisfeer

4. ⓐ icicel   ⓒ icicles
   ⓑ icycles   ⓓ icycels

5. ⓐ invenshun   ⓒ invension
   ⓑ invencion   ⓓ invention

6. ⓐ nowlege   ⓒ knowlege
   ⓑ knowledge   ⓓ nowledge

7. ⓐ schedual   ⓒ scedule
   ⓑ schedule   ⓓ skedual

8. ⓐ deserving   ⓒ desserveing
   ⓑ deserveing   ⓓ desserving

9. ⓐ broshure   ⓒ brochure
   ⓑ brosure   ⓓ brossure

10. ⓐ younique   ⓒ unieque
    ⓑ yuneek   ⓓ unique

11. ⓐ huzband   ⓒ husband
    ⓑ husbend   ⓓ huzbend

12. ⓐ cartredge   ⓒ cartrege
    ⓑ cartridge   ⓓ cartrage

13. ⓐ diseases   ⓒ diseazes
    ⓑ dizeases   ⓓ deseases

Review Test (Side B)

Read each set of words. Fill in the circle next to the word that is spelled correctly.

14. ⓐ inshure   © insure
    ⓑ inssure   ⓓ inchure

15. ⓐ parcial   © parsial
    ⓑ partial   ⓓ parshal

16. ⓐ composure   © cumpossure
    ⓑ cumposure   ⓓ compossure

17. ⓐ intelligient   © intelligent
    ⓑ intelligant   ⓓ inteligent

18. ⓐ chorus   © choris
    ⓑ choress   ⓓ coris

19. ⓐ casuel   © cashuel
    ⓑ cashual   ⓓ casual

20. ⓐ afford   © afourd
    ⓑ aford   ⓓ afored

21. ⓐ knealt   © nealt
    ⓑ kneelt   ⓓ knelt

22. ⓐ phisician   © phisitian
    ⓑ physician   ⓓ phystian

23. ⓐ ashaimmed   © ashaimed
    ⓑ ashammed   ⓓ ashamed

24. ⓐ cristal   © crystal
    ⓑ crystle   ⓓ cristle

25. ⓐ recipee   © recipe
    ⓑ resippy   ⓓ resipe

Take It Home 1

Your child has learned to spell many new words and would enjoy sharing them with you and your family. The following activities will provide both a review of the words in lessons 1–5 and a lot of family fun!

Homey Words

School isn't the only place where spelling words are found—there may be dozens of them floating around your house! Encourage your child to collect these words by looking for them in books, magazines, and newspapers, and by listening for them on the radio or TV. Keep a piece of paper and a pencil handy to jot down each spelling word he or she finds.

Lesson 1

1. acknowledge	12. locksmith
2. antique	13. qualify
3. banquet	14. quantity
4. chemistry	15. remarkable
5. chorus	16. required
6. chrome	17. schedule
7. echoes	18. technical
8. headache	19. technique
9. keyboard	20. unique
10. knelt	
11. knowledge	

Lesson 2

1. advantage	12. icicles
2. angle	13. intelligent
3. budget	14. language
4. carbon	15. magical
5. cartridge	16. medicine
6. celebration	17. pledges
7. conjugate	18. processed
8. crystal	19. recipe
9. engaged	20. refrigerator
10. genuine	
11. guesses	

Lesson 3

1. afford	12. pamphlet
2. coffee	13. photographed
3. effective	14. phrase
4. emphasize	15. physician
5. fifteen	16. prefer
6. fragrant	17. saxophone
7. hemisphere	18. sufficient
8. hyphenate	19. toughen
9. laughable	20. triumphant
10. magnificent	
11. officer	

Lesson 4

1. casual	12. position
2. composure	13. purpose
3. deserving	14. resemble
4. desirable	15. seasonal
5. diseases	16. treasury
6. gymnasium	17. trousers
7. husband	18. usually
8. instructor	19. version
9. instruments	20. visual
10. leisurely	
11. measuring	

Lesson 5

1. accomplish	12. machinery
2. appreciate	13. negotiate
3. ashamed	14. nourish
4. assure	15. official
5. brochure	16. parachute
6. convention	17. partial
7. exploration	18. potential
8. facial	19. quotient
9. information	20. social
10. insure	
11. invention	

Word Decoding

Can you and your child decode the secret writing? Use the key to help you write the spelling words represented by the numbers and symbols. Then, use the letters in the boxes to complete the message.

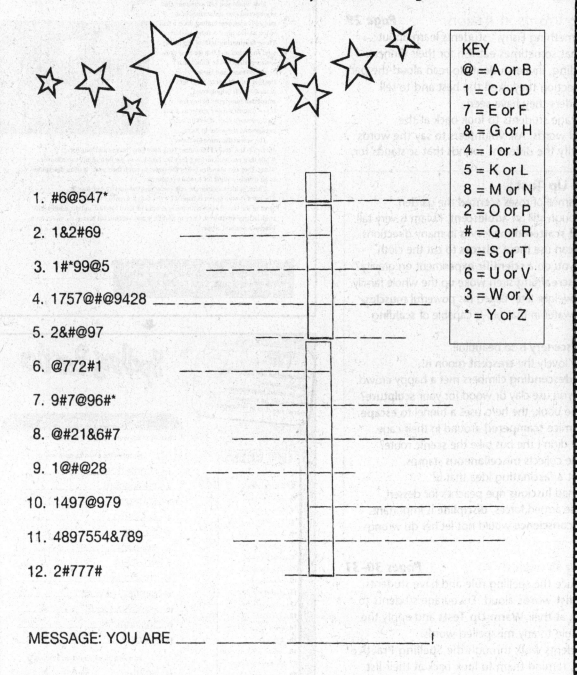

1. #6@547*   _ _ _ _ _ _ _

2. 1&2#69   _ _ _ _ _ _

3. 1#*99@5   _ _ _ _ _ _ _

4. 1757@#@9428   _ _ _ _ _ _ _ _ _ _ _

5. 2&#@97   _ _ _ _ _ _

6. @772#1   _ _ _ _ _ _

7. 9#7@96#*   _ _ _ _ _ _ _ _

8. @#21&6#7   _ _ _ _ _ _ _ _

9. 1@#@28   _ _ _ _ _ _

10. 1497@979   _ _ _ _ _ _ _

11. 4897554&789   _ _ _ _ _ _ _ _ _ _

12. 2#777#   _ _ _ _ _ _

MESSAGE: YOU ARE _ _ _   _ _ _ _ _   _ _ _ _ _ _ _ _!

Objective
To spell words with the letters *sc*

 Correlated Phonics Lesson
MCP Phonics, Level F, Lesson 6

Spelling Words in Action   Page 29
In "Something Fishy," students learn about spiders that sometimes eat fish for their dinners. After reading, invite students to read aloud the part of the selection they liked the best and to tell about spiders they have seen.

Encourage students to look back at the boldfaced words. Ask volunteers to say the words and identify the different sounds that *sc* stands for.

Warm-Up Test
1. The smell of roses **scented** the garden.
2. Although still an **adolescent**, Khiam is very tall.
3. Wind **scattered** the leaves in many directions.
4. You can use these **scissors** to cut the cloth.
5. Did you do a **scientific** experiment on gravity?
6. The **screaming** siren woke up the whole family.
7. The weight lifter flexed his powerful **muscles**.
8. The water in that tap is capable of **scalding** you.
9. This **scenery** is so beautiful!
10. How lovely the **crescent** moon is!
11. The **descending** climbers met a happy crowd.
12. Will you use clay or wood for your **sculpture**?
13. In the book, the hero uses a tunnel to **escape**.
14. The mice **scampered** around in their cage.
15. Why didn't the bus take the **scenic** route?
16. Marie collects **miscellaneous** stamps.
17. What a **fascinating** idea that is!
18. We had **luscious** ripe peaches for dessert.
19. In the armed forces, **discipline** is important.
20. Her **conscience** would not let her do wrong.

Spelling Practice   Pages 30–31
Introduce the spelling rule and have students read the **list words** aloud. Encourage students to look back at their **Warm-Up Tests** and apply the spelling rule to any misspelled words.

As students work through the **Spelling Practice** exercises, remind them to look back at their **list words** or in their dictionaries if they need help.

 See Picture Clues, page 15
for ESL students

34

Spelling Words in Action

How are fisher spiders like and unlike other spiders?

Something Fishy

What would you call a creature that **scampered** over the surface of a stream before **descending** upon a fish twice its own size? A fisher spider! These **fascinating** spiders live on the land and water and fish for their prey. Fisher spiders can be found near ponds, streams, and lakes. Besides eating insects, they can actually catch tadpoles and **miscellaneous** types of tiny fish. If you disturb a fisher spider as it sits by the water's edge, it will probably **escape** into the water to hide.

The **scientific** name for fisher spiders is the family Pisauridae. They have large bodies and long legs. While they can hunt on land, they are best known for their ability to walk over water. They can also dive below the water to catch their prey. It takes **discipline** to sit quietly waiting for a meal to swim by.

Fisher spiders include the raft spider and the nursery-web spider. The nursery-web spider is named for the web it weaves to hold its egg sac. Most of the time it stays with the eggs until all have hatched and the **adolescent** spiders have **scattered**. Once in a while it may venture out across the water for a **luscious** seafood supper!

Say the boldfaced words in the selection. How many different sounds can you find made by the letters sc?

29

Spelling Practice

TIP
The letters sc can make three different sounds:
the **sk** sound, as in escape
the **s** sound, as in scissors
the **sh** sound, as in conscience

LIST WORDS
1. scented
2. adolescent
3. scattered
4. scissors
5. scientific
6. screaming
7. muscles
8. scalding
9. scenery
10. crescent
11. descending
12. sculpture
13. escape
14. scampered
15. scenic
16. miscellaneous
17. fascinating
18. luscious
19. discipline
20. conscience

Words with sc

Write each **list word** under the sound sc makes.

sc spells the **s** sound, as in scene
1. scented
2. adolescent
3. scissors
4. scientific
5. muscles
6. scenery
7. crescent
8. descending
9. scenic
10. miscellaneous
11. fascinating
12. discipline

sc spells the **sk** sound, as in scoop
13. scattered   14. screaming
15. scalding   16. sculpture
17. escape   18. scampered

sc spells the **sh** sound, as in unconscious
19. luscious   20. conscience

30   Lesson 7 • Words with sc

Complete the Paragraph

Use **list words** to fill in the blanks in the paragraph. Write the words on the lines.

My friend Andrew Smith was sitting on a dock near the lake last week, enjoying the ___scenery___, when he noticed a large spider next to him. He jumped up, ___screaming___, and ran back home as fast as his ___muscles___ would carry him. He told his father about his narrow ___escape___. "Let's go back and look at the spider," Mr. Smith suggested. "It sounds ___fascinating___!" When they reached the dock, the spider was nowhere to be found. Then Mr. Smith pointed to the water, where the spider ___scampered___ rapidly over the surface. "It's a fisher spider," he said. "They are very interesting from a ___scientific___ point of view because they can walk on water. I bet this one is looking for a ___luscious___ tadpole!"

Solve the Riddles

Use the **list words** to solve the riddles.

1. I can describe soap, a candle, or bath oil. ___scented___
2. You could say that I'm all over the place. ___scattered___
3. I'm quite a cut-up, especially when I'm around paper. ___scissors___
4. I'm not a child, yet I'm not a grown-up. ___adolescent___
5. I'm too hot to handle! ___scalding___
6. The moon sometimes appears to take my shape. ___crescent___
7. When you listen to me, you remember the right thing to do. ___conscience___
8. I'm a synonym for hard work or self-control. ___discipline___
9. I'm going down, not up. ___descending___
10. I'm lovely to look at, especially when you're outdoors. ___scenic___
11. I'm a work of art that has been carved or modeled. ___sculpture___
12. I don't fit in anywhere. ___miscellaneous___

Spelling and Writing

Proofreading

These nature poems have ten mistakes. Use the proofreading marks to correct them. Then, write the misspelled **list words** correctly on the lines.

Proofreading Marks
- ⬭ spelling mistake
- ⌄ add apostrophe
- ⌃ add something

The Fassenating Spider
She uses thread, but doesn't need sizzors;
She is making a skulpcher with no tools but her legs;
And though the lines she forms are thin,
They're so strong that a fly can't eskape them!

1. ___fascinating___   2. ___scissors___
3. ___sculpture___   4. ___escape___

Hungry Night
Crecint Moon, the night
Has taken abite from you.
What a lussious meal!

5. ___crescent___   6. ___luscious___

Writing a Poem

Write a nature poem. You might write about a fascinating creature, your favorite season, or a scenic place. Use any **list words** that you can. Remember to proofread your poem and fix any mistakes.

_____
_____
_____
_____
_____
_____

BONUS WORDS

scrimp
ascend
scour
conscious
scheme

Spelling Strategy

Write several cloze sentences on the board using **list words**. Next to each sentence, include the sound that *sc* stands for in the missing **list word**. For example: "A squirrel _____ along the branch." *sk* sound

Call on volunteers to read each sentence, write the correct word, and circle the letters *sc*.

BONUS WORDS

You may want to suggest that students create a crossword puzzle that includes each of the bonus words by drawing a blank grid and writing clues. Tell them to use their dictionaries if they need help. Then, have them switch puzzles with a partner and fill in the answer.

Spelling and Writing   *Page 32*

The **Proofreading** exercise will help students prepare to proofread their poems. As students complete the writing activity, encourage them to brainstorm ideas, write a first draft, revise, and proofread their work. To publish their writing, students may want to submit their poetry to a magazine that publishes children's work, such as *Stone Soup*. Its guidelines can be found on its Web site at http://www.stonesoup.com/main2/guidelines.html.

Writer's Corner Encourage students to research other interesting spiders by using the library or the Internet. Students can create a booklet to show what they learned.

Final Test

1. Those strawberries look absolutely **luscious**!
2. Don't let the rabbit **escape** when you feed it.
3. Only a **crescent** of the moon remained visible.
4. Please put the **scissors** back when you finish.
5. We looked at the **scenery** from the window.
6. The odor of mothballs **scented** the entire attic.
7. A clear **conscience** is a pleasant companion.
8. I need to buy **miscellaneous** school supplies.
9. Be careful **descending** the stairs!
10. Susan lifts weights to strengthen her **muscles**.
11. An **adolescent** boy gave us directions.
12. Why are papers **scattered** around your room?
13. The puppy **scampered** across the lawn.
14. It requires **discipline** to exercise daily.
15. That river is one of our **scenic** attractions.
16. I read a **fascinating** book about firefighting.
17. Did you see the artist's marble **sculpture**?
18. We are making a **scientific** study.
19. Don't burn yourself with that **scalding** water!
20. They were **screaming** with laughter.

Objective
To spell words with *gn*, *wr*, and *tch*

Correlated Phonics Lesson
MCP Phonics, Level F, Lesson 8

Spelling Words in Action   *Page 33*
In "The Last Voyage of the *Hindenburg*," students may be surprised to learn that people once traveled via airship. Invite students to discuss why the *Hindenburg* disaster ended the era of travel by airship.

Ask volunteers to say each boldfaced word and identify the letters that stand for the sound of *n, r,* or *ch*.

Warm-Up Test
1. Do you do warm-up **stretches** before you run?
2. The book **designer** chose a heavy cream paper.
3. That antique **wristwatch** is really beautiful!
4. The dog **fetched** the stick from the stream.
5. The family ate breakfast at the **kitchen** counter.
6. We found **wreckage** from the ship.
7. How is **wrestling** scored?
8. I returned the **crutches** after my leg healed.
9. The scout used a **hatchet** to split the logs.
10. The villagers feared the **wrath** of their leader.
11. The two runners are **unmatched** in ability.
12. Rita dabbed some **cologne** behind her ears.
13. The puppy **scratched** a hole in the screen door.
14. He **resigned** after twenty years in his job.
15. Some artists do all their **sketching** outdoors.
16. They helped the **foreigner** find his hotel.
17. Did you see the **campaign** posters?
18. The shutters were blown **awry** by the wind.
19. What a **gnarled** appearance that tree has!
20. Queen Victoria **reigned** for many years.

Spelling Practice   *Pages 34–35*
Introduce the spelling rule and have students read the **list words** aloud. Point out the correct pronunciation of *awry* and give its meaning and the meanings of other unfamiliar words (*gnarled, wrath*). Then, encourage students to look back at their **Warm-Up Tests** and apply the spelling rule to any misspelled words.

As students work through the **Spelling Practice** exercises, remind them to look back at their **list words** or in their dictionaries if they need help.

for ESL students **See Spelling Aloud, page 14**

Spelling Words in Action

How is the story of the *Hindenburg* disaster like other famous disasters?

The Last Voyage of the **Hindenburg**

On May 6, 1937, people at the landing field at Lakehurst, New Jersey, waited for the *Hindenburg* to arrive. Over 800 feet long, the great airship **reigned** over the Atlantic Ocean travel route. The luxurious craft had everything from a **kitchen** to a baby grand piano.

The flight was one of the routine **stretches** crossing the Atlantic Ocean. It had dropped off an airbag over Cologne, Germany, the city which gave perfumed **cologne** its name. Then it headed across the Atlantic. As the airship swung low over the landing field in Lakehurst, something went **awry**. The *Hindenburg* burst into flames and fell to the ground. Within a minute, nothing was left but **gnarled**, melted **wreckage**. Thirty-five of the 97 people on board lost their lives.

Some people blamed the **wrath** of nature. They believed that a spark of lightning had ignited the *Hindenburg*'s hydrogen gas. People **resigned** themselves to the end of airship travel. Later investigations suggested the airship's **designer** was at fault. The aircraft's fabric cover might have burst into flame. Whatever is to blame, the accident was one of the great disasters of the 20th century.

Look back at the boldfaced words in the selection. Say the words. Listen for the sounds of n, r, and ch. What do you notice about how these sounds are spelled?

33

TIP
Sometimes you don't hear every letter in a word. The letters gn can spell the n sound, as in designer, but the g is silent. The letters wr can spell the r sound, as in wrath, but the w is silent. The letters tch can spell the ch sound, as in scratched, but the t is silent.

Spelling Practice

Words with gn, wr, and tch
Write each **list word** under the correct heading. One word will be written twice.

LIST WORDS
1. stretches
2. designer
3. wristwatch
4. fetched
5. kitchen
6. wreckage
7. wrestling
8. crutches
9. hatchet
10. wrath
11. unmatched
12. cologne
13. scratched
14. resigned
15. sketching
16. foreigner
17. campaign
18. awry
19. gnarled
20. reigned

gn spells the n sound
1. designer
2. cologne
3. resigned
4. foreigner
5. campaign
6. gnarled
7. reigned

wr spells the r sound
8. wristwatch   9. wreckage
10. wrestling   11. wrath
12. awry

tch spells the ch sound
13. stretches   14. wristwatch
15. fetched   16. kitchen
17. crutches   18. hatchet
19. unmatched   20. scratched
21. sketching

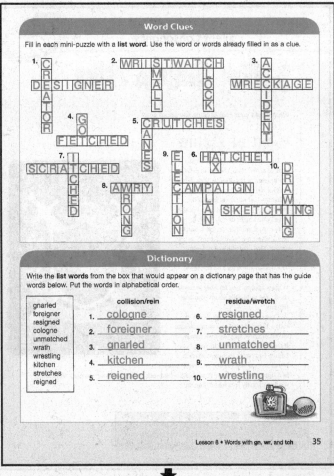

Word Clues

Fill in each mini-puzzle with a **list word**. Use the word or words already filled in as a clue.

1. CREATOR / DESIGNER
2. WRISTWATCH / SMALL / CLOCK
3. ACCIDENT / WRECKAGE
4. GO / FETCHED
5. CRUTCHES / CANES
6. HATCHET
7. ITCHED / SCRATCHED
8. AWRY / WRONG
9. ELECTION
6. HATCHET / FIX
10. DRAWING / SKETCHING / CAMPAIGN / PLAN

Dictionary

Write the **list words** from the box that would appear on a dictionary page that has the guide words below. Put the words in alphabetical order.

gnarled
foreigner
resigned
cologne
unmatched
wrath
wrestling
kitchen
stretches
reigned

collision/rein
1. cologne
2. foreigner
3. gnarled
4. kitchen
5. reigned

residue/wretch
6. resigned
7. stretches
8. unmatched
9. wrath
10. wrestling

Spelling and Writing

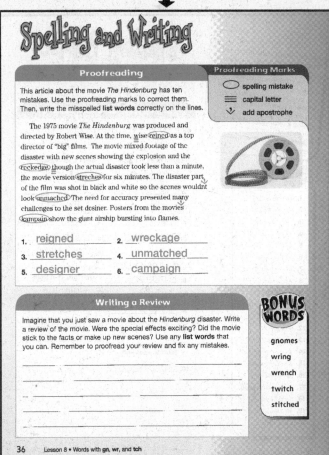

Proofreading

This article about the movie *The Hindenburg* has ten mistakes. Use the proofreading marks to correct them. Then, write the misspelled **list words** correctly on the lines.

Proofreading Marks
- ◯ spelling mistake
- ≡ capital letter
- ⌄ add apostrophe

The 1975 movie *The Hindenburg* was produced and directed by Robert Wise. At the time, wise reincd as a top director of "big" films. The movie mixed footage of the disaster with new scenes showing the explosion and the reckedge though the actual disaster took less than a minute, the movie version streches for six minutes. The disaster part of the film was shot in black and white so the scenes wouldnt look unmatced The need for accuracy presented many challenges to the set desiner. Posters from the movies kampain show the giant airship bursting into flames.

1. reigned
2. wreckage
3. stretches
4. unmatched
5. designer
6. campaign

Writing a Review

Imagine that you just saw a movie about the *Hindenburg* disaster. Write a review of the movie. Were the special effects exciting? Did the movie stick to the facts or make up new scenes? Use any **list words** that you can. Remember to proofread your review and fix any mistakes.

_____
_____
_____
_____

BONUS WORDS

gnomes
wring
wrench
twitch
stitched

Spelling Strategy

With a partner, students can write *gn*, *wr*, and *tch* on separate cards. Then, they can take turns saying the **list words** aloud and using them in sentences. For each word, the partner who is listening holds up the appropriate card or cards—to show whether *gn*, *wr*, and/or *tch* is in the word—and spells the word aloud.

BONUS WORDS
You may want to suggest that students write a riddle for each bonus word, leaving a space for the answer. Then, have them switch riddles with a partner and see if each can fill in the correct answers.

Spelling and Writing   Page 36

The **Proofreading** exercise will help students prepare to proofread their reviews. As students complete the writing activity, encourage them to brainstorm ideas, write a first draft, revise, and proofread their work. To publish their writing, students may want to create and illustrate their own movie posters, incorporating the reviews.

Writer's Corner Encourage students to look in an encyclopedia or a library book to learn more about famous aircraft, including planes, hot-air balloons, and airships. Students can create "flight" cards based on their favorite aircraft, and then share or trade their cards with one another.

Final Test

1. The character's **wrath** is shown in Chapter 1.
2. Was the **wreckage** from the storm removed?
3. Those pine trees have **gnarled** trunks.
4. Do you see the artist **sketching** the tree?
5. Al needed **crutches** after his sprain.
6. Jane **stretches** before she runs.
7. We'll eat dinner at the **kitchen** table.
8. This French **cologne** smells wonderful!
9. Queen Elizabeth II has **reigned** since 1953.
10. Why can't a **foreigner** visit that site?
11. The tablecloth was blown **awry** in the wind.
12. That old **hatchet** is too dull.
13. My new **wristwatch** is waterproof.
14. Fundy's tides are **unmatched** by any in the world.
15. Yuka **resigned** from her job.
16. A political **campaign** takes time and money.
17. The sharp chair legs **scratched** the wood floor.
18. Is sumo **wrestling** a popular sport in Japan?
19. This suit was made by a famous **designer**.
20. A student **fetched** a chair for the guest.

Objective
To spell words that contain silent consonants

 Correlated Phonics Lesson
MCP Phonics, Level F, Lesson 9

Spelling Words in Action   *Page 37*

In this selection, students find out about a "coat" that isn't a piece of clothing. Ask students what kinds of symbols people wear today (e.g., brand names, T-shirt slogans) and what their coat of arms would look like if they had one.

Encourage students to look back at the boldfaced words. Ask volunteers to say each word and identify the silent consonant or consonants.

Warm-Up Test

1. I **doubt** that I will attend the party.
2. **Knickers** are sometimes worn by golfers.
3. Can you read the date on that old **tombstone**?
4. A streak of **lightning** lit up the evening sky.
5. If you borrow money, you are in **debt**.
6. A water **softener** removes iron from water.
7. The people believed that the king was **almighty**.
8. We made a **solemn** promise.
9. **Fasten** the leash on the dog's collar.
10. We heard the teakettle **whistling** on the stove.
11. What fabulous **castles** we saw in Europe!
12. Louisa added the numbers in the **column**.
13. Did Mozart write any **hymns**?
14. An owl uses its sharp **eyesight** to find food.
15. Felipe was **listening** to a talk show.
16. Uncle Bert is a very successful **plumber**.
17. Lorraine Hansberry was a famous **playwright**.
18. When did the city **condemn** that old building?
19. **Moisten** the envelope before sealing it.
20. Lamar coated the fish fillet with bread **crumbs**.

Spelling Practice   *Pages 38–39*

Introduce the spelling rule and have students read the **list words** aloud, identifying the silent consonant in each word. Then, encourage students to look back at their **Warm-Up Tests** and apply the spelling rule to any misspelled words.

As students work through the **Spelling Practice** exercises, remind them to look back at their **list words** or in their dictionaries if they need help.

for ESL students **See Tape Recording, page 15**

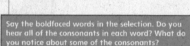

What would your coat of arms say about you?

Coat of Arms

Does your school or city have a coat of arms? If so, they're in **debt** to the knights of the Middle Ages. When knights defended their kings' **castles**, uniforms had not been invented. Nobody's **eyesight** was keen enough to tell one knight dressed in full armor from another. So, each knight would **fasten** a "coat of arms" to his armor. This coat showed a design identified with the knight's family. The design could also be displayed on a shield or flag. When a **column** of knights approached another in battle, there was no **doubt** about who was fighting.

Coats of arms are still in use today. Imagine how you would design a coat of arms for your own family. If there was a **plumber** in your family, you might include a wrench. If you were a fast runner, you might put in a **lightning** bolt. Your coat could be **solemn** or silly, showing anything from a flag waving proudly to a **whistling** cat!

Say the boldfaced words in the selection. Do you hear all of the consonants in each word? What do you notice about some of the consonants?

37

TIP
Use the following rules to help you spell words with silent consonants:
- Silent **t** often comes before **en** or **le**, as in **fasten** and **castles**.
- Silent **b** often comes before **t**, as in **debt**, or after **m**, as in **crumbs**.
- Silent **n** often follows **m**, as in **hymns**.
- Silent **k** often comes before **n**, as in **knickers**.
- Silent **gh** often follows **i**, as in **eyesight**.

Spelling Practice

LIST WORDS
1. doubt
2. knickers
3. tombstone
4. lightning
5. debt
6. softener
7. almighty
8. solemn
9. fasten
10. whistling
11. castles
12. column
13. hymns
14. eyesight
15. listening
16. plumber
17. playwright
18. condemn
19. moisten
20. crumbs

Words with Silent Consonants

Write each **list word** in the category that tells what silent consonant or consonants it contains.

silent b, as in thumb
1. doubt
2. tombstone
3. debt
4. plumber
5. crumbs

silent n, as in autumn
6. solemn
7. column
8. hymns
9. condemn

silent k, as in knife
10. knickers

silent t, as in glisten
11. softener
12. fasten
13. whistling
14. castles
15. listening
16. moisten

silent gh, as in flight
17. lightning
18. almighty
19. eyesight
20. playwright

Comparing Words

Study the relationship between the first two underlined words. Then, write a **list word** that has the same relationship with the third underlined word.

1. poem is to poet as play is to _playwright_
2. birds are to nests as kings are to _castles_
3. vegetables are to peas as songs are to _hymns_
4. shoe is to tie as seatbelt is to _fasten_
5. big is to huge as powerful is to _almighty_
6. music is to hearing as colors are to _eyesight_
7. water is to drops as bread is to _crumbs_
8. shoes are to sandals as pants are to _knickers_
9. keep is to promise as pay is to _debt_
10. television is to watching as radio is to _listening_

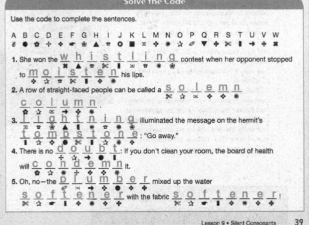

Solve the Code

Use the code to complete the sentences.

A B C D E F G H I J K L M N O P Q R S T U V W

1. She won the **w h i s t l i n g** contest when her opponent stopped to **m o i s t e n** his lips.
2. A row of straight-faced people can be called a **s o l e m n** **c o l u m n**.
3. **l i g h t n i n g** illuminated the message on the hermit's **t o m b s t o n e**: "Go away."
4. There is no **d o u b t**: If you don't clean your room, the board of health will **c o n d e m n** it.
5. Oh, no—the **p l u m b e r** mixed up the water **s o f t e n e r** with the fabric **s o f t e n e r**!

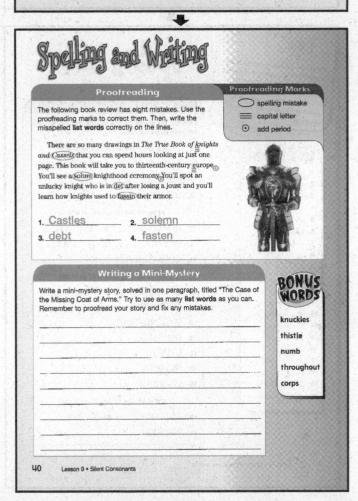

Spelling and Writing

Proofreading

The following book review has eight mistakes. Use the proofreading marks to correct them. Then, write the misspelled **list words** correctly on the lines.

There are so many drawings in *The True Book of knights and Cassels* that you can spend hours looking at just one page. This book will take you to thirteenth-century europe. You'll see a solum knighthood ceremony. You'll spot an unlucky knight who is in det after losing a joust and you'll learn how knights used to fassin their armor.

Proofreading Marks
- ⬭ spelling mistake
- ≡ capital letter
- ⊙ add period

1. _Castles_   2. _solemn_
3. _debt_   4. _fasten_

Writing a Mini-Mystery

Write a mini-mystery story, solved in one paragraph, titled "The Case of the Missing Coat of Arms." Try to use as many **list words** as you can. Remember to proofread your story and fix any mistakes.

BONUS WORDS

knuckles
thistle
numb
throughout
corps

Spelling Strategy

Invite students to pair up with a partner and write the **list words**. Then, partners can pronounce each word, point to the silent consonant or consonants, and explain the spelling rule that applies to the silent letter or letters. Challenge students to think of other words that contain a silent *b*, *n*, *k*, *t*, or *gh*.

BONUS WORDS

You may want to suggest that students write an exclamatory sentence that includes each of the bonus words. Then, have them erase the bonus words and switch papers with a partner to fill in the missing words.

Spelling and Writing   *Page 40*

The **Proofreading** exercise will help students prepare to proofread their mini-mystery stories. As students complete the writing activity, encourage them to brainstorm ideas, write a first draft, revise, and proofread their work. To publish their writing, students may want to

- present their mystery stories as skits
- create a mystery-story magazine.

Writer's Corner Students might be interested in looking at *Coat of Arms* by Catherine Daly-Weir or a similar book to help them design their own coat of arms or personal seal.

Final Test
1. The **tombstone** was made of pink granite.
2. The chorus recorded several old **hymns**.
3. A witness takes a **solemn** oath to tell the truth.
4. Teachers must **condemn** disruptive behavior.
5. Hannah is **whistling** a song.
6. I finally paid my **debt** to the bank!
7. Pigeons ate the **crumbs** on the ground.
8. Who's **listening** to the ballgame on the radio?
9. Please **fasten** the latch on the door.
10. Glaucoma is a disease that affects **eyesight**.
11. Dew will **moisten** the grass.
12. Did **lightning** strike the tower?
13. If you **doubt** the truth of a fact, look it up.
14. That wave just destroyed two sand **castles**!
15. When did your aunt become a **plumber**?
16. Fabric **softener** makes clothes soft and fluffy.
17. In the 1920s, men's **knickers** were fashionable.
18. The **almighty** ruler promised to bring peace.
19. Arthur Miller is an American **playwright**.
20. The words are listed in a long **column**.

Objective

To spell words in which _ear_ spells the sound of /ur/ as in _earth_ and the sound of /ir/ as in _clear_, _are_ spells the sound of /er/ as in _care_; and _air_ spells the sound of /er/ as in _chair_

Correlated Phonics Lessons
MCP Phonics, Level F, Lessons 9–10

Spelling Words in Action   _Page 41_

In this selection, students read about an exciting Olympic event called luging. After reading, invite students to tell about their favorite Olympic events.

Encourage students to look back at the boldfaced words. Ask volunteers to say each word and identify the sound spelled by _ear_, _are_, or _air_.

Warm-Up Test

1. In 1849 many miners were **searching** for gold.
2. Black clouds suddenly **appeared** in the sky.
3. The **millionaire** donated funds to the hospital.
4. Sulfur in the air can tarnish **silverware**.
5. Have you **compared** a luge and a bobsled?
6. Watch your step on the **stairway**.
7. Pottery made of baked clay is called **earthenware**.
8. LuAnn followed the directions **carefully**.
9. We **barely** arrived in time!
10. A checkerboard has red and black **squares**.
11. The mechanic replaced the engine's **gears**.
12. Jake is **earning** money for college.
13. The pitcher thought the umpire ruled **unfairly**.
14. I was **unaware** that you were away last week.
15. Donna designs and makes **earrings**.
16. I have an **earnest** desire to become a doctor.
17. Are the students doing **research** in the library?
18. Don't **despair** over the loss of a game.
19. We filled out a **questionnaire** for the class.
20. Did the **rehearsal** for the school play go well?

Spelling Practice   _Pages 42–43_

Introduce the spelling rule and have students read the **list words** aloud. You may also want to point out that _earthenware_ contains two of the sounds being studied. Then, encourage students to look back at their **Warm-Up Tests** and apply the spelling rule to any misspelled words.

As students work through the **Spelling Practice** exercises, remind them to look back at their **list words** or in their dictionaries if they need help.

 See Student Dictation, page 14

Spelling Words in Action

How does luge racing differ from sledding?

Super Sledding

Imagine whizzing down an ice-covered course on a sled traveling 90 miles an hour, **earning** cheers from admiring onlookers! That's what the sport of luge racing is all about. A luge is a fast, lightweight sled that holds one person. It can be **compared** to a bobsled in some ways, but a luger lies on his or her back on the sled.

A luger can reach incredible speeds for a vehicle with no motor or **gears**. To steer the sled down the course's twists and turns, the rider **carefully** moves his or her legs and shoulders. These movements are **barely** noticeable to others.

The riders wear helmets with face shields and form-fitting rubber suits. The idea is to reduce air friction. Racers **despair** when they lose even a few hundredths of a second off their finish times.

Though Europeans had been luging for centuries, Americans were **unaware** of the sport until modern times. Luge racing first **appeared** in the Winter Olympics in 1964. Coaches and athletes searched for new talent. The best athletes got to train on ice courses as a **rehearsal** for competitions. These Olympic hopefuls practiced in **earnest** for the chance to compete with the world's best lugers.

Look back at the boldfaced words in the selection. Say the words. Compare the sound made by the letters _ear_, _are_, and _air_.

41

TIP

Sometimes the letters _ear_ make the /ir/ sound, as in _years_ and _appeared_. The letters _ear_ can also make the /ur/ sound, as in _earnest_ and _earning_. Sometimes the /er/ sound can be spelled _are_, as in _barely_, or _air_, as in _stairway_.

Spelling Practice

Words with _ear_, _are_, and _air_

Write the **list words** that contain the sound given. You will write one word twice.

LIST WORDS

1. searching
2. appeared
3. millionaire
4. silverware
5. compared
6. stairway
7. earthenware
8. carefully
9. barely
10. squares
11. gears
12. earning
13. unfairly
14. unaware
15. earrings
16. earnest
17. research
18. despair
19. questionnaire
20. rehearsal

ear spells the /ur/ sound, as in _earth_

1. searching   2. earthenware
3. earning   4. earnest
5. research   6. rehearsal

air spells the /er/ sound, as in _chair_

7. millionaire   8. stairway
9. unfairly   10. despair
11. questionnaire

are spells the /er/ sound, as in _care_

12. silverware
13. compared
14. earthenware
15. carefully
16. barely
17. squares
18. unaware

ear spells the /ir/ sound, as in _clear_

19. appeared   20. gears
21. earrings

Missing Words

Write the **list word** that completes each sentence.

1. A rescue team is <u>searching</u> for the lost boy.
2. Mountain bikes are equipped with several <u>gears</u>.
3. She is saving part of the money she is <u>earning</u> every month.
4. Although the <u>earthenware</u> pot was very old, it had no cracks.
5. The younger brother didn't appreciate being <u>compared</u> to his older brother.
6. The sun was shining while it was showering, and a rainbow <u>apeared</u>.
7. I was so sick I could <u>barely</u> get out of bed.
8. Since she had no idea about the surprise party, it caught her <u>unaware</u>.
9. The angry defendant felt that he had been treated <u>unfairly</u> by the judge.
10. He gave an <u>earnest</u> and moving speech about his fight with the disease.
11. Members will fill out a <u>questionnaire</u> to participate in the survey.
12. When the economy is strong, it's easier to become a <u>millionaire</u>.

Riddles

Choose the **list word** that answers each riddle. Write it on the line. The words in bold are contained in the answers.

1. A **search** for information can be called this. <u>research</u>
2. How to handle a box **full** of dynamite. <u>carefully</u>
3. What to call **silver** knives, forks, and spoons. <u>silverware</u>
4. How to describe the attitude of a gloomy **pair** of friends. <u>despair</u>
5. If you **are** shapes with four equal sides, you are these. <u>squares</u>
6. If **he** needs more practice, this is where he should go. <u>rehearsal</u>
7. It's the **way** up to the second floor. <u>stairway</u>
8. What jewelry for your **ear** can be called. <u>earrings</u>

Spelling and Writing

Proofreading

These how-to directions for a Trivia Olympics have eleven mistakes. Use the proofreading marks to correct them. Then, write the misspelled **list words** correctly on the lines.

1. You will need two teams and a a judge.
2. Each team has to resrch five questions for the other team to answer. Start by surching through reference books. List the books where the information appeared. Work cairfully.
3. Each correctly answered question is worth 50 points.
4. Each incorrectly answered question results in the opposite team teming a 25-point bonus.
5. At the end of the game, the scores are compared. The team with the most points wins.

Proofreading Marks

◯ spelling mistake
⊙ add period
ꝰ take out something

1. <u>research</u>   2. <u>searching</u>
3. <u>appeared</u>   4. <u>carefully</u>
5. <u>earning</u>   6. <u>compared</u>

Writing a Questionnaire

Think of a sport that you feel should be in the Olympics. Write a questionnaire about the sport. The questionnaire could follow a question-and-answer format or multiple choice. Use any **list words** that you can. Remember to proofread your questionnaire and fix any mistakes.

_____
_____
_____
_____
_____
_____

BONUS WORDS

concessionaire
smeared
yearn
impair
welfare

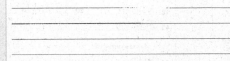

Spelling Strategy

On separate sheets of paper, write *ear*—sound of /ʉr/ (*earth*); *ear*—sound of /ir/ (*clear*); *are*—sound of /er/ (*care*); and *air*—sound of /er/ (*chair*) in large letters. Tape each sheet in a different corner of the classroom. Then, call out each **list word** and have students point to the appropriate sheet for the word's vowel sound and spelling. Ask a volunteer to write each **list word** on the correct sheet.

BONUS WORDS You may want to suggest that students write a mystery-story title for each bonus word. Then, have them erase the bonus word from each title. Have them switch titles with a partner and see if they can fill in the missing words correctly.

Spelling and Writing   Page 44

The **Proofreading** exercise will help students prepare to proofread their questionnaires. As students complete the writing activity, encourage them to brainstorm ideas, write a first draft, revise, and proofread their work. To publish their writing, students may want to submit the results of their questionnaires to the local newspaper.

Writer's Corner Invite groups of students to consult an almanac to find each Olympic winning time or distance for a particular competitive event. Students can make line graphs to show the results of an event for several successive competitions.

Final Test

1. Rinse the **silverware** with hot water.
2. Josie was **unaware** that she dropped her scarf.
3. Tio used a **questionnaire** to gather opinions.
4. I was **barely** able to lift the box by myself.
5. Astronomers do **research** to learn about stars.
6. Lovely **earthenware** is made in Spain.
7. How is the group **earning** money?
8. After the storm, a beautiful rainbow **appeared**.
9. The tailor **carefully** stitched the trousers.
10. The **millionaire** left all her money to charity.
11. I felt that the author was criticized **unfairly**.
12. What **despair** that terrible storm left behind!
13. Yesterday she lost one of her favorite **earrings**.
14. **Squares** have four equal sides.
15. Have you **compared** the book with the movie?
16. The orchestra will hold a **rehearsal** today.
17. Daryl helped out by vacuuming the **stairway**.
18. I am **searching** for facts to use in my report.
19. Roberto has an **earnest** way of speaking.
20. Karen adjusted the **gears** on her racing bike.

Words with the Sound of Long e

Objective
To spell words with the long *e* sound

 Correlated Phonics Lessons
MCP Phonics, Level F,
Lessons 15, 17–18

Spelling Words in Action   *Page 45*

In "Olympic Gold," students learn about the athletes in a unique kind of competition. After reading, invite students to discuss competitions in which they have participated.

Ask volunteers to say the boldfaced words and identify the different letters that spell the long *e* sound.

Warm-Up Test
1. An **athlete** must train regularly.
2. The police officer signaled the car to **proceed**.
3. Please **delete** my name from the list of runners.
4. That animal is in **extreme** danger of extinction.
5. Amy **repeated** the good news to her family.
6. This award is a token of our **esteem** for you.
7. Try to find a **reasonable** solution.
8. Leon **revealed** the secret only to his friend.
9. My collection of models is finally **complete**!
10. Let me wash that **greasy** pan for you.
11. Painting my room was quite an **achievement**!
12. The governor **squeezed** my hand firmly.
13. What do you charge for overnight **delivery**?
14. The students rode a **trolley** car to school.
15. **Ecology** is the study of the environment.
16. How many **nieces** and nephews does he have?
17. Grandpa **concealed** my present under his coat.
18. The jeweler will **guarantee** my watch.
19. The jury found the witness's story **believable**.
20. Jamie finally **succeeded** at doing a handstand.

Spelling Practice   *Pages 46–47*

Introduce the spelling rule and have students read the **list words** aloud. Encourage students to look back at their **Warm-Up Tests** and apply the spelling rule to any misspelled words.

As students work through the **Spelling Practice** exercises, remind them to look back at their **list words** or in their dictionaries if they need help. Explain that *delete, revealed,* and *delivery* can be pronounced with the long *e* or the short *i* sound in the first syllable. *Believable* can be pronounced with the long *e* sound or the schwa sound.

 See Variant Spellings, page 14

42

Spelling Words in Action

Who are the competitors in the Special Olympics?

OLYMPIC GOLD

There are some very special athletes who know they have **succeeded** every time they compete. They are part of the Special Olympics. Each **athlete** in the competition is mentally challenged, yet all have developed the skills and the **esteem** it takes to make them winners.

The Special Olympics began in 1968. Eunice Kennedy Shriver **revealed** the need for a contest for athletes with mental retardation. She believed the benefits for the athletes, including physical fitness and self-confidence, would be **extreme**. Today, about a million athletes compete in over 140 countries. There are more than 20 events.

Every two years, either the World Winter Games or the World Summer Games are **repeated**. Thousands of athletes take part. The games begin with a parade. Friends, parents, **nieces** or nephews, and other fans watch the athletes enter proudly. Then they are ready to **proceed**. After every event, the top three athletes are presented with gold, silver, or bronze medals. Everyone's **achievement** is recognized. All contestants are awarded a well-deserved ribbon.

Most athletes only have to compete against one another. Athletes in the Special Olympics go one step further. They compete against themselves. Their efforts **guarantee** that they will win.

Say the boldfaced words in the selection. What vowel sound do you hear in each of these words? How many ways can you find to spell that sound?

45

TIP
The long e sound can be spelled different ways:
e, as in ecology   ee, as in proceed
ea, as in repeated   ie, as in nieces
e_e, as in athlete   y, as in delivery
ey, as in trolley

Words with the Sound of Long e

Write each **list word** under the spelling of its long *e* sound. Some **list words** are used more than once.

LIST WORDS
1. athlete
2. proceed
3. delete
4. extreme
5. repeated
6. esteem
7. reasonable
8. revealed
9. complete
10. greasy
11. achievement
12. squeezed
13. delivery
14. trolley
15. ecology
16. nieces
17. concealed
18. guarantee
19. believable
20. succeeded

ee, as in succeed
1. proceed
2. esteem
3. squeezed
4. guarantee
5. succeeded

e, as in equal
15. delete
16. revealed
17. delivery
18. ecology
19. believable

ea, as in speak
6. repeated
7. reasonable
8. revealed
9. greasy
10. concealed

ie, as in piece
20. achievement
21. nieces
22. believable

y, as in apology
11. greasy
12. delivery
13. ecology

e_e, as in scheme
23. athlete
24. delete
25. extreme
26. complete

ey, as in volleyball
14. trolley

46   Lesson 11 • Words with the Sound of Long e

Classification

Write the **list word** that belongs in each group.

1. omit, erase, _delete_
2. pressed, kneaded, _squeezed_
3. respect, admiration, _esteem_
4. farthest, utmost, _extreme_
5. total, whole, _complete_
6. train, bus, _trolley_
7. sisters, aunts, _nieces_
8. feat, accomplishment, _achievement_
9. uncovered, unveiled, _revealed_
10. did again, persisted, _repeated_
11. warranty, promise, _guarantee_
12. fair, sensible, _reasonable_
13. true, likely, _believable_
14. oily, slick, _greasy_
15. advance, move ahead, _proceed_
16. hid, obscured, _concealed_

Solve the Code

Use the code to complete the jokes.

A B C D E F G H I J K L M N O P Q R S T U V W X Y Z
✗ ✳ ⚬ ✢ ✳ ✢ ⚬ + ⊙ ✢ ✳ ✢ ⚬ ✳ ⚬ ✢ ✳ ⚬ ☆ ★ ✓ ✳ ⚬ ⇨ ⇨ ☆

1. I _s u c c e e d e d_ in crossing a parrot and a centipede . . . now
      ☆ + ⚬ ⚬ ✳ ✳ ✢ ✳ +
   I have a walkie talkie!

2. Q: What _a t h l e t e_ can jump higher than a stop sign?
          ✗ ★ + ✢ ✳ ★ ✳
   A: All of them—stop signs can't jump!

3. Teacher: Class, today we'll study the _e c o l o g y_ of the rain forest.
                                          ✳ ⚬ ⚬ ✢ ⚬ ⚬ ⇨
   Who knows what tree frogs like to eat?

   Student: Lollihops!

4. Patient: Doctor, Doctor, I can't decide if I'm a comedian or a mailman!

   Doctor: Well, keep working on your _d e l i v e r y_!
                                       ✢ ✳ ✢ ⊙ ✳ ✳ ⇨

Spelling and Writing

Proofreading

This speech presenting an award to an athlete has twelve mistakes. Use the proofreading marks to correct them. Then, write the misspelled **list words** correctly on the lines.

Proofreading Marks

◯ spelling mistake
≡ capital letter
⤸ take out something

Most Improved Athleet of the Year

P. S. 321 recognizes Russell Ice for his acheivment in track. although Russ did not win any races, he suceded in winning our admiration. At at first, Russ could not even complete a 100-yard dash. instead of quitting or giving up, Russ ran each day, even under the most extream weather conditions. At Field Day, Russ came in third in the the 3-mile race. He has truly earned our our highest esteem.

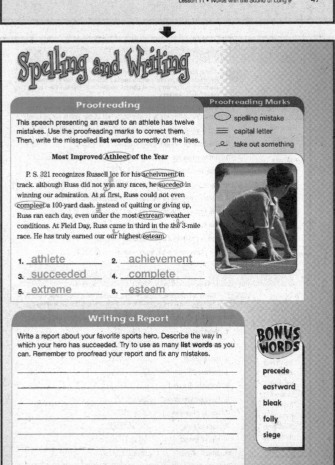

1. _athlete_
2. _achievement_
3. _succeeded_
4. _complete_
5. _extreme_
6. _esteem_

Writing a Report

Write a report about your favorite sports hero. Describe the way in which your hero has succeeded. Try to use as many **list words** as you can. Remember to proofread your report and fix any mistakes.

_____

_____

_____

_____

_____

BONUS WORDS

precede

eastward

bleak

folly

siege

Spelling Strategy

To call attention to the different ways to spell long *e*, write each **list word** on the board and circle the letter or letters that stand for the long *e* sound or sounds. Ask volunteers to suggest other words that illustrate each of the spelling patterns.

BONUS WORDS

You may want to suggest that students write each list word, then work with a partner to list at least one synonym and one antonym for each word. Have them use a thesaurus or an unabridged dictionary to check their work, and ask them how many additional synonyms and antonyms they can find.

Spelling and Writing   Page 48

The **Proofreading** exercise will help students prepare to proofread their reports. As students complete the writing activity, encourage them to brainstorm ideas, write a first draft, revise, and proofread their work. To publish their writing, students may want to

• use their reports to create a display
• read their reports aloud as TV broadcasts.

Writer's Corner Students may enjoy writing fan letters to sports figures they admire. A reference librarian can help them locate appropriate addresses. Be sure to tell students that not all the celebrities will respond to their letters.

Final Test

1. Linda **squeezed** lemons to make lemonade.
2. Your plan sounds like a **reasonable** one.
3. When the rain stops, our game can **proceed**.
4. On Saturdays, our mail **delivery** is very early.
5. A curtain **concealed** the prize.
6. Have you **succeeded** in starting the mower?
7. Two of my **nieces** were born on the same day.
8. Once, this **trolley** was pulled by a horse.
9. The teacher **repeated** each spelling word.
10. Good nutrition is important for an **athlete**.
11. I read the **complete** book in only an hour!
12. The store will **guarantee** the radio for a year.
13. We are learning about **ecology** in science class.
14. My hands are **greasy** from working on the car.
15. Draw a line through words you want to **delete**.
16. The play's plot was not **believable**.
17. The flashlight's beam **revealed** a cat.
18. Do you have a warm coat for **extreme** cold?
19. You should be proud of this **achievement**!
20. The mayor is held in high **esteem**.

Objectives

To review spelling words with *sc*; *gn*, *wr*, and *tch*; silent consonants; *ear*, *are*, *air*; and the sound of long *e*

Check Your
Spelling Notebook   *Page 49–52*

Based on your observations, note which words are giving students the most difficulty and offer assistance for spelling them correctly. Here are some frequently misspelled words to watch for: *scissors, muscles, cologne, campaign, solemn, column, despair, athlete,* and *achievement.*

To give students extra help and practice in taking standardized tests, you may want to have them take the **Review Test** for this lesson on pages 46–47. After scoring the tests, return them to students so that they can record their misspelled words in their spelling notebooks.

After practicing their troublesome words, students can work through the exercises for lessons 7–11 and the cumulative review, **Show What You Know.** Before they begin each exercise, you may want to go over the spelling rule.

Take It Home

Invite students to listen for the **list words** in lessons 7–11 as they watch TV news and weather programs. Students can also use **Take It Home** Master 2 on pages 48–49 to help them do the activity. (A complete list of the spelling words is included on page 48 of the **Take It Home** Master.) Invite students to bring their lists to class and to compare them, noting which words were used most frequently.

In lessons 7 through 11, you learned that some words are spelled differently than you expect. The letters **sc** and **ear** can stand for more than one sound. In addition, one sound, like **er**, **n**, **r**, **ch**, or long **e**, may be spelled in many different ways. Some words contain silent consonants.

Check Your Spelling Notebook

Look at the words in your spelling notebook. Which words for lessons 7 through 11 did you have the most trouble with? Write them here.

_____

Practice writing your troublesome words with a partner. Erase certain letters from the words, trade papers with your partner, and fill in the missing letters.

Lesson 7

 TIP The letters **sc** can stand for three different sounds: the **sk** sound, as in <u>scalding</u>; the **s** sound, as in <u>muscles</u>; and the **sh** sound, as in <u>luscious</u>.

List Words

scented
scattered
discipline
scissors
screaming
muscles
scalding
scenic
crescent
descending
escape
luscious

Study the relationship between the first two underlined words. Then, write a **list word** that has the same relationship with the third underlined word or phrase. Not all the words will be used.

1. <u>catch</u> is to <u>throw</u> as <u>capture</u> is to __escape__
2. <u>draw</u> is to <u>sketch</u> as <u>tasty</u> is to __luscious__
3. <u>sew</u> is to <u>needle</u> as <u>cut</u> is to __scissors__
4. <u>reading</u> is to your <u>mind</u> as <u>exercise</u> is to your __muscles__
5. <u>cool</u> is to <u>chilly</u> as <u>hot</u> is to __scalding__
6. <u>up</u> is to <u>down</u> as <u>climbing</u> is to __descending__
7. <u>whispering</u> is to <u>murmuring</u> as <u>yelling</u> is to __screaming__
8. <u>whole</u> is to <u>part</u> as <u>full moon</u> is to __crescent__ moon
9. <u>food</u> is to <u>flavored</u> as <u>flower</u> is to __scented__
10. <u>gathered</u> is to <u>spread</u> as <u>collected</u> is to __scattered__

49

Lesson 8

TIP The **n** sound can be spelled with **gn** but the **g** is silent, as in <u>gnarled</u>. The **r** sound can be spelled with **wr** but the **w** is silent, as in <u>awry</u>. The **ch** sound can be spelled with **tch** but the **t** is silent, as in <u>kitchen</u>.

List Words

stretches
fetched
wrath
cologne
wristwatch
gnarled
resigned
sketching
kitchen
foreigner
awry
wreckage

Find the **list words** that mean the same as the underlined words in the sentences. Write the words on the lines. Not all the words will be used.

1. By my <u>small clock</u>, it's almost twelve o'clock. __wristwatch__
2. The apology ended my <u>fury</u>. __wrath__
3. Tim <u>reaches</u> for the box on the top shelf. __stretches__
4. That tree is so <u>twisted</u>! __gnarled__
5. Eileen <u>quit</u> after a week. __resigned__
6. He is a <u>stranger</u> to our land. __foreigner__
7. Kirk <u>brought</u> the book I had left behind. __fetched__
8. The storm left <u>damage</u> everywhere. __wreckage__
9. Dad is <u>drawing</u> a boat. __sketching__
10. Our plans for the trip went <u>wrong</u>. __awry__

Lesson 9

TIP Some words contain silent letters, such as the **t** in <u>softener</u>, the **b** in <u>plumber</u>, the **n** in <u>column</u>, the **k** in <u>knickers</u>, and the **gh** in <u>almighty</u>.

List Words

doubt
knickers
softener
lightning
debt
solemn
column
fasten
hymns
condemn
moisten
crumbs

Write the **list word** to match each clue. Not all the words will be used.

1. short pants — __knickers__
2. declare unfit for use — __condemn__
3. make damp — __moisten__
4. comes with thunder — __lightning__
5. something owed — __debt__
6. be uncertain about — __doubt__
7. songs of praise — __hymns__
8. not laughing — __solemn__
9. bits of bread — __crumbs__
10. attach or join — __fasten__

50   Lesson 12 • Review

Lesson 10

TIP The letters **ear** make the /ir/ sound, as in <u>ear</u>rings, and the /ur/ sound, as in res<u>ear</u>ch. The /er/ sound is sometimes spelled **are**, as in un<u>aware</u>, or **air**, as in unf<u>air</u>ly.

List Words

searching
appeared
stairway
millionaire
carefully
earthenware
earrings
earning
unfairly
questionnaire
despair
rehearsal

Each word below is hidden in a **list word**. Write the **list words** on the lines. Not all the words will be used.

1. mill   <u>millionaire</u>
2. fully   <u>carefully</u>
3. earn   <u>earning</u>
4. fair   <u>unfairly</u>
5. hear   <u>rehearsal</u>
6. pair   <u>despair</u>
7. rings   <u>earrings</u>
8. arch   <u>searching</u>
9. pear   <u>appeared</u>
10. then   <u>earthenware</u>

Lesson 11

TIP The long e sound can be spelled several ways: **e**, as in <u>e</u>cology; **ee**, as in est<u>ee</u>m; **ea**, as in rev<u>ea</u>led; **ie**, as in bel<u>ie</u>vable; **e_e**, as in d<u>e</u>let<u>e</u>; **y**, as in deliver<u>y</u>; and **ey**, as in troll<u>ey</u>.

List Words

trolley
delivery
delete
greasy
reasonable
revealed
concealed
squeezed
nieces
succeeded
repeated
achievement

Write a **list word** to complete each sentence. Not all the words will be used.

1. These dirty dishes are <u>greasy</u>
2. What an <u>achievement</u> it was to win first prize!
3. We can ride on the <u>trolley</u>
4. My baby sister finally <u>succeeded</u> in walking.
5. No one heard, so I <u>repeated</u> the question.
6. Send it by special <u>delivery</u>
7. Just <u>delete</u> the extra names.
8. Ty <u>revealed</u> the winner's name to us.
9. Jon <u>squeezed</u> the sponge dry.
10. The actor's face was <u>concealed</u> by a beard.

Lesson 12 • Review   51

Show What You Know

Lessons 7–11 Review

One word is misspelled in each set of **list words**. Fill in the circle next to the **list word** that is spelled incorrectly.

1. ○ wrestling ○ searching ○ whistling ○ screaming ● silverwair
2. ○ fascinating ○ unfairly ○ softener ● resined ○ scenic
3. ○ listening ○ scenery ○ delivery ● skratched ○ condemn
4. ○ descending ● ristwatch ○ achievement ○ nieces ○ reasonable
5. ○ earthenware ○ crumbs ● misellaneous ○ earnest ○ awry
6. ● playwrite ○ trolley ○ hymns ○ sketching ○ sculpture
7. ○ research ○ scattered ● garanty ○ muscles ○ solemn
8. ○ doubt ○ appeared ○ earrings ○ revealed ● deziner
9. ○ succeeded ○ luscious ● kichen ○ moisten ○ extreme
10. ● adolesent ○ tombstone ○ questionnaire ○ conscience ○ proceed
11. ● cairfully ○ wrath ○ scissors ○ castles ○ squares
12. ○ listening ○ esteem ○ escape ○ gnarled ● greesy
13. ○ crutches ○ gears ○ foreigner ● dispair ○ athlete
14. ○ debt ○ cologne ● cressent ○ scientific ○ earning
15. ○ compared ● compleate ○ millionaire ○ believable ○ plumber
16. ○ wreckage ○ scalding ○ unaware ● ecologey ○ scented
17. ● campane ○ fetched ○ almighty ○ barely ○ eyesight
18. ○ stairway ○ delete ○ reigned ○ hatchet ● rehersal
19. ○ concealed ○ scampered ○ repeated ○ discipline ● fascen
20. ○ column ○ squeezed ● streches ○ knickers ○ unmatched

Final Test

1. That water is **scalding**, so let it cool.
2. There is a **crescent**-shaped moon tonight.
3. Going up the hill may be easier than **descending**.
4. The magician could **escape** from any trap.
5. Those berries we picked are **luscious**!
6. This belt **stretches** enough to fit my father.
7. I bought a **wristwatch** with a big face.
8. Pedro **fetched** his mother's purse for her.
9. Investigators studied the **wreckage** for clues.
10. His tone of voice was filled with **wrath**.
11. I have no **doubt** that I will finish on time.
12. In the picture, Grandfather is wearing **knickers**.
13. **Lightning** just lit up the sky!
14. No one should go into **debt** for luxury items.
15. His face was serious and **solemn**.
16. Mom lost one of her new **earrings**.
17. The money I am **earning** will pay for a bike.
18. Did you think the other team played **unfairly**?
19. Their **despair** lifted when they spotted the ship.
20. Today we are having a **rehearsal** for our play.
21. My parents are proud of my **achievement**.
22. Finally, the judges **revealed** the winning poster.
23. Tom **succeeded** at swimming ten laps.
24. The chef **squeezed** the lemons.
25. How easily the disguise **concealed** my identity!
26. The smell of fresh bread **scented** the house.
27. Papers were **scattered** around the room.
28. Don't use those **scissors** for cutting paper.
29. The children are **screaming** with delight.
30. Seth's **muscles** were sore after the race.
31. No one ever **resigned** from this job.
32. Mr. Dubois is **sketching** plans for a house.
33. No **foreigner** may vote in our elections.
34. The curtains were blown **awry** by the breeze.
35. How **gnarled** those old tree branches are!
36. Please **fasten** the gate when you leave.
37. Which composer wrote those **hymns**?
38. The judge will **condemn** such behavior.
39. If the mixture seems dry, **moisten** it with water.
40. The hikers left only **crumbs** on their plates.
41. The rescue ship began **searching** at once.
42. When the people **appeared**, the deer vanished.
43. That mansion must belong to a **millionaire**!
44. Make sure you pack that fragile vase **carefully**.
45. The potter made **earthenware** vases.
46. Did you enjoy riding the old **trolley**?
47. Make sure this **delivery** is made before noon.
48. Remember to **delete** the extra word in the title.
49. We **repeated** the song for the audience.
50. Don't touch the sofa with those **greasy** hands!

Name _____

Read each set of phrases. Fill in the circle next to the phrase with an underlined word that is spelled correctly.

1. ⓐ sketching the tree   ⓒ schetching on paper
    ⓑ scetching some fruit   ⓓ skeching with a pencil

2. ⓐ doub the facts   ⓒ doute the story
    ⓑ dowt the witness   ⓓ doubt her word

3. ⓐ resgned as chairperson   ⓒ a risgned attitude
    ⓑ resigned from office   ⓓ rezined himself to it

4. ⓐ that gnarled branch   ⓒ those gnrled trees
    ⓑ the narld hand   ⓓ these narled vines

5. ⓐ special delivary   ⓒ daily dellivary
    ⓑ weekly delivery   ⓓ monthly deliverry

6. ⓐ these lusious grapes   ⓒ one luscious honeydew
    ⓑ those lucious pears   ⓓ some luscous strawberries

7. ⓐ treated unfarely   ⓒ scolded unfarly
    ⓑ handled unfairley   ⓓ punished unfairly

8. ⓐ the loud hymms   ⓒ the old hymns
    ⓑ those grand himms   ⓓ familiar hims

9. ⓐ the skreming monkeys   ⓒ excited, skreaming fans
    ⓑ those screeming arguers   ⓓ the screaming infant

10. ⓐ this new ristwach   ⓒ a digital wristwatch
    ⓑ an antique wristwach   ⓓ a waterproof ristwatch

11. ⓐ his courageous excape   ⓒ their ingenious escape
    ⓑ her daring escaipe   ⓓ an unsuccessful eskape

12. ⓐ these sharp scisors   ⓒ the tailor's scissors
    ⓑ those children's scissers   ⓓ these blunt sissors

13. ⓐ frantically serching   ⓒ sertching the area
    ⓑ seartching for clues   ⓓ intensely searching

Name _____

Read each set of phrases. Fill in the circle next to the phrase with an underlined word that is spelled correctly.

14. ⓐ appeared at dawn   ⓒ suddenly appeered
    ⓑ quietly apeered   ⓓ mysteriously apeared

15. ⓐ your outstanding acheivement   ⓒ their extraordinary achievment
    ⓑ my academic acheivmment   ⓓ this incredible achievement

16. ⓐ squeezed the orange   ⓒ squeased the handle
    ⓑ squezed the pillow   ⓓ squeesed between them

17. ⓐ deleat this word   ⓒ dellete one paragraph
    ⓑ delete that letter   ⓓ delleat that phrase

18. ⓐ my greasy hands   ⓒ greasey bicycle chain
    ⓑ this gresey pizza   ⓓ gresy cooking utensils

19. ⓐ moysten the towel   ⓒ moysen the plant
    ⓑ moisen the sponge   ⓓ moisten your hands

20. ⓐ those scattered toys   ⓒ the skattered crumbs
    ⓑ the scaterred pages   ⓓ these skatered documents

21. ⓐ pay a det   ⓒ a small deabt
    ⓑ owe a debt   ⓓ to be in dett

22. ⓐ many engine geers   ⓒ the airplane's gears
    ⓑ these bicycle geares   ⓓ my wristwatch's geres

23. ⓐ his solemn promise   ⓒ her solumn look
    ⓑ that solum moment   ⓓ this sollumn occasion

24. ⓐ the visiting foureigner   ⓒ a lost fourener
    ⓑ introduce the foregner   ⓓ that interesting foreigner

25. ⓐ these quilted squares   ⓒ those wooden scuairs
    ⓑ some plastic squars   ⓓ the orange scuares

Take It Home 2

Your child has learned to spell many new words and would like to share them with you and your family. Here are some ideas for having family fun as you help your child review the words in lessons 7–11.

Word Scoop

What's new in the news? Spelling words! Encourage your child to scoop up spelling words while listening to TV news and weather programs.
Remind him or her to keep a list of the words.

Lesson 7

1. adolescent
2. conscience
3. crescent
4. descending
5. discipline
6. escape
7. fascinating
8. luscious
9. miscellaneous
10. muscles
11. scalding
12. scampered
13. scattered
14. scenery
15. scenic
16. scented
17. scientific
18. scissors
19. screaming
20. sculpture

Lesson 8

1. awry
2. campaign
3. cologne
4. crutches
5. designer
6. fetched
7. foreigner
8. gnarled
9. hatchet
10. kitchen
11. reigned
12. resigned
13. scratched
14. sketching
15. stretches
16. unmatched
17. wrath
18. wreckage
19. wrestling
20. wristwatch

Lesson 9

1. almighty
2. castles
3. column
4. condemn
5. crumbs
6. debt
7. doubt
8. eyesight
9. fasten
10. hymns
11. knickers
12. lightning
13. listening
14. moisten
15. playwright
16. plumber
17. softener
18. solemn
19. tombstone
20. whistling

Lesson 10

1. appeared
2. barely
3. carefully
4. compared
5. despair
6. earnest
7. earning
8. earrings
9. earthenware
10. gears
11. millionaire
12. questionnaire
13. rehearsal
14. research
15. searching
16. silverware
17. squares
18. stairway
19. unaware
20. unfairly

Lesson 11

1. achievement
2. athlete
3. believable
4. complete
5. concealed
6. delete
7. delivery
8. ecology
9. esteem
10. extreme
11. greasy
12. guarantee
13. nieces
14. proceed
15. reasonable
16. repeated
17. revealed
18. squeezed
19. succeeded
20. trolley

Crossword Puzzle Challenge

See how fast you and your child can complete this crossword puzzle.

proceed	concealed	despair	wristwatch	gears
scissors	unmatched	fasten	moisten	earning

ACROSS

3. Rhymes with tears
4. Being paid
6. Hidden
8. A device worn on the wrist
9. To make slightly wet
10. To go on

DOWN

1. A loss of hope
2. Unequalled
5. Used to cut paper
7. Attach

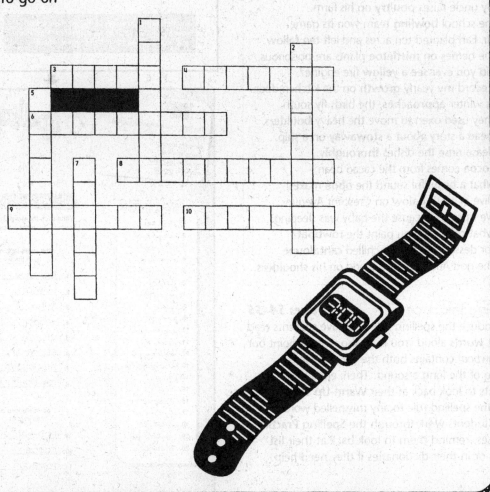

Words with the Sound of Long o

Objective

To spell words in which *oa*, *oe*, *ou*, and *ow* spell the long *o* sound

 Correlated Phonics Lesson
MCP Phonics, Level F, Lesson 16

Spelling Words in Action Page 53

In this selection, students read about ancient paintings in the Lascaux cave. Ask students what they think life might have been like for the prehistoric artists.

Encourage students to look back at the boldfaced words. Ask volunteers to say the words and identify the different ways to spell the long *o* sound.

Warm-Up Test

1. The **borrower** promptly paid back the debt.
2. Gloria mixed the **doughnut** batter.
3. **Although** Pam got off to a bad start, she won.
4. My uncle raises **poultry** on his farm.
5. The school **bowling** team won its game.
6. Mr. Earl planted ten acres and left ten **fallow**.
7. The berries on **mistletoe** plants are poisonous.
8. Did you ever see a **yellow** fire engine?
9. I record my yearly **growth** on the kitchen door.
10. As winter **approaches**, the birds fly south.
11. They used oxen to move the heavy **boulders**.
12. I read a story about a **stowaway** on a ship.
13. Please rinse the dishes **thoroughly**.
14. **Cocoa** comes from the cacao bean.
15. What a beautiful sound the **oboe** makes!
16. I live in a **bungalow** on Crescent Avenue.
17. We **tiptoed** because the baby was sleeping.
18. What color did you paint the **rowboat**?
19. For dessert, we'll have chilled **cantaloupe**.
20. The god Atlas held the world on his **shoulders**.

Spelling Practice Pages 54–55

Introduce the spelling rule and have students read the **list words** aloud. You may also wish to point out that *rowboat* contains both the *ow* and the *oa* spelling of the long *o* sound. Then, encourage students to look back at their **Warm-Up Tests** and apply the spelling rule to any misspelled words.

As students work through the **Spelling Practice** exercises, remind them to look back at their **list words** or in their dictionaries if they need help.

for ESL students See Variant Spellings, page 14

50

Spelling Words in Action

Why might prehistoric artists have made paintings of animals?

Cave of Wonders

Imagine making one of the greatest archaeological discoveries of all time. You may shrug your **shoulders** at the idea, but that really happened to four French teenagers in 1940. While exploring the woods of Lascaux (Lah-SKO), France, the boys slid past **boulders** into an underground cave. As they **tiptoed** farther into the cave, they were **thoroughly** surprised by what they found. The walls had beautiful paintings of enormous mammoths, reindeer, horses, bulls, and other animals. Later, they learned that prehistoric artists drew these 17,000 years ago! The prehistoric artists had made paint by mixing animal fat with red and **yellow** earth.

The cave had lain **fallow** for years, but now it was opened to the public. Hundreds of thousands of people entered it to marvel at the realistic paintings. **Although** nobody meant to damage the cave, the **approaches** of so many people harmed the paintings. In 1963, the cave was closed. Plans were made to build a copy of the cave nearby. The **growth** of the cave continued for several years, and finally, "Lascaux II" was opened in 1983. Any modern artist who visits the site must consider himself a **borrower** of techniques dating back thousands of years.

Say the boldfaced words in the selection. What vowel sound do you hear in each word? How many ways can you find to spell that vowel sound?

53

Spelling Practice

TIP
The long *o* sound can be spelled many ways:
oa, as in <u>rowboat</u>
oe, as in <u>oboe</u>
ou, as in <u>doughnut</u>
ow, as in <u>growth</u>

LIST WORDS

1. borrower
2. doughnut
3. although
4. poultry
5. bowling
6. fallow
7. mistletoe
8. yellow
9. growth
10. approaches
11. boulders
12. stowaway
13. thoroughly
14. cocoa
15. oboe
16. bungalow
17. tiptoed
18. rowboat
19. cantaloupe
20. shoulders

Words with the Long o Sound

Write each **list word** under the spelling of its long *o* sound. One word will be used twice.

ow spells long o, as in <u>throw</u>	**ou** spells long o, as in <u>dough</u>
1. borrower	12. doughnut
2. bowling	13. although
3. fallow	14. poultry
4. yellow	15. boulders
5. growth	16. thoroughly
6. stowaway	17. cantaloupe
7. bungalow	18. shoulders
8. rowboat	

oa spells long o, as in <u>boat</u>	**oe** spells long o, as in <u>toe</u>
9. approaches	19. mistletoe
10. cocoa	20. oboe
11. rowboat	21. tiptoed

Find the Words

The underlined word in each sentence does not make sense. Replace the word with a **list word** that does make sense. Write the **list word** on the line.

1. Would you like a steaming cup of boulders?   <u>cocoa</u>
2. In the story, the boy was a secret rowboat aboard the ship.   <u>stowaway</u>
3. The tiptoed is a melon with light orange flesh.   <u>cantaloupe</u>
4. The farmer made a wall out of cocoa.   <u>boulders</u>
5. Bungalow is a sport the whole family enjoys.   <u>Bowling</u>
6. Stand back when the train shoulders the station.   <u>approaches</u>
7. Thoroughly I tried, I couldn't lift the rock.   <u>Although</u>
8. The doughnut paid back the money I loaned her.   <u>borrower</u>
9. He oboe softly down the hall.   <u>tiptoed</u>

Classification

Write the **list word** that belongs in each group.

1. red, blue, — <u>yellow</u>
2. increase, development, — <u>growth</u>
3. barren, unplanted, — <u>fallow</u>
4. ranch, townhouse, — <u>bungalow</u>
5. hen, rooster, — <u>poultry</u>
6. completely, totally, — <u>thoroughly</u>
7. holly, cactus, — <u>mistletoe</u>
8. elbows, knees, — <u>shoulders</u>
9. pancake, waffle, — <u>doughnut</u>
10. flute, clarinet, — <u>oboe</u>
11. canoe, sailboat, — <u>rowboat</u>

Spelling and Writing

Proofreading

Proofreading Marks
◯ spelling mistake
☰ capital letter
⌃ add something

This journal entry about making an archaeological discovery has ten mistakes. Use the proofreading marks to correct them. Then, write the misspelled **list words** correctly on the lines.

July 30

As I was climbing around the boulders, my yelloe camera strap became wedged between two rocks. I was trying to pull it out when I noticed the opening to a passage. Thorohly intrigued, I called to my parents. althow the boulder was large, we were able to move it together. the hole was just wide enough for my showelders to pass through. It led to a small cave, and when I tiptoad farther inside I saw the jars that held the ancient scrolls.

1. <u>boulders</u>   2. <u>yellow</u>
3. <u>Thoroughly</u>   4. <u>Although</u>
5. <u>shoulders</u>   6. <u>tiptoed</u>

Writing a Descriptive Paragraph

Imagine a painting that shows objects found in the **list words**, such as a boulder, a rowboat, or a stowaway. Write a paragraph describing the painting. Try to use as many **list words** as you can. Remember to proofread your paragraph and fix any mistakes.

_____
_____
_____
_____
_____
_____

BONUS WORDS

overgrown
woeful
approach
borough
mellow

Spelling Strategy

Write each **list word** on the board. Then, ask a volunteer to come to the front of the class and
- pronounce the word
- circle the letters that spell the long o sound
- suggest another word in which the same letter pair spells long o.

BONUS WORDS

You may want to suggest that students write a sentence for each bonus word. Then, have them erase the letters that make the long o sound in each word. Have them trade papers with a partner and fill in the missing letters in each other's words.

Spelling and Writing   *Page 56*

The **Proofreading** exercise will help students prepare to proofread their paragraphs. As students complete the writing activity, encourage them to brainstorm ideas, write a first draft, revise, and proofread their work. To publish their writing, students may want to create pictures of their imagined paintings and make a bulletin board display titled "Envisioning Art."

Writer's Corner You might want to bring in reproductions of famous paintings and show them to the class. Invite students to write about their feelings as they look at the paintings.

Final Test

1. Columbus introduced Europeans to **cocoa**.
2. A **cantaloupe** has a rind that is very rough.
3. What store sells the freshest **poultry**?
4. Look at all the new **growth** since the last rain.
5. The **oboe** was developed in France.
6. My **shoulders** got sunburned at the beach.
7. Let's go **bowling** on Saturday.
8. As spring **approaches**, the flowers bloom.
9. During the fall, the leaves turn red and **yellow**.
10. We pulled the **rowboat** up on the shore.
11. **Although** it is sunny now, it may rain later.
12. Jennifer cleaned her room **thoroughly**.
13. The family rented a **bungalow** near the sea.
14. Last year the farmer let that field lie **fallow**.
15. A **borrower** pays monthly interest on a loan.
16. Don't climb up on those **boulders**!
17. Where on the ship was the **stowaway** hiding?
18. She made a bouquet of holly and **mistletoe**.
19. Grandfather fed **doughnut** crumbs to the birds.
20. We **tiptoed** up to the window.

Vowel Digraphs ei and ie and Vowel Pair ei

Objective
To spell words with vowel digraphs *ei* and *ie* and vowel pair *ei*

Phonics Correlated Phonics Lessons
MCP Phonics, Level F,
Lessons 15, 18–19

Spelling Words in Action   Page 57
Students may enjoy learning about bonsai in "Tiny Trees." After reading, ask students why they would or would not like to have a bonsai tree.

Call on volunteers to say each boldfaced word and tell whether it contains *ei* or *ie*.

Warm-Up Test
1. In the fable, **conceit** caused a lot of trouble.
2. The **sleigh** sped over the snow-covered road.
3. The school nurse measures your **height**.
4. A **veil** of clouds hid the mountains.
5. Last night the army **seized** the fort.
6. She **yields** the right of way.
7. The explorer saw **weird** shadows in the cave.
8. We promise to stay out of **mischief**!
9. Greeting others warmly is a **neighborly** act.
10. Can **reindeer** pull several hundred pounds?
11. The hurricane winds blew **fiercely**.
12. That character's actions were **unbelievable**!
13. We met **briefly** at a party last week.
14. The knight's armor was never **pierced**.
15. Many cars now have **diesel** engines.
16. We **perceived** a problem with the project.
17. I was **relieved** when the long flight was over.
18. Foods high in **protein** include fish.
19. Were these stones part of an **ancient** castle?
20. Carl must **retrieve** the book he left behind.

Spelling Practice   Pages 58–59
Introduce the spelling rule and have students read the **list words** aloud. Encourage students to look back at their **Warm-Up Tests** and apply the spelling rule to any misspelled words.

As students work through the **Spelling Practice** exercises, remind them to look back at their **list words** or in their dictionaries if they need help. You may want to review analogies by writing this example on the board: *leaf* is to *tree* as *feather* is to *bird*. Help students conclude that a leaf covers a branch of a tree as a feather covers part of a bird.

 for ESL students See Picture Clues, page 15

52

Spelling Words in Action

Why might people enjoy bonsai trees?

Tiny Trees

Growing bonsai trees is an **ancient** art that comes from Asia. The word "bonsai" means "tray planting." Gardeners train their plants to look like miniature and very beautifully shaped trees.

The art of bonsai began in China over a thousand years ago. It spread to Japan about 800 years ago. More and more people have **seized** this beautiful and unusual form of gardening.

A picture of a bonsai tree on a plain background might be **perceived** to be as large as a giant oak. It is perfectly formed. Yet, a bonsai tree is usually no more than a few feet in **height**. A bonsai maple tree, for example, might reach three feet tall and **yields** very small leaves.

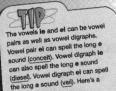

The life span of these tiny trees is **unbelievable**. One tree can live in a small pot for 200 years or more. Some are handed down in families from parent to child. Each generation takes its turn bending and pruning the branches to keep the tree from growing larger. It isn't surprising that growers are **fiercely** proud of their art.

If you're looking for a hobby to pursue **briefly**, growing these tiny trees is not for you. Keeping a bonsai plant looking its best takes time and energy. If you are interested in this long-term pastime, you'll be **relieved** to know that classes are available. You can **retrieve** information from the Internet or at your local library.

Look back at the boldfaced words. Notice the vowel sounds made by the letters <u>ei</u> and <u>ie</u>. How many different sounds do you hear?

57

Spelling Practice

TIP
The vowels **ie** and **ei** can be vowel pairs as well as vowel digraphs. Vowel pair **ei** can spell the long **e** sound (conceit). Vowel digraph **ie** can also spell the long **e** sound (diesel). Vowel digraph **ei** can spell the long **a** sound (veil). Here's a helpful rule:
I before **E** except after **C** or when sounded like **A** as in neighborly or sleigh. There are exceptions to this rule, as in weird and height.

LIST WORDS
1. conceit
2. sleigh
3. height
4. veil
5. seized
6. yields
7. weird
8. mischief
9. neighborly
10. reindeer
11. fiercely
12. unbelievable
13. briefly
14. pierced
15. diesel
16. perceived
17. relieved
18. protein
19. ancient
20. retrieve

Words with ei and ie
Write each **list word** under the correct heading.

ie as in thief
1. yields
2. fiercely
3. unbelievable
4. briefly
5. pierced
6. diesel
7. relieved
8. retrieve

ei after c
9. conceit
10. perceived

ei as in weigh
11. sleigh
12. veil
13. neighborly
14. reindeer

ie or ei—no rule
15. height
16. seized
17. weird
18. mischief
19. protein
20. ancient

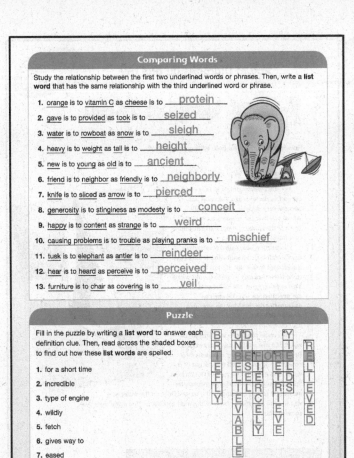

Comparing Words

Study the relationship between the first two underlined words or phrases. Then, write a **list word** that has the same relationship with the third underlined word or phrase.

1. orange is to vitamin C as cheese is to _____ protein
2. gave is to provided as took is to _____ seized
3. water is to rowboat as snow is to _____ sleigh
4. heavy is to weight as tall is to _____ height
5. new is to young as old is to _____ ancient
6. friend is to neighbor as friendly is to _____ neighborly
7. knife is to sliced as arrow is to _____ pierced
8. generosity is to stinginess as modesty is to _____ conceit
9. happy is to content as strange is to _____ weird
10. causing problems is to trouble as playing pranks is to _____ mischief
11. tusk is to elephant as antler is to _____ reindeer
12. hear is to heard as perceive is to _____ perceived
13. furniture is to chair as covering is to _____ veil

Puzzle

Fill in the puzzle by writing a **list word** to answer each definition clue. Then, read across the shaded boxes to find out how these **list words** are spelled.

1. for a short time
2. incredible
3. type of engine
4. wildly
5. fetch
6. gives way to
7. eased

Crossword grid answers: BRIEFLY, UNBELIEVABLE, BEFORE, DIESEL, FIERCELY, YIELDS, RETRIEVE, RELIEVED

Lesson 14 • Vowel Digraphs ei and ie and Vowel Pair ei   59

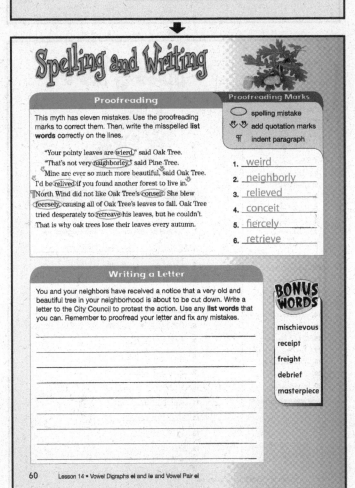

Spelling and Writing

Proofreading

This myth has eleven mistakes. Use the proofreading marks to correct them. Then, write the misspelled **list words** correctly on the lines.

"Your pointy leaves are wierd," said Oak Tree.
"That's not very naighborley," said Pine Tree.
Mine are ever so much more beautiful, said Oak Tree. I'd be relived if you found another forest to live in.
North Wind did not like Oak Tree's conseit. She blew feersely, causing all of Oak Tree's leaves to fall. Oak Tree tried desperately to retreave his leaves, but he couldn't. That is why oak trees lose their leaves every autumn.

Proofreading Marks
⬭ spelling mistake
✓✓ add quotation marks
¶ indent paragraph

1. weird
2. neighborly
3. relieved
4. conceit
5. fiercely
6. retrieve

Writing a Letter

You and your neighbors have received a notice that a very old and beautiful tree in your neighborhood is about to be cut down. Write a letter to the City Council to protest the action. Use any **list words** that you can. Remember to proofread your letter and fix any mistakes.

_____
_____
_____
_____
_____
_____
_____
_____
_____

BONUS WORDS

mischievous
receipt
freight
debrief
masterpiece

60   Lesson 14 • Vowel Digraphs ei and ie and Vowel Pair ei

Spelling Strategy

Ask the class to identify the **list words** in which *i* comes before *e*. Write these words on the board and underline the letters *ie*. Then, read the Tip and ask students to name the **list words** in which *ei* spells the long *a* sound or follows *c*. Add the words to the board, underlining *ei*. Point out to students that some of the **list words** (*weird, height, ancient, seized, protein*) do not follow the spelling rule.

BONUS WORDS You may want to suggest that students write a tongue twister for each bonus word, leaving a blank where the word should go. Have them trade papers and fill in the missing words. Ask them to read the completed twisters aloud.

Spelling and Writing   Page 60

The **Proofreading** exercise will help students prepare to proofread their letters. As students complete the writing activity, encourage them to brainstorm ideas, write a first draft, revise, and proofread their work. To publish their writing, students may want to use their letters to develop a play called *Spare That Tree!*

Writer's Corner Explain to students that origami, or paper-folding, is a popular art form in Japan. Encourage students to read a book about origami and to make their own origami figures. Students can write a verse or a short poem to display with their artwork.

Final Test

1. Grace **pierced** the leather with a needle.
2. The dogs get into **mischief** often.
3. Allen shows self-confidence but no **conceit**.
4. We were **relieved** to hear that you arrived.
5. Can Mika **retrieve** the kite from that tree?
6. The **weird** sounds scared us.
7. The lion defended her young **fiercely**.
8. The **veil** on this wedding gown is lace.
9. We rode in a horse-drawn **sleigh**.
10. Through the fog, the sailor **perceived** a ship.
11. The light flickered **briefly** and then went out.
12. From this **height** you can see the entire city.
13. The car on the left **yields**.
14. Was Pompeii an important **ancient** city?
15. Tim's story was **unbelievable**!
16. A **diesel** engine uses a special kind of fuel.
17. They were **neighborly** when we stopped by.
18. Thirsty runners **seized** the cups of water.
19. Eggs contain **protein**.
20. In Lapland, **reindeer** roam in large herds.

Vowel Digraphs au and aw

Objective
To spell words with the *aw* sound spelled *au* and *aw*

 Phonics

Correlated Phonics Lesson
MCP Phonics, Level F, Lesson 19

Spelling Words in Action   Page 61

In "New Wave," students read about a sport called windsurfing, which is a combination of sailing and surfboarding. After reading, invite students to tell why they would or would not like to try this sport.

Encourage students to look back at the boldfaced words. Ask volunteers to say each word and identify the vowel sound they hear.

Warm-Up Test
1. The **brawny** athlete raised the barbells.
2. Chang helped me fold the clean **laundry**.
3. Rosa **taught** the alphabet to her little brother.
4. He **paused** before he began to speak.
5. Why do leaves change color in **autumn**?
6. We stood in the shade of the striped **awning**.
7. Climbing Mt. Everest is an **awesome** task!
8. Soon the shuttle will be **launched**.
9. In space, **astronauts** experience weightlessness.
10. The farmer heard the chickens **squawking**.
11. Being small is not a **drawback** for gymnasts.
12. After the relay race, the team was **exhausted**.
13. Marty heated the soup in the **saucepan**.
14. Does the fire alarm go off **automatically**?
15. Why did the **dinosaur** become extinct?
16. Is this old coin **authentic**?
17. Her **withdrawal** from the race caused surprise.
18. A **thesaurus** contains synonyms and antonyms.
19. Careful drivers take **precautions**.
20. We gave the dancers a round of **applause**.

Spelling Practice   Pages 62–63

Introduce the spelling rule and have students read the **list words** aloud. Discuss the meanings of unfamiliar words (*brawny, awning, authentic*). Then, encourage students to look back at their **Warm-Up Tests** and apply the spelling rule to any misspelled words.

As students work through the **Spelling Practice** exercises, remind them to look back at their **list words** or in their dictionaries if they need help.

 See Student Dictation, page 14

54

Vowel Digraphs au and aw   Lesson 15

Spelling Words in Action

How is windsurfing like both sailing and surfing?

NEW WAVE

Although windsurfing was **launched** only a few decades ago, the sport has become very popular. Depending on where you live, the sailing season might begin in the spring and run into **autumn**, or it might be year-round.

Windsurfing, also called boardsailing, uses a craft called a sailboard. It looks like a surfboard with a sail. It's not necessary to be big or **brawny** to guide the sailboard! This exciting sport has its hazards. There are **precautions** to take, such as **automatically** checking the wind and weather forecast. If it's too windy or stormy, it's best not to go windsurfing.

You can be **taught** to windsurf in the water, but this method has a **drawback**. Beginners can be quickly **exhausted** by constantly having to pull the sail out of the water. You might prefer to start out on land. Special equipment can almost recreate the **authentic** feeling of being on the waves. Once on the water, you will feel the **awesome** power of the wind and waves. You might even hear some **applause**!

Look back at the boldfaced words in the selection. What vowel sound do you hear in each word?

61

TIP
The vowel digraphs **au** and **aw** sound alike. They both spell the *aw* sound you hear in <u>paused</u> and <u>awesome</u>.

Spelling Practice

LIST WORDS
1. brawny
2. laundry
3. taught
4. paused
5. autumn
6. awning
7. awesome
8. launched
9. astronauts
10. squawking
11. drawback
12. exhausted
13. saucepan
14. automatically
15. dinosaur
16. authentic
17. withdrawal
18. thesaurus
19. precautions
20. applause

Words with au and aw

Write the **list words** in the correct category.

vowel digraph **au**		vowel digraph **aw**	
1. laundry		15. brawny	
2. taught		16. awning	
3. paused		17. awesome	
4. autumn		18. squawking	
5. launched		19. drawback	
6. astronauts		20. withdrawal	
7. exhausted			
8. saucepan			
9. automatically			
10. dinosaur			
11. authentic			
12. thesaurus			
13. precautions			
14. applause			

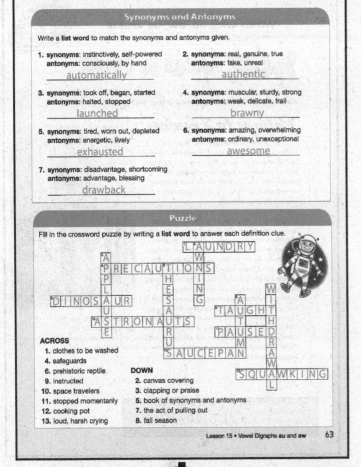

Synonyms and Antonyms

Write a **list word** to match the synonyms and antonyms given.

1. synonyms: instinctively, self-powered
   antonyms: consciously, by hand
   __automatically__

2. synonyms: real, genuine, true
   antonyms: fake, unreal
   __authentic__

3. synonyms: took off, began, started
   antonyms: halted, stopped
   __launched__

4. synonyms: muscular, sturdy, strong
   antonyms: weak, delicate, frail
   __brawny__

5. synonyms: tired, worn out, depleted
   antonyms: energetic, lively
   __exhausted__

6. synonyms: amazing, overwhelming
   antonyms: ordinary, unexceptional
   __awesome__

7. synonyms: disadvantage, shortcoming
   antonyms: advantage, blessing
   __drawback__

Puzzle

Fill in the crossword puzzle by writing a **list word** to answer each definition clue.

ACROSS
1. clothes to be washed
4. safeguards
6. prehistoric reptile
9. instructed
10. space travelers
11. stopped momentarily
12. cooking pot
13. loud, harsh crying

DOWN
2. canvas covering
3. clapping or praise
5. book of synonyms and antonyms
7. the act of pulling out
8. fall season

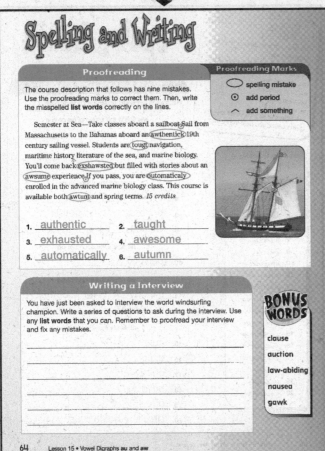

Spelling and Writing

Proofreading

The course description that follows has nine mistakes. Use the proofreading marks to correct them. Then, write the misspelled **list words** correctly on the lines.

Semester at Sea—Take classes aboard a sailboat. Sail from Massachusetts to the Bahamas aboard an awthentick 19th century sailing vessel. Students are tought navigation, maritime history literature of the sea, and marine biology. You'll come back exshawsted but filled with stories about an awsume experience. If you pass, you are automatically enrolled in the advanced marine biology class. This course is available both awtum and spring terms. *15 credits*

Proofreading Marks
○ spelling mistake
⊙ add period
∧ add something

1. __authentic__
2. __taught__
3. __exhausted__
4. __awesome__
5. __automatically__
6. __autumn__

Writing a Interview

You have just been asked to interview the world windsurfing champion. Write a series of questions to ask during the interview. Use any **list words** that you can. Remember to proofread your interview and fix any mistakes.

BONUS WORDS
clause
auction
law-abiding
nausea
gawk

Spelling Strategy

Write each **list word** on the board, leaving out the digraph *au* or *aw*. For each word, ask a volunteer to come to the board, name the missing letters, and complete the word by filling in the digraph. Have the class check each spelling against the **list words** in their *Spelling Workout* books.

BONUS WORDS You may want to suggest that students write a sentence for each bonus word, then erase the bonus words and trade papers with a partner. Ask them if they can correctly fill in each other's bonus words.

Spelling and Writing   Page 64

The **Proofreading** exercise will help students prepare to proofread their interview questions. As students complete the writing activity, encourage them to brainstorm ideas, write a first draft, revise, and proofread their work. To publish their writing, students may want to get together with a partner to role-play an interview with a windsurfer.

Writer's Corner Students might enjoy inventing a sport that combines two existing sports. Encourage them to research various sports at the library and to write about their new activity in a style similar to the entries in the book *Eyewitness: Sports* by Tim Hammond.

Final Test
1. We took **precautions** to avoid the storm.
2. He made a **withdrawal** from his bank.
3. Ken made a **dinosaur** model for the science fair.
4. Lena poured the gravy into the **saucepan**.
5. A poor memory is a **drawback** during a test.
6. The first **astronauts** were considered heroes.
7. Her triple somersault in midair was **awesome**!
8. When was the space shuttle **launched**?
9. Mr. Li unrolled the **awning** in front of his store.
10. She **paused** in the middle of her speech.
11. Does Franny do her own **laundry**?
12. **Applause** is an inspiration to performers.
13. A **thesaurus** is a useful reference book.
14. The chair was an **authentic** antique from 1750.
15. The door opens **automatically**.
16. The farmer was **exhausted** after working all day.
17. The **squawking** birds are making a loud racket.
18. How cool and crisp the air is in **autumn**!
19. My mother **taught** me how to weave.
20. He was once frail, but now he's **brawny**.

Objective
To spell words with the sounds of *yoo*, *oo*, short *i* spelled *oo, ew, ue, ui*

 Correlated Phonics Lessons
MCP Phonics, Level F,
Lessons 20, 21, 25

Spelling Words in Action   **Page 65**
In this selection, students learn about the Underground Railroad. After reading, invite students to share any facts they might know about the Underground Railroad and its heroes.

Encourage students to look back at the boldfaced words. Ask volunteers to say each word and tell whether it has the sound of *oo* in *poodle* or the sound of *i* in *build*.

Warm-Up Test
1. Dampness can cause **mildew** to form.
2. Stuart played his **guitar** at my sister's party.
3. The rainy day made the old house look **gloomy**.
4. Grandma is going on an ocean **cruise**.
5. The jury found the defendant **guilty** as charged.
6. What time is **curfew** at summer camp?
7. These old spoons are made from **pewter**.
8. What a **juicy** hamburger that was!
9. Use fine sandpaper to make the wood **smoother**.
10. Maria **bruised** her knee sliding into first base.
11. Bonnie made a **quilted** bedspread from scraps.
12. The bank **building** is behind the post office.
13. The parents' committee had a **fruitful** meeting.
14. Is this **shampoo** good for sun-damaged hair?
15. Soft music can be **soothing** after a busy day.
16. In summer, a cotton blanket is a **suitable** cover.
17. The dog **pursued** the cat around the house.
18. Daryl enjoyed the **biscuit** my mother baked.
19. Earth's **circuit** around the sun takes a year.
20. That ringing phone upstairs is a real **nuisance**!

Spelling Practice   **Pages 66–67**
Introduce the spelling rule and have students read the **list words** aloud. Encourage students to look back at their **Warm-Up Tests** and apply the spelling rule to any misspelled words.

As students work through the **Spelling Practice** exercises, remind them to look back at their **list words** or in their dictionaries if they need help.

 See Letter Cards, page 15

56

Spelling Words in Action

Was the name "Underground Railroad" a good one? Why or why not?

Passage to Freedom
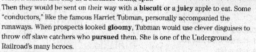

In the years before slavery was illegal, the Underground Railroad helped escaping slaves to find freedom in the north. Everyone who took part in the Underground Railroad was **guilty** of breaking the law, but their efforts were **fruitful**. An estimated 40,000 to 100,000 escaped slaves reached freedom this way.

On the plantations, slaves readied themselves in many ways. They listened to stories or songs about escape routes. Other clues might have come in **quilted** form. It is possible that quilt patterns showed the slaves how to prepare for the journey.

The success of the "railroad" depended on its "conductors." Some helped the runaways by **building** hiding places for them. The houses along the Underground Railroad were known as "stations." **Bruised** and hungry runaways would reach a station and stay in a **suitable** hiding spot. Then they would be sent on their way with a **biscuit** or a **juicy** apple to eat. Some "conductors," like the famous Harriet Tubman, personally accompanied the runaways. When prospects looked **gloomy**, Tubman would use clever disguises to throw off slave catchers who **pursued** them. She is one of the Underground Railroad's many heroes.

Say the boldfaced words in the selection. Which words have the sound you hear in poodle? Which words have the sound you hear in build?

65

TIP
The sound of **yoo**, as in *curfew*, can be spelled **ew**.
The **oo** sound, as in *smoother*, can be spelled in the following ways:
ew, as in *mildew*
ue, as in *pursued*
oo, as in *gloomy*
ui, as in *fruitful*
The letters **ui** also can spell the short i sound you hear in *biscuit*.

LIST WORDS
1. mildew
2. guitar
3. gloomy
4. cruise
5. guilty
6. curfew
7. pewter
8. juicy
9. smoother
10. bruised
11. quilted
12. building
13. fruitful
14. shampoo
15. soothing
16. suitable
17. pursued
18. biscuit
19. circuit
20. nuisance

Spelling Practice

Words with oo, ew, ue, and ui
Write each **list word** under the correct heading.

ew spells the sound of oo or yoo
1. mildew
2. curfew
3. pewter

ui spells the sound of oo
4. cruise   5. juicy
6. bruised   7. fruitful
8. suitable   9. nuisance

ue spells the sound of oo
10. pursued

oo spells the sound of oo
11. gloomy   12. smoother
13. shampoo   14. soothing

ui spells the short i sound
15. guitar
16. guilty
17. quilted
18. building
19. biscuit
20. circuit

Complete the Paragraph

Use the **list words** below to fill in the blanks in the paragraphs. Write the words on the lines.

In my family, we have an old mug made of ___pewter___ that has a very special story. It once played a part in helping people to escape on the Underground Railroad! My ancestors had been ___building___ a small room behind a wall to hide the fleeing slaves. Though they tried to conceal the door, it was ___smoother___ than the rest of the wall. The first time people were hidden in the room, they were followed by an official who had ___pursued___ them for miles. When he came to the house, he became suspicious about the wall. My great-great-great-grandmother Anne distracted the man by offering him a ___juicy___ piece of apple pie and a hot ___biscuit___ on her best plate, with a cool drink of cider in the mug. He said the refreshments were ___suitable___ for a king, and he apologized for being a ___nuisance___ before he left the house. The runaways were safe, thanks to Anne's quick thinking and ___soothing___ ways!

Word Building

Add and subtract letters to form **list words**.

1. mild + few – f = ___mildew___
2. gust – st + silt – s + y = ___guilty___
3. quill – l + wanted – wan = ___quilted___
4. go – o + suit – s + art – t = ___guitar___
5. brush – ush + disguised – disg = ___bruised___
6. curtain – tain + f + new – n = ___curfew___
7. shame – e + pool – l = ___shampoo___
8. circus – s + item – em = ___circuit___
9. g + look – k + enemy – ene = ___gloomy___
10. crust – st + bruise – bru = ___cruise___
11. fry – y + quit – q + fully – ly = ___fruitful___

Spelling and Writing

Proofreading

This scene from a TV show about the Underground Railroad has nine mistakes. Use the proofreading marks to fix the mistakes. Then, write the misspelled **list words** correctly on the lines.

MAMA: "This way, George! Move quickly, now, because I think we are are being persooed!"

GEORGE: "I'm running as fast as I can, Mama. I brewsed my my foot, and I'm so hungry. I'd do anything for a biskit or a joocy piece of fruit."

MAMA (in a suithing tone): "We'll eat after we meet up with our conductor. Where could she be? At the the last station, they said we'd find her holding a lantern and waiting by a big oak tree!"

GEORGE: "Mama, look! That's her her, right over there!"

Proofreading Marks

◯ spelling mistake
⌖ take out something

1. ___pursued___
2. ___bruised___
3. ___biscuit___
4. ___juicy___
5. ___soothing___

Writing a Journal Entry

Write a journal entry from the point of view of a young person helping his or her family to participate in the Underground Railroad. Use any **list words** that you can. Remember to proofread your paragraph and fix any mistakes.

_____
_____
_____
_____
_____
_____

BONUS WORDS

steward
typhoon
undue
recruit
monsoon

Spelling Strategy

To help students practice spelling the **list words**, invite them to get together with a partner and take turns

- writing the **list words**
- pronouncing the words they write
- circling the letters *ew*, *ue*, *oo*, or *ui*
- telling the sound the letters stand for.

BONUS WORDS You may want to suggest that students write a clue for each bonus word, then trade papers with a partner and write the bonus words that match the clues.

Spelling and Writing   Page 68

The **Proofreading** exercise will help students prepare to proofread their journal entries. As students complete the writing activity, encourage them to brainstorm ideas, write a first draft, revise, and proofread their work. To publish their writing, students may want to use their journal entries to create a classroom display.

Writer's Corner Encourage students to work in groups to research the life of a hero of the Underground Railroad, such as Levi Coffin, Thomas Garrett, or Harriet Tubman. Invite them to write a short biography of their subject to present to the class.

Final Test

1. Please buy a bottle of **shampoo** at the store.
2. Each year, my parents and I agree on a **curfew**.
3. Linda is taking **guitar** lessons after school.
4. People stopped to stare at the strange **building**.
5. Don't feel **guilty**, because it wasn't your fault.
6. Those insects are beginning to be a **nuisance**.
7. The lawyer **pursued** one line of questioning.
8. **Mildew** grows in warm, damp places.
9. This **juicy** orange is delicious!
10. Steam rose from the **biscuit** as I cut it.
11. The coat was made of a blue, **quilted** material.
12. That restaurant serves salads on **pewter** dishes.
13. Our trip to the library was most **fruitful**.
14. Did the lights go out when the **circuit** failed?
15. Some of the music by Brahms is very **soothing**.
16. Stir the batter until it's a little **smoother**.
17. This weekend, let's take a **cruise** on the bay.
18. The house sure looks **gloomy** without a light!
19. I **bruised** my ankle when I tripped over a branch.
20. Did you wear **suitable** shoes for walking?

Objective

To spell words in which *ay* or *ai* spells the long *a* sound; *oi* or *oy* spells the sound of *oi*

 Correlated Phonics Lessons
MCP Phonics, Level F, Lessons 14, 23

Spelling Words in Action   Page 69

In this selection, students discover that the eggshell is the world's best-designed container. Afterward, invite students to discuss other facts they know about eggs and to share their favorite ways to eat eggs.

Ask volunteers to say the boldfaced words and to compare the vowel sounds they hear.

Warm-Up Test

1. Ralph Waldo Emerson wrote many **essays**.
2. Donna **boiled** two eggs for her breakfast.
3. Pearls are sometimes found in **oysters**.
4. Is the crew responsible for road **maintenance**?
5. Juanita is searching for summer **employment**.
6. She decorated the pillow with **embroidery**.
7. Would you like to borrow my **crayons**?
8. The hero had one daring **exploit** after another.
9. At rush hour, the station is in **turmoil**.
10. The nurse put **ointment** on my poison ivy.
11. Please rinse the strawberries in a **strainer**.
12. The principal **praised** us for our hard work.
13. What **disappointment** I felt when I lost!
14. Put the **container** of milk into the refrigerator.
15. I put the **remainder** of the salad on a plate.
16. Franklin Roosevelt had a **faithful** dog, Fala.
17. By wearing seat belts, they **avoided** injury.
18. We are **rejoicing** over Alicia's victory.
19. I'd like a ham sandwich with **mayonnaise**.
20. He is a business **acquaintance** of my father.

Spelling Practice   Pages 70–71

Introduce the spelling rule and have students read the **list words** aloud. Point out that *mayonnaise* contains both *ay* and *ai*, and call students' attention to the double *p* in *disappointment* and the double *n* in *mayonnaise*. Then, encourage students to look back at their **Warm-Up Tests** and apply the spelling rule to any misspelled words.

As students work through the **Spelling Practice** exercises, remind them to look back at their **list words** or in their dictionaries if they need help.

 See Charades/Pantomime, page 15

Spelling Words in Action

What other kinds of animals lay eggs besides birds?

The World's Best Container

The world's most **praised** and well-designed **container** is not a gift-wrapped box. It's an eggshell. An eggshell may seem fragile, but it's able to withstand a lot of pressure. Try holding an egg in the palm of your hand and squeezing it tightly. It usually won't break. Don't drop the egg, though, unless you want **disappointment**—and a big mess!

Hens lay most of the eggs that we eat, though people also eat eggs from ducks, geese, and other birds. Raising poultry to produce eggs requires a great deal of **maintenance**. The birds need proper nutrition, and the temperature and lighting of their cages must be controlled. Under the right conditions, hens are **faithful** layers. One chicken can produce about 300 eggs a year. Of the billions of eggs produced in America each year, two-thirds are sold whole and the **remainder** are used in various food products.

People eat eggs many ways. Entire **essays** have been written about how to make scrambled eggs! Eggs can also be **boiled** or fried. They are used to make everything from cake to **mayonnaise**. Eating eggs that are raw or undercooked should be **avoided** because they might be contaminated with bacteria. To enjoy your eggs, cook them thoroughly!

> Say the boldfaced words in the selection. What vowel sound do you hear in each word? How are the vowel sounds alike? How are they different?

69

TIP
The letters **ay** and **ai** make the long *a* sound you hear in <u>crayons</u> and <u>praised</u>.
The letters **oy** and **oi** make the **oi** sound you hear in <u>oysters</u> and <u>rejoicing</u>.

Spelling Practice

LIST WORDS

1. essays
2. boiled
3. oysters
4. maintenance
5. employment
6. embroidery
7. crayons
8. exploit
9. turmoil
10. ointment
11. strainer
12. praised
13. disappointment
14. container
15. remainder
16. faithful
17. avoided
18. rejoicing
19. mayonnaise
20. acquaintance

Words with ai, ay, oi, and oy

Write each **list word** under the spelling of its long *a* or *oi* sound. One word is used twice.

ai spells the long a sound, as in <u>train</u>	oi spells the oi sound, as in <u>oil</u>
1. maintenance	12. boiled
2. strainer	13. embroidery
3. praised	14. exploit
4. container	15. turmoil
5. remainder	16. ointment
6. faithful	17. disappointment
7. mayonnaise	18. avoided
8. acquaintance	19. rejoicing

ay spells the long a sound, as in <u>play</u>	oy spells the oi sound, as in <u>toy</u>
9. essays	20. oysters
10. crayons	21. employment
11. mayonnaise	

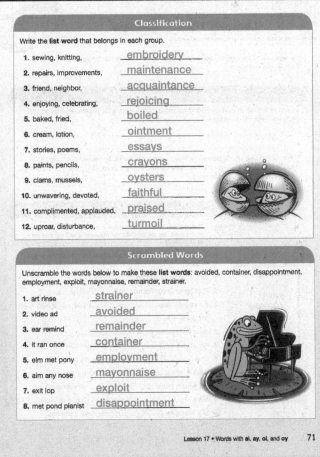

Classification

Write the **list word** that belongs in each group.

1. sewing, knitting, ___embroidery___
2. repairs, improvements, ___maintenance___
3. friend, neighbor, ___acquaintance___
4. enjoying, celebrating, ___rejoicing___
5. baked, fried, ___boiled___
6. cream, lotion, ___ointment___
7. stories, poems, ___essays___
8. paints, pencils, ___crayons___
9. clams, mussels, ___oysters___
10. unwavering, devoted, ___faithful___
11. complimented, applauded, ___praised___
12. uproar, disturbance, ___turmoil___

Scrambled Words

Unscramble the words below to make these **list words**: avoided, container, disappointment, employment, exploit, mayonnaise, remainder, strainer.

1. art rinse ___strainer___
2. video ad ___avoided___
3. ear remind ___remainder___
4. it ran once ___container___
5. elm met pony ___employment___
6. aim any nose ___mayonnaise___
7. exit lop ___exploit___
8. met pond pianist ___disappointment___

Lesson 17 • Words with ai, ay, oi, and oy   71

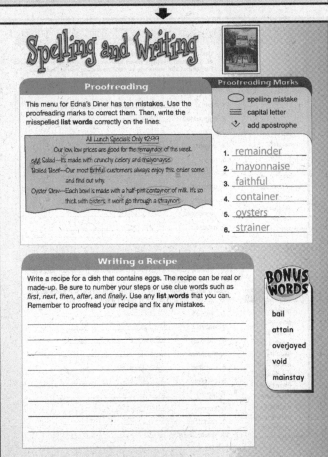

Spelling and Writing

Proofreading

This menu for Edna's Diner has ten mistakes. Use the proofreading marks to correct them. Then, write the misspelled **list words** correctly on the lines.

Proofreading Marks
- ◯ spelling mistake
- ≡ capital letter
- ⌄ add apostrophe

All Lunch Specials Only $2.99

Our low low prices are good for the remayndor of the week.
egg Salad—Its made with crunchy celery and mayonayse.
Boiled Beef—Our most faithfull customers always enjoy this. order some and find out why.
Oyster Stew—Each bowl is made with a half-pint contaynor of milk. It's so thick with oisters, it won't go through a straynor!

1. ___remainder___
2. ___mayonnaise___
3. ___faithful___
4. ___container___
5. ___oysters___
6. ___strainer___

Writing a Recipe

Write a recipe for a dish that contains eggs. The recipe can be real or made-up. Be sure to number your steps or use clue words such as *first, next, then, after,* and *finally.* Use any **list words** that you can. Remember to proofread your recipe and fix any mistakes.

_____
_____
_____
_____
_____
_____
_____

BONUS WORDS
bail
attain
overjoyed
void
mainstay

72   Lesson 17 • Words with ai, ay, oi, and oy

Spelling Strategy

With a partner, students can fold a piece of paper in half lengthwise to make two columns. Have them label the columns *long a* and *oi* and write each **list word** in the appropriate column, circling the letters that stand for the long *a* or *oi* sound. Encourage students to exchange papers with another set of partners and check the other pair's work.

BONUS WORDS
You may want to suggest that students write a newspaper headline for each bonus word and erase the bonus word in each headline. Then, have them trade headlines with a partner and fill in each other's missing words.

Spelling and Writing   Page 72

The **Proofreading** exercise will help students prepare to proofread their recipes. As students complete the writing activity, encourage them to brainstorm ideas, write a first draft, revise, and proofread their work. To publish their writing, students may want to

- use their recipes to create a cookbook
- take their recipes home and try them, with adult supervision.

Writer's Corner Invite students to invent a container that would protect an egg from breaking if it were dropped from 10 feet off the ground. Ask them to draw a picture of their egg container and write a paragraph about why it would work.

Final Test
1. The crowds at the sale created **turmoil**.
2. My aunt has a recipe for **mayonnaise**.
3. Jim bought a small **container** of sardines.
4. Is **maintenance** of your car expensive?
5. Eight divided by three equals two, with a **remainder** of two.
6. Mother found **employment** at the store.
7. The veterinarian put **ointment** in the cat's ears.
8. Kim is an **acquaintance** of mine from Chicago.
9. The astronaut told about his exciting **exploit**.
10. I felt **disappointment** when we lost the game.
11. Try the **oysters** when you visit Key West.
12. The fans were **rejoicing** after the game.
13. Henry David Thoreau wrote many **essays**.
14. Will you pour the broth through a **strainer**?
15. How thankful I am for my **faithful** friends!
16. We saw a beautiful exhibit of old **embroidery**.
17. Grandfather **boiled** the corn in a big pot.
18. Each child at the party got a box of **crayons**.
19. The driver barely **avoided** an accident.
20. The teacher **praised** Nicole for her fine report.

Objectives
To review spelling words with long *o*; *oa, oe, ou*, and *ow*; *ei* and *ie*; *au* and *aw*; *oo, ew, ue*, and *ui*; *ai, ay, oi*, and *oy*

Check Your
Spelling Notebook **Pages 73–76**

Based on your observations, note which words are giving students the most difficulty and offer assistance for spelling them correctly. Here are some frequently misspelled words to watch for: *although, shoulders, conceit, weird, exhausted, pursued, biscuit,* and *maintenance*.

To give students extra help and practice in taking standardized tests, you may want to have them take the **Review Test** for this lesson on pages 62–63. After scoring the tests, return them to students so that they can record their misspelled words in their spelling notebooks.

After practicing their troublesome words, students can work through the exercises for lessons 13–17 and the cumulative review, **Show What You Know**. Before they begin each exercise, you may want to go over the spelling rule.

Take It Home

Invite students to choose a **list word** from lessons 13–17 for each day of the week. Students can tell their families that they are going to use a "secret word" in conversation each day. At night, students can ask their family members to name the word. They can also use **Take It Home** Master 3 on pages 64–65 to help them do the activity. (A complete list of the spelling words is included on page 64 of the **Take It Home** Master.) In class, students can share their experiences and discuss which list words were easy and which were difficult to use in conversation.

60

In lessons 13 through 17, you learned that vowel sounds can be spelled many different ways.

Check Your Spelling Notebook

Look at the words in your spelling notebook. Which words for lessons 13 through 17 did you have the most trouble with? Write them here.

_____

Practice writing your troublesome words with a partner. Write the words on slips of paper and put them in a container. Take turns drawing a word, illustrating it, and having the other person guess the word.

Lesson 13

 TIP The long **o** sound can be spelled in more than one way: **oa**, as in <u>coa</u>t; **oe**, as in <u>mistletoe</u>; **ou**, as in <u>boulders</u>; and **ow**, as in <u>bowling</u>.

List Words
- bowling
- yellow
- growth
- approaches
- boulders
- although
- thoroughly
- cocoa
- oboe
- borrower
- rowboat
- shoulders

Write a **list word** to complete each sentence. Not all the words will be used.

1. School buses are often ___yellow___.
2. That jacket is tight across your ___shoulders___.
3. If a strange dog ___approaches___ you, you should never scream or run.
4. Wear a life jacket in the ___rowboat___.
5. An ___oboe___ is a woodwind instrument.
6. These ___boulders___ are blocking the hiking trail.
7. Make sure the ___cocoa___ is not too hot.
8. I'm getting better at ___bowling___ with our team.
9. Plant ___growth___ depends upon light and water.
10. Mix the batter ___thoroughly___ to make it smooth.

73

Lesson 14

 TIP Use the spelling rule you learned when spelling words with **ie** or **ei**. It will help you spell words such as <u>pierce</u>, <u>ceiling</u>, and <u>weigh</u>. Remember that some words, such as <u>ancient</u>, are exceptions.

List Words
- ancient
- seized
- conceit
- veil
- height
- relieved
- fiercely
- briefly
- perceived
- sleigh
- neighborly
- weird

Write a **list word** that means the opposite of the word given. Not all the words will be used.

1. normal ___weird___
2. aggravated ___relieved___
3. width ___height___
4. lengthily ___briefly___
5. new ___ancient___
6. sweetly ___fiercely___
7. unfriendly ___neighborly___
8. modesty ___conceit___
9. overlooked ___perceived___
10. released ___seized___

Lesson 15

TIP The **aw** sound can be spelled with **au**, as in <u>dinosaur</u>, and **aw**, as in <u>drawback</u>.

List Words
- brawny
- paused
- autumn
- awesome
- laundry
- exhausted
- squawking
- drawback
- saucepan
- authentic
- withdrawal
- applause

Write a **list word** that means the same or almost the same as the word given. Not all the words will be used.

1. fatigued ___exhausted___
2. waited ___paused___
3. clapping ___applause___
4. muscular ___brawny___
5. clucking ___squawking___
6. genuine ___authentic___
7. fall ___autumn___
8. removal ___withdrawal___
9. wonderful ___awesome___
10. shortcoming ___drawback___

Lesson 16

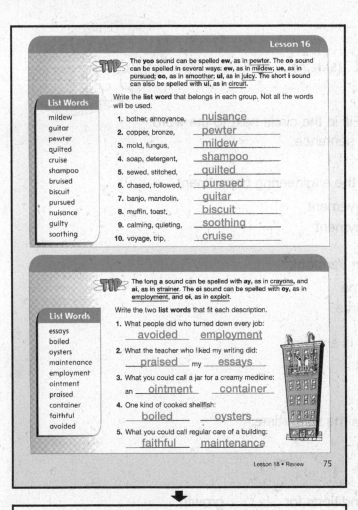

TIP — The **yoo** sound can be spelled **ew**, as in pewter. The **oo** sound can be spelled in several ways: **ew**, as in mildew; **ue**, as in pursued; **oo**, as in smoother; **ui**, as in juicy. The short **i** sound can also be spelled with **ui**, as in circuit.

List Words

mildew
guitar
pewter
quilted
cruise
shampoo
bruised
biscuit
pursued
nuisance
guilty
soothing

Write the **list word** that belongs in each group. Not all the words will be used.

1. bother, annoyance, _nuisance_
2. copper, bronze, _pewter_
3. mold, fungus, _mildew_
4. soap, detergent, _shampoo_
5. sewed, stitched, _quilted_
6. chased, followed, _pursued_
7. banjo, mandolin, _guitar_
8. muffin, toast, _biscuit_
9. calming, quieting, _soothing_
10. voyage, trip, _cruise_

TIP — The long **a** sound can be spelled with **ay**, as in crayons, and **ai**, as in strainer. The **oi** sound can be spelled with **oy**, as in employment, and **oi**, as in exploit.

List Words

essays
boiled
oysters
maintenance
employment
ointment
praised
container
faithful
avoided

Write the two **list words** that fit each description.

1. What people did who turned down every job:
avoided _employment_
2. What the teacher who liked my writing did:
praised my _essays_
3. What you could call a jar for a creamy medicine:
an _ointment_ _container_
4. One kind of cooked shellfish:
boiled _oysters_
5. What you could call regular care of a building:
faithful _maintenance_

Lesson 18 • Review   75

Show What You Know

Lessons 13—17 Review

One word is misspelled in each set of **list words**. Fill in the circle next to the **list word** that is spelled incorrectly.

1. ○ faithful ○ suitable ● unbeleivable ○ bungalow ○ disappointment
2. ● sqawking ○ growth ○ smoother ○ pursued ○ awning
3. ○ perceived ● mayonnase ○ conceit ○ cantaloupe ○ cruise
4. ○ applause ○ crayons ● gilty ○ ancient ○ veil
5. ○ borrower ○ dinosaur ● deisel ○ essays ○ cocoa
6. ● nuesance ○ saucepan ○ oysters ○ boulders ○ strainer
7. ○ building ● brauny ○ seized ○ mischief ○ withdrawal
8. ○ fallow ○ taught ● biskit ○ turmoil ○ launched
9. ● raindeer ○ mistletoe ○ pewter ○ rejoicing ○ employment
10. ○ shampoo ○ doughnut ● peirced ○ drawback ○ acquaintance
11. ● remaneder ○ yields ○ stowaway ○ guitar ○ poultry
12. ○ thesaurus ● proteen ○ tiptoed ○ quilted ○ paused
13. ○ sleigh ○ boiled ○ oboe ● precawtions ○ yellow
14. ● mildoo ○ weird ○ avoided ○ laundry ○ bowling
15. ○ praised ○ neighborly ○ relieved ○ circuit ● oyntment
16. ○ rowboat ○ automatically ○ authentic ● gluemy ○ bruised
17. ● shoalders ○ astronauts ○ exploit ○ juicy ○ approaches
18. ○ maintenance ○ soothing ● awtumn ○ awesome ○ container
19. ● feircely ○ although ○ briefly ○ fruitful ○ embroidery
20. ○ curfew ● retreive ○ exhausted ○ height ○ thoroughly

Final Test

1. The book's ending left me **thoroughly** confused.
2. After skiing, this **cocoa** will warm you up.
3. An **oboe** makes a soft, mellow sound.
4. We pulled the **rowboat** onto the dock.
5. I wear pads on my **shoulders** for football.
6. The lion was **fiercely** protective of its cubs.
7. Rain fell **briefly**, but then it was sunny again.
8. The scout **perceived** movement in the bushes.
9. People in this area are very **neighborly**.
10. The sky changed to a **weird** shade of gray.
11. The **brawny** workers moved the heavy boxes.
12. We **paused** at the door to speak to Pedro.
13. Will those flowers bloom until **autumn**?
14. The Grand Canyon is **awesome** to see.
15. The chickens' **squawking** woke us early.
16. I think that bottle of **shampoo** is empty.
17. Don't eat that **biscuit** because it's burned.
18. The dog **pursued** the cat across the field.
19. These tiny buttons are a **nuisance** to use!
20. Don't you find the sound of waves **soothing**?
21. Everyone wrote **essays** on different topics.
22. We are having **boiled** potatoes with chicken.
23. Only very fresh raw **oysters** are safe to eat.
24. Cars run better with regular **maintenance**.
25. The ads were run by **employment** agencies.
26. On Saturdays my friends and I go **bowling**.
27. Let's paint the room a cheerful **yellow**.
28. This city's **growth** has been very rapid.
29. Watch as the bird **approaches** the feeder.
30. Aren't those **boulders** too large to move?
31. I was **relieved** to hear that he had arrived.
32. The **ancient** castle was hundreds of years old.
33. Elise's **conceit** about her work is unfortunate.
34. I **seized** the chance to thank the speaker.
35. Make sure the **height** of the fence is six feet.
36. I can find only one **drawback** to your plan.
37. Everyone was **exhausted** after the soccer game.
38. Is that an **authentic** Ming vase?
39. Judy made a cash **withdrawal** from the bank.
40. The symphony ended and the **applause** began.
41. Scrub hard to remove that **mildew**.
42. Would you please play your **guitar** for me?
43. These old plates are made of **pewter**.
44. What a beautiful **quilted** bedspread!
45. The travel agent told us about a **cruise**.
46. You can buy that **ointment** in a tube or a jar.
47. Everyone **praised** the lasagna that I made.
48. Carry the juice in a **container** with a lid.
49. Jody was a **faithful** companion during the trip.
50. We **avoided** standing near the edge of the cliff.

Name _____

Read each sentence and set of words. Fill in the circle next to the word that is spelled correctly to complete the sentence.

1. This applicant is seeking _____ in the engineering department.
   - ⓐ emploiment
   - ⓒ employement
   - ⓑ employmint
   - ⓓ employment

2. Autumn foliage is an _____ sight in Vermont.
   - ⓐ ausome
   - ⓒ awsome
   - ⓑ awesome
   - ⓓ auesome

3. The _____ of modern skyscrapers is amazing.
   - ⓐ hight
   - ⓒ height
   - ⓑ haight
   - ⓓ heit

4. Hot _____ is a popular beverage in the wintertime.
   - ⓐ coacoe
   - ⓒ cocoa
   - ⓑ cocoe
   - ⓓ coaco

5. A damp cellar provides favorable conditions for _____ growth.
   - ⓐ mildew
   - ⓒ mildue
   - ⓑ milldew
   - ⓓ milldue

6. Athletes must train _____ to participate in the Olympics.
   - ⓐ fiersely
   - ⓒ fircely
   - ⓑ fiercely
   - ⓓ feircely

7. When the basement for our house was excavated, huge _____ were uncovered.
   - ⓐ boalders
   - ⓒ bolders
   - ⓑ boulders
   - ⓓ boleders

8. The bride wore a beautiful white _____.
   - ⓐ veil
   - ⓒ vaile
   - ⓑ vayl
   - ⓓ viel

Name _____

Review Test (Side B)

Read each sentence and set of words. Fill in the circle next to the word that is spelled correctly to complete the sentence.

9. Some of the town's historic buildings require costly _____.
   - ⓐ maintenence
   - ⓑ maintenance
   - ⓒ maintanence
   - ⓓ maintainance

10. An infant's _____ is carefully recorded by a physician.
    - ⓐ growthe
    - ⓑ groath
    - ⓒ groth
    - ⓓ growth

11. His sister has _____ a career in dentistry.
    - ⓐ pursued
    - ⓑ persood
    - ⓒ pursood
    - ⓓ persued

12. Consult a jeweler to determine whether the diamond is _____.
    - ⓐ authentic
    - ⓑ awthentick
    - ⓒ authentick
    - ⓓ awthentic

13. This _____ is formulated to shield skin from the sun's harmful rays.
    - ⓐ oyntment
    - ⓑ ountment
    - ⓒ ointement
    - ⓓ ointment

14. That _____ blanket was hand-stitched by my stepmother.
    - ⓐ quielted
    - ⓑ kwuilted
    - ⓒ cuilted
    - ⓓ quilted

15. The comedian appreciated the audience's exuberant _____.
    - ⓐ aplause
    - ⓑ applawse
    - ⓒ applause
    - ⓓ aplawse

Take It Home 3

Your child has learned to spell many new words and would like to share them with you and your family. Here are some ideas that will make reviewing the words in lessons 13–17 fun for everyone.

Secrets of Spelling

Every day this week, try to guess the secret spelling word that your child has chosen and is using in conversations. After you guess each word, don't keep its spelling to yourself—spell it aloud together!

Lesson 13

1. although
2. approaches
3. borrower
4. boulders
5. bowling
6. bungalow
7. cantaloupe
8. cocoa
9. doughnut
10. fallow
11. growth
12. mistletoe
13. oboe
14. poultry
15. rowboat
16. shoulders
17. stowaway
18. thoroughly
19. tiptoed
20. yellow

Lesson 14

1. ancient
2. briefly
3. conceit
4. diesel
5. fiercely
6. height
7. mischief
8. neighborly
9. perceived
10. pierced
11. protein
12. reindeer
13. relieved
14. retrieve
15. seized
16. sleigh
17. unbelievable
18. veil
19. weird
20. yields

Lesson 15

1. applause
2. astronauts
3. authentic
4. automatically
5. autumn
6. awesome
7. awning
8. brawny
9. dinosaur
10. drawback
11. exhausted
12. launched
13. laundry
14. paused
15. precautions
16. saucepan
17. squawking
18. taught
19. thesaurus
20. withdrawal

Lesson 16

1. biscuit
2. bruised
3. building
4. circuit
5. cruise
6. curfew
7. fruitful
8. gloomy
9. guilty
10. guitar
11. juicy
12. mildew
13. nuisance
14. pewter
15. pursued
16. quilted
17. shampoo
18. smoother
19. soothing
20. suitable

Lesson 17

1. acquaintance
2. avoided
3. boiled
4. container
5. crayons
6. disappointment
7. embroidery
8. employment
9. essays
10. exploit
11. faithful
12. maintenance
13. mayonnaise
14. ointment
15. oysters
16. praised
17. rejoicing
18. remainder
19. strainer
20. turmoil

Sky Spelling

Encourage your child to complete the spelling words that the skywriters have begun.

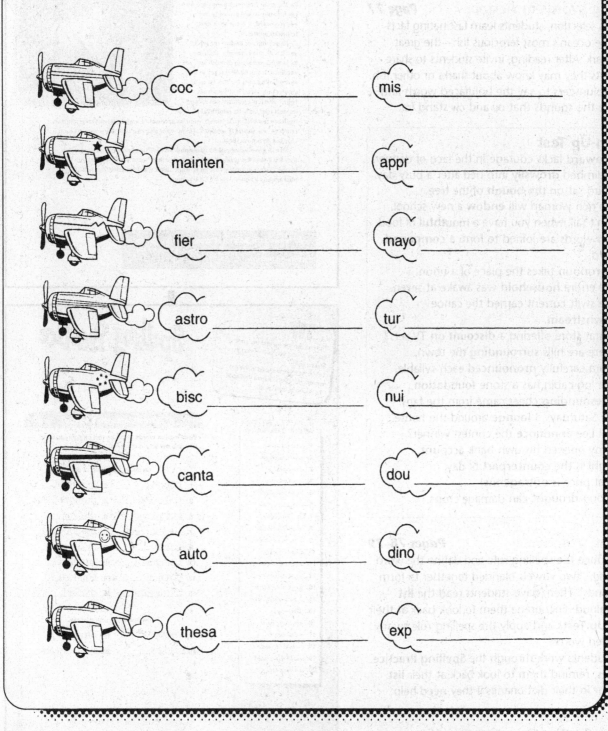

coc _____

mainten _____

fier _____

astro _____

bisc _____

canta _____

auto _____

thesa _____

mis _____

appr _____

mayo _____

tur _____

nui _____

dou _____

dino _____

exp _____

Lesson 19

Words with Diphthongs ou and ow

Objective
To spell words with the *ow* sound spelled by the diphthongs *ou* and *ow*

Correlated Phonics Lesson
MCP Phonics, Level F, Lesson 24

Spelling Words in Action   Page 77
In this selection, students learn fascinating facts about the ocean's most ferocious fish—the great white shark. After reading, invite students to share other facts they may know about sharks or other fish.

Ask volunteers to say the boldfaced words and compare the sounds that *ou* and *ow* stand for.

Warm-Up Test
1. A **coward** lacks courage in the face of danger.
2. Al climbed **drowsily** into bed after a busy day.
3. A bird sat on the **bough** of the tree.
4. The rich woman will **endow** a new school.
5. Don't talk when you have a **mouthful** of food.
6. Two words are joined to form a **compound** word.
7. A **pronoun** takes the place of a noun.
8. The entire **household** was awake at seven.
9. The swift current carried the canoe **downstream**.
10. Is that store offering a **discount** on TV sets?
11. There are hills **surrounding** the town.
12. Laura carefully **pronounced** each syllable.
13. The log cabin has a stone **foundation**.
14. A **resounding** cheer came from the fans!
15. On Saturdays, I **lounge** around the house.
16. Will Lee **announce** the contest winner?
17. Leroy opened his own bank **account**.
18. Night is the **counterpart** of day.
19. That price is **outrageous**!
20. A long **drought** can damage crops.

Spelling Practice   Pages 78–79
Introduce the spelling rule and define the word *diphthong*: "two vowels blended together to form one sound." Then, have students read the **list words** aloud. Encourage them to look back at their **Warm-Up Tests** and apply the spelling rule to any misspelled words.

As students work through the **Spelling Practice** exercises, remind them to look back at their **list words** or in their dictionaries if they need help.

 for ESL students   See Tape Recording, page 15

66

Spelling Words in Action

Why is the great white shark considered the sea's most ferocious animal?

Great White Shark

Ask everyone in your **household** to name the most feared animal in the ocean. You may get a **resounding** vote for the great white shark. Anyone who ran into one would probably feel like a **coward**. It is the sea's most ferocious animal.

Nature did not **endow** the white shark with good eyesight. Rather, its hearing and sense of smell are excellent. It can smell its prey in the **surrounding** area from as far as a quarter-mile away. It strikes from below, and few creatures can escape its steel-trap jaws. Its **mouthful** of 3,000 teeth are razor-sharp. If you've heard an **account** of a white shark eating a human, however, you should **discount** it. Great white sharks attack a few humans each year but do not eat them.

Sharks are elasmobranchs (**pronounced** i-LAZ-ma-branks). Unlike true fish, they have skeleton made of cartilage rather than bones. A white shark can grow to over 20 feet in length. One great white shark was found that weighed an **outrageous** amount—about 7,000 pounds!

Look back at the boldfaced words in the selection. Say the words. Compare the sounds made by the letters ou and ow.

77

TIP
The diphthongs **ou** and **ow** spell the **ow** sound you hear in <u>bough</u> and <u>coward</u>.
Listen for the **ow** sound in the **list words**. Notice the letters that spell the sound in each word.

Spelling Practice

LIST WORDS
1. coward
2. drowsily
3. bough
4. endow
5. mouthful
6. compound
7. pronoun
8. household
9. downstream
10. discount
11. surrounding
12. pronounced
13. foundation
14. resounding
15. lounge
16. announce
17. account
18. counterpart
19. outrageous
20. drought

Words with ou and ow
Write the **list words** in the correct category to show how the **ow** sound is spelled.

ou spells the sound of ow
1. bough
2. mouthful
3. compound
4. pronoun
5. household
6. discount
7. surrounding
8. pronounced
9. foundation
10. resounding
11. lounge
12. announce
13. account
14. counterpart
15. outrageous
16. drought

ow spells the sound of ow
17. coward
18. drowsily
19. endow
20. downstream

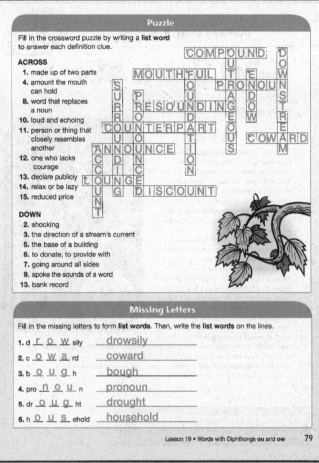

Puzzle

Fill in the crossword puzzle by writing a **list word** to answer each definition clue.

ACROSS
1. made up of two parts
4. amount the mouth can hold
8. word that replaces a noun
10. loud and echoing
11. person or thing that closely resembles another
12. one who lacks courage
13. declare publicly
14. relax or be lazy
15. reduced price

DOWN
2. shocking
3. the direction of a stream's current
5. the base of a building
6. to donate; to provide with
7. going around all sides
9. spoke the sounds of a word
13. bank record

Crossword answers: COMPOUND, MOUTHFUL, PRONOUN, OUTRAGEOUS, DOWNSTREAM, SURROUNDING, RESOUNDING, COUNTERPART, FOUNDATION, COWARD, ANNOUNCE, ACCOUNT, LOUNGE, DISCOUNT, ENDOW, PRONOUNCED

Missing Letters

Fill in the missing letters to form **list words**. Then, write the **list words** on the lines.

1. d **r o w** sily   drowsily
2. c **o w a** rd   coward
3. b **o u g** h   bough
4. pro **n o u** n   pronoun
5. dr **o u g** ht   drought
6. h **o u s** ehold   household

Lesson 19 • Words with Diphthongs **ou** and **ow**   79

Spelling and Writing

Proofreading

This flyer for an aquarium has ten mistakes. Use the proofreading marks to correct them. Then, write the misspelled **list words** correctly on the lines.

Proofreading Marks
- ◯ spelling mistake
- ⌃ add something

Where can you have your picture taken with a white shark, a penguin, or a seal? Where can everyone in your howshold have outrajous fun watching a dolphin do tricks? Where can you follow a river donstreem in a glass-bottomed boat? Where can you lownge around and enjoy the ocean view? The answer is at the Marine Life Aquarium. We are pleased to announse that we now give a discownt to students, senior citizens, and aquarium members.

1. household
2. outrageous
3. downstream
4. lounge
5. announce
6. discount

Writing a Tall Tale

Write a brief tall tale that features a shark. Make yourself the hero. The more outrageous your exaggerations, the better your tale will be. Try to use as many **list words** as you can. Remember to proofread your tall tale and fix any mistakes.

_____
_____
_____
_____
_____
_____

BONUS WORDS

profound
counsel
founder
cauliflower
scowl

Spelling Strategy

Write *touch, flower, shout, soup, frown, dough, flown,* and *mountain* on the board. Ask students to identify the words that contain the *ow* sound (*flower, shout, frown, mountain*). As each word is said, call students' attention to the *ow* sound spelled by *ou* or *ow*. Then, invite students to call out **list words**, identifying the diphthong that spells the sound.

BONUS WORDS — You may want to suggest that students create a crossword puzzle using the bonus words. Have them write clues and draw an empty grid. Then, have them trade puzzles with a partner and try to solve each other's puzzles.

Spelling and Writing   **Page 80**

The **Proofreading** exercise will help students prepare to proofread their tall tales. As students complete the writing activity, encourage them to brainstorm ideas, write a first draft, revise, and proofread their work. To publish their writing, students may want to plan a "Festival of Tall Tales" and invite their families or another class.

Writer's Corner Students may enjoy reading a book about sharks such as *Eyewitness: Shark* by Miranda MacQuitty. Encourage students to take notes on the most interesting facts they learn.

Final Test

1. Due to the **drought**, there is a water ban.
2. What an **outrageous** costume Sue wore!
3. I'd like to thank my **counterpart** for his help.
4. Only a **coward** would have run away like that.
5. The cat sat **drowsily** in the sun.
6. The **bough** of the tree is covered with flowers.
7. Will you put that check into a savings **account**?
8. Nature may **endow** any of us with special talents.
9. I will **announce** the names of the winners.
10. She took a big **mouthful** of pizza.
11. I like to **lounge** in the hammock.
12. Are there two subjects in a **compound** sentence?
13. We gave Jerry a **resounding** round of applause.
14. Please replace that noun with a **pronoun**.
15. This house was built on a concrete **foundation**.
16. Every member of our **household** has chores.
17. Santos **pronounced** each word slowly.
18. We stopped rowing and drifted **downstream**.
19. **Surrounding** the field was a fence.
20. Does this store sell shoes at **discount** prices?

Objective

To spell words with the prefixes *ir*, *in*, *il*, and *im*

 Phonics

Correlated Phonics Lessons
MCP Phonics, Level F,
Lessons 29–30

Spelling Words in Action   Page 81

In "About Face," students learn about the connection between the ancient Roman god Janus and the modern custom of making New Year's resolutions. Afterward, invite students to discuss New Year's resolutions that they have made.

Ask volunteers to say the boldfaced words and to identify the prefixes.

Warm-Up Test

1. No one took the **incredible** story seriously.
2. The work of great artists is **immortal**.
3. Some people are **intolerant** of new ideas.
4. She was an **immigrant** from England.
5. Doesn't their hasty decision seem **illogical**?
6. **Immature** trees need plenty of water to grow.
7. It is **illegal** to go over the speed limit.
8. I put the model car together **improperly**.
9. Babies are **incapable** of caring for themselves.
10. Some singular nouns have **irregular** plural forms.
11. Did waiting for the bus make you **impatient**?
12. The people in the theater behaved **impolitely**.
13. We took an **indirect** route.
14. We left our plans **indefinite** so we could relax.
15. Her testimony at the trial was **immaterial**.
16. Liz is teaching an **illiterate** man how to read.
17. Why do you think that our plan is **impractical**?
18. Forgetting to lock the door is **irresponsible**!
19. The angry man became **irrational**.
20. Please correct any words that are **illegible**.

Spelling Practice   Pages 82–83

Introduce the spelling rule and ask students to read the **list words** aloud, having them define each word using *not*, or *to* or *into*. Then, encourage students to look back at their **Warm-Up Tests** and apply the spelling rule to any misspelled words.

As students work through the **Spelling Practice** exercises, remind them to look back at their **list words** or in their dictionaries if they need help.

 for ESL students See Comparing/Contrasting, page 15

68

Spelling Words in Action

Why do we make New Year's resolutions?

About Face

To the ancient Romans, Janus was an **immortal** god who represented new beginnings. Janus was portrayed as a figure with two faces. One face looked west— toward the setting sun. The other face looked east—toward the new day. The face that looked at the past, toward the setting sun, was old. The one facing the dawn was that of an **immature** youth.

The idea of a two-faced figure seems **incredible** today. However, the god Janus still has an **indirect** influence on customs that people observe in modern times. January, the first month of the year, is named in honor of Janus. On January 1, people continue to review the past and look forward to the new year with hope.

Though it may be **illogical**, people make New Year's resolutions every January 1. On this day, people become **intolerant** of their imperfections. They may vow never to be **irresponsible** again. They may decide to stop being **impatient** or to stop gobbling down **irregular** snacks. Deciding to be perfect is an **impractical** goal, however. No one, not even Janus, can do a complete about-face!

Look back at the boldfaced words in the selection. These words have prefixes at the beginning of each word. How many prefixes can you find?

81

Spelling Practice

TIP

The prefixes **ir, in, il,** and **im** usually mean *not*, as in *irregular, incapable, illegal,* and *immature.*
The prefix **im** can also mean *to* or *into,* as in *immigrant.*
Here are some helpful spelling rules.

Words that follow:	begin with:
The prefix **im**	m, p, or b
The prefix **il**	l
The prefix **ir**	r
The prefix **in**	different letters

LIST WORDS

1. incredible
2. immortal
3. intolerant
4. immigrant
5. illogical
6. immature
7. illegal
8. improperly
9. incapable
10. irregular
11. impatient
12. impolitely
13. indirect
14. indefinite
15. immaterial
16. illiterate
17. impractical
18. irresponsible
19. irrational
20. illegible

Words with ir, in, il, and im

Add a prefix to each of these words. Then, write each **list word** under the correct heading.

1. legible   **illegible**
2. mature   **immature**
3. capable   **incapable**
4. logical   **illogical**
5. properly   **improperly**
6. responsible   **irresponsible**
7. direct   **indirect**
8. practical   **impractical**
9. tolerant   **intolerant**
10. politely   **impolitely**
11. patient   **impatient**
12. credible   **incredible**
13. rational   **irrational**
14. migrant   **immigrant**
15. material   **immaterial**
16. legal   **illegal**
17. literate   **illiterate**
18. definite   **indefinite**
19. mortal   **immortal**
20. regular   **irregular**

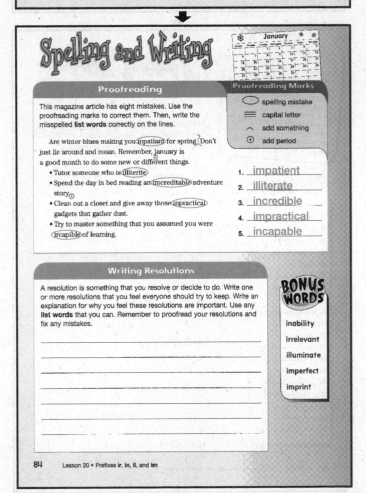

Missing Words

Write a **list word** to complete each sentence. Prefix clues are provided.

1. A person who acts childishly is ___immature___ . (im)
2. A person who has little patience is ___impatient___ . (im)
3. An ___illiterate___ person cannot read and write. (il)
4. Something that is ___illegal___ is against the law. (il)
5. A person who moves to a new country is an ___immigrant___ . (im)
6. Something that will never die is called ___immortal___ . (Im)
7. A piece of writing that is impossible to read is ___illegible___ . (ll)
8. A poor plan is ___impractical___ or ___irrational___ . (im, ir)
9. Something that really doesn't matter is ___immaterial___ . (im)
10. Someone who doesn't tolerate new ideas is ___intolerant___ . (in)
11. A badly paved road was done ___improperly___ and may look ___irregular___ . (im, ir)
12. Someone who can't be trusted is ___irresponsible___ . (ir)

Word Clues

Fill in each mini-puzzle with a **list word**. Use the word or words already filled in as a clue.

13. INCREDIBLE
14. ILLOGICAL / ABSURD
15. INCAPABLE
16. UNCERTAIN / INDEFINITE
17. IMPOLITELY
18. ROUNDABOUT / INDIRECT
UNBELIEVABLE
RUDELY
HELPLESS

Lesson 20 • Prefixes ir, in, ll, and im   83

Spelling and Writing

Proofreading

This magazine article has eight mistakes. Use the proofreading marks to correct them. Then, write the misspelled **list words** correctly on the lines.

Are winter blues making you (inpatiant) for spring? Don't just lie around and moan. Remember, january is a good month to do some new or different things.

• Tutor someone who is (illiterite)
• Spend the day in bed reading an (incredible) adventure story.
• Clean out a closet and give away those (inpractical) gadgets that gather dust.
• Try to master something that you assumed you were (ircapible) of learning.

Proofreading Marks
- ⬭ spelling mistake
- ≡ capital letter
- ⌃ add something
- ⊙ add period

1. ___impatient___
2. ___illiterate___
3. ___incredible___
4. ___impractical___
5. ___incapable___

Writing Resolutions

A resolution is something that you resolve or decide to do. Write one or more resolutions that you feel everyone should try to keep. Write an explanation for why you feel these resolutions are important. Use any **list words** that you can. Remember to proofread your resolutions and fix any mistakes.

BONUS WORDS

inability
irrelevant
illuminate
imperfect
imprint

84   Lesson 20 • Prefixes ir, in, ll, and im

Spelling Strategy

With a partner, students can write the list words and
- circle the prefix in each word
- point to and name the letter that immediately follows the prefix
- orally complete this sentence: "Base words that follow the prefix ____ begin with ____."

BONUS WORDS

You may want to pair students and suggest that they divide the list of **bonus words** between them. Ask partners to write a real and a made-up definition for each of their words. Then, have them try to match each of their partner's words with its correct definition.

Spelling and Writing   *Page 84*

The **Proofreading** exercise will help students prepare to proofread their resolutions and explanations. As students complete the writing activity, encourage them to brainstorm ideas, write a first draft, revise, and proofread their work. To publish their writing, students may want to have a class discussion based on their resolutions.

Writer's Corner Students may enjoy reading a mythology book, such as *Tales of the Greek Heroes* by Roger Lancelyn Green. Encourage them to take notes as they read and to share the information they gather with their classmates.

Final Test

1. The coat of an **immature** deer is spotted.
2. All human beings are born **illiterate**.
3. I become **impatient** when I have to wait.
4. Frank's artistic talents are **incredible**!
5. Did you find the plot of the movie **illogical**?
6. That fact is **immaterial** to the case.
7. Write slowly or your answers may be **illegible**.
8. This strange pumpkin has an **irregular** shape.
9. The child was **incapable** of lifting the trunk.
10. The schedule for our summer trip is **indefinite**.
11. Anger may make a person **irrational**.
12. My neighbor is an **immigrant** from Russia.
13. At first, I held the chopsticks **improperly**.
14. I'm **intolerant** of the barking dog next door.
15. I won't accept an **indirect** answer.
16. It's **irresponsible** to leave the keys in a car.
17. The poems of Emily Dickinson are **immortal**.
18. Is it **illegal** to own an unlicensed dog?
19. Teaching cows to read is totally **impractical**!
20. I'm sorry I acted **impolitely** at lunch.

Lesson 21

Prefixes <u>de</u>, <u>pre</u>, <u>pro</u>, <u>con</u>, <u>com</u>, and <u>mis</u>

Objective
To spell words with the prefixes *de*, *pre*, *pro*, *con*, *com*, and *mis*

Correlated Phonics Lessons
MCP Phonics, Level F,
Lessons 31, 34

Spelling Words in Action   **Page 85**

In this selection, students find out how once-deadly fights with a sword have evolved into the sport of fencing. After reading, ask students why they would or wouldn't like to try fencing.

Call on volunteers to say the boldfaced words and identify the different prefixes.

Warm-Up Test
1. Jim uses a pole when **propelling** his raft.
2. Who were the **competitors** in the contest?
3. There is a **provision** for shelter if it rains.
4. Mrs. Lu is attending a **conference**.
5. We talked on a **previous** occasion.
6. Danita will **dedicate** this song to Ali.
7. We **deposited** the check today.
8. What a silly **complaint** they made!
9. The lion cubs **depended** on their mother.
10. I felt better when the humidity **decreased**.
11. Has the weather forecaster **predicted** snow?
12. Computers have helped industry to **progress**.
13. I **misunderstood** the directions and got lost.
14. The driver was **confused** about the route.
15. I **presume** that you are tired after your trip.
16. Some medicines require a **prescription**.
17. The tourist **mispronounced** some words.
18. A fence **prevented** the cows from straying.
19. The witness felt **compelled** to tell the truth.
20. Is there any **confirmation** of that fact?

Spelling Practice   **Pages 86–87**

Introduce the spelling rule and have students read the **list words** aloud. Encourage students to look back at their **Warm-Up Tests** and apply the spelling rule to any misspelled words.

As students work through the **Spelling Practice** exercises, remind them to look back at their **list words** or in their dictionaries if they need help. You may want to write *product*, *induct*, and *conduct* on the board to remind students that a new word can be formed by using a different prefix.

 See Charades/Pantomime, page 15

70

Spelling Words in Action

How is modern fencing different from duels fought long ago?

Touché

Imagine that you're in a duel. There is no way your opponent's next move can be **predicted**. If you make a wrong move, you could be jabbed with a foil, a flexible blade sometimes used in fencing.

Fencing is somewhat of a **misunderstood** sport. Those who **dedicate** their time to the sport do not want their fans to be **confused**. Some fans **presume** that the **competitors** get hurt. That is not the case today.

Fencing competitors used to engage in a duel to settle an argument. Only the winner survived. Modern fencing, however, does not involve danger. Injuries are **prevented** in several ways. Fencers wear protective clothing, and the points of the swords are covered. Another sign of **progress** in the sport is the use of electrical judging. Swords are wired to help judges determine how many touches, or hits, have been made. When the electrified sword touches the other fencer's vest or mask, a light appears on the scoring machine in **confirmation** of the hit.

One **complaint** from spectators new to the sport is that fencing is hard to follow. A good way to watch a fencing bout is to concentrate on just one fencer's actions. If you follow the sport long enough, you will learn to appreciate its fast pace!

> Say the boldfaced words in the selection. These words have prefixes at the beginning of each word. How many prefixes can you find?

85

Spelling Practice

TIP
The prefixes **pre** and **pro** usually mean before. **Pro** can also mean forward, as in progress.
The prefix **de** means down, not, or reverse. **De** can also mean apart or aside, as in dedicate.
The prefixes **con** and **com** mean with or together.
The prefix **mis** usually means bad or badly or wrong or wrongly.

LIST WORDS
1. propelling
2. competitors
3. provision
4. conference
5. previous
6. dedicate
7. deposited
8. complaint
9. depended
10. decreased
11. predicted
12. progress
13. misunderstood
14. confused
15. presume
16. prescription
17. mispronounced
18. prevented
19. compelled
20. confirmation

Words with de, pre, pro, con, com, and mis

Write the **list words** under the correct category.

Words with the prefix pre or pro
1. propelling
2. provision
3. previous
4. predicted
5. progress
6. presume
7. prescription
8. prevented

Words with the prefix con or com
15. competitors
16. conference
17. complaint
18. confused
19. compelled
20. confirmation

Words with the prefix de
9. dedicate
10. deposited
11. depended
12. decreased

Words with the prefix mis
13. misunderstood
14. mispronounced

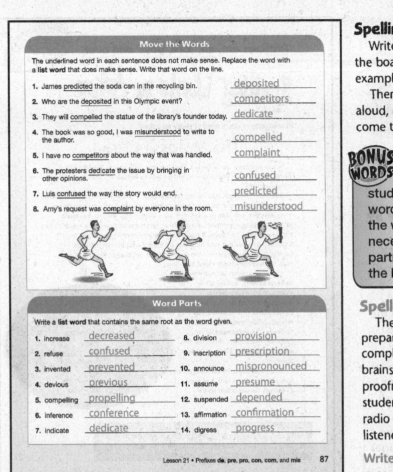

Move the Words

The underlined word in each sentence does not make sense. Replace the word with a **list word** that does make sense. Write that word on the line.

1. James <u>predicted</u> the soda can in the recycling bin.
2. Who are the <u>deposited</u> in this Olympic event?
3. They will <u>compelled</u> the statue of the library's founder today.
4. The book was so good, I was <u>misunderstood</u> to write to the author.
5. I have no <u>competitors</u> about the way that was handled.
6. The protesters <u>dedicate</u> the issue by bringing in other opinions.
7. Luis <u>confused</u> the way the story would end.
8. Amy's request was <u>complaint</u> by everyone in the room.

deposited
competitors
dedicate
compelled
complaint
confused
predicted
misunderstood

Word Parts

Write a **list word** that contains the same root as the word given.

1. increase — decreased
2. refuse — confused
3. invented — prevented
4. devious — previous
5. compelling — propelling
6. inference — conference
7. indicate — dedicate
8. division — provision
9. inscription — prescription
10. announce — mispronounced
11. assume — presume
12. suspended — depended
13. affirmation — confirmation
14. digress — progress

Lesson 21 • Prefixes de, pre, pro, con, com, and mis   87

Spelling and Writing

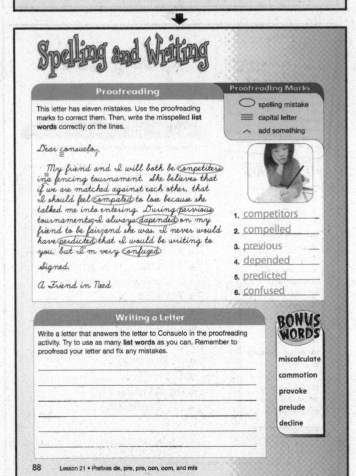

Proofreading

This letter has eleven mistakes. Use the proofreading marks to correct them. Then, write the misspelled **list words** correctly on the lines.

Dear consuelo,

My friend and I will both be ~competitors~ in a fencing tournament. She believes that if we are matched against each other, that I should feel ~compelled~ to lose because she talked me into entering. During ~pervious~ tournaments, I always ~dapended~ on my friend to be fair, and she was. I never would have ~predicted~ that I would be writing to you, but I'm very ~confused~.

Signed,

A Friend in Need

Proofreading Marks

◯ spelling mistake
☰ capital letter
∧ add something

1. competitors
2. compelled
3. previous
4. depended
5. predicted
6. confused

Writing a Letter

Write a letter that answers the letter to Consuelo in the proofreading activity. Try to use as many **list words** as you can. Remember to proofread your letter and fix any mistakes.

_____
_____
_____
_____
_____
_____
_____

BONUS WORDS

miscalculate
commotion
provoke
prelude
decline

88   Lesson 21 • Prefixes de, pre, pro, con, com, and mis

Spelling Strategy

Write several sentences containing **list words** on the board, but leave blanks for the prefixes. For example: "I ____ pronounced the word."

Then, invite the class to read each sentence aloud, completing the **list word**. Ask a volunteer to come to the board and fill in the missing prefix.

BONUS WORDS

You may want to suggest that students write a definition for each bonus word, then write a question for each of the words, referring to their definitions if necessary. Have them trade papers with a partner and answer each question, using the bonus word in their response.

Spelling and Writing   **Page 88**

The **Proofreading** exercise will help students prepare to proofread their letters. As students complete the writing activity, encourage them to brainstorm ideas, write a first draft, revise, and proofread their work. To publish their writing, students may want to use their letters to create a radio show called "Ask Consuelo," in which listeners call in for on-the-air advice.

Writer's Corner Students might enjoy learning more about fencing by reading *Fencing* (*Know the Sport*) by Allan Skipp, or a similar book. Encourage them to write a compare-and-contrast paragraph telling what they thought about fencing before and after they read the book.

Final Test

1. Theo's explanation **confused** me.
2. The wind is **propelling** debris across the road.
3. I received **confirmation** that my letter arrived.
4. **Competitors** from ten countries came to race.
5. I **presume** that you know you are late.
6. We felt **compelled** to tell you the news.
7. A **provision** for a garage is in the house plans.
8. Sherelle **misunderstood** what I said.
9. Will the **conference** focus on health issues?
10. We discussed our plans at a **previous** meeting.
11. Bad weather **prevented** us from hiking.
12. We'd like to **dedicate** this song to our parents.
13. My baby brother **mispronounced** my name.
14. Jill **deposited** half her allowance in the bank.
15. Will Dr. Saka write a **prescription** for you?
16. We made a **complaint** about the poor service.
17. Gramps **predicted** rain whenever his knee hurt.
18. She **decreased** the car's speed on the curve.
19. The farmer **depended** on rain for a good crop.
20. What **progress** we've made on this project!

Lesson 22

Prefixes em, en, fore, post, and over

Objective

To spell words with the prefixes *em, en, fore, post,* and *over*

 Phonics

Correlated Phonics Lessons
MCP Phonics, Level F,
Lessons 30, 35–36

Spelling Words in Action

Page 89

In this selection, students find out about the deadly molasses flood of 1919. After reading, ask students what they would have done to help clean up the mess.

Call on volunteers to say the boldfaced words, identify the different prefixes, and suggest how the prefixes change the meanings of the base words.

Warm-Up Test

1. Are those sounds the **forewarning** of a storm?
2. Janelle added a **postscript** to her letter.
3. The generals agreed to a **postwar** treaty.
4. Phil tries to **encourage** his brother to study.
5. Passengers paid extra for **overweight** baggage.
6. Turn off the water or the sink will **overflow**.
7. A leader must have **foresight** to govern well.
8. Cindy will **embellish** her story with a few jokes.
9. We will **emblazon** our ties with the motto.
10. A jeweler can **engrave** your bracelet.
11. Bad habits can **endanger** your health.
12. He is in the **foreground** of the photo.
13. A life of hardship can **embitter** a person.
14. Your library books are three days **overdue**.
15. We had **foreknowledge** of the event.
16. Parents sometimes **overprotect** their children.
17. Rosa fished from the river **embankment**.
18. We must **embattle** our village against attack.
19. His **enlistment** in the Navy made us proud.
20. An atlas can **enlighten** you about geography.

Spelling Practice

Pages 90–91

Introduce the spelling rule and have students read the **list words** aloud. Discuss the meanings of less familiar words, such as *emblazon* and *embattle*. Then, encourage students to look back at their **Warm-Up Tests** and apply the spelling rule to any misspelled words.

As students work through the **Spelling Practice** exercises, remind them to look back at their **list words** or in their dictionaries if they need help.

 for ESL students **See Words in Context, page 14**

72

Prefixes em, en, fore, post, and over

 Lesson 22

Spelling Words in Action

How would you stop a flood of sticky molasses?

The Molasses Flood

It was a January day in Boston. The year was 1919, shortly after the end of World War I. A story that people would tell and **embellish** for years to come was about to unfold.

At around noontime, without any **forewarning**, a 52-foot-tall storage tank holding over 2 million gallons of molasses began to split apart. As chunks of metal flew in every direction, **postwar** veterans must have thought they were back in battle. Molasses began to **overflow** onto the street. An enormous gooey wave nearly 15 feet high swept down the streets. It began to **endanger** everything in its path. It destroyed houses and even hit one of the supports for the elevated train. Luckily, the engineer glimpsed the disaster ahead and stopped the train in time. His **foreknowledge** saved many lives.

The cleanup effort lasted for weeks. Workers hired to fight the sticky substance were knee-deep in molasses. Wishing they had had the **foresight** to do it earlier, city officials finally brought in nearby fireboats. The **enlistment** of the fireboats, which hosed down the area with saltwater, finally helped to clean the streets.

As a **postscript**, the company that owned the molasses tank was fined $1 million. An inspection on the tank had been long **overdue**.

Say the boldfaced words in the selection. Each boldfaced word has a prefix. How many prefixes can you find? How do the prefixes change the meanings of the base words?

89

TIP

The prefixes **em** and **en** can mean <u>in</u> or <u>into</u>, as in endanger. They can also mean <u>cause to be</u>, as in embitter, or <u>to make</u>, as in engrave. The prefix **fore** means <u>front</u> or <u>before</u>, as in foresight.
The prefix **post** means <u>after</u>, as in postwar.
The prefix **over** usually means <u>too much</u> or <u>above</u>, as in overdue.

Spelling Practice

LIST WORDS

1. forewarning
2. postscript
3. postwar
4. encourage
5. overweight
6. overflow
7. foresight
8. embellish
9. emblazon
10. engrave
11. endanger
12. foreground
13. embitter
14. overdue
15. foreknowledge
16. overprotect
17. embankment
18. embattle
19. enlistment
20. enlighten

Words with em, en, fore, post, and over

Write each **list word** under the correct category.

Words with the prefix em or en

1. encourage
2. embellish
3. emblazon
4. engrave
5. endanger
6. embitter
7. embankment
8. embattle
9. enlistment
10. enlighten

Words with the prefix fore

11. forewarning
12. foresight
13. foreground
14. foreknowledge

Words with the prefix over

15. overweight
16. overflow
17. overdue
18. overprotect

Words with the prefix post

19. postscript
20. postwar

90   Lesson 22 • Prefixes em, en, fore, post, and over

Comparing Words

Study the relationship between the first two underlined words. Then, write a **list word** that has the same relationship with the third underlined word.

1. road is to curb as river is to ___embankment___
2. hinder is to discourage as help is to ___encourage___
3. lake is to flood as bathtub is to ___overflow___
4. careful is to careless as protect is to ___endanger___
5. wood is to carve as metal is to ___engrave___
6. Mr. is to Mister as p.s. is to ___postscript___
7. far is to near as background is to ___foreground___
8. prompt is to timely as late is to ___overdue___
9. advice is to caution as hint is to ___forewarning___
10. yesterday is to tomorrow as prewar is to ___postwar___

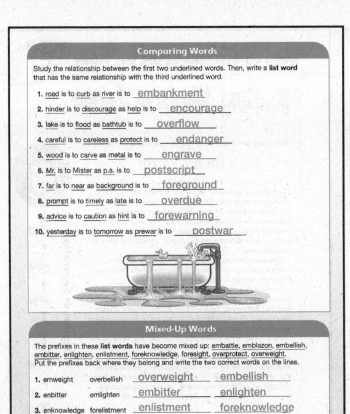

Mixed-Up Words

The prefixes in these **list words** have become mixed up: embattle, emblazon, embellish, embitter, enlighten, enlistment, foreknowledge, foresight, overprotect, overweight. Put the prefixes back where they belong and write the two correct words on the lines.

1. emweight   overbellish   ___overweight___   ___embellish___
2. enbitter   emlighten   ___embitter___   ___enlighten___
3. enknowledge   forelistment   ___enlistment___   ___foreknowledge___
4. forebattle   emsight   ___foresight___   ___embattle___
5. overblazon   emprotect   ___overprotect___   ___emblazon___

Lesson 22 • Prefixes **em, en, fore, post,** and **over**   91

Spelling and Writing

Proofreading

This pamphlet on storm safety tips has ten mistakes. Use the proofreading marks to correct them. Then, write the misspelled **list words** correctly on the lines.

When a storm is coming, you cant overpertect yourself. With forsite and planning you can remain safe. If you don't have a portable radio, you're overdew to get one. Follow any forwarning about flooding if you live in a low-lying area. Keep batteries bottled water, and candles on hand. During the storm, encairage everyone to keep away from windows electrical appliances, and telephones. after the storm, don't endanger yourself by going near downed wires.

Proofreading Marks
- ◯ spelling mistake
- ≡ capital letter
- ⌃ add something
- ⌄ add apostrophe

1. ___overprotect___   2. ___foresight___   3. ___overdue___
4. ___forewarning___   5. ___encourage___   6. ___endanger___

Writing Quotations

What do you think people who were on the train that nearly plunged into the molasses flood might have said? Write quotations for several different people who may have experienced this train ride. Use any **list words** that you can. Remember to proofread your quotations and fix any mistakes.

_____
_____
_____
_____

BONUS WORDS

empower
encompass
foremost
oversensitive
overemotional

92   Lesson 22 • Prefixes **em, en, fore, post,** and **over**

Spelling Strategy

You may want to write the definitions in the Tip box on the board and ask students to name the prefix or prefixes that go with each definition. Then, challenge students to name **list words** for each prefix and define and spell each word.

BONUS WORDS You may want to suggest that students write a question for each bonus word that they will use to interview a person who survived "The Molasses Flood." Have them take turns role-playing the parts of interviewer and survivor.

Spelling and Writing   Page 92

The **Proofreading** exercise will help students prepare to proofread their quotations. As students complete the writing activity, encourage them to brainstorm ideas, write a first draft, revise, and proofread their work. To publish their writing, students may want to use their quotations to create a TV "person-on-the-scene" news report.

Writer's Corner To request a free student kit containing general information on water, waste, pollution, etc., the class can write to: Public Access, The Environmental Protection Agency, 401 M St., SW, Washington, DC 20460.

Final Test

1. Mr. Chi will **enlighten** us about the election.
2. I received **forewarning** that I was failing math.
3. What did the soldiers do after **enlistment**?
4. Celeste signed the letter and added a **postscript**.
5. The **postwar** calm was a relief to the villagers.
6. They will **embattle** themselves against the enemy.
7. We slid down the **embankment** to the river.
8. I want to **encourage** everyone to attend.
9. A mother dog may **overprotect** her pups.
10. **Foreknowledge** of the hurricane reduced injuries.
11. Was the **overweight** wrestler disqualified?
12. Don't let the tub **overflow**!
13. With **foresight**, we may avoid many problems.
14. Pat will **embellish** her tales with scary noises.
15. What is the fine on these **overdue** books?
16. His harsh words may **embitter** his audience.
17. We will **emblazon** the walls with our paintings.
18. She'll **engrave** the date on the silver plate.
19. Chemical waste can **endanger** public health.
20. I stood in the **foreground**, with Mom in back.

Lesson 23

Prefixes anti, counter, super, sub, ultra, trans, and semi

Objective

To spell words with the prefixes *anti, counter, super, sub, ultra, trans,* and *semi*

Correlated Phonics Lessons
MCP Phonics, Level F,
Lessons 32, 36–38

Spelling Words in Action   *Page 93*

In this selection, students learn about the "small world" theory. Ask students if they have ever experienced the "small world" theory in action, and invite them to share their stories.

Ask volunteers to say the boldfaced words and identify the different prefixes.

Warm-Up Test

1. Mark put **antifreeze** in the car.
2. Who will **supervise** the building of the house?
3. Our team played in the **semifinal** tournament.
4. Rita applied an **antiseptic** to her scraped knee.
5. Window glass is a **transparent** material.
6. My **substitution** of ingredients improved the pie.
7. For some poisons, milk is an **antidote**.
8. Radar helped the ship locate the **submarine**.
9. The cut looked bad, but it was only **superficial**.
10. Did you get a magazine **subscription** as a gift?
11. The boys sat in a **semicircle** around the fire.
12. Aspirin is often used to **counteract** pain.
13. The army staged a clever **counterattack**.
14. The proofreader put a **semicolon** in the sentence.
15. Do **supersonic** jets exceed the speed of sound?
16. A **transistor** is an electronic device in radios.
17. The sun's **ultraviolet** rays are invisible.
18. Keneesha **transferred** to a new school.
19. The FBI investigates **counterfeit** money.
20. Blood produces **antibodies** to destroy bacteria.

Spelling Practice   *Pages 94–95*

Introduce the spelling rule and have students read the **list words** aloud. Encourage students to look back at their **Warm-Up Tests** and apply the spelling rule to any misspelled words.

As students work through the **Spelling Practice** exercises, remind them to look back at their **list words** or in their dictionaries if they need help.

See Spelling Aloud, page 14

74

Lesson 23

Spelling Words in Action

How closely are people connected from all around the world?

It's a Small World

Did you ever hear of the "small world" theory, sometimes called "six degrees of separation"? Here's how it works. Say you read a letter from a girl in Ohio, Jill Romero, in a magazine to which you have a **subscription**. Jill wrote the letter as an **antidote** to **counteract** the idea that nothing exciting ever happens in her town. Her letter tells how her brother Will scored the winning basket in his **semifinal** basketball playoffs when he was put in for a **substitution**.

How many "people connections," or *degrees of separation,* would it take to get from you to Jill? The small world theory says that on the average, it would take no more than six.

You start by asking your mom whom she knows in Ohio. Mom is the *first* person connecting you to Jill. She offers to ask her friend Josie (the 2nd person). Josie is the gas station attendant who put **antifreeze** in Mom's car. She lived in Ohio before her husband was **transferred** to your city's **submarine** base.

Josie doesn't know the Romeros, so she calls her friend Mary in Ohio. Mary (the 3rd person) helps to **supervise** her son Frank's basketball team. Frank (the 4th person) turns out to have a **superficial** acquaintance with Jill's brother, Will (the 5th person). Will, of course, knows Jill, for the sixth and last connection. There you have it—six "people connections," or degrees of separation, between you and Jill Romero. It's a small world after all!

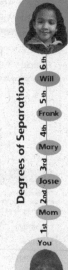

Look back at the boldfaced words in the selection. Each word has a prefix at the beginning of the word. How many different prefixes can you find?

93

Spelling Practice

TIP

anti = against; opposite
ultra = beyond; very
sub = under; below; not quite
semi = half; partly
counter = against; opposite
super = over; very; greater than others
trans = across; over; beyond

LIST WORDS

1. antifreeze
2. supervise
3. semifinal
4. antiseptic
5. transparent
6. substitution
7. antidote
8. submarine
9. superficial
10. subscription
11. semicircle
12. counteract
13. counterattack
14. semicolon
15. supersonic
16. transistor
17. ultraviolet
18. transferred
19. counterfeit
20. antibodies

Words with Prefixes

Write each **list word** under the correct heading.

Words with the prefixes anti and counter

1. antifreeze
2. antiseptic
3. antidote
4. counteract
5. counterattack
6. counterfeit
7. antibodies

Words with the prefix super

8. supervise
9. superficial
10. supersonic

Words with the prefix ultra

11. ultraviolet

Words with the prefix sub

12. substitution
13. submarine
14. subscription

Words with the prefix trans

15. transparent
16. transistor
17. transferred

Words with the prefix semi

18. semifinal
19. semicircle
20. semicolon

94   Lesson 23 • Prefixes anti, counter, super, sub, ultra, trans, and semi

Definitions

Write a **list word** to match each definition.

1. something that works against a poison — antidote
2. takes place before a final match or round — semifinal
3. limited to the surface area — superficial
4. device that controls the flow of electric current — transistor
5. attack that is a response to a fight — counterattack
6. to oversee or direct work — supervise
7. moved from one person, place, or thing to another — transferred
8. the act of putting one thing in place of another — substitution
9. see-through — transparent
10. beyond the speed of sound — supersonic
11. half of a round shape — semicircle
12. something that acts against germs — antiseptic
13. to act directly against — counteract

Solve the Riddles

Use the **list words** to solve the riddles. Write the words on the lines.

1. This helps keep your car running in the winter. — antifreeze
2. It can describe a sandwich or an underwater boat. — submarine
3. You might use this to get newspapers, tickets, or magazines. — subscription
4. Without this, you wouldn't pause as long when you read certain sentences. — semicolon
5. You don't want to get a dollar bill that is one of these. — counterfeit
6. The rays this describes cannot be seen. — ultraviolet
7. They help your body to fight colds. — antibodies

Proofreading

The following paragraph has eleven mistakes. Use the proofreading marks to fix each mistake. Then, write the misspelled **list words** correctly on the lines.

Proofreading Marks
- ◯ spelling mistake
- ℒ take out something
- ∧ add something
- ⩔ add apostrophe

When my parents volunteered to to supervise their high school reunion, they couldnt locate two classmates. "What should we do" they wondered. They advertised the reunion in the local newspaper, but it seemed that neither of the the missing classmates had a subscription. One had been transferred to a Naval submereen base, so Dad wrote to a friend in the in Navy. Another one had a superfishal role in a Broadway play, so Mom wrote to a relative who was an actor. Their efforts paid off when the two classmates addresses were found.

1. supervise
2. subscription
3. transferred
4. submarine
5. superficial

Writing an Advertisement

Imagine that it's 20 years in the future, and you are writing a newspaper advertisement to help find students from your class for a reunion. What would you say? Create an ad that would encourage your classmates to contact you. Use any **list words** that you can. Remember to proofread your advertisement and fix any mistakes.

_____

_____

_____

_____

_____

BONUS WORDS

antisocial
counterbalance
subcontract
transaction
semiprecious

Spelling Strategy

Write *anti, counter, sub, super, ultra, trans,* and *semi* on the board as separate column headings. For each of the **list words**, tell students a root or base word and ask which prefix they would add to it to form a **list word**. Ask a volunteer to write the complete word on the board in the correct column and to give its meaning.

BONUS WORDS

You may want to suggest that students write a sentence for each bonus word, then erase the prefixes. Have them pair up to trade papers and rewrite each other's sentences, adding the prefixes. Ask them to talk about how the prefixes change the meanings of the words.

Spelling and Writing   Page 96

The **Proofreading** exercise will help students prepare to proofread their advertisements. As students complete the writing activity, encourage them to brainstorm ideas, write a first draft, revise, and proofread their work. To publish their writing, students can illustrate their ads and combine their drawings and ads into a newspaper page.

Writer's Corner Invite students to interview a senior citizen. Encourage them to find out about friends or classmates of their guests who went on to do surprising things. Ask students to share what they learned.

Final Test

1. Vaccines cause the blood to produce **antibodies**.
2. Bo **transferred** money into the account.
3. **Transistor** radios were popular in the 1960s.
4. This sentence does not need a **semicolon**.
5. A smile may **counteract** Jan's sadness.
6. When does this magazine **subscription** expire?
7. The **submarine** slowly surfaced.
8. The **substitution** of salt for sugar was horrible!
9. An **antiseptic** will prevent infection.
10. Roland will **supervise** the children.
11. We bought **antifreeze** at the gas station.
12. Mom attended our **semifinal** tennis match.
13. The silky curtain material is **transparent**.
14. The doctor carried an **antidote** for snake bites.
15. The accident caused only a **superficial** wound.
16. Draw a full circle, and then draw a **semicircle**.
17. The chess player pondered his **counterattack**.
18. Some pilots are trained to fly **supersonic** jets.
19. The sun's **ultraviolet** rays may be harmful.
20. Don't be fooled by **counterfeit** bills.

Lesson 24

Lessons 19–23 · Review

Objectives

To review spelling words with *ou* and *ow*, prefixes *ir*, *in*, *il*, *im*, *de*, *pre*, *pro*, *con*, *com*, *mis*, *em*, *en*, *fore*, *post*, *over*, *anti*, *counter*, *super*, *sub*, *ultra*, *trans*, and *semi*

Check Your Spelling Notebook
Page 97–100

Based on your observations, note which words are giving students the most difficulty and offer assistance for spelling them correctly. Here are some frequently misspelled words to watch for: *outrageous, drought, incredible, illiterate, irresponsible, compelled, encourage,* and *antiseptic.*

To give students extra help and practice in taking standardized tests, you may want to have them take the **Review Test** for this lesson on pages 78–79. After scoring the tests, return them to students so that they can record their misspelled words in their spelling notebooks.

After practicing their troublesome words, students can work through the exercises for lessons 19–23 and the cumulative review, **Show What You Know**. Before they begin each exercise, you may want to go over the spelling rule.

Take It Home

Invite students to locate **list words** from lessons 19–23 in books, magazines, and newspapers they read at home. Students can also use **Take It Home** Master 4 on pages 80–81 to help them do the activity. (A complete list of the spelling words is included on page 80 of the **Take It Home** Master.) Invite students to share their lists with the class.

76

Lessons 19–23 · Review

Lesson 24

In lessons 19 through 23, you learned more about the spelling of vowel sounds in words. You also learned about words with prefixes added to the base word. Look at those words again and think about what the prefixes mean.

Check Your Spelling Notebook

Look at the words in your spelling notebook. Which words for lessons 19 through 23 did you have the most trouble with? Write them here.

_____

_____

Practice writing your troublesome words with a partner. Say a sentence for each word and spell the word aloud for your partner.

Lesson 19

 The **ow** sound can be spelled two ways: **ou**, as in surrounding, and **ow**, as in drowsily.

Write a **list word** to match each clue. Not all the words will be used.

List Words
coward
bough
mouthful
compound
downstream
pronoun
discount
foundation
lounge
endow
announce
outrageous

1. tree part	bough
2. a room to relax in	lounge
3. a bargain price	discount
4. base of a house	foundation
5. shocking; excessive	outrageous
6. proclaim, make known	announce
7. don't talk with this	mouthful
8. he, she, they, or it	pronoun
9. mixture made of two or more parts	compound
10. person who lacks courage	coward

97

Lesson 20

 The prefixes **ir**, **in**, **il**, and **im** usually mean not, as in irresponsible, indirect, illogical, and immaterial. The prefix **im** can also mean to or into, as in immigrant.

Write the **list word** that has the same base word or root as the word given. Not all the words will be used.

List Words
immortal
irregular
intolerant
indirect
illegal
immature
illegible
immigrant
incapable
irrational
impatient
indefinite

1. definitely	indefinite
2. migrate	immigrant
3. capability	incapable
4. mortality	immortal
5. legalize	illegal
6. tolerate	intolerant
7. patience	impatient
8. regulate	irregular
9. direction	indirect
10. legibility	illegible

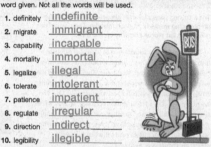

Lesson 21

 pre, pro = before con, com = with or together
pro = forward mis = bad or badly, or wrong or wrongly
de = down, not, reverse, apart, aside

Write five **list words** that could be found listed between each set of dictionary guide words given. Write the words in alphabetical order. Not all the words will be used.

List Words
prevented
depended
compelled
confused
predicted
complaint
provision
conference
prescription
decreased
progress
misunderstood

compile/deposit		mistake/protect	
1. complaint	6.	misunderstood
2. conference	7.	predicted
3. confused	8.	prescription
4. decreased	9.	prevented
5. depended	10.	progress

98 Lesson 24 • Review

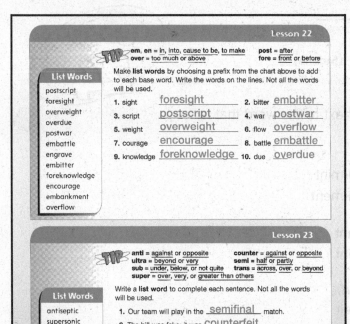

TIP em, en = in, into, cause to be, to make   post = after
over = too much or above   fore = front or before

List Words

postscript
foresight
overweight
overdue
postwar
embattle
engrave
embitter
foreknowledge
encourage
embankment
overflow

Make **list words** by choosing a prefix from the chart above to add to each base word. Write the words on the lines. Not all the words will be used.

1. sight   foresight
2. bitter   embitter
3. script   postscript
4. war   postwar
5. weight   overweight
6. flow   overflow
7. courage   encourage
8. battle   embattle
9. knowledge   foreknowledge
10. due   overdue

TIP anti = against or opposite   counter = against or opposite
ultra = beyond or very   semi = half or partly
sub = under, below, or not quite   trans = across, over, or beyond
super = over, very, or greater than others

List Words

antiseptic
supersonic
antifreeze
ultraviolet
semifinal
semicolon
semicircle
submarine
transparent
subscription
counterfeit
counterattack

Write a **list word** to complete each sentence. Not all the words will be used.

1. Our team will play in the semifinal match.
2. The bill was fake; it was counterfeit.
3. We put antifreeze in the car in the winter.
4. After we ate half the pie, a semicircle shape was left.
5. A submarine travels underwater.
6. Use a semicolon to separate those clauses.
7. The nurse uses an antiseptic to kill germs.
8. Our subscription to that magazine is for one year.
9. That window is transparent; you can see through it.
10. A supersonic aircraft exceeds the speed of sound.

Lesson 24 • Review   99

Show What You Know

Lessons 19–23 Review

One word is misspelled in each set of **list words**. Fill in the circle next to the **list word** that is spelled incorrectly.

1. ○ drought ○ immortal ○ antifreeze ○ semicolon ● confrence
2. ○ depended ● illegul ○ downstream ○ progress ○ foreground
3. ○ propelling ○ impractical ● risounding ○ antibodies ○ overdue
4. ○ lounge ○ impolitely ○ previous ● indefinate ○ semifinal
5. ○ substitution ○ coward ● poastwar ○ misunderstood ○ transistor
6. ● forknowledge ○ embattle ○ competitors ○ bough ○ indirect
7. ○ pronoun ● counterract ○ foresight ○ superficial ○ prevented
8. ○ incapable ○ supervise ● counterfit ○ enlistment ○ incredible
9. ○ intolerant ● overwait ○ pronounced ○ irrational ○ engrave
10. ○ forewarning ○ immaterial ○ illogical ● confurmation ○ account
11. ○ confused ○ mouthful ○ compelled ● drously ○ enlighten
12. ○ counterpart ○ provision ○ antidote ○ overprotect ● impashunt
13. ○ illiterate ● enblazon ○ transparent ○ compound ○ complaint
14. ○ antiseptic ○ overflow ○ illegible ● perscription ○ discount
15. ○ predicted ○ ultraviolet ● semcircle ○ outrageous ○ dedicate
16. ○ immature ○ embellish ● submareen ○ embitter ○ presume
17. ○ supersonic ● diposited ○ improperly ○ foundation ○ decreased
18. ○ encourage ○ household ○ endanger ○ transferred ● annownce
19. ○ counterattack ● imigrant ○ surrounding ○ irregular ○ postscript
20. ● endough ○ subscription ○ embankment ○ irresponsible ○ mispronounced

Final Test   Page 100

1. The **foundation** of a house must be strong.
2. Please carry that **lounge** chair into the shade.
3. Do you have some news to **announce**?
4. Some **compound** words are hyphenated.
5. What an **outrageous** thing to say!
6. Books can make an author's ideas **immortal**.
7. Don't be **intolerant** of ideas that are different.
8. A natural pond has an **irregular** shape.
9. That route is **indirect**, but it's beautiful.
10. It is **illegal** to go through a stop sign.
11. You have made a lot of **progress** in your work.
12. I'm sorry that I **misunderstood** your message.
13. Joe was **confused** by the unclear directions.
14. The drugstore has your **prescription** ready.
15. What **prevented** you from being here earlier?
16. Mom added a **postscript** to Dad's letter.
17. I had the **foresight** to pack a warm coat.
18. I paid extra because my bag was **overweight**.
19. Your library books are a week **overdue**.
20. We will **embattle** the fort against the invaders.
21. We put **antifreeze** in the car before winter.
22. She won the **semifinal** tennis match easily.
23. Use an **antiseptic** to kill any germs.
24. Here is a **transparent** cover for your drawing.
25. The **submarine** stayed underwater for days.
26. Alan was careful, but he was no **coward**.
27. During the storm, a **bough** fell from the tree.
28. Lawanda took a **mouthful** of spinach soup.
29. A singular **pronoun** replaces a singular noun.
30. Why don't you buy a radio at a **discount** store?
31. The signature on that contract is **illegible**.
32. My father came here as an **immigrant**.
33. They seem **incapable** of learning to swim.
34. Please don't be so **impatient**!
35. Are your weekend plans still **indefinite**?
36. My mother is at a business **conference**.
37. Put your **complaint** in writing.
38. The symphony orchestra **depended** on donations.
39. The number of accidents has **decreased**.
40. No one **predicted** the tied score.
41. I want you to **engrave** my name on this cup.
42. The rain-swollen river overran its **embankment**.
43. Paul's bad luck did not **embitter** him.
44. We will **encourage** her at the swim meet.
45. Watch out or the water will **overflow**!
46. A magazine **subscription** is a thoughtful present.
47. This lotion will **counteract** that itching.
48. Use a period instead of a **semicolon**.
49. What time will the **supersonic** plane arrive?
50. These jewels must be **counterfeit**!

Review Test (Side A)

Read each set of words. Fill in the circle next to the word that is spelled correctly.

1.   ⓐ ebankment   ⓒ embankmint
     ⓑ enbankment   ⓓ embankment

2.   ⓐ intolerent   ⓒ intolerant
     ⓑ imtolerent   ⓓ intolarent

3.   ⓐ counterfeit   ⓒ cownterfit
     ⓑ counterfit   ⓓ conterfeit

4.   ⓐ compound   ⓒ compounde
     ⓑ compownde   ⓓ compownd

5.   ⓐ countract   ⓒ kounteract
     ⓑ counteract   ⓓ counreact

6.   ⓐ imortal   ⓒ immortal
     ⓑ immortle   ⓓ imortale

7.   ⓐ presiption   ⓒ precription
     ⓑ prescription   ⓓ perscription

8.   ⓐ compleint   ⓒ complant
     ⓑ complaynt   ⓓ complaint

9.   ⓐ anownce   ⓒ anounce
     ⓑ announce   ⓓ annonce

10. ⓐ submarin   ⓒ submareen
     ⓑ sebmarine   ⓓ submarine

11. ⓐ conference   ⓒ confrence
     ⓑ conferance   ⓓ comference

12. ⓐ imigrant   ⓒ immigrant
     ⓑ imigrante   ⓓ imagrant

13. ⓐ transparnt   ⓒ transparint
     ⓑ transperent   ⓓ transparent

Name _____

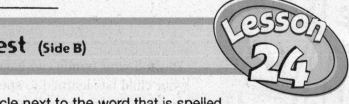
Read each set of words. Fill in the circle next to the word that is spelled correctly.

14. ⓐ bugh   ⓒ bowgh
    ⓑ bough   ⓓ bogh

15. ⓐ foresite   ⓒ forsight
    ⓑ foresight   ⓓ forasite

16. ⓐ dacreased   ⓒ decresed
    ⓑ decraesed   ⓓ decreased

17. ⓐ incapeble   ⓒ incapable
    ⓑ incapabile   ⓓ imcapable

18. ⓐ overweight   ⓒ overwayt
    ⓑ overwait   ⓓ overwieght

19. ⓐ foundation   ⓒ fowndation
    ⓑ fondation   ⓓ foundashun

20. ⓐ enbitter   ⓒ embitter
    ⓑ embiter   ⓓ imbitter

21. ⓐ irregular   ⓒ ireguler
    ⓑ iregular   ⓓ irreguler

22. ⓐ confuesed   ⓒ confussed
    ⓑ confused   ⓓ comfused

23. ⓐ owtrageous   ⓒ outrajous
    ⓑ outrageus   ⓓ outrageous

24. ⓐ encourage   ⓒ encurage
    ⓑ encarouge   ⓓ encuorage

25. ⓐ supersonik   ⓒ soopersonic
    ⓑ supersonic   ⓓ supersenic

Take It Home 4

You and your family can have fun sharing the new words that your child has learned to spell at school. You'll find some ideas on these pages for helping your child review the words in lessons 19–23.

Read All About It!

Keep a piece of paper and a pencil handy in the room where your family usually gathers to read. Encourage your child to look for spelling words while reading books, magazines, and newspapers and to write each one he or she finds on the paper.

Lesson 19

1. account
2. announce
3. bough
4. compound
5. counterpart
6. coward
7. discount
8. downstream
9. drought
10. drowsily
11. endow
12. foundation
13. household
14. lounge
15. mouthful
16. outrageous
17. pronoun
18. pronounced
19. resounding
20. surrounding

Lesson 20

1. illegal
2. illegible
3. illiterate
4. illogical
5. immaterial
6. immature
7. immigrant
8. immortal
9. impatient
10. impolitely
11. impractical
12. improperly
13. incapable
14. incredible
15. indefinite
16. indirect
17. intolerant
18. irrational
19. irregular
20. irresponsible

Lesson 21

1. compelled
2. competitors
3. complaint
4. conference
5. confirmation
6. confused
7. decreased
8. dedicate
9. depended
10. deposited
11. mispronounced
12. misunderstood
13. predicted
14. prescription
15. presume
16. prevented
17. previous
18. progress
19. propelling
20. provision

Lesson 22

1. embankment
2. embattle
3. embellish
4. embitter
5. emblazon
6. encourage
7. endanger
8. engrave
9. enlighten
10. enlistment
11. foreground
12. foreknowledge
13. foresight
14. forewarning
15. overdue
16. overflow
17. overprotect
18. overweight
19. postscript
20. postwar

Lesson 23

1. antibodies
2. antidote
3. antifreeze
4. antiseptic
5. counteract
6. counterattack
7. counterfeit
8. semicircle
9. semicolon
10. semifinal
11. submarine
12. subscription
13. substitution
14. superficial
15. supersonic
16. supervise
17. transferred
18. transistor
19. transparent
20. ultraviolet

Word Search

There are twelve spelling words hidden in this puzzle. How many can you and your child find? Remember to look horizontally, vertically, and diagonally.

immature	indirect	coward	downstream
announce	progress	presume	engrave
embattle	antidote	supervise	depended

V	B	J	F	E	M	U	S	E	R	P	Z
B	U	T	C	E	R	I	D	N	I	K	T
E	L	T	T	A	B	M	E	G	I	X	W
R	C	S	V	T	T	R	P	R	M	I	U
D	O	W	N	S	T	R	E	A	M	K	M
B	W	G	G	A	O	H	N	V	A	N	G
R	A	R	C	G	A	N	D	E	T	W	M
M	R	Y	R	N	O	Y	E	E	U	S	G
U	D	E	R	U	I	M	D	I	R	I	J
H	S	A	N	T	I	D	O	T	E	Z	Z
S	Q	C	T	M	V	F	P	I	X	I	U
V	E	S	I	V	R	E	P	U	S	Z	V

Prefixes uni, mono, bi, tri, and mid

Objective
To spell words with the prefixes *uni*, *mono*, *bi*, *tri*, and *mid*

 Correlated Phonics Lessons
MCP Phonics, Level F,
Lessons 38–39

Spelling Words in Action   *Page 101*

The meaning of *barnstorming* becomes clear in this selection about the hazardous early days of "flying machines." After reading, invite students to read aloud the part of the selection they liked the best.

Encourage students to look back at the boldfaced words. Ask volunteers to say the words, identify the different prefixes, and suggest their meanings.

Warm-Up Test
1. The flag of Italy is **tricolor**.
2. Illinois is one of America's **midwestern** states.
3. Membership in the science club has **tripled**.
4. Wittenberg is a **university** in Springfield, Ohio.
5. Where did you go on your **midsummer** trip?
6. The committee meets on a **biweekly** basis.
7. The clown rode a **unicycle** in the circus parade.
8. A high-speed **monorail** runs through Japan.
9. Each staff member wears an identical **uniform**.
10. The diameter line **bisects** a circle into halves.
11. One of the earliest airplanes was the **biplane**.
12. Mother cut the meat pie into **triangular** pieces.
13. I enjoy watching birds through my **binoculars**.
14. How well the chorus sings in **unison**!
15. Three books in a series make up a **trilogy**.
16. Was driving across the desert **monotonous**?
17. The word **monosyllable** means "one syllable."
18. The students worked for **universal** peace.
19. Please fill out the application in **triplicate**.
20. The reunion is a **biannual** event.

Spelling Practice   *Pages 102–103*

Introduce the spelling rule and have students read the **list words** aloud. Encourage students to look back at their **Warm-Up Tests** and apply the spelling rule to any misspelled words.

As students work through the **Spelling Practice** exercises, remind them to look back at their **list words** or in their dictionaries if they need help.

for ESL students **See Questions/Answers, page 15**

82

Spelling Words in Action

How did barnstorming get its name?

BARNSTORMING

Picture yourself on a **midsummer** afternoon in the 1920s. You've just heard that some of those new flying machines would be landing at Farmer Jones's field in your **midwestern** town. You hop in your Model-T and drive off.

There they are—half a dozen biplanes sitting on the field. You pick out faces in the growing crowd, including the president of the local **university**. The audience has **tripled** by the time you hear an announcer's **monotonous** voice droning over the loudspeaker.

The **biplane** speeds down the grassy "runway." It lifts off, carrying a pilot and one passenger. Then you see the passenger step out onto the wing. You're glad you brought your **binoculars** to get a close-up look. Everyone gasps in **unison** as the passenger, a stuntwoman, hangs from a ladder below the plane.

Another plane takes off, and then another. These planes don't carry stuntmen. Instead, they fly in a **triangular** pattern, zigzagging through the clouds. Then the engine of one of the planes starts to make a sputtering sound. It's falling in a spiral down toward the earth. The pilot leaps out and safely floats to the ground in his parachute. The plane, however, crashes through the farmer's barn and neatly **bisects** the roof. At that moment, it's perfectly clear to you why this type of flying is called "barnstorming."

Look back at the boldfaced words in the selection. Find the different prefixes in the words. Try coming up with the meaning for each prefix.

101

TIP
The prefixes **uni** and **mono** mean one or single.
The prefix **bi** means two or twice.
The prefix **tri** means three or three times.
The prefix **mid** means in the middle of.

Spelling Practice

LIST WORDS
1. tricolor
2. midwestern
3. tripled
4. university
5. midsummer
6. biweekly
7. unicycle
8. monorail
9. uniform
10. bisects
11. biplane
12. triangular
13. binoculars
14. unison
15. trilogy
16. monotonous
17. monosyllable
18. universal
19. triplicate
20. biannual

Words with uni, mono, bi, tri, and mid

Write each **list word** in the correct category to show the prefix it contains.

uni	bi
1. university	11. biweekly
2. unicycle	12. bisects
3. uniform	13. biplane
4. unison	14. binoculars
5. universal	15. biannual

mono	tri
6. monorail	16. tricolor
7. monotonous	17. tripled
8. monosyllable	18. triangular
	19. trilogy
mid	20. triplicate
9. midwestern	
10. midsummer	

Definitions

Write a **list word** to solve each definition clue.

1. once every two weeks — biweekly
2. multiplied by three — tripled
3. plane with one wing above the other — biplane
4. twice a year — biannual
5. having three sides — triangular
6. train with one track — monorail
7. something made of three colors — tricolor
8. boring and repetitive — monotonous
9. one-wheeled vehicle — unicycle
10. three copies — triplicate
11. divides into two parts — bisects
12. the middle of the summer — midsummer

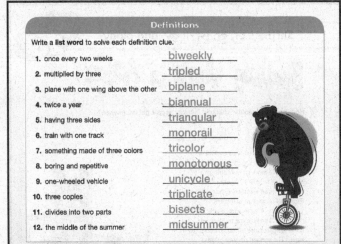

Scrambled Words

What **list word** can be made from the letters in each of these phrases? Write the word on the line.

1. survey in it — university
2. end sew trim — midwestern
3. in forum — uniform
4. is noun — unison
5. glory it — trilogy
6. mall by lone so — monosyllable
7. lunar vise — universal
8. boa curls in — binoculars

binoculars
midwestern
monosyllable
trilogy
uniform
unison
universal
university

Spelling and Writing

Proofreading

This biography has ten mistakes. Use the proofreading marks to correct them. Then, write the misspelled **list words** correctly on the lines.

Bessie Coleman was the first African American woman to become a pilot. Tired of monotenus work, Coleman wanted to fly a byplane. Prejudice nearly stopped her, but she earned a license in Europe. Her first exhibition was in a middwesdern city in 1922. Her stunts won her unaversl acclaim. Can you imagine Coleman in her Pilot's unaform standing before a cheering crowd If only we had a pair of magic binockulars that would enable us to see her soar across the sky.

Proofreading Marks
- ◯ spelling mistake
- ∧ add something
- ℓ take out something
- / make small letter

1. monotonous   2. biplane
3. midwestern   4. universal
5. uniform   6. binoculars

Writing a Comparison

Write a paragraph comparing and contrasting two of the following means of transportation: a biplane, a monorail, and a unicycle. Be sure to include the advantages and disadvantages of each of these. Try to use as many **list words** as you can. Remember to proofread your paragraph and fix any mistakes.

_____
_____
_____
_____
_____

BONUS WORDS
- unilateral
- monogram
- bifocals
- trilingual
- midpoint

Spelling Strategy

Write the numbers 1, 2, and 3 on the board as separate column headings. Then, ask volunteers to name **list words** whose prefixes indicate these numbers. Write each word on the board in the correct column and circle the prefix.

BONUS WORDS You may want to suggest that students write a definition or draw a simple sketch for each bonus word, using their dictionaries if they need help with a meaning. Then, have them trade papers with a partner and write the word that fits each clue.

Spelling and Writing   *Page 104*

The **Proofreading** exercise will help students prepare to proofread their paragraphs. As students complete the writing activity, encourage them to brainstorm ideas, write a first draft, revise, and proofread their work. To publish their writing, students may want to illustrate or draw a diagram of each type of transportation and display their paragraphs with their artwork.

Writer's Corner You may want to bring in newspaper clippings about events such as air shows, bicycle races, or truck rallies. Invite students to write a paragraph telling which event they would have liked to attend and why.

Final Test
1. The theater presented a **trilogy** of plays.
2. Our family gathered for the **biannual** reunion.
3. This line **bisects** the square into two triangles.
4. Where shall we have our **midsummer** picnic?
5. Does France have a **tricolor** flag?
6. The call of the catbird is somewhat **monotonous**.
7. The museum has a model of an early **biplane**.
8. We clean the apartment on a **biweekly** schedule.
9. Chicago is a lovely **midwestern** city.
10. The acrobat stood on his head on a **unicycle**.
11. The word **monosyllable** contains five syllables.
12. How many **triangular** patches are in the quilt?
13. The police officer wore a bright blue **uniform**.
14. What a great **university** Harvard is!
15. The students recited the poem in **unison**.
16. She filled out the order form in **triplicate**.
17. We'll take the **monorail** at the airport.
18. Our annual profits have **tripled** over five years.
19. We can look ahead to **universal** space travel.
20. I used **binoculars** to watch the fielder's catch.

Lesson 26

Suffixes or, er, ist, logy, and ology

Objective
To spell words with the suffixes or, er, ist, logy, and ology

Phonics
Correlated Phonics Lesson
MCP Phonics, Level F, Lesson 51

Spelling Words in Action   Page 105

In this selection, students learn how technology has changed the delivery of information over the years. Ask students what they think media equipment will be able to do in the future.

Ask volunteers to say the boldfaced words, identify the suffixes, and tell how many different suffixes there are.

Warm-Up Test
1. A **juror** became ill during the trial.
2. A **consumer** should spend carefully.
3. **Biology** is the study of plants and animals.
4. Sam asked the **jeweler** to repair his watch.
5. Charles Lindbergh was a famous **aviator**.
6. Would you rather be a **spectator** or a player?
7. An **insulator** does not conduct electricity.
8. She asked the **typist** to compose a letter.
9. A **transformer** alters the voltage of electricity.
10. We put up the **projector** to view our slides.
11. The **machinist** repaired the printing press.
12. Aretha is a **geologist** who studies volcanos.
13. The **florist** created a beautiful bridal bouquet.
14. The **divisor** is a number divided into another.
15. I enjoy columns by that **journalist**.
16. Modern **technology** has brought us computers.
17. Achilles is a hero of Greek **mythology**.
18. Let's take the **escalator** to the fifth floor.
19. Which **manufacturer** made that video game?
20. My mother is a police **investigator**.

Spelling Practice   Pages 106–107

Introduce the spelling rule and have students read the **list words** aloud. Call on volunteers to look up such difficult words as *insulator* and *transformer* and read the definitions aloud. Then, encourage students to look back at their **Warm-Up Tests** and apply the spelling rule to any misspelled words.

As students work through the **Spelling Practice** exercises, remind them to look back at their **list words** or in their dictionaries if they need help.

for ESL students See Student Dictation, page 14

84

Spelling Words in Action

How has the computer changed the way people get information?

Ancient Machines

Imagine that you want to find out how information reached people in the days before modern **technology**. You decide to visit a history museum. After riding an **escalator**, you reach a room full of ancient machines.

A guide points to a tall black machine. "The printing press was a great **transformer** of information," he says. "The earliest presses printed books and pamphlets. Eventually, presses were used to print newspapers. A **journalist** would write about important events. Then a **machinist** would set the letters for the story on a metal sheet. The process took a day, so a **consumer** bought a newspaper to read yesterday's news." His words almost sound like **mythology** as you think of what it's like to get news today. Although a journalist is still an **investigator**, he or she is also the **typist** who writes the story on a computer.

Next the man points to a machine with two wheels. "That's a film **projector**," he says. "It was invented by Thomas A. Edison. Pretty different from watching movies on a VCR, isn't it? But one thing hasn't changed. People still love to read the news and watch movies!"

Look back at the boldfaced words in the selection. These words have word parts, called suffixes, at the end of each word. How many suffixes can you find?

105

Spelling Practice

TIP
The suffixes **or** and **er** mean something or someone that does something, as in projector, juror, and jeweler. The suffix **ist** also means someone who does something, as in typist.

The suffixes **logy** and **ology** mean the study of, as in biology.

LIST WORDS
1. juror
2. consumer
3. biology
4. jeweler
5. aviator
6. spectator
7. insulator
8. typist
9. transformer
10. projector
11. machinist
12. geologist
13. florist
14. divisor
15. journalist
16. technology
17. mythology
18. escalator
19. manufacturer
20. investigator

Words with or, er, ist, logy, and ology

Write a **list word** that has the same root as the word given.

1. mythical — mythology
2. biosphere — biology
3. consume — consumer
4. machine — machinist
5. geology — geologist
6. investigate — investigator
7. escalate — escalator
8. type — typist
9. inspect — spectator
10. jewel — jeweler
11. aviation — aviator
12. flower — florist
13. journal — journalist
14. jury — juror
15. technique — technology
16. divide — divisor
17. factory — manufacturer
18. form — transformer
19. project — projector
20. insulate — insulator

Describing Words

Write a **list word** to name the person whose work involves the items given.

1. rocks and minerals — geologist
2. bracelets and rings — jeweler
3. flowers — florist
4. machines and wrenches — machinist
5. clues and fingerprints — investigator
6. keyboards — typist
7. news stories — journalist
8. airplanes — aviator
9. trials and juries — juror
10. any sort of manufactured goods — manufacturer

Rhyming Words

Fill in the blanks with a word that rhymes with the underlined word or words.

1. I heard a <u>rumor</u> that you are a careful **consumer**
2. She showed us how hummingbirds drink <u>nectar</u> on the overhead **projector**
3. I feel much <u>wiser</u>, now that I know which number is the **divisor**
4. The study of animals, <u>zoology</u>, is a branch of the science called **biology**
5. When you went to see the <u>skater</u>, were you in the crowd as a **spectator**?
6. Who was the <u>informer</u> who reported the broken **transformer**?
7. What is the <u>chronology</u> of the growth of computer **technology**?
8. From the field of <u>archaeology</u> we've learned much about Greek and Roman **mythology**
9. Please stand <u>straighter</u> when you ride on the **escalator**
10. The heat in the apartment was <u>greater</u> because of the new **insulator**

Lesson 26 • Suffixes **or**, **er**, **ist**, **logy**, and **ology**   107

Proofreading

Proofreading Marks
◯ spelling mistake
⌃ add something

This article has ten mistakes. Use the proofreading marks to fix each mistake. Then, write the misspelled **list words** correctly on the lines.

There is a story in the school newspaper about a local spice manufackturer called Spicy's. The company makesmany different spices to flavor food. Thesespices include cinnamon garlic, and pepper. They are used to flavor vinegar mustard different sauces, and pickles. In the article, the journalist said that Spicy's also produces some artificial flavorings. Using modern technolgy and current knowledge in biahlogy, they can make flavors that a consumor cannot tell from natural spices.

1. manufacturer   2. journalist   3. technology
4. biology   5. consumer

Writing a News Story

Write the lead paragraph of a news story about an interesting event in your school or your community. Try to tell the *who, what, where, when,* and *why* of the story. Use any **list words** that you can. Remember to proofread your paragraph and fix any mistakes.

_____
_____
_____
_____
_____
_____

BONUS WORDS

counselor

zoology

lecturer

hypnotist

theology

108   Lesson 26 • Suffixes **or**, **er**, **ist**, **logy**, and **ology**

Spelling Strategy

Use the definitions in the Tip box to help create clues for several of the **list words**, such as "something that insulates." Then say each clue aloud and invite the class to guess the matching **list word**. Call on a volunteer to write the word on the board, circle the suffix, and give the meaning of the suffix.

BONUS WORDS You may want to suggest that students write a sentence for each bonus word and underline the word. Then, have them write either "person" or "field of study" according to the meaning of the suffix.

Spelling and Writing   *Page 108*

The **Proofreading** exercise will help students prepare to proofread their news stories. As students complete the writing activity, encourage them to brainstorm ideas, write a first draft, revise, and proofread their work. To publish their writing, students may want to use their news stories to make a newsletter.

Writer's Corner You may want to bring in articles from magazines and newspapers. Ask students to work in pairs to discuss how the way a story is reported might be different 100 years ago and 100 years in the future. Invite them to jot down key phrases and present their ideas to the class.

Final Test

1. The **jeweler** repaired Grandmother's ring.
2. The **divisor** seven goes into fourteen twice.
3. We had no power when the **transformer** broke.
4. My uncle is a clothing **manufacturer.**
5. The movie **projector** needs a new lightbulb.
6. That **aviator** pilots her own plane.
7. Russell Baker is a famous American **journalist.**
8. Mr. Flynn is an **investigator** for the FBI.
9. The **biology** teacher held a test tube.
10. Did a **florist** arrange that bouquet?
11. We took the **escalator** up to the third floor.
12. A secretary needs to be an excellent **typist.**
13. Will each **consumer** receive a refund?
14. Glass can be an effective **insulator.**
15. Hector is a hero in Greek **mythology.**
16. A **geologist** studies the earth's composition.
17. Was your mother a **juror** on that case?
18. My aunt worked as a **machinist** in Toledo.
19. He fixed it using the latest in **technology.**
20. Every **spectator** in the stands cheered.

85

Suffixes er, est, and ness

Objective

To spell words with the suffixes er, est, and ness

Correlated Phonics Lessons
MCP Phonics, Level F,
Lessons 52, 55

Spelling Words in Action   Page 109

"Weaving Stories" gives students some tips for good storytelling. Call on volunteers to give brief summaries of stories they would like to tell or of favorite stories they have heard.

Ask volunteers to say the boldfaced words, identify the base words, and describe any spelling changes that occurred in the base words when the suffixes were added.

Warm-Up Test

1. The children's **happiness** was clearly evident.
2. The river is **muddiest** after a rainstorm.
3. Is this pair of shoes **tighter** than that pair?
4. Our **cruelest** winter storm was in January.
5. The **noisiest** part of the school day is recess.
6. This TV show is even **crazier** than ever!
7. Earl felt some **stiffness** in his elbow.
8. The **dampness** of the air makes me sneeze.
9. The chef checked the **sharpness** of her knives.
10. Her sergeant was the **strictest** of all.
11. The **brightest** star is often the North Star.
12. Barry wants the **thickest** jacket he can buy.
13. Our voices echoed in the room's **emptiness**.
14. This puppy is **tinier** than that one.
15. The **firmest** cucumbers will be the freshest.
16. When writing jokes, **cleverness** is important.
17. Those plants are **healthier** under Lenny's care.
18. Answer the **simplest** test questions first.
19. **Cleanliness** is important to good health.
20. Do you have the quality of **promptness**?

Spelling Practice   Pages 110–111

Introduce the spelling rule and have students read the **list words** aloud. Encourage students to look back at their **Warm-Up Tests** and apply the spelling rule to any misspelled words.

As students work through the **Spelling Practice** exercises, remind them to look back at their **list words** or in their dictionaries if they need help.

for ESL students   **See Change or No Change, page 15**

86

Spelling Words in Action

If you were a storyteller, what stories would you tell?

Weaving Stories

Storytelling is an art, but even people who tell the **simplest** stories can be storytellers. A good story touches an audience with humor, drama, wisdom, or all these things. A story can bring listeners **happiness** or even a healthier outlook on life.

You can sharpen your own storytelling skills. First, you should find a story you would enjoy telling. The library is a good place to start. Myths, tall tales, and folktales can all be fun to tell aloud. You might choose a folktale about the **noisiest** animal in the forest, or the **cruelest** or **strictest** king, or the **brightest** young woman in a land. Other stories tell about a character who is **tinier** than other people, like Thumbelina or Tom Thumb. Often, these tiny characters solve their problems through **cleverness**.

Learning a story doesn't have to be hard. Reading it over and over and picturing each of the events will help you to remember the story. It's not necessary to memorize it. In fact, telling a story in your own words helps you avoid **stiffness** in your speech. You might also want to shorten parts of a story, making it **tighter** to keep the plot moving along. Remember that small groups or large ones can be great audiences. With a story and an audience, a storyteller is always ready to perform.

Say the boldfaced words in the selection. These words have suffixes. See if you notice any spelling changes in the base words when the suffixes are added.

109

Spelling Practice

TIP

The suffix **er** means *more*, as in *tighter*. It is used to compare two things. The suffix **est** means *most*, as in *cruelest*. It is used to compare more than two things. The suffix **ness** changes an adjective into a noun, as in *damp-dampness*. To add suffixes to words ending in **y**, change the **y** to an **i**: *tiny-tinier*. To add suffixes to words ending in **e**, drop the **e**: *simple-simplest*.

Words with er, est and ness

Write a **list word** under the correct heading.

LIST WORDS

1. happiness
2. muddiest
3. tighter
4. cruelest
5. noisiest
6. crazier
7. stiffness
8. dampness
9. sharpness
10. strictest
11. brightest
12. thickest
13. emptiness
14. tinier
15. firmest
16. cleverness
17. healthier
18. simplest
19. cleanliness
20. promptness

Words with the suffix er

1. tighter
2. crazier
3. tinier
4. healthier

Words with the suffix est

5. muddiest
6. cruelest
7. noisiest
8. strictest
9. brightest
10. thickest
11. firmest
12. simplest

Words that were changed from adjectives to nouns with the suffix ness

13. happiness
14. stiffness
15. dampness
16. sharpness
17. emptiness
18. cleverness
19. cleanliness
20. promptness

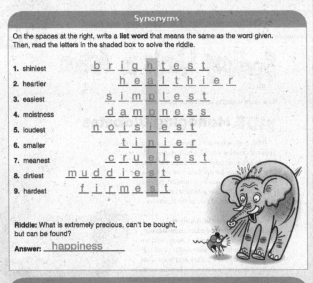

Synonyms

On the spaces at the right, write a **list word** that means the same as the word given. Then, read the letters in the shaded box to solve the riddle.

1. shiniest — b r i g h t e s t
2. heartier — h e a l t h i e r
3. easiest — s i m p l e s t
4. moistness — d a m p n e s s
5. loudest — n o i s i e s t
6. smaller — t i n i e r
7. meanest — c r u e l e s t
8. dirtiest — m u d d i e s t
9. hardest — f i r m e s t

Riddle: What is extremely precious, can't be bought, but can be found?

Answer: _happiness_

Word Parts

Add a suffix to each base word to form a **list word**. Write the word on the line.

1. tight — tighter
2. empty — emptiness
3. thick — thickest
4. clean — cleanliness
5. sharp — sharpness
6. clever — cleverness
7. tiny — tinier
8. muddy — muddiest
9. stiff — stiffness
10. noisy — noisiest
11. bright — brightest
12. strict — strictest
13. prompt — promptness
14. crazy — crazier

Lesson 27 • Suffixes er, est, and ness   111

Spelling and Writing

Proofreading

This paragraph from a travel book has nine mistakes. Use the proofreading marks to fix each mistake. Then, write the misspelled **list words** on the lines.

Hapyness mightbe listening to a story at the National Storytelling Festival in Jonesborough, tennessee. This was the first such festival in the country and it is still the best-known. What can you do there? You can see the brietest storytellers turn the simplest stories into the most fascinating tales you've ever heard. You will be amazed by their cleverness.

Proofreading Marks
- ⬭ spelling mistake
- ∧ add something
- ≡ captial letter

1. Happiness 2. brightest
3. simplest 4. cleverness

Writing a Summary

Stories can take you anywhere, anytime—even to places that do not exist. Do you have a favorite story? Perhaps you have an idea for a story. Write a paragraph that summarizes what your story is about. Try to use as many **list words** as you can. Remember to proofread your story summary and fix any mistakes.

_____
_____
_____
_____
_____
_____
_____

BONUS WORDS
bitterness
coarsest
filthier
gentler
painfulness

112   Lesson 27 • Suffixes er, est, and ness

Spelling Strategy

Ask the class to identify each **list word** in which the base word changed when the suffix was added. Write students' responses on the board. Then, call on volunteers to write each word as an equation (*noisy - y + i + est = noisiest; simple - e + est = simplest*), explaining the rule that applies to the spelling change as they do so.

BONUS WORDS

You may want to suggest that students write a paragraph using the bonus words, then erase the suffixes. Have them trade papers with a partner and read the partner's paragraph, adding the correct suffixes to the bonus words.

Spelling and Writing   Page 112

The **Proofreading** exercise will help students prepare to proofread their summaries. As students complete the writing activity, encourage them to brainstorm ideas, write a first draft, revise, and proofread their work. To publish their writing, students may want to create a dust jacket for a book based on their story idea.

Writer's Corner You may wish to read students a story by a well-known reteller of folk tales such as Joseph Bruchac or Robert D. San Souci, having them take notes as they listen. Encourage students to study their notes to help them retell the story to a friend or to family members.

Final Test

1. Cats are known for their **cleanliness**.
2. He is exercising and eating **healthier** foods.
3. Did you use your **firmest** voice to scold her?
4. When my friends left, I felt an **emptiness** inside.
5. This red shirt is the **brightest** one I own.
6. After falling, Ann had a **stiffness** in her arm.
7. Monkeys are the **noisiest** animals in the zoo.
8. Can you make this bolt **tighter**?
9. My parents care about my **happiness**.
10. Don't walk in the **muddiest** part of the path.
11. Snow in May is the **cruelest** of nature's jokes.
12. I had never heard a **crazier** idea.
13. A warm fire will get rid of the **dampness**.
14. The **strictest** rules were made for our safety.
15. This cafe serves the **thickest** steaks in town.
16. The sliver of ice cream got **tinier** as it melted.
17. His invention is an example of his **cleverness**.
18. Which problem was the **simplest**?
19. Mom praised me for my **promptness**.
20. We heard a **sharpness** in her voice.

Lesson 28

Suffixes able, ible, ful, hood, ship, and ment

Objective
To spell words with the suffixes *able*, *ible*, *ful*, *hood*, *ship*, and *ment*

 Phonics Correlated Phonics Lessons
MCP Phonics, Level F,
Lessons 55, 57

Spelling Words in Action **Page 113**

In this selection, students learn what diabetes is. Invite students to share facts they may know about diabetes.

Ask volunteers to say the boldfaced words and point out any spelling changes that occurred in the base words when the suffixes were added.

Warm-Up Test
1. Is Victor's new dog friendly and **likable**?
2. I have an **appointment** with the dentist.
3. The rewards of **parenthood** are many.
4. Good **sportsmanship** means playing fair.
5. The weather is extremely **changeable**.
6. When you reach **adulthood**, you can vote.
7. These glasses are highly **breakable**.
8. Is **enrollment** in college one of your goals?
9. She was in a **fanciful** mood.
10. There are **noticeable** stains on the tablecloth.
11. What a **successful** writer he has become!
12. Sharing tasks will make the project **manageable**.
13. Your **assignment** is to write a poem.
14. I need an **adjustment** to my schedule.
15. The lawyer gave her final **argument**.
16. The delay of the plane was **unavoidable**.
17. This coat is **reversible**.
18. Elise really enjoys her old red **convertible**.
19. The apple harvest was so **bountiful** this year!
20. Brenda was awarded a college **scholarship**.

Spelling Practice **Pages 114–115**

Introduce the spelling rule and have students read the **list words** aloud. Encourage students to look back at their **Warm-Up Tests** and apply the spelling rule to any misspelled words.

As students work through the **Spelling Practice** exercises, remind them to look back at their **list words** or in their dictionaries if they need help. Review the rules for changing base words (*bounty*, *reverse*). Point out that *manage*, *change*, and *notice* do not drop the final *e* when the suffix is added.

 for ESL students See Words in Context, page 14

88

Suffixes able, ible, ful, hood, ship, and ment

Lesson 28

Spelling Words in Action

How does diabetes affect a person's life?

KIDS Managing Diabetes

What is diabetes? It's a disease in which a person's body does not produce enough of a hormone called *insulin*. Insulin helps the body to use sugar for energy. There is no cure for diabetes, and the disease is not **reversible**. It can be controlled, however. Eating proper foods regularly, taking insulin, and exercising are all part of the treatment for diabetes.

Diabetes can start in **adulthood** or childhood. The disease offers **unavoidable** challenges to young people. Usually, kids with diabetes soon become **successful** at testing their blood sugar level. They also learn what kinds of food and exercise are healthy for them. The tricky part for diabetics is balancing all those things to keep their blood sugar levels within the right range. These levels are **changeable**, so it takes some **adjustment** for diabetic kids to stay on track with their illness. For instance, they can show great **sportsmanship**, but they may need to eat something before exercising. They may need to catch up on an **assignment** they missed in order to make a doctor's **appointment**. Friends can help by offering support. Friends should never put up an **argument** when diabetics say they need to take a blood test or get a snack.

For diabetic kids, education and knowledge about managing their disease puts them in control so they can be kids first and diabetics second.

Say the boldfaced words in the selection. Each boldfaced word has a suffix. What spelling changes in the base words occur when the suffixes are added?

113

Spelling Practice

TIP
The suffixes **able** and **ible** usually mean *can* or *able to be*. The suffix **ful** means *full of* or *having a tendency to be*. The suffix **hood** usually means *the state or condition of being*. The suffix **ship** means *having the qualities of*. The suffix **ment** means *act of* or *state of*. Before adding the suffix to some words that end in **e** or **y**, drop the **e** or change **y** to **i**, as in like + **able** = likable, and fancy + **ful** = fanciful.

LIST WORDS
1. likable
2. appointment
3. parenthood
4. sportsmanship
5. changeable
6. adulthood
7. breakable
8. enrollment
9. fanciful
10. noticeable
11. successful
12. manageable
13. assignment
14. adjustment
15. argument
16. unavoidable
17. reversible
18. convertible
19. bountiful
20. scholarship

Adding Suffixes

Write each list word in the correct category to show the suffix it contains.

able
1. likable
2. changeable
3. breakable
4. noticeable
5. manageable
6. unavoidable

ible
7. reversible
8. convertible

hood
9. parenthood
10. adulthood

ment
11. appointment
12. enrollment
13. assignment
14. adjustment
15. argument

ful
16. fanciful
17. successful
18. bountiful

ship
19. sportsmanship
20. scholarship

Classification

Write the **list word** that belongs in each group.

1. inescapable, unmistakable, __unavoidable__
2. fairness, generosity, __sportsmanship__
3. visible, remarkable, __noticeable__
4. friendly, kind, __likable__
5. homework, book report, __assignment__
6. date, meeting, __appointment__
7. victorious, excellent, __successful__
8. unreliable, shifting, __changeable__
9. sedan, station wagon, __convertible__
10. abundant, rich, __bountiful__
11. quarrel, feud, __argument__
12. fragile, delicate, __breakable__

Mixed-up Words

The suffixes in these **list words** have become mixed up: adjustment, adulthood, enrolment, fanciful, manageable, parenthood, reversible, scholarship. Put the suffixes back where they belong and write the two correct words on the line.

1. fanciment   enrollful   __fanciful__   __enrollment__
2. adultible   revershood   __adulthood__   __reversible__
3. parentable   managehood   __parenthood__   __manageable__
4. adjustship   scholarment   __adjustment__   __scholarship__

Spelling and Writing

Proofreading

This biographical sketch has nine mistakes. Use the proofreading marks to fix each mistake. Then, write the misspelled **list words** correctly on the lines.

The actress Mary Tyler Moore was famous for the (likeble) roles she played on two long-running TV shows, "The Dick Van Dyke Show" and "The Mary Tyler Moore Show" Her fans thought this (successfull) woman was possessed with (bountifel) good health, like the energetic characters she played In fact, Moores health was a challenge to her because she had been diagnosed with diabetes in (adulthode). She decided to do something for children with diabetes As the Juvenile Diabetes Foundations international chairperson, she has helped to raise millions of dollars toward researching a cure for the disease.

Proofreading Marks

- ◯ spelling mistake
- ⊙ add period
- ⍀ add apostrophe

1. __likable__
2. __successful__
3. __bountiful__
4. __adulthood__

Writing a Descriptive Paragraph

How do you meet challenges in your own life? Write a paragraph that describes something you found difficult or challenging, and what you did to overcome that challenge. Use any **list words** that you can. Remember to proofread your paragraph and fix any mistakes.

_____
_____
_____
_____
_____

BONUS WORDS

digestible
inflatable
livelihood
fellowship
ailment

Spelling Strategy

With a partner, students can fold a piece of paper in half lengthwise, write the base word for each **list word** in the first column, and write the **list word** in the second column. Point out to students that for *unavoidable* they will be adding both a suffix and a prefix (*un*) to form the **list word**. Then, have students circle the **list words** in which a spelling change occurred in the base word when the suffix was added. Ask them to discuss the rule that applies to each spelling change.

BONUS WORDS

You may want to suggest that students write a newspaper headline for each bonus word. Have them trade papers with a partner and make up a brief story to go with one of the headlines.

Spelling and Writing   *Page 116*

The **Proofreading** exercise will help students prepare to proofread their paragraphs. As students complete the writing activity, encourage them to brainstorm ideas, write a first draft, revise, and proofread their work. To publish their writing, students may want to display their paragraphs on a bulletin board titled "We Meet Our Challenges."

Writer's Corner You may want to invite a local doctor to speak to the class about diabetes. Before the visit, students can prepare a list of questions they would like to ask.

Final Test

1. **Changeable** winds made sailing difficult.
2. I overheard an **argument** about the game.
3. The paint made a **noticeable** improvement.
4. Did you apply for a college **scholarship**?
5. Your grandmother is a very **likable** person.
6. I know you'll be **successful** in your career.
7. When I reached **adulthood**, I moved to Tucson.
8. Some mistakes are totally **unavoidable**.
9. This book discusses **parenthood**.
10. What is the homework **assignment**?
11. Jay applied for **enrollment** at the university.
12. Becky drove her **convertible** in the parade.
13. Dad made an **adjustment** on my bicycle.
14. The **fanciful** story told about a timid dragon.
15. The team showed good **sportsmanship**.
16. **Bountiful** rainfall helped the crops.
17. Plan ahead to make the project **manageable**.
18. Pack the **breakable** goods in newspaper.
19. When is your doctor's **appointment**?
20. Miguel's new jacket is **reversible**.

Lesson 29

Suffixes ion, ation, ition, ance, ence, ive, and ity

Objective
To spell words with the suffixes *ion*, *ation*, *ition*, *ance*, *ence*, *ive*, and *ity*

 Phonics Correlated Phonics Lessons
MCP Phonics, Level F, Lessons 58–59

Spelling Words in Action   Page 117

In "Twister!," students read about the destruction caused by the Tri-State Tornado. Ask students to share their opinions on how modern weather prediction and mass communication systems might prevent another tornado disaster like this one.

Ask volunteers to say the boldfaced words, identify the base words, and point out any spelling changes that occurred in the bases when the suffixes were added.

Warm-Up Test
1. I know the **difference** between snow and sleet.
2. Coretta wrote a **composition** about her family.
3. Many homes are heated by **electricity**.
4. Our country has an **abundance** of resources.
5. Yesterday I had a **conversation** with Dr. Winter.
6. Do you believe in the **existence** of unicorns?
7. Reading is a relaxing **activity**.
8. **Communication** is a key to friendship.
9. The **excellence** of that restaurant is well known.
10. In **addition** to swimming, I enjoy baseball.
11. Use a **combination** of oil and vinegar.
12. In my spare time, I enjoy **creative** writing.
13. Was the teacher's **explanation** clear?
14. Spectator sports provide **passive** recreation.
15. I learned a **quotation** by Benjamin Franklin.
16. Fans provided for the **circulation** of fresh air.
17. That **destructive** cat just chewed up my glove!
18. The howling dog created a **disturbance**.
19. Do you have any work **experience**?
20. I was firm in my **resistance** to breaking rules.

Spelling Practice   Pages 118–119

Introduce the spelling rule and have students read the **list words** aloud. Encourage students to look back at their **Warm-Up Tests** and apply the spelling rule to any misspelled words.

As students work through the **Spelling Practice** exercises, remind them to look back at their **list words** or in their dictionaries if they need help. You may wish to point out that the suffix *ion*, not *ation*, is used for words ending in *ate*.

 for ESL students See Tape Recording, page 15

90

Spelling Words in Action

What made the Tri-State Tornado the worst ever to hit the U.S.?

TWISTER!

The United States has more **experience** with tornado **activity** than any other country. Many experts believe that the most **destructive** tornado ever to hit the U.S. was the 1925 Tri-State Tornado. In just hours, it roared through three states: Missouri, Illinois, and Indiana. Experts still aren't sure if the Tri-State Tornado was one twister or a group of twisters, because it is so hard to tell the **difference**. Still, this tornado qualifies as the worst in the U.S. for a **combination** of reasons. It was on the ground continuously for three and a half hours, the longest time ever recorded. In **addition**, it had the longest track of any tornado—219 miles. Tragically, the Tri-State Tornado claimed nearly 700 lives, more than any other U.S. tornado.

One **explanation** for the massive destruction caused by the Tri-State Tornado is that people had very little warning that the twister was coming their way. For much of its path, it looked like rolling clouds—not the funnel shape that people associate with a twister. Fortunately, with the **excellence** of modern weather prediction and the **existence** of mass **communication** systems, another tornado disaster of this magnitude should never occur again.

Look back at the boldfaced words in the selection. What are the base words? What spelling changes in the base words occur when the suffixes are added?

117

TIP
ion, *ation*, and *ition* = the act of or the condition of being, as in conversation and composition
ance, *ence*, and *ity* = quality or fact of being, as in resistance, experience, and activity
ive = likely to or having to do with, as in destructive and creative

Spelling Practice

LIST WORDS
1. difference
2. composition
3. electricity
4. abundance
5. conversation
6. existence
7. activity
8. communication
9. excellence
10. addition
11. combination
12. creative
13. explanation
14. passive
15. quotation
16. circulation
17. destructive
18. disturbance
19. experience
20. resistance

Adding Suffixes

Write the **list words** that contain the suffixes given.

ence
1. difference   2. existence
3. excellence   4. experience

ation
5. conversation   6. combination
7. explanation   8. quotation

ance
9. abundance   10. disturbance
11. resistance

ion
12. communication
13. circulation

ive
14. creative   15. passive
16. destructive

ition
17. composition   18. addition

ity
19. electricity   20. activity

Missing Words

Write the **list word** that belongs in each sentence.

1. Soccer is a recreational __activity__.
2. The __destructive__ storm caused heavy damage.
3. Tom's __experience__ as a tutor will help him to be a teacher.
4. The heart controls the __circulation__ of blood.
5. The title of his __composition__ was "Sources of Energy."
6. The telephone is a __communication__ tool.
7. Winnie received an award for __excellence__ in science.
8. The __existence__ of computer technology has greatly helped weather prediction.
9. I memorized the __combination__ to the lock for my locker.
10. Our long-distance phone __conversation__ lasted an hour!
11. We needed a more detailed __explanation__ to fully understand how the machine worked.
12. That group was asked to leave because they were causing a __disturbance__.
13. We take __electricity__ for granted until the power goes out.
14. I'm going to cite this famous __quotation__ by Albert Einstein in my report.

Puzzle

This is a crossword puzzle without clues. Use the length and spacing of six **list words** to complete the puzzle.

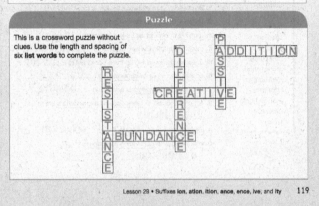

(Crossword answers: PASSIVE, ADDITION, DIFFERENCE, RESISTANCE, CREATIVE, ABUNDANCE)

Spelling and Writing

Proofreading

The news report below has ten mistakes. Use the proofreading marks to fix each mistake. Then, write the misspelled **list words** correctly on the lines.

¶ The tornado that swooped through the area last night was quite a destructive storm. As one resident described it, "I heard a roar like a huge freight train, and then it hit." A conversashion with another witness resulted in this quotasion: "My daughter Anna and I ran for the cellar as the electrisity flickered, and the tornado tore off the roof."

It was a very frightening experience for many residents. Camunication systems were knocked out for several hours until the disturbence passed.

Proofreading Marks

⬭ spelling mistake
∧ add something
⤾⤿ add quotation marks
¶ insert paragraph

1. __destructive__   2. __conversation__
3. __quotation__   4. __electricity__
5. __Communication__   6. __disturbance__

Writing Advice

What do you think people should do to prepare for a big storm? Write a paragraph stating your advice for someone who experiences a tornado, hurricane, blizzard, or flood. Use complete sentences and use any **list words** that you can. Remember to proofread your paragraph and fix any mistakes.

_____
_____
_____
_____
_____

BONUS WORDS

legislation
inspection
correspondence
radiance
originality

Spelling Strategy

Write roots or base words contained in the **list words** on the board. Then ask students which ending (*ion, ation, ition, ance, ence, ive,* or *ity*) goes with each word or word part to spell a **list word**. Call on a volunteer to come to the board and write the entire word, giving its meaning. Discuss base words that had spelling changes before the suffixes were added.

BONUS WORDS

You may want to suggest that students write a sentence for each bonus word, then trade papers with a partner. Ask them to take turns saying what the entire word means, and then what the suffix means.

Spelling and Writing   **Page 120**

The **Proofreading** exercise will help students prepare to proofread their advice. As students complete the writing activity, encourage them to brainstorm ideas, write a first draft, revise, and proofread their work. To publish their writing, students may want to read their paragraphs to the class.

Writer's Corner Students may be interested in reading more about tornadoes in *Eyewitness: Hurricane and Tornado* by Jack Challoner or a similar book. Encourage groups of students to make maps tracking the path of a particular tornado.

Final Test

1. Write a **composition** for homework tonight.
2. Alaska has an **abundance** of natural resources.
3. There are many Web sites in **existence**.
4. The telegraph is a system of **communication**.
5. Are **addition** problems easy for you?
6. An elderly man wrote this **creative** story.
7. What does **passive** smoking mean?
8. Tight clothes may cut off blood **circulation**.
9. What a **disturbance** the barking dog caused!
10. Stainless steel has strong **resistance** to rust.
11. What is the **difference** between tin and steel?
12. My alarm clock is powered by **electricity**.
13. I'd like to have a **conversation** with that artist.
14. Swimming is my favorite summertime **activity**.
15. The movie won several awards for **excellence**.
16. Fire and wind are a dangerous **combination**.
17. Will you accept my **explanation** for being late?
18. Connie read a **quotation** by Shakespeare.
19. The most **destructive** flood happened last year.
20. Our hiking trip was a great **experience**.

Lesson 30

Lessons 25–29 · Review

Objectives

To review spelling words with the prefixes *uni, mono, bi, tri,* and *mid;* and with the suffixes *or, er, ist, logy, ology, er, est, ness, able, ible, ful, hood, ship, ment, ion, ation, ition, ance, ence, ive,* and *ity*

Check Your Spelling Notebook

Page 121–124

Based on your observations, note which words are giving students the most difficulty and offer assistance for spelling them correctly. Here are some frequently misspelled words to watch for: *manufacturer, likable, changeable, existence,* and *experience.*

To give students extra help and practice in taking standardized tests, you may want to have them take the **Review Test** for this lesson on pages 94–95. After scoring the tests, return them to students so that they can record their misspelled words in their spelling notebooks.

After practicing their troublesome words, students can work through the exercises for Lessons 25–29 and the cumulative review, **Show What You Know.** Before they begin each exercise, you may want to go over the spelling rule.

 Take It Home

Invite students to listen for the **list words** in lessons 25–29 in television shows, movies, and music videos. Students can also use **Take It Home** Master 5 on pages 96–97 to help them do the activity. (A complete list of the spelling words is included on page 96 of the **Take It Home** Master.) Invite students to bring their lists to class and to compare them with other students' lists.

In lessons 25 through 29, you learned about words with prefixes and suffixes. Look at those words again, and think about how the prefixes and suffixes can change the meanings and the spelling of some base words.

Check Your Spelling Notebook

Look at the words in your spelling notebook. Which words for lessons 25 through 29 did you have the most trouble with? Write them here.

Practice writing your troublesome words with a partner. Write a sentence for each word. Trade papers, circle the prefixes or suffixes, and tell the meaning of each prefix or suffix.

Lesson 25

TIP uni, mono = one, single   bi = two, twice
tri = three, three times   mid = in the middle of

List Words
- unicycle
- bisects
- biplane
- tricolor
- triangular
- binoculars
- monotonous
- midsummer
- triplicate
- monosyllable
- universal
- trilogy

Write a **list word** to match each clue. Not all the words will be used.

1. Wednesday is to midweek as July is to ___ midsummer
2. unites is to joins as divides is to ___ bisects
3. round is to circular as three-sided is to ___ triangular
4. tricycle is to bicycle as bicycle is to ___ unicycle
5. three artists are to trio as three books are to ___ trilogy
6. double is to triple as duplicate is to ___ triplicate
7. computer is to typewriter as jet is to ___ biplane
8. astronomers are to telescopes as bird watchers are to ___ binoculars
9. illegal is to unlawful as global is to ___ universal
10. interesting is to captivating as boring is to ___ monotonous

121

Lesson 26

TIP or, er = one who or something that
ist = one who   logy, ology = the study of

List Words
- consumer
- biology
- jeweler
- juror
- aviator
- spectator
- typist
- florist
- journalist
- technology
- manufacturer
- investigator

Write a **list word** that means the same or almost the same as the word or phrase given. Not all the words will be used.

1. maker ___ manufacturer
2. jury member ___ juror
3. detective ___ investigator
4. reporter ___ journalist
5. pilot ___ aviator
6. onlooker ___ spectator
7. technical knowledge ___ technology
8. buyer or user ___ consumer
9. keyboarder ___ typist
10. life science ___ biology

Lesson 27

TIP er = more, as in healthier   est = most, as in simplest
ness changes an adjective into a noun

List Words
- tighter
- noisiest
- dampness
- brightest
- thickest
- emptiness
- tinier
- cleverness
- crazier
- simplest
- muddiest
- cleanliness

Write the **list word** that belongs in each group. Not all the words will be used.

1. small, little, ___ tinier
2. loud, ear-splitting, ___ noisiest
3. broad, wide, ___ thickest
4. easy, plain, ___ simplest
5. firm, snug, ___ tighter
6. bareness, blankness, ___ emptiness
7. wet, moist, ___ dampness
8. intelligence, wit, ___ cleverness
9. spotless, sanitary, ___ cleanliness
10. brilliant, shining, ___ brightest

122   Lesson 30 • Review

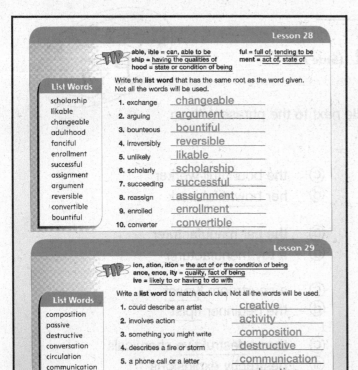

Lesson 28

TIP: able, ible = can, able to be
ship = having the qualities of
hood = state or condition of being
ful = full of, tending to be
ment = act of, state of

List Words

scholarship
likable
changeable
adulthood
fanciful
enrollment
successful
assignment
argument
reversible
convertible
bounteous

Write the **list word** that has the same root as the word given. Not all the words will be used.

1. exchange — changeable
2. arguing — argument
3. bounteous — bountiful
4. irreversibly — reversible
5. unlikely — likable
6. scholarly — scholarship
7. succeeding — successful
8. reassign — assignment
9. enrolled — enrollment
10. converter — convertible

Lesson 29

TIP: ion, ation, ition = the act of or the condition of being
ance, ence, ity = quality, fact of being
ive = likely to or having to do with

List Words

composition
passive
destructive
conversation
circulation
communication
explanation
abundance
activity
excellence
addition
creative

Write a **list word** to match each clue. Not all the words will be used.

1. could describe an artist — creative
2. involves action — activity
3. something you might write — composition
4. describes a fire or storm — destructive
5. a phone call or a letter — communication
6. tells why something happened — explanation
7. more than enough — abundance
8. 2 plus 2 — addition
9. talking between people — conversation
10. the highest level of success — excellence

Lesson 30 • Review   123

Show What You Know

Lessons 25–29 Review

One word is misspelled in each set of **list words**. Fill in the circle next to the **list word** that is spelled incorrectly.

1. ○ investigator ○ argument ○ bisects ● adjustmint ○ electricity
2. ○ consumer ○ conversation ○ emptiness ● kreativ ○ triangular
3. ○ university ○ communication ○ adulthood ● uneforum ○ happiness
4. ○ dampness ○ escalator ○ convertible ○ addition ● parenthod
5. ○ florist ● crazyer ○ passive ○ triplicate ○ strictest
6. ● diffirince ○ manageable ○ tighter ○ unicycle ○ simplest
7. ○ transformer ○ likable ● machinest ○ divisor ○ monosyllable
8. ○ reversible ● clevernus ○ activity ○ juror ○ unison
9. ○ tinier ● aveeator ○ circulation ○ scholarship ○ muddiest
10. ○ biology ○ sportsmanship ● trycolor ○ firmest ○ spectator
11. ○ cruelest ○ midwestern ○ explanation ○ thickest ● tipist
12. ○ geologist ○ bountiful ○ biweekly ○ cleanliness ● tecknologee
13. ● trylogy ○ existence ○ noisiest ○ breakable ○ biplane
14. ○ universal ● experiance ○ excellence ○ projector ○ appointment
15. ● promptniss ○ tripled ○ manufacturer ○ enrollment ○ resistance
16. ○ composition ○ unavoidable ○ changeable ● notissible ○ stiffness
17. ○ jeweler ○ monorail ● britest ○ mythology ○ combination
18. ○ healthier ○ binoculars ○ sharpness ○ abundance ● biennuel
19. ○ journalist ○ disturbance ● fancyfull ○ midsummer ○ successful
20. ● distructiv ○ assignment ○ insulator ○ monotonous ○ quotation

124   Lesson 30 • Review

Final Test   Page 121–124

1. How **monotonous** the speaker's voice is!
2. My family is having a **midsummer** party in July.
3. Please fill out this form in **triplicate**.
4. Our goal is **universal** literacy.
5. Did you read the last book in the **trilogy**?
6. These features will improve **consumer** safety.
7. In **biology** we studied the digestive system.
8. Any **jeweler** can fix that ring for you.
9. What kind of plane does that **aviator** fly?
10. Will you be a **spectator** at the game today?
11. Footsteps echoed in the **emptiness** of the house.
12. Some dollhouses are even **tinier** than this one.
13. My dog's **cleverness** surprised the trainer.
14. This route is the **simplest** but not the shortest.
15. In a hospital, **cleanliness** is vital.
16. Your parents are certainly **likable** people.
17. The weather here is very **changeable**.
18. My aunt spent her **adulthood** traveling.
19. Our class **enrollment** increases every year.
20. Good planning resulted in a **successful** vacation.
21. Our principal spoke of striving for **excellence**.
22. I can do simple **addition** without a calculator.
23. What a **creative** performer Julie is!
24. The citizens wanted an **explanation** of the tax.
25. The storm was **destructive** to the garden.
26. Look at Camille ride that **unicycle**!
27. The bicycle path **bisects** the park.
28. At the air show, they watched a **biplane**.
29. Use a **triangular** piece of cloth to make a sling.
30. With these new **binoculars** I can see the islands.
31. The **typist** quickly entered the new data.
32. Each **journalist** wrote a separate story.
33. Computer **technology** changes so rapidly!
34. Return the defective radio to the **manufacturer**.
35. The **investigator** found the cause of the fire.
36. Can you tie that knot a little **tighter**?
37. This is the **noisiest** classroom in the building.
38. **Dampness** bothers me more than the cold does.
39. Which star in the sky is the **brightest**?
40. My history book is the **thickest** one in the pile.
41. Tonight's **assignment** is to read two chapters.
42. Her quick answer prevented an **argument**.
43. This is a **reversible** coat so I wear it often.
44. Who owns that new **convertible** in the lot?
45. What a **bountiful** harvest we had this year!
46. My teacher liked my last **composition**.
47. Our tree has an **abundance** of fruit on it.
48. Alex and Mom had a long **conversation**.
49. I like any **activity** that involves the ocean.
50. The climbers sent one **communication** a day.

Name _____

Review Test (Side A)

Read each set of phrases. Fill in the circle next to the phrase with an underlined word that is spelled correctly.

1. ⓐ bountiful food
   ⓑ a bountyful harvest
   ⓒ the bountifull worker
   ⓓ her bowntiful work

2. ⓐ this computer manufacterer
   ⓑ an appliance mannufacturer
   ⓒ the car manufacturer
   ⓓ a toy menufacturer

3. ⓐ this fast typist
   ⓑ an accurate typeist
   ⓒ a courtroom typest
   ⓓ the beginner tipist

4. ⓐ the distructive tornado
   ⓑ destructive earthquakes
   ⓒ those destruktive chemicals
   ⓓ destructiv explosions

5. ⓐ expensive binoculers
   ⓑ these large binnoculars
   ⓒ powerful binoculars
   ⓓ the sophisticated benoculars

6. ⓐ one possible exeplanation
   ⓑ their fanciful explanashun
   ⓒ a reasonable explaination
   ⓓ a complicated explanation

7. ⓐ byology class
   ⓑ our biolojy teacher
   ⓒ the biology experiments
   ⓓ a bilogy paper

8. ⓐ good communecation
   ⓑ radio comunication
   ⓒ her comunication skills
   ⓓ an important communication

9. ⓐ one universal language
   ⓑ yuniversal instructions
   ⓒ some uneversal desires
   ⓓ universel laws

10. ⓐ consistent cleaneliness
    ⓑ habit of cleanlines
    ⓒ importance of clenliness
    ⓓ the bedroom's cleanliness

11. ⓐ the thickkest piece
    ⓑ the thickest fur
    ⓒ your thickist coat
    ⓓ his thickst socks

12. ⓐ that movie trilogy
    ⓑ the book trilegy
    ⓒ trillogy of events
    ⓓ trilogee of plays

13. ⓐ the noiziest fans
    ⓑ the noysiest music
    ⓒ the noisyest siren
    ⓓ the noisiest pets

Name _____

Review Test (Side B)

Read each set of phrases. Fill in the circle next to the phrase with an underlined word that is spelled correctly.

14. ⓐ these <u>enrolement</u> procedures   ⓒ sports <u>inrollment</u>
    ⓑ this class's <u>enrolmint</u>   ⓓ college <u>enrollment</u>

15. ⓐ a <u>monotonous</u> task   ⓒ <u>monottonous</u> music
    ⓑ this <u>menotonous</u> sound   ⓓ that <u>monotonus</u> voice

16. ⓐ the <u>simplist</u> method   ⓒ the <u>simplest</u> activity
    ⓑ the <u>simpelest</u> solution   ⓓ his <u>simmplest</u> reason

17. ⓐ the <u>revursible</u> sweater   ⓒ a <u>reversible</u> pillowcase
    ⓑ that <u>riversible</u> puppet   ⓓ his <u>reversable</u> jacket

18. ⓐ a <u>tinier</u> model   ⓒ the <u>tynier</u> one
    ⓑ <u>tinyer</u> than yours   ⓓ <u>tineer</u> pages

19. ⓐ <u>abundanse</u> of animals   ⓒ <u>abundence</u> of resources
    ⓑ <u>abundance</u> of plants   ⓓ a profitable <u>abunndance</u>

20. ⓐ his <u>trinegular</u> hat   ⓒ a <u>triangular</u> pattern
    ⓑ the <u>triengular</u> locket   ⓓ <u>trianglear</u> blocks

21. ⓐ her red <u>convertible</u>   ⓒ <u>convertibble</u> fuel
    ⓑ a sporty <u>convertable</u>   ⓓ this fast <u>konvertible</u>

22. ⓐ breakthrough in <u>teknology</u> ⓒ computer <u>tecknology</u>
    ⓑ foreign <u>technology</u>   ⓓ complicated <u>technolugy</u>

23. ⓐ a skilled <u>aveator</u>   ⓒ an experienced <u>aviater</u>
    ⓑ the famous <u>aviator</u>   ⓓ that young <u>avator</u>

24. ⓐ the <u>chaingeable</u> schedule ⓒ this <u>changable</u> weather
    ⓑ a <u>changible</u> design   ⓓ many <u>changeable</u> plans

25. ⓐ an <u>addition</u> problem   ⓒ <u>addishion</u> of spices
    ⓑ a new <u>adition</u>   ⓓ <u>addision</u> and subtraction

Take It Home

5

Your child has learned to spell many new words and would enjoy sharing them with you and your family. The following activities will help your child review the words in lessons 25–29 and provide some family fun, too.

Spelling Star

Your child can "star" in a TV show or music video! Here's how. Encourage your child to write down spelling words as you watch television programs, movies, and music videos. Invite your child to become a "spelling star" by spelling aloud the words he or she listed.

Lesson 25

1. biannual	12. trilogy
2. binoculars	13. tripled
3. biplane	14. triplicate
4. bisects	15. trilogy
5. biweekly	16. unicycle
6. midsummer	17. uniform
7. monorail	18. unison
8. monosyllable	19. universal
9. monotonous	20. university
10. triangular	
11. tricolor	

Lesson 26

1. aviator	12. juror
2. biology	13. machinist
3. consumer	14. manufacturer
4. divisor	15. mythology
5. escalator	16. projector
6. florist	17. spectator
7. geologist	18. technology
8. insulator	19. transformer
9. investigator	20. typist
10. jeweler	
11. journalist	

Lesson 27

1. brightest	12. noisiest
2. cleanliness	13. promptness
3. cleverness	14. sharpness
4. crazier	15. simplest
5. cruelest	16. stiffness
6. dampness	17. strictest
7. emptiness	18. thickest
8. firmest	19. tighter
9. happiness	20. tinier
10. healthier	
11. muddiest	

Lesson 28

1. adjustment	12. likable
2. adulthood	13. manageable
3. appointment	14. noticeable
4. argument	15. parenthood
5. assignment	16. reversible
6. bountiful	17. scholarship
7. breakable	18. sportsmanship
8. changeable	19. successful
9. convertible	20. unavoidable
10. enrollment	
11. fanciful	

Lesson 29

1. abundance	12. disturbance
2. activity	13. electricity
3. addition	14. excellence
4. circulation	15. existence
5. combination	16. experience
6. communication	17. explanation
7. composition	18. passive
8. conversation	19. quotation
9. creative	20. resistance
10. destructive	
11. difference	

What's My Line?

How many occupations can you and your child guess? Write the spelling word that best answers each play on words. Use the underlined words to help you.

manufacturer	machinist	typist	jeweler	florist
investigator	spectator	juror	aviator	geologist

1. Who's turning over a new leaf?_____

2. Who's a cog in a wheel? _____

3. Who's taking wing? _____

4. Who's just looking? _____

5. Who's a real gem? _____

6. Who's a rock hound? _____

7. Who's all keyed up? _____

8. Who doesn't have a clue? _____

9. Who's got the goods? _____

10. Who takes sides? _____

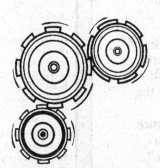

Objective
To spell words in which the final consonant is doubled or the final e dropped before adding the ending or suffix

 Correlated Phonics Lessons
MCP Phonics, Level F, Lessons 62–63

Spelling Words in Action   **Page 125**

In this selection, students read about a unique museum that helps visitors understand the importance of civil rights. Afterward, ask students why they might like to visit the museum.

Call on volunteers to say each boldfaced word, identify the base word, and explain how the spelling of the base word changed when the ending was added.

Warm-Up Test
1. How quickly the puddles **evaporated** in the heat!
2. When **combining** the ingredients, use a mixer.
3. Juan's sister **graduated** from high school today.
4. How long will that road remain **unpaved**?
5. My teacher **approved** the topic for my report.
6. The cashier **referred** me to the store manager.
7. Ted found homes for the puppies by **advertising**.
8. Lionel's suitcase was **crammed** with clothes.
9. Each class **produced** its own yearbook.
10. Her new bicycle comes **equipped** with a canteen.
11. The class election **occurred** yesterday.
12. Who **memorized** the longest poem?
13. The lion tamer easily **controlled** ten big cats.
14. That new adventure movie is **exciting**!
15. Many of the words in this note are **abbreviated**.
16. By my **calculation**, there should be rain soon.
17. With no **hesitation**, she dived into the pool.
18. Vina is busy **organizing** her photo collection.
19. The wig and glasses **disguised** Sandy's identity.
20. He **realized** that his coat was still on the bus.

Spelling Practice   **Pages 126–127**

Introduce the spelling rule and have students read the **list words** aloud. Encourage students to look back at their **Warm-Up Tests** and apply the spelling rule to any misspelled words.

As students work through the **Spelling Practice** exercises, remind them to look back at their **list words** or in their dictionaries if they need help. Explain that the spelling rules also apply to the list words that have the suffix *ion* (*calculation, hesitation*).

 See Comparing/Contrasting, page 15

Spelling Words in Action

Have you ever been to a museum like the National Civil Rights Museum?

The National Civil Rights Museum

On April 4, 1968, a terrible tragedy **occurred** at the Lorraine Motel in Memphis, Tennessee. This is the place where Dr. Martin Luther King, Jr., was assassinated. On that spot now stands a moving tribute to Dr. King and all who fought for African Americans' equal rights.

When the Lorraine was going to be sold in 1982, a group of dedicated people **approved** a decision to buy the motel. They wanted to help preserve Dr. King's memory. In 1991, the National Civil Rights Museum opened there. It was the first museum in the country to show the history of the civil rights movement through exhibits. By **organizing** key legal challenges, marches, and other protests, the movement's leaders helped to change laws that treated African Americans unfairly.

In this museum, visitors don't just look at pictures or cases **crammed** with objects. It is **equipped** with many **exciting** interactive exhibits. To tell about Rosa Parks, for example, the museum **produced** an exhibit **combining** sights and sounds. Visitors can board a bus like the one Mrs. Parks once rode in Montgomery, Alabama. Just as Mrs. Parks did, visitors hear the voice of a bus driver telling them to move to the back of the bus. While many of the museum's visitors have **memorized** facts about the civil rights movement, this place brings those facts to life. It has truly **realized** the dream of its founders.

Look back at the boldfaced words in the selection. Find the base word in each word. What happened to the spelling of the base word when the suffixes were added?

125

TIP
When a short-vowel word or syllable ends in a single consonant, usually double the consonant before adding a suffix or ending that begins with a vowel, as in equip + ed = equipped. When you add a suffix or ending that begins with a vowel to a word that ends with e, usually drop the e before adding the suffix or ending, as in unpave + ed = unpaved and combine + ing = combining.

Spelling Practice

LIST WORDS
1. evaporated
2. combining
3. graduated
4. unpaved
5. approved
6. referred
7. advertising
8. crammed
9. produced
10. equipped
11. occurred
12. memorized
13. controlled
14. exciting
15. abbreviated
16. calculation
17. hesitation
18. organizing
19. disguised
20. realized

Adding Suffixes and Endings

Write the **list words** in which the final consonant was doubled before the suffix or ending was added.
1. referred
2. crammed
3. equipped
4. occurred
5. controlled

Write the **list words** in which the final **e** was dropped before the suffix or ending was added.
6. evaporated
7. combining
8. graduated
9. unpaved
10. approved
11. advertising
12. produced
13. memorized
14. exciting
15. abbreviated
16. calculation
17. hesitation
18. organizing
19. disguised
20. realized

Missing Words

Write a **list word** to complete each sentence.

1. The word "pound" is **abbreviated** as "lb."
2. She **referred** us to an excellent dentist.
3. Tony **memorized** the poem so he would not need notes.
4. The chef is **combining** all the ingredients in a large bowl.
5. Without any **hesitation**, the firefighter rushed into the burning building.
6. What could have **occurred** in the meeting to change everyone's mind?
7. Dad made a quick **calculation** to figure out how much grocery money we would need.
8. Aunt Betsy **disguised** herself as my cousin's favorite book character for the birthday party.
9. Consuelo will be **organizing** a new file system for the office files.
10. A giant billboard was **advertising** the company's new fruit drink.
11. I was so proud of my brother when he **graduated** at the top of his class.
12. The water in our science experiment **evaporated** overnight.

Rhyming Words

Write the **list word** that rhymes with each word or phrase.

1. cup moved   **approved**
2. deduced   **produced**
3. we shipped   **equipped**
4. one rolled   **controlled**
5. Rex biting   **exciting**
6. meal sized   **realized**
7. slammed   **crammed**
8. one waved   **unpaved**

Spelling and Writing

Proofreading

Proofreading Marks
- ⟋ spelling mistake
- / make small letter
- ⌃ add something
- ⌄ add apostrophe

The following article has ten mistakes. Use the proofreading marks to fix each mistake. Then, write the misspelled **list words** on the lines.

One of the worlds longest borders along which conflict has rarely ocured is in North America. The lasting peace between Canada and the United States has produced a beautiful place that is refared to as the International Peace Garden. The garden sits on the border between the two countries in the Turtle Mountains. Aprooved in 1931, the garden is a symbol of peace, combineing beauty with a message. What kinds of things will you see there? For one thing, youll see an exciteing clock made of flowers that keeps the park's official time.

1. **occurred**   2. **produced**   3. **referred**
4. **Approved**   5. **combining**   6. **exciting**

Writing a Persuasive Paragraph

Write a paragraph telling what you think should be done about prejudice and intolerance and why your ideas would work. Use any **list words** that you can. Remember to proofread your paragraph and fix any mistakes.

_____
_____
_____
_____
_____
_____

BONUS WORDS

challenged
relating
patrolling
tolerated
admitted

Spelling Strategy

Write *calculate, combine, produce, occur, graduate, control, cram,* and *organize* on the board and ask volunteers to add *ed, ing,* or *ion* to form a **list word**. For each word, have the volunteer explain how the spelling of the base word was changed in order to add the ending or suffix. Point out that *controlled* is an exception to the rule because the second syllable contains a long vowel, not a short vowel.

BONUS WORDS Have students write stories with partners using the bonus words. Then, have them erase the bonus words and put them in the wrong places. Partner teams trade papers with other teams and rewrite the story, using the bonus words correctly.

Spelling and Writing   *Page 128*

The **Proofreading** exercise will help students prepare to proofread their paragraphs. As students complete the writing activity, encourage them to brainstorm ideas, write a first draft, revise, and proofread their work. To publish their writing, students may want to submit the paragraph to a local newspaper.

Writer's Corner Students might enjoy requesting a pen pal from the Student Letter Exchange, 211 Broadway, Suite 201, Lynbrook, NY 11563, or via the Web at www.pen-pal.com/.

Final Test
1. The artist was **combining** colors.
2. The **unpaved** road is rough and bumpy.
3. James **referred** to me in his speech.
4. We **crammed** all our bags into the trunk.
5. The campers were **equipped** with sleeping bags.
6. The actors **memorized** their lines in the play.
7. What an **exciting** roller coaster ride that was!
8. How long will it take to do the **calculation**?
9. Is Carlos **organizing** a baseball game?
10. No one **realized** how far we'd have to walk.
11. I **disguised** myself as an alien from outer space.
12. Being nervous, he spoke with **hesitation**.
13. Mai **abbreviated** many words in her letter.
14. She expertly **controlled** the horses.
15. The accident **occurred** on the first of June.
16. The factory **produced** men's clothing.
17. Is the grocery store **advertising** for cashiers?
18. Dad **approved** our plans to go to the beach.
19. Heather **graduated** from college last year.
20. The water **evaporated**, forming clouds.

Objective
To spell words in which suffixes or endings have been added to base words ending in y

Correlated Phonics Lessons
MCP Phonics, Level F, Lessons 65–66

Spelling Words in Action   **Page 129**
In this selection, students learn about the history of cranberries and how they are grown. After reading, invite students to describe dishes they like that contain cranberries or other fruit.

Ask volunteers to say the boldfaced words and identify any changes that occurred in the base words when the suffixes or endings were added.

Warm-Up Test
1. Many **companies** make donations to charity.
2. We picked strawberries to make **jellies**.
3. He poured the soup **sloppily**, so it spilled.
4. Are the engineers **surveying** the vacant lot?
5. The astronomer wrote **theories** about quasars.
6. Denise ran **steadily**, maintaining an even pace.
7. The Nile River is one of the longest **waterways**.
8. We **identified** several birds on our walk.
9. Which seats in this row are **occupied**?
10. The dog **disobeyed** and followed me to school.
11. Some folk **remedies** may be effective.
12. After jogging, I drank the juice **thirstily**.
13. Let's cut the **decaying** branches off the tree.
14. The teacher **modified** our schedule.
15. The universe has several **galaxies**.
16. What are the major **industries** in Turkey?
17. Our **attorneys** met with us to discuss the case.
18. How **dismayed** we were when our team lost!
19. The microscope **magnified** the bacteria.
20. The actor has **portrayed** many characters.

Spelling Practice   **Pages 130–131**
Introduce the spelling rule and have students read the **list words** aloud. Encourage students to look back at their **Warm-Up Tests** and apply the spelling rule to any misspelled words.

As students work through the **Spelling Practice** exercises, remind them to look back at their **list words** or in their dictionaries if they need help.

 See Charades/Pantomime, page 15

100

Spelling Words in Action

How are cranberries grown?

A "Berry" Interesting Fruit

Native Americans were the first people in North America to discover the many uses of the cranberry. They used the berries to make food, dye, and even **remedies** to treat wounds. It was the Pilgrims who **identified** the berries as "crane-berries." They thought the cranberries' pink flowers looked like the heads of cranes.

Anyone who ate a cranberry right after it had been picked would probably be **dismayed** by the waxy coating and sour taste. The taste is **modified** greatly when cranberries are used in recipes and food products.

Various **companies** produce about 5 million barrels of cranberries each year. Cranberry growing is one of the most important **industries** in Massachusetts. The berries are also grown in other parts of the U.S. and Canada.

Cranberries grow in sandy marshes known as bogs. During the growing season, growers are **occupied** by the need to protect the vines from frost. In very cold weather, water runs **steadily** over the plants to keep them from freezing. Harvesting begins in the fall, when the bogs are flooded with water. Stirring the water causes the berries to float to the surface, where they are gathered. Refrigeration keeps them from **decaying**. Some berries are sold as fresh fruit, while others are made into cranberry juice, jams, **jellies**, and other delicious foods.

Look back at the boldfaced words in the selection. Each of these words ends in a suffix. What happens to the root words that end in y when the suffixes are added?

129

TIP
If a word ends in:
- a **vowel** and **y**, add **ed** or **s** without changing the base word, as in *disobeyed*.
- a **consonant** and **y**, change the **y** to **i** before adding **ed**, **es**, or **ly**, as in *occupied*, *remedies*, or *sloppily*.
- **y**, add **ing** without changing the base word, as in *decaying*.

LIST WORDS
1. companies
2. jellies
3. sloppily
4. surveying
5. theories
6. steadily
7. waterways
8. identified
9. occupied
10. disobeyed
11. remedies
12. thirstily
13. decaying
14. modified
15. galaxies
16. industries
17. attorneys
18. dismayed
19. magnified
20. portrayed

Spelling Practice

Adding Suffixes and Endings
Add a suffix or ending to each word to form a **list word**. Write the **list word** on the line.

1. attorney   attorneys
2. modify   modified
3. company   companies
4. magnify   magnified
5. waterway   waterways
6. identify   identified
7. industry   industries
8. occupy   occupied
9. survey   surveying
10. galaxy   galaxies
11. steady   steadily
12. theory   theories
13. portray   portrayed
14. dismay   dismayed
15. jelly   jellies
16. decay   decaying
17. thirsty   thirstily
18. sloppy   sloppily
19. remedy   remedies
20. disobey   disobeyed

Synonyms and Antonyms

Write the **list word** that is the synonym or antonym of the word or phrase given.

1. antonym for <u>neatly</u> — sloppily
2. synonym for <u>adjusted</u> — modified
3. antonym for <u>periodically</u> — steadily
4. synonym for <u>lawyers</u> — attorneys
5. antonym for <u>without thirst</u> — thirstily
6. synonym for <u>enlarged</u> — magnified
7. antonym for <u>empty, vacant</u> — occupied
8. synonym for <u>alarmed, surprised</u> — dismayed
9. antonym for <u>behaved</u> — disobeyed
10. synonym for <u>named</u> — identified

Move the Words

The underlined word in each sentence does not make sense. Replace the word with a **list word** that does make sense. Write that word on the line.

1. Refrigeration is used to keep food from <u>portrayed</u>. decaying
2. This garden contains many of the plants that the early settlers used for <u>companies</u> when they were ill. remedies
3. Many <u>galaxies</u> offer summer internships for college students. companies
4. Not everyone knows that cranberry production is one of Wisconsin's <u>jellies</u>. industries
5. He is <u>decaying</u> the property where the new house will be built. surveying
6. I like the way the actress <u>industries</u> the main character in that movie. portrayed
7. The St. Lawrence Seaway is one of our most important <u>theories</u>. waterways
8. There are many <u>surveying</u> about the best growing methods. theories
9. In the science-fiction story, astronauts carried cranberries to distant <u>remedies</u>. galaxies
10. My aunt is famous for the jams and <u>waterways</u> she makes from cranberries. jellies

Spelling and Writing

Proofreading

This article has eleven mistakes. Use the proofreading marks to fix the mistakes. Then, write the misspelled **list words** correctly on the lines.

Along the watewayes of the Great Lakes region, a special harvest takes place in the summer. The Ojibway people begin survaying the Wild rice beds to plan their their harvest. Two people ride ride in each canoe, and one steedily pushes it through the water with a long pole. The Ojibway have occupyed thisarea and gathered wild rice for about 400 years. Their methods have not been modifyed very much over the years. They pull the stalks over, knock the tops, and send the grains into the bottom of the canoe. Nothing isdone slaupily.

Proofreading Marks

- ◯ spelling mistake
- / make small letter
- ∧ add something
- ℯ take something out

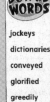

1. waterways
2. surveying
3. steadily
4. occupied
5. modified
6. sloppily

Writing a Menu

Write a menu for a meal that features three different ways to serve cranberries. You might include a beverage, bread, side dish, main course, or dessert. Describe each item on your menu, using as many **list words** as you can. Remember to proofread your menu and fix any mistakes.

_____
_____
_____
_____
_____

BONUS WORDS

jockeys
dictionaries
conveyed
glorified
greedily

Spelling Strategy

Write *consonant-y* on one side of the board and *vowel-y* on the other. Say the base word in each **list word** and have students

- point to the side of the board that applies to the last two letters in the base word
- using the spelling rules, add a suffix or ending to the base word to form a **list word**
- spell the **list word** aloud.

BONUS WORDS

You may want to suggest that students write a sentence with the base word for each bonus word. Have partners trade papers, then add the suffixes or endings to make the bonus words, and write new sentences.

Spelling and Writing   Page 132

The **Proofreading** exercise will help students prepare to proofread their menus. As students complete the writing activity, encourage them to brainstorm ideas, write a first draft, revise, and proofread their work. To publish their writing, students may want to combine their passages to create a book of menus.

Writer's Corner Encourage students to research in an encyclopedia or on the Internet to find out what your state's major crops are. Suggest that they make a map to show what crops are grown in different regions of the state.

Final Test

1. The train compartment is fully **occupied**.
2. Are geologists **surveying** the field?
3. Have you **modified** your travel plans yet?
4. The photo is **magnified** many times.
5. The dog **disobeyed** and turned left, not right.
6. Scientists try to test their **theories**.
7. Who **portrayed** Queen Victoria in the movie?
8. How exciting it would be to explore **galaxies**!
9. **Attorneys** attend law school for many years.
10. The farm horse drank **thirstily** from the pail.
11. I'd like to explore America's **waterways**.
12. Janet sells homemade **jellies**.
13. Water poured **steadily** from the broken pipe.
14. Several **companies** manufacture dishwashers.
15. Are there any new **remedies** for poison ivy?
16. Many people work in steel **industries**.
17. I cook **sloppily** when I'm rushed.
18. I **identified** Grandpa in his old school photo.
19. The **decaying** leaves will make rich garden soil.
20. We were **dismayed** to miss your party.

Objective
To spell the plurals of nouns ending in *f*, *fe*, and *o*; and nouns whose singular and plural forms are the same

 Correlated Phonics Lessons
MCP Phonics, Level F, Lessons 67–68

Spelling Words in Action — Page 133
In this selection, students read about shopping on the Internet. Ask students if they have ever bought anything online and how they feel about online stores.

Ask volunteers to say each boldfaced word, identify the singular form, and tell whether or not the spelling of the plural form is different.

Warm-Up Test
1. Many towns hold **rodeos** in the summer.
2. **Kangaroos** are such fascinating animals!
3. The band members were all wearing **tuxedos**.
4. The hotel's **patios** are cool places to sit.
5. Does this store sell car **stereos**?
6. Nina bought two **avocados** at the store.
7. We enjoy discussing our different **beliefs**.
8. The tale of forty **thieves** is one of my favorites.
9. Do importers of jewelry pay high **tariffs**?
10. Some plant **species** have become extinct.
11. The waiters in the Mexican cafe wore **ponchos**.
12. We played a game of **dominoes** after school.
13. These shells are **mementos** from our vacation.
14. **Embargoes** were put on certain goods.
15. I prefer my **broccoli** with lemon.
16. Aunt Ann made sauce for the **spaghetti**.
17. Let's look for a store that sells **jackknives**.
18. Jill's aunt gave her several **handkerchiefs**.
19. The **Eskimos** trimmed their jackets with fur.
20. The **mosquitoes** are so annoying!

Spelling Practice — Pages 134–135
Introduce the spelling rule and have students read the **list words** aloud. Encourage students to look back at their **Warm-Up Tests** and apply the spelling rule to any misspelled words.

As students work through the **Spelling Practice** exercises, remind them to look back at their **list words** or in their dictionaries if they need help. After students complete the exercises, you may want to explain that another name for *Eskimo* is *Inuit*.

for ESL students **See Picture Clues, page 15**

Spelling Words in Action

What can be bought on the Internet?

Open for Business

Buying products on the Internet is very popular, and for good reason. Online stores are open 24 hours a day, and items are delivered right to the buyer's doorstep.

What are people buying online? High-tech items such as **stereos** and computers are very popular. Some buyers also like to order food over the Internet. Internet grocery stores offer everything from fresh pears and **avocados** to ordinary boxes of **spaghetti**. Toys are also popular with online consumers, from **dominoes** to stuffed **kangaroos**.

Online auction services do a lively business selling collectibles such as sports **mementos**. The motto here is "Let the buyer beware," as there are Internet **thieves**! One person stole over $37,000 from customers on an Internet auction site.

Specialty clothing can be found easily on the Internet, from **tuxedos** for a wedding to **ponchos** for camping. No item is overlooked, from fine linen **handkerchiefs** to designer suspenders.

Of course, the Internet isn't the solution to every shopping need. When people need a quart of milk, they still head to the nearest grocery store!

Look back at the boldfaced words in the selection. Say the singular form of each plural word. What do you notice about the spelling of some plural forms of words?

Spelling Practice

TIP
Some words remain the same in singular and plural form, as in *species*. For most words ending in *f* or *fe*, change the *f* or *fe* to *v* and add *es* to form the plural, as in *thieves* or *knives*. For some exceptions, form the plural by adding *s*, as in *beliefs* or *tariffs*. For most words ending in *o*, add *s* to form the plural, as in *tuxedos*. Some exceptions add *es*, as in *mosquitoes* or *dominoes*.

LIST WORDS
1. rodeos
2. kangaroos
3. tuxedos
4. patios
5. stereos
6. avocados
7. beliefs
8. thieves
9. tariffs
10. species
11. ponchos
12. dominoes
13. mementos
14. embargoes
15. broccoli
16. spaghetti
17. jackknives
18. handkerchiefs
19. Eskimos
20. mosquitoes

Plural Words
Write the **list words** under the correct headings.

Words that do not change to form the plural	Words that end in f, ff, or o and just add s to form the plural
1. species	9. rodeos
2. broccoli	10. kangaroos
3. spaghetti	11. tuxedos

Words that change f or fe to v and add es to form the plural	
4. thieves	12. patios
5. jackknives	13. stereos
	14. avocados

Words that end in o and add es to form the plural	
6. dominoes	15. beliefs
7. embargoes	16. tariffs
8. mosquitoes	17. ponchos
	18. mementos
	19. handkerchiefs
	20. Eskimos

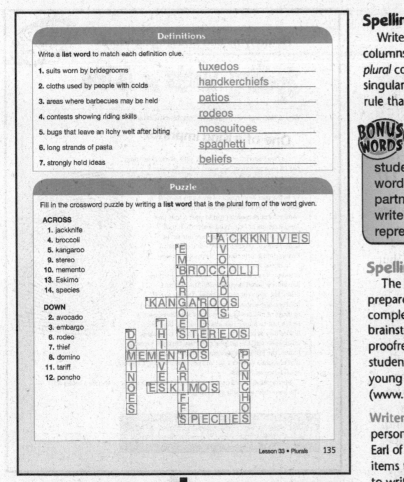

Definitions

Write a **list word** to match each definition clue.

1. suits worn by bridegrooms — tuxedos
2. cloths used by people with colds — handkerchiefs
3. areas where barbecues may be held — patios
4. contests showing riding skills — rodeos
5. bugs that leave an itchy welt after biting — mosquitoes
6. long strands of pasta — spaghetti
7. strongly held ideas — beliefs

Puzzle

Fill in the crossword puzzle by writing a **list word** that is the plural form of the word given.

ACROSS
1. jackknife
4. broccoli
5. kangaroo
9. stereo
10. memento
13. Eskimo
14. species

DOWN
2. avocado
3. embargo
6. rodeo
7. thief
8. domino
11. tariff
12. poncho

Crossword answers: JACKKNIVES, BROCCOLI, KANGAROOS, STEREOS, MEMENTOS, DOMINOES, ESKIMOS, PONCHO, SPECIES

Lesson 33 • Plurals   135

Spelling and Writing

Proofreading

The journal entry below has ten mistakes. Use the proofreading marks to fix each mistake. Then, write the misspelled **list words** on the lines.

Proofreading Marks
- ◯ spelling mistake
- / make small letter
- ⌄ add apostrophe

May 7

   Today William and I took our first cooking class. We made a pasta dish with Spagetti, broccoli, and other vegetables. We also learned a new way to serve avocadoes Each of us received a chefs hat to wear, and we got to keep them as mementose of the Class. Afterward, we walked over to Williams house. It was raining, so we wore ponchoes We had fun playing a game of dominows

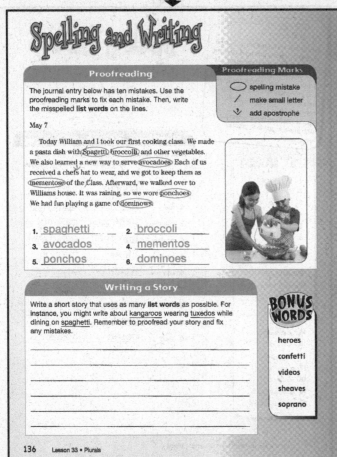

1. spaghetti
2. broccoli
3. avocados
4. mementos
5. ponchos
6. dominoes

Writing a Story

Write a short story that uses as many **list words** as possible. For instance, you might write about kangaroos wearing tuxedos while dining on spaghetti. Remember to proofread your story and fix any mistakes.

_____

_____

_____

_____

_____

BONUS WORDS

heroes
confetti
videos
sheaves
soprano

136   Lesson 33 • Plurals

Spelling Strategy

Write *singular* and *plural* at the top of two columns on the board. Write each **list word** in the *plural* column and call on a volunteer to write the singular form in the other column, then explain the rule that applies to forming the plural.

BONUS WORDS
You may want to suggest that students write a sentence for each bonus word, then compare their sentences with a partner. Have partners work together to write a spelling rule for each type of plural represented.

Spelling and Writing   Page 136

The **Proofreading** exercise will help students prepare to proofread their writing. As students complete the writing activity, encourage them to brainstorm ideas, write a first draft, revise, and proofread their work. To publish their short stories, students may want to send them to a publisher of young people's writing, such as Stone Soup (www.stonesoup.com).

Writer's Corner Explain that an eponym is a person for whom something is named, such as the Earl of *Sandwich*. Encourage students to think of items that might be named after them. Ask them to write descriptions of the items for an online store's Web site.

Final Test

1. Many **Eskimos** live in Alaska.
2. All the campers carried **jackknives**.
3. Raw **broccoli** is a good vegetable snack.
4. Danielle has many **mementos** of her trip.
5. Does this store sell rain **ponchos**?
6. **Tariffs** were placed on the imported goods.
7. We get along because we share many **beliefs**.
8. I looked at a lot of **stereos** before buying one.
9. The ushers at the wedding all wore t**uxedos**.
10. The cowboys participated in **rodeos**.
11. **Kangaroos** carry their babies in pouches.
12. All the houses on our street have **patios**.
13. Guacamole is made with ripe **avocados**.
14. How quickly the police arrested the t**hieves**!
15. Dinosaurs are an extinct **species**.
16. All the **dominoes** in the row fell.
17. **Embargoes** were placed on every ship.
18. The chef boiled the **spaghetti**.
19. People waved **handkerchiefs** in farewell.
20. We moved inside because of the **mosquitoes**.

Objective
To spell words that are homonyms or other words that are often confused, referred to here as "challenging words"

Spelling Words in Action   *Page 137*

In "One of a Kind Imprints," students read about fingerprinting. Ask students to suggest other types of personal identification.

Call on volunteers to say each boldfaced word and name another word that sounds the same, but has a different spelling and meaning.

Warm-Up Test
1. He was so tired that he slept **through** the movie.
2. Seth **threw** the empty can into the recycling bin.
3. We will have to **wait** an hour for the next bus.
4. The man will guess your **weight** for a penny.
5. She refused on **principle** to pay the high price.
6. The **principal** praised the graduating class.
7. Mike can easily jump up and touch the **ceiling**.
8. Mrs. Chang is **sealing** the package with tape.
9. The **weather** is so beautiful today!
10. Do you know **whether** or not he is coming?
11. Shall I use **coarse** sandpaper on this wood?
12. The university offers a **course** on the Civil War.
13. Several **patients** are waiting to see the doctor.
14. Having **patience** is not easy for young children.
15. Everyone arrived on time **except** Ji-Li.
16. Will you please **accept** my apology?
17. Patty ate yogurt for **dessert**.
18. The sun beat down on the white **desert** sand.
19. That question is too **personal** for me to answer.
20. To apply for a job, go to the **personnel** office.

Spelling Practice   *Pages 138–139*

Introduce the spelling rule and have students read the **list words** aloud. Encourage students to look back at their **Warm-Up Tests** and apply the spelling rule to any misspelled words.

As students work through the **Spelling Practice** exercises, remind them to look back at their **list words** or in their dictionaries if they need help. Make sure students understand that they should first write the **list word** that goes with the clue.

for ESL students See Rhymes and Songs, page 14

Spelling Words in Action

Why is fast, accurate fingerprint matching important?

One of a Kind Imprints

No two fingerprints are exactly alike. Every fingerprint has its own pattern of loops and swirls. Because fingerprints don't change as people age, they are truly a **personal** form of identification.

In the past, fingerprints were rarely used by police, **except** in really serious crimes. Law enforcement **personnel** had to **wait** a long time for the results of fingerprint searches. It took a great deal of **patience** to compare one set of fingerprints to another. Now, police use digital fingerprinting technology to help solve crimes.

In digital fingerprinting, prints are first scanned. Every place where the **course** of a ridge line ends is noted electronically. The digitized prints are then sent to a database. Thanks to the Internet, one suspect's fingerprints can be compared to those of millions of others to see **whether** or not a match can be found. Humans still look at the prints before they **accept** a final match, but the technology greatly shortens the process of sorting **through** records. In fact, the FBI's search engine is so powerful, it can take into account a suspect's age and physical features, including appearance and **weight**.

Maybe someday fingerprints will be used to unlock a door or operate a bank's ATM. The know-how is already at our fingertips.

Say the boldfaced words in the selection. Can you think of another word that sounds the same, but is spelled differently and has a different meaning?

137

TIP

Words that sound the same, but are spelled differently and have different meanings, are called homonyms, as in through and threw.
Some words have similar spellings and pronunciations, but different meanings, as in personnel and personal.
The best way to become familiar with these words is to practice using them.

Spelling Practice

LIST WORDS
1. through
2. threw
3. wait
4. weight
5. principle
6. principal
7. ceiling
8. sealing
9. weather
10. whether
11. coarse
12. course
13. patients
14. patience
15. except
16. accept
17. dessert
18. desert
19. personal
20. personnel

Homonyms and Challenging Words

Write a **list word** to match each clue. Then, write another **list word** that is the word's homonym or has a similar spelling.

1. rough	coarse	course
2. rule	principle	principal
3. calmness	patience	patients
4. private	personal	personnel
5. pitched	threw	through
6. rain	weather	whether
7. scale	weight	wait
8. roof	ceiling	sealing
9. receive	accept	except
10. sand	desert	dessert

Spelling Strategy

You may want to write one-half of each **list word** pair on the board. Ask students to spell the second word aloud, and write it on the board as they do so. Then, call on volunteers to use each word in the pair in a sentence.

BONUS WORDS

You may want to suggest that students work with partners to make a list of the bonus words and write a homonym for each word. One partner can write sentences for the bonus words, and the other can write sentences for the homonyms. Then, have them compare sentences.

Spelling and Writing   Page 140

The **Proofreading** exercise will help students prepare to proofread their letters. As students complete the writing activity, encourage them to brainstorm ideas, write a first draft, revise, and proofread their work. To publish their writing, students may want to illustrate their inventions, then use their letters and drawings or diagrams to make a bulletin-board display.

Writer's Corner Students may enjoy turning their thumbprints into drawings by following the directions in *Ed Emberley's Great Thumbprint Drawing Book*. Encourage students to write a story for younger children, using their thumbprint artwork as the illustrations.

Final Test

1. The juggler **threw** five balls into the air.
2. I gain **weight** more easily than my sister.
3. Mrs. Hundert is the **principal** of the school.
4. The judges are **sealing** their votes in envelopes.
5. Will you tell me **whether** or not I am right?
6. Lynda is taking an auto repair **course**.
7. You must try to have more **patience**!
8. The candidate will **accept** the nomination.
9. Cactus plants grow well in the **desert**.
10. Your application is in the **personnel** office.
11. Liz looked at the eagle **through** binoculars.
12. We will **wait** ten more minutes for Teresita.
13. He makes it a **principle** never to tell a lie.
14. Water leaked through the crack in the **ceiling**.
15. What time is the **weather** forecast shown on TV?
16. The burlap material is stiff and **coarse**.
17. The doctor has time to see four more **patients**.
18. The store is open every day **except** Sunday.
19. The waiter asked if we had room for **dessert**.
20. Can we discuss the **personal** matter in private?

Abbreviations

Objective
To spell abbreviations of words

Spelling Words in Action   Page 141

Students might enjoy deciphering Joe Quick's letter in "Short and Sweet." After reading, invite students to read the sentences they liked the best, saying the words that the abbreviations represent.

Ask volunteers to identify the words that the boldfaced abbreviations stand for.

Warm-Up Test

1. The **government** collects taxes. *(govt.)*
2. Linda was elected class **president**. *(pres.)*
3. Pat works in a big **department** store. *(dept.)*
4. Did you interview with that **company**? *(co.)*
5. Mom's business recently **incorporated**. *(inc.)*
6. A pronoun is the **subject** of the sentence. *(subj.)*
7. Is there a new **edition** of that dictionary? *(ed.)*
8. **Volume** 8 of the encyclopedia is missing. *(vol.)*
9. Sue read a **biography** of Lincoln. *(biog.)*
10. They live at **number** 26 Hale Street. *(no.)*
11. My report, for **example**, is about Alaska. *(ex.)*
12. It's the Suns **versus** the Jets tonight. *(vs.)*
13. Does the small pitcher hold a **pint** of milk? *(pt.)*
14. A **quart** is one-fourth of a gallon. *(qt.)*
15. The recipe calls for an **ounce** of butter. *(oz.)*
16. We need a **pound** of meat for the stew. *(lb.)*
17. John is the **manager** of a bank. *(mgr.)*
18. Ed was promoted to **assistant** supervisor. *(asst.)*
19. I can't wait to open the **package**! *(pkg.)*
20. The clerk stacked the **merchandise**. *(mdse.)*

Spelling Practice   Pages 142–143

Introduce the spelling rule and help students identify the words that the abbreviations in the **list words** box represent, emphasizing those spelled with letters not found in the complete words (*oz.*, *lb.*, and *no.*). Then, encourage students to look back at their **Warm-Up Tests** and apply the spelling rule to any misspelled words.

As students work through the **Spelling Practice** exercises, remind them to look back at their **list words** or in their dictionaries if they need help. You may want to do the first few items with students, checking that they write a period at the end of each abbreviation.

for ESL students   **See Words in Context, page 14**

Spelling Words in Action

Can you figure out Joe Quick's message to Mrs. X?

Short and Sweet

Here's the letter that Mrs. X received from Joe Quick.

Speedy Co., Inc., 1001 Fast Blvd. Velocity, NY 00240

Dear Mrs. X,

As **Pres.** of Speedy **Co., Inc.,** I have read your **biog.** along with those of a **no.** of other applicants. I am pleased that you have applied for a position with us **vs.** one with the **govt.**; however, I believe that an **oz.** of experience is worth more than a pound of ability. Because the **vol.** of your experience is extremely limited, the only position I could possibly offer is **asst.** to our **mdse. mgr.** in the shipping **dept.** As an **ex.** of what the job entails, you might be asked to ship a two **oz. pkg.** to Taiwan, or a three **lb. pkg.** to Timbuktu. Let me know what you think as soon as possible. I'm a very busy guy.

Sincerely,
Joe Quick, Pres.
Speedy Co., Inc.

Look back at all the boldfaced abbreviations in the selection. Try to say all the words written in abbreviated form.

141

TIP
An abbreviation is the shortened form of a word that ends with a period. Most are spelled with the first letters of the word, as in company ➤ co. Some are spelled with a combination of letters from the word, as in package ➤ pkg. Others are spelled with letters not found in the original word, as in ounce ➤ oz. and pound ➤ lb.

Spelling Practice

LIST WORDS
1. govt.
2. pres.
3. dept.
4. co.
5. inc.
6. subj.
7. ed.
8. vol.
9. biog.
10. no.
11. ex.
12. vs.
13. pt.
14. qt.
15. oz.
16. lb.
17. mgr.
18. asst.
19. pkg.
20. mdse.

Abbreviations
Write a **list word** that is an abbreviation for the word given.

1. manager   mgr.
2. incorporated   inc.
3. merchandise   mdse.
4. versus   vs.
5. assistant   asst.
6. department   dept.
7. ounce   oz.
8. volume   vol.
9. subject   subj.
10. quart   qt.
11. number   no.
12. biography   biog.
13. pound   lb.
14. company   co.
15. government   govt.
16. example   ex.
17. package   pkg.
18. pint   pt.
19. edition   ed.
20. president   pres.

Abbreviations

Write a **list word** that is the abbreviation for the underlined word in each sentence.

1. The tour guide showed us an <u>example</u> of a fossil. — ex.
2. We found information about England in <u>volume</u> 6 of the encyclopedia. — vol.
3. The first <u>edition</u> of a classic would be priceless. — ed.
4. Martin wants to work for the <u>government</u> when he graduates. — govt.
5. Dr. Tripp introduced us to her young <u>assistant</u>. — asst.
6. The delivery service left the <u>package</u> on our doorstep. — pkg.
7. I bought a <u>pint</u> of milk to go with my lunch. — pt.
8. Carlos applied for a job at my aunt's <u>company</u>. — co.
9. Have you read the <u>biography</u> of Amelia Earhart? — biog.
10. Seth was elected <u>president</u> of the student council. — pres.

Solve the Code

Use the code to find the **list words** that will complete the sentences. Write the **list words** on the lines.

A B C D E F G H I J K L M N O P Q R S T U V W X Y Z

1. Is it true that an <u>o z</u>. of prevention is worth a <u>l b</u>. of cure?
2. He is the <u>m g r</u>. of a printing company called Ink, <u>I n c</u>.
3. The company softball game will feature the sales staff <u>v s</u>. the art <u>d e p t</u>.
4. When you buy the <u>m d s e</u>. for the camping trip, can you include a 2-<u>q t</u>. water bottle?
5. George Washington has been the <u>s u b j</u>. of a <u>n o</u>. of books.

Spelling and Writing

Proofreading

The following made-up recipe has nine mistakes. Use the proofreading marks to fix each mistake. Then, write the misspelled **list words** on the lines.

Golden Coconut Bread
1/4 cup butter
1/4 cup milk
3 os. shredded coconut
1 pakg. yeast
3 cups flour

Mix ingredients together and cover. Set the bowl bowl aside and allow the dough to to rise. Then punch knead, and push the dough. Put it in a loaf pan and bake for 1 hour. (Recipe from Breads vrs, Muffins, Second edi, New Com, Valley Books, Inc., Anytown New York.)

1. oz.   2. pkg.
3. vs.   4. ed.
5. Co.

Proofreading Marks

◯ spelling mistake
∧ add something
℮ take out something

Writing an Informative Paragraph

Why do you think people use abbreviations? Write your ideas in an informative paragraph. Be sure to explain why they are useful or why they create problems. Try to use as many **list words** as you can. Remember to proofread your paragraph and fix any mistakes.

_____
_____
_____
_____
_____
_____

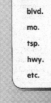
BONUS WORDS

blvd.
mo.
tsp.
hwy.
etc.

Spelling Strategy

With a partner, students can take turns telling each other the words that the **list word** abbreviations stand for. The partner who is listening repeats the word and then spells its abbreviation, saying the word *period* at the end.

BONUS WORDS

You may want to suggest that students use their dictionaries to find out what the abbreviations mean. Tell them to spell out each abbreviation as a complete word in a sentence. Then, have them trade papers with a partner and replace the complete words with their abbreviations.

Spelling and Writing   Page 144

The **Proofreading** exercise will help students prepare to proofread their paragraphs. As students complete the writing activity, encourage them to brainstorm ideas, write a first draft, revise, and proofread their work. To publish their writing, students may want to use their paragraphs to conduct a class debate on the pros and cons of using abbreviations.

Writer's Corner Students might enjoy looking at dictionaries of acronyms and abbreviations. Check the school library for copies. Afterward, invite students to write a message using their favorite entries and then share the message with a classmate.

Final Test

1. Give an **example** of a mammal. (*ex.*)
2. Write a **biography** of your best friend. (*biog.*)
3. What **edition** of the paper is this? (*ed.*)
4. The company recently **incorporated**. (*inc.*)
5. The sales **department** gave its report. (*dept.*)
6. The FBI is a **government** agency. (*govt.*)
7. A **pint** of liquid spilled on the table. (*pt.*)
8. There is an **ounce** of gold in that nugget. (*oz.*)
9. She is the **manager** of the store. (*mgr.*)
10. That **package** is wrapped beautifully! (*pkg.*)
11. All the **merchandise** is on sale. (*mdse.*)
12. The magician's **assistant** laughed. (*asst.*)
13. I'd like one **pound** of seedless grapes. (*lb.*)
14. There is a **quart** of milk on the counter. (*qt.*)
15. It was Kim **versus** Jose in the finals. (*vs.*)
16. She wore **number** 425 in the bicycle race. (*no.*)
17. Who has **volume** 3 of the encyclopedia? (*vol.*)
18. Find the **subject** of the sentence. (*subj.*)
19. Jim's **company** makes computer parts. (*co.*)
20. The **president** greeted the diplomats. (*pres.*)

Lessons 31-35 · Review

Objectives
To review spelling words with suffixes, plurals of words, homonyms and challenging words, and abbreviations

Check Your Spelling Notebook   *Pages 145–148*

Based on your observations, note which words are giving students the most difficulty and offer assistance for spelling them correctly. Here are some frequently misspelled words to watch for: *equipped, occurred, attorneys, portrayed, mosquitoes, personnel,* and *whether.*

To give students extra help and practice in taking standardized tests, you may want to have them take the **Review Test** for this lesson on pages 110–111. After scoring the tests, return them to students so that they can record their misspelled words in their spelling notebooks.

After practicing their troublesome words, students can work through the exercises for lessons 31–35 and the cumulative review, **Show What You Know.** Before they begin each exercise, you may want to go over the spelling rule.

Take It Home

Invite students to write down **list words** from lessons 31–35 and to locate the words on signs and labels at the grocery store. Students can also use **Take It Home** Master 6 on pages 112–113 to help them do the activity. (A complete list of the spelling words is included on page 112 of the **Take It Home** Master.) In class, they can share their lists and discuss the words they found.

In lessons 31 through 35, you learned how words are spelled when suffixes are added to words that end in single consonants, e, or y. You also learned how plurals are formed and how to spell homonyms, challenging words, and abbreviations.

Check Your Spelling Notebook

Look at the words in your spelling notebook. Which words for lessons 31 through 35 did you have the most trouble with? Write them here.

_____

_____

Practice writing your troublesome words with a partner. Take turns saying the base words for words with suffixes, the singular form for plural words, homonyms, and the complete words for abbreviations.

Lesson 31

TIP Before adding a suffix to a word, sometimes you need to double the final consonant, as in referred, or drop the final e, as in organizing.

List Words

combining
approved
referred
crammed
evaporated
produced
occurred
advertising
controlled
exciting
hesitation
realized

Write a **list word** that means the same or almost the same as the word given. Not all the words will be used.

1. happened   occurred
2. blending   combining
3. understood   realized
4. thrilling   exciting
5. accepted   approved
6. crowded   crammed
7. created   produced
8. uncertainty   hesitation
9. mentioned   referred
10. managed   controlled

145

Lesson 32

TIP Before adding a suffix or ending to a word that ends in a consonant and y, change the y to i, as in jellies and magnified. If the word ends in a vowel and y, add ed or s without changing the base word, as in dismayed.

List Words

jellies
theories
thirstily
steadily
waterways
remedies
decaying
modified
industries
attorneys
magnified
galaxies

Circle the correctly spelled **list word**. Write the word on the line. Not all the words will be used.

1. (jellies) jellys   jellies
2. decaing (decaying)   decaying
3. magnifyed (magnified)   magnified
4. (attorneys) attornies   attorneys
5. (waterways) waterwaies   waterways
6. theorys (theories)   theories
7. (modified) modifyed   modified
8. steadyly (steadily)   steadily
9. industryes (industries)   industries
10. (remedies) remedyes   remedies

Lesson 33

TIP Some words are the same in both the singular and plural form. To form the plural of most words that end in f or fe, change the f or fe to v and add es. For some words, including words that end in ff, just add s. Some words that end in o take es to form the plural, while others just take an s.

List Words

tuxedos
patios
stereos
kangaroos
thieves
rodeos
tariffs
species
ponchos
mementos
spaghetti
mosquitoes

Write the **list words** that would be found between these dictionary guide words in alphabetical order. Not all the words will be used.

mariner/triumph

1. mementos   2. mosquitoes
3. patios   4. ponchos
5. rodeos   6. spaghetti
7. species   8. stereos
9. tariffs   10. thieves

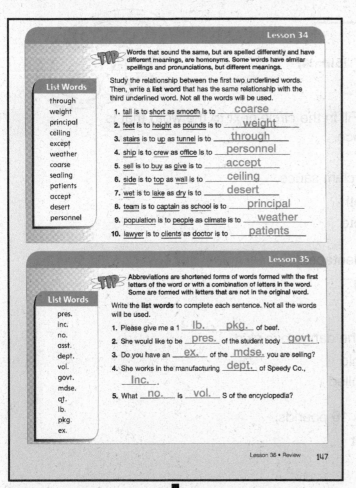

Lesson 34

TIP: Words that sound the same, but are spelled differently and have different meanings, are homonyms. Some words have similar spellings and pronunciations, but different meanings.

List Words

through
weight
principal
ceiling
except
weather
coarse
sealing
patients
accept
desert
personnel

Study the relationship between the first two underlined words. Then, write a **list word** that has the same relationship with the third underlined word. Not all the words will be used.

1. tall is to short as smooth is to _coarse_
2. feet is to height as pounds is to _weight_
3. stairs is to up as tunnel is to _through_
4. ship is to crew as office is to _personnel_
5. sell is to buy as give is to _accept_
6. side is to top as wall is to _ceiling_
7. wet is to lake as dry is to _desert_
8. team is to captain as school is to _principal_
9. population is to people as climate is to _weather_
10. lawyer is to clients as doctor is to _patients_

Lesson 35

TIP: Abbreviations are shortened forms of words formed with the first letters of the word or with a combination of letters in the word. Some are formed with letters that are not in the original word.

List Words

pres.
inc.
no.
asst.
dept.
vol.
govt.
mdse.
qt.
lb.
pkg.
ex.

Write the **list words** to complete each sentence. Not all the words will be used.

1. Please give me a 1 _lb._ _pkg._ of beef.
2. She would like to be _pres._ of the student body _govt._
3. Do you have an _ex._ of the _mdse._ you are selling?
4. She works in the manufacturing _dept._ of Speedy Co., _Inc._
5. What _no._ is _vol._ S of the encyclopedia?

Lesson 36 • Review   147

Show What You Know

Lessons 31–35 Review

One word is misspelled in each set of **list words**. Fill in the circle next to the **list word** that is spelled incorrectly.

1. ○ qt. ● pursonal ○ principle ○ occurred ○ jellies
2. ○ identified ○ except ● attornies ○ vs. ○ exciting
3. ○ no. ○ coarse ○ embargoes ● seeling ○ evaporated
4. ○ referred ● theeries ○ rodeos ○ govt. ○ mosquitoes
5. ○ pres. ● portrayd ○ mgr. ○ galaxies ○ tuxedos
6. ○ patience ● hesitashun ○ ed. ○ disguised ○ species
7. ○ desert ○ memorized ○ sloppily ○ blog. ● avocadoes
8. ○ oz. ○ weather ○ Eskimos ● unpayved ○ ex.
9. ○ inc. ○ patients ● companees ○ realized ○ approved
10. ○ threw ○ mdse. ○ spaghetti ○ occupied ● tarrifs
11. ○ dept. ○ patios ○ dismayed ○ produced ● cramed
12. ○ ceiling ○ organizing ● remedyes ○ beliefs ○ dessert
13. ● dicaying ○ vol. ○ steadily ○ calculation ○ stereos
14. ○ lb. ○ course ○ thieves ○ modified ● handkerchievs
15. ○ graduated ○ personnel ○ surveying ● pcg. ○ ponchos
16. ○ co. ○ wait ● kangeroos ○ magnified ○ accept
17. ○ whether ● abbreviated ○ subj. ○ thirstily ○ mementos
18. ● dominows ○ broccoli ○ waterways ○ advertising ○ asst.
19. ○ pt. ○ disobeyed ● combineing ○ industries ○ controlled
20. ● throgh ○ principal ○ equipped ○ weight ○ jackknives

148   Lesson 36 • Review

Final Test   Page 148

1. Suddenly the same idea **occurred** to both of us.
2. A series of gates **controlled** the flow of water.
3. Our last game was the most **exciting** one of all.
4. After a moment's **hesitation**, I started speaking.
5. No one **realized** how late it had gotten.
6. Can you use the grapes to make **jellies**?
7. What unbelievable **theories** those are!
8. Rain fell **steadily** for three days.
9. Some inland **waterways** are used by large boats.
10. Those **remedies** for hiccups sound quite odd.
11. Several **species** of birds are yellow.
12. The riders brought **ponchos** in case of rain.
13. A scrapbook can help you keep **mementos**.
14. My neighbor always makes his own **spaghetti**.
15. One bat can eat thousands of **mosquitoes**.
16. Push those letters **through** the slot in the door.
17. The doctor wrote down my height and **weight**.
18. Our school **principal** spoke at the assembly.
19. Did Arlene decide to paint the **ceiling**?
20. The **weather** report begins at nine o'clock.
21. Meet the **president** of our organization. (*pres.*)
22. Where is the sports **department**? (*dept.*)
23. Our company was **incorporated** in 1990. (*inc.*)
24. This set is missing volume 2. (*vol.*)
25. We are looking for shipment **number** 17. (*no.*)
26. Be careful when **combining** chemicals!
27. The mayor **approved** the new design for City Hall.
28. The footnote **referred** to a book about animals.
29. We **crammed** our uniforms into one bag.
30. A small generator **produced** electricity.
31. The **decaying** wood provided shelter for insects.
32. Each owner **modified** the building in some way.
33. Our state tries to attract various **industries**.
34. Several **attorneys** volunteered their time.
35. The tin roof **magnified** the sound of the rain.
36. All the men wore **tuxedos** to the formal dance.
37. These bricks are used to build decks and **patios**.
38. Today there are many different kinds of **stereos**.
39. Were the **thieves** caught quickly?
40. The government recently changed its **tariffs**.
41. Her jacket was made from some **coarse** material.
42. Most of the **patients** look forward to visitors.
43. John was pleased to **accept** our offer of help.
44. Most **desert** animals survive with little water.
45. My job is to interview all new **personnel**.
46. The recipe calls for one **quart** of milk. (*qt.*)
47. This packet holds an **ounce** of yeast. (*oz.*)
48. That is a 50-**pound** bag of sand. (*lb.*)
49. Ms. Fujimura is the **assistant** manager. (*asst.*)
50. I took the **package** to the post office. (*pkg.*)

Name _____

Read each sentence and set of words. Fill in the circle next to the word that is spelled correctly to complete the sentence.

1. Tisha made _____ with garlic and clam sauce.
   - ⓐ spagetti
   - ⓒ spageti
   - ⓑ spaghetti
   - ⓓ spagete

2. The _____ contains books and videotapes.
   - ⓐ pckg.
   - ⓒ packg.
   - ⓑ pkg.
   - ⓓ pkge.

3. The driver _____ her car through the dangerous skid.
   - ⓐ controld
   - ⓒ cuntrold
   - ⓑ controled
   - ⓓ controlled

4. The black and white cat's _____ is 16 pounds.
   - ⓐ wieght
   - ⓒ waight
   - ⓑ weight
   - ⓓ wayt

5. The _____ on the imported products were significant.
   - ⓐ tarrifs
   - ⓒ tariffs
   - ⓑ tariphs
   - ⓓ tarifs

6. The customer service _____ were extremely helpful.
   - ⓐ personell
   - ⓒ personnel
   - ⓑ personel
   - ⓓ personnell

7. After leaving the bus, Ken _____ he'd lost his lunch.
   - ⓐ relized
   - ⓒ reilized
   - ⓑ reelized
   - ⓓ realized

8. The gravel on the driveway is very _____.
   - ⓐ corse
   - ⓒ corce
   - ⓑ coorse
   - ⓓ coarse

Name _____

Read each sentence and set of words. Fill in the circle next to the word that is spelled correctly to complete the sentence.

9. We drove _____ the tunnel to get to the city.
   - ⓐ thrugh
   - ⓑ throu
   - ⓒ throogh
   - ⓓ through

10. The repair _____ can fix your computer.
   - ⓐ depmt.
   - ⓑ dept.
   - ⓒ deptmt.
   - ⓓ deprtmt.

11. The water rose _____ until it reached flood levels.
   - ⓐ stedily
   - ⓑ stedduly
   - ⓒ steadily
   - ⓓ steadilee

12. Do you know _____ or not you want to join us?
   - ⓐ whether
   - ⓑ weather
   - ⓒ wether
   - ⓓ wethir

13. Mike's business will be _____ in 2004.
   - ⓐ inc
   - ⓑ inc.
   - ⓒ incorp.
   - ⓓ incorptd.

14. _____ can transmit different diseases to people.
   - ⓐ Masquitos
   - ⓑ Mosquitos
   - ⓒ Mosquitoes
   - ⓓ Musquitos

15. My _____ around the pot holes cost me the race.
   - ⓐ hesitasion
   - ⓑ hesitashion
   - ⓒ hesitashun
   - ⓓ hesitation

Take It Home 6

Your child has learned to spell many new words in lessons 31–35 and would enjoy sharing them with you and your family. The activity ideas below can make reviewing those words fun for the whole family.

Shop-N-Spell

The next time you make out a shopping list for items such as broccoli, spaghetti, and avocados, ask your child to prepare a list of spelling words that might be found on products in stores or shopping centers. Then, you and your child can "shop" for the words on signs and labels.

Lesson 31

1. abbreviated	12. graduated
2. advertising	13. hesitation
3. approved	14. memorized
4. calculation	15. occurred
5. combining	16. organizing
6. controlled	17. produced
7. crammed	18. realized
8. disguised	19. referred
9. equipped	20. unpaved
10. evaporated	
11. exciting	

Lesson 32

1. attorneys	12. occupied
2. companies	13. portrayed
3. decaying	14. remedies
4. dismayed	15. sloppily
5. disobeyed	16. steadily
6. galaxies	17. surveying
7. identified	18. theories
8. industries	19. thirstily
9. jellies	20. waterways
10. magnified	
11. modified	

Lesson 33

1. avocados	12. patios
2. beliefs	13. ponchos
3. broccoli	14. rodeos
4. dominoes	15. spaghetti
5. embargoes	16. species
6. Eskimos	17. stereos
7. handkerchiefs	18. tariffs
8. jackknives	19. thieves
9. kangaroos	20. tuxedos
10. mementos	
11. mosquitoes	

Lesson 34

1. accept	12. principal
2. ceiling	13. principle
3. coarse	14. sealing
4. course	15. threw
5. desert	16. through
6. dessert	17. wait
7. except	18. weather
8. patience	19. weight
9. patients	20. whether
10. personal	
11. personnel	

Lesson 35

1. asst.	12. no.
2. biog.	13. oz.
3. co.	14. pkg.
4. dept.	15. pres.
5. ed.	16. pt.
6. ex.	17. qt.
7. govt.	18. subj.
8. inc.	19. vol.
9. lb.	20. vs.
10. mdse.	
11. mgr.	

Word Clue

Can you and your child complete each mini-puzzle with a spelling word? The words that are already given are clues.

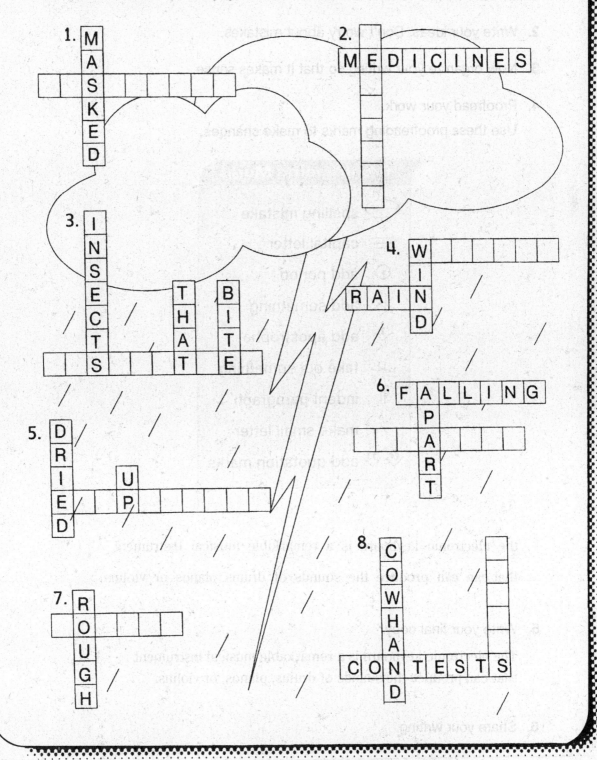

1. M A S K E D

2. M E D I C I N E S

3. I N S E C T S / T H A T / B I T E

4. W I N D / R A I N

5. D R I E D / U P

6. F A L L I N G / A P A R T

7. R O U G H

8. C O W H A N D / C O N T E S T S

Writing and Proofreading Guide

1. Choose a topic to write about.

2. Write your ideas. Don't worry about mistakes.

3. Now organize your writing so that it makes sense.

4. Proofread your work.
   Use these proofreading marks to make changes.

Proofreading Marks

⬯	spelling mistake
≡	capital letter
⊙	add period
⌃	add something
⌄	add apostrophe
ℒ	take out something
¶	indent paragraph
/	make small letter
⌄⌄ ⌄⌄	add quotation marks

the electronic keyboard is a 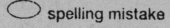 musical instrument
that can ear produce the sounds of drums, pianos, or violins⊙

5. Write your final copy.

   The electronic keyboard is a remarkable musical instrument
   that can produce the sounds of drums, pianos, or violins.

6. Share your writing.

Using Your Dictionary

The *Spelling Workout* Dictionary shows you many things about your spelling words.

The **entry word** listed in alphabetical order is the word you are looking up.

The **sound-spelling** or **respelling** tells how to pronounce the word.

The **part of speech** is given as an abbreviation.

im·prove (im pro͞ov′) *v.* **1** to make or become better [Business has *improved*.] **2** to make good use of [She *improved* her spare time by reading.] —**im·proved im·prov′ing**

Sample sentences or **phrases** show how to use the word.

Other **forms** of the word are given.

The **definition** tells what the word means. There may be more than one definition.

Pronunciation Key

SYMBOL	KEY WORDS	SYMBOL	KEY WORDS	SYMBOL	KEY WORDS	SYMBOL	KEY WORDS
a	ask, fat	͝oo	look, pull	b	bed, dub	t	top, hat
ā	ape, date	y͞oo	unite, cure	d	did, had	v	vat, have
ä	car, lot	͞oo	ooze, tool	f	fall, off	w	will, always
		y͞oo	cute, few	g	get, dog	y	yet, yard
e	elf, ten	ou	out, crowd	h	he, ahead	z	zebra, haze
er	berry, care			j	joy, jump		
ē	even, meet	u	up, cut	k	kill, bake	ch	chin, arch
		ʉ	fur, fern	l	let, ball	ŋ	ring, singer
i	is, hit			m	met, trim	sh	she, dash
ir	mirror, here	ə	a in ago	n	not, ton	th	thin, truth
ī	ice, fire		e in agent	p	put, tap	*th*	then, father
			e in father	r	red, dear	zh	s in pleasure
			i in unity	s	sell, pass		
ō	open, go		o in collect				
ô	law, horn		u in focus				
oi	oil, point						

An Americanism is a word or usage of a word that was born in this country. An open star (☆) before an entry word or definition means that the word or definition is an Americanism.

ab·bre·vi·ate (ə brē′vē āt) **v.** to make shorter by cutting out part [The word "Street" is often *abbreviated* to "St."] —**ab·bre′vi·at·ed, ab·bre′vi·at·ing**

ab·stract (ab strakt′ *or* ab′strakt) **adj.** 1 thought of apart from a particular act or thing [A just trial is a fair one, but justice itself is an *abstract* idea.] 2 formed with designs taken from real things, but not actually like any real object or being [an *abstract* painting]

a·bun·dance (ə bun′dəns) **n.** a great supply; an amount more than enough [Where there is an *abundance* of goods, prices are supposed to go down.]

ac·cel·er·a·tor (ak sel′ər āt′ ər) **n.** a thing that accelerates an action; especially, the foot pedal that can make an automobile go faster by feeding the engine more gasoline

ac·cept (ak sept′) **v.** 1 to take what is offered or given [Will you *accept* $20 for that old bicycle?] 2 to answer "yes" to [We *accept* your invitation.] 3 to believe to be true [to *accept* a theory]

ac·cess (ak′ses) **n.** 1 a way of approach [The *access* to the park is by this road.] 2 the right or ability to approach, enter, or use [Do the students have *access* to a good library?]

ac·com·plish (ə käm′plish) **v.** to do; carry out [The task was *accomplished* in one day.]

ac·cor·di·on (ə kôr′dē ən) **n.** a musical instrument with keys, metal reeds, and a bellows: it is played by pulling out and pressing together the bellows to force air through the reeds, which are opened by fingering the keys

ac·count (ə kount′) **v.** 1 to give a detailed record of money handled [Our treasurer can *account* for every penny spent.] 2 to give a satisfactory reason; explain [How do you *account* for your absence from school?] ➤**n.** 1 *often* **accounts,** *pl.* a statement of money received, paid, or owed; record of business dealings 2 a report or story [The book is an *account* of their travels.]

a·chieve·ment (ə chēv′mənt) **n.** 1 the act of achieving something [his *achievement* of a lifelong dream] 2 something achieved by skill, work, courage, etc. [The landing of spacecraft on the moon was a remarkable *achievement.*]

ac·knowl·edge (ak näl′ij) **v.** 1 to admit to be true [I *acknowledge* that you are right.] 2 to recognize the authority of [They *acknowledged* him as their king.] 3 to recognize and answer or express one's thanks for [She *acknowledged* my greeting by smiling. Have you written to your uncle to *acknowledge* his gift?] —**ac·knowl′edged, ac·knowl′edg·ing**

ac·quaint·ance (ə kwānt′ns) **n.** 1 knowledge of a thing or person got from one's own experience [She has some *acquaintance* with modern art.] 2 a person one knows but not as a close friend

ac·tiv·i·ty (ak tiv′ə tē) **n.** 1 the condition of being active; action; motion [There was not much *activity* in the shopping mall today.] 2 normal power of mind or body; liveliness; alertness [His mental *activity* at age eighty was remarkable.] 3 something that one does besides one's regular work [We take part in many *activities* after school.] —*pl.* **ac·tiv′i·ties**

ad·di·tion (ə dish′ən) **n.** 1 an adding of numbers to get a sum or total 2 a joining of one thing to another thing [The lemonade was improved by the *addition* of sugar.] 3 a thing or part added [The gymnasium is a new *addition* to our school.]

ad·just·ment (ə just′mənt) **n.** 1 a changing or settling of things to bring them into proper order or relation [She made a quick *adjustment* to her new job.] 2 a way or device by which parts are adjusted [An *adjustment* on our television set can make the picture brighter.]

ad·mit (ad mit′) **v.** 1 to permit or give the right to enter [One ticket *admits* two persons.] 2 to accept as being true; confess [Lucy will not *admit* her mistake.] —**ad·mit′ted, ad·mit′ting**

ad·o·les·cent (ad′ə les′ ənt) **adj.** growing up; developing from a child to an adult ➤**n.** a boy or girl between childhood and adulthood; teenage person

a·dult (ə dult′ *or* ad′ult) **adj.** grown up; having reached full size and strength [an *adult* person or plant] ➤**n.** 1 a man or woman who is fully grown up; mature person 2 an animal or plant that is fully developed —**a·dult′hood**

ad·van·tage (ad van′tij) **n.** 1 a more favorable position; better chance [My speed gave me an *advantage* over them.] 2 a thing, condition, or event that can help one; benefit [What are the *advantages* of a smaller school?]

ad·ver·tise (ad′vər tīz) **v.** 1 to tell about a product in public and in such a way as to make people want to buy it [to *advertise* cars on television] 2 to announce or ask for publicly, as in a newspaper [to *advertise* a house for rent; to *advertise* for a cook] —**ad′ver·tised, ad′ver·tis·ing** —**ad′ver·tis′er n.**

ad·ver·tis·ing (ad′vər tīz′iŋ) **n.** 1 an advertisement or advertisements 2 the work of preparing advertisements and getting them printed or on radio and TV [*Advertising* is a major industry in this country.]

a	ask, fat
ā	ape, date
ä	car, lot
e	elf, ten
ē	even, meet
i	is, hit
ī	ice, fire
ō	open, go
ô	law, horn
oi	oil, point
͡oo	look, pull
͡ōo	ooze, tool
ou	out, crowd
u	up, cut
u	fur, fern
ə	a in ago
	e in agent
	e in father
	i in unity
	o in collect
	u in focus
ch	chin, arch
ŋ	ring, singer
sh	she, dash
th	thin, truth
th	then, father
zh	s in pleasure

ad·vise (ad vīz´) *v.* **1** to give advice or an opinion to [The doctor *advised* me to have an operation.] **2** to notify; inform [The letter *advised* us of the time of the meeting.] —**ad·vised´, ad·vis´ing**

af·fec·tion (ə fek´shən) *n.* fond or tender feeling; warm liking

af·ford (ə fôrd´) *v.* **1** to have money enough to spare for: *usually used with* can *or* be able [Can we *afford* a new car?] **2** to be able to do something without taking great risks [I can *afford* to speak frankly.]

ag·ri·cul·tur·al (ag´ri kul´chər əl) *adj.* of agriculture; of growing crops and raising livestock; farming

ail·ment (āl´mənt) *n.* an illness; sickness

al·li·ga·tor (al´ə gāt´ər) *n.* a large lizard like the crocodile, found in warm rivers and marshes of the U.S. and China

al·might·y (ôl mīt´ē) *adj.* having power with no limit; all-powerful

al·though (ôl thō´) *conj.* in spite of the fact that; even if; though [*Although* the sun is shining, it may rain later.]

an·a·lyze (an´ə līz) *v.* to separate or break up any thing or idea into its parts so as to examine them and see how they fit together [to *analyze* the causes of war] —**an´a·lyz´er** *n.*

an·cient (ān´chənt *or* ān´shənt) *adj.* **1** of times long past; belonging to the early history of people, before about 500 A.D. **2** having lasted a long time; very old [their *ancient* quarrel]

an·gle (aŋ´gəl) *n.* **1** the shape made by two straight lines meeting in a point, or by two surfaces meeting along a line **2** the way one looks at something; point of view [Consider the problem from all *angles*.] ◆*v.* to move or bend at an angle —**an´gled, an´gling**

an·nounce (ə nouns´) *v.* **1** to tell the public about; proclaim [to *announce* the opening of a new store] **2** to say; tell [Mother *announced* she wasn't going with us.] —**an·nounced´, an·nounc´ing**

an·ten·na (an ten´ə) *n.* **1** either of a pair of slender feelers on the head of an insect, crab, lobster, etc. —*pl.* **an·ten·nae** (an ten´ē) *or* **an·ten´nas 2** a wire or set of wires used in radio and television to send and receive signals; aerial —*pl.* **an·ten´nas**

an·ti·bod·y (an´ti bäd´ e) *n.* a specialized protein that is formed in the body to neutralize a particular foreign substance that is harmful, making the body immune to it —*pl.* **an´ti·bod´ies**

an·tic·i·pate (an tis´ə pāt´) *v.* to look forward to; expect [We *anticipate* a pleasant trip.] —**an·tic´i·pat·ed, an·tic´i·pat·ing** —**an·tic´i·pa´tion** *n.*

an·ti·dote (an´ti dōt) *n.* **1** a substance that is taken to work against the effect of a poison **2** anything that works against an evil or unwanted condition [The party was a good *antidote* to the sadness we felt.]

☆**an·ti·freeze** (an´ti frēz´) *n.* a liquid with a low freezing point, such as alcohol, put in the water of automobile radiators to prevent freezing

an·tique (an tēk´) *adj.* very old; of former times; made or used a long time ago ◆*n.* a piece of furniture or silverware, a tool, etc. made many years ago [They sell *antiques* of colonial America.]

an·ti·sep·tic (an´ti sep´tik) *adj.* **1** preventing infection by killing germs **2** free from living germs; sterile [an *antiseptic* room] ◆*n.* any substance used to kill germs or stop their growth, as alcohol or iodine

an·ti·so·cial (an´ti sō´shəl) *adj.* not liking to be with other people [Are you so *antisocial* that you never have visitors?]

ap·par·el (ə per´əl) *n.* clothing; garments; dress [They sell only children's *apparel*.] ◆*v.* to dress; clothe [The king was *appareled* in purple robes.] —**ap·par´eled** *or* **ap·par´elled, ap·par´el·ing** *or* **ap·par´el·ling**

ap·pear (ə pir´) *v.* **1** to come into sight or into being [A ship *appeared* on the horizon. Leaves appear on the tree every spring.] **2** to seem; look [He *appears* to be in good health.] **3** to come before the public [The actor will *appear* on television. The magazine *appears* monthly.] —**ap·peared´**

ap·plause (ə plôz´ *or* ə pläz´) *n.* the act of showing that one enjoys or approves of something, especially by clapping one's hands

ap·point·ment (ə point´mənt) *n.* **1** the act of appointing or the fact of being appointed [the *appointment* of Jones as supervisor] **2** an arrangement to meet someone or be somewhere at a certain time [an *appointment* for lunch]

ap·pre·ci·ate (ə prē´shē āt´) *v.* **1** to think well of; understand and enjoy [I now *appreciate* modern art.] **2** to recognize and be grateful for [We *appreciate* all you have done for us.] —**ap·pre´ci·at·ed, ap·pre´ci·at·ing** —**ap·pre´ci·a´tion** *n.*

ap·proach (ə prōch´) *v.* to come closer or draw nearer [We saw three riders *approaching*. Vacation time *approaches*.] —**ap·proach´a·ble** *adj.*

ap·prove (ə proov´) *v.* **1** to think or say to be good, worthwhile, etc.; be pleased with: *often used with* of [She doesn't *approve* of smoking.] **2** to give one's consent to [Has the mayor *approved* the plans?] —**ap·proved´, ap·prov´ing**

ar·gu·ment (är´gyōō mənt) *n.* **1** the act of arguing; discussion in which people disagree; dispute **2** a reason given for or against something [What are your *arguments* for wanting to study mathematics?]

ar·range·ment (ə rānj′mənt) *n.* **1** the act of arranging or putting in order **2** the way in which something is arranged [a new *arrangement* of pictures on the wall] **3** a preparation; plan: *usually used in pl.*, **arrangements** [*Arrangements* have been made for the party.]

as·cend (ə send′) *v.* to go up; move upward; rise; climb [The procession *ascended* the hill.]

a·shamed (ə shāmd′) *adj.* feeling shame because something bad, wrong, or foolish was done [They were *ashamed* of having broken the window.]

as·sign·ment (ə sīn′mənt) *n.* **1** the act of assigning **2** something assigned, as a lesson

asst. *abbreviation for* **assistant**

as·sure (ə shoor′) *v.* **1** to make a person sure of something; convince [What can we do to *assure* you of our friendship?] **2** to tell or promise positively [I *assure* you I'll be there.] **3** to make a doubtful thing certain; guarantee [Their gift of money *assured* the success of our campaign.] —**as·sured′, as·sur′ing**

as·ter·isk (as′tər isk) *n.* a sign in the shape of a star (*) used in printing and writing to call attention to a footnote or other explanation or to show that something has been left out

as·ter·oid (as′tər oid) *n.* any of the many small planets that move in orbits around the sun between the orbits of Mars and Jupiter

as·tro·naut (as′trə nôt *or* as′trə nät) *n.* a person trained to make rocket flights in outer space

ath·lete (ath′lēt) *n.* a person who is skilled at games, sports, or exercises in which one needs strength, skill, and speed

at·tain (ə tān′) *v.* to get by working hard; gain; achieve [to *attain* success]

at·tor·ney (ə tur′nē) *n.* a lawyer —*pl.* **at·tor′neys**

auc·tion (ôk′shən *or* äk′shən) *n.* a public sale at which each thing is sold to the person offering to pay the highest price ◆*v.* to sell at an auction [They *auctioned* their furniture instead of taking it with them.]

Aus·tral·ia (ô strāl′yə *or* ä strāl′yə) **1** an island continent in the Southern Hemisphere, southeast of Asia **2** a country made up of this continent and Tasmania —**Aus·tral′ian** *adj., n.*

au·then·tic (ô then′tik *or* ä then′tik) *adj.* **1** that can be believed; reliable; true [an *authentic* news report] **2** that is genuine; real [an *authentic* antique] —**au·then′ti·cal·ly** *adv.*

au·to·mat·ic (ôt′ə mat′ik *or* ät′ə mat′ik) *adj.* **1** done without thinking about it, as though by a machine; unconscious [Breathing is usually *automatic*.] **2** moving or working by itself [*automatic* machinery] —**au′to·mat′i·cal·ly** *adv.*

au·tumn (ôt′əm *or* ät′əm) *n.* the season of the year that comes between summer and winter; fall ◆*adj.* of or like autumn —**au·tum·nal** (ô tum′n'l) *adj.*

a·vi·a·tor (ā′vē āt′ ər) *n.* a person who flies airplanes; pilot

☆**av·o·ca·do** (av′ ə kä′ dō *or* äv′ ə kä′ dō) *n.* a tropical fruit that is shaped like a pear and has a thick, green or purplish skin and a single large seed: its yellow, buttery flesh is used in salads, sauces, dips, etc. —*pl.* **av′o·ca′ dos**

a·void (ə void′) *v.* **1** to keep away from; get out of the way of; shun [to *avoid* crowds] **2** to keep from happening [Try to *avoid* spilling the milk.] —**a·void′ ed** —**a·void′a·ble** *adj.* —**a·void′ance** *n.*

awe·some (ô′ səm *or* ä′ səm) *adj.* **1** causing one to feel awe [The burning building was an *awesome* sight.] **2** showing awe [He had an *awesome* look on his face.]

awn·ing (ôn′ iŋ *or* än′ iŋ) *n.* a covering made of canvas, metal, or wood fixed to a frame over a window, door, etc. to keep off the sun and rain

a·wry (ə rī′) *adv., adj.* **1** twisted to one side; askew [The curtains were blown *awry* by the wind.] **2** wrong; amiss [Our plans went *awry*.]

ax·le (ak′səl) *n.* **1** a rod on which a wheel turns, or one connected to a wheel so that they turn together **2** the bar joining two opposite wheels, as of an automobile

back·gam·mon (bak′gam ən) *n.* a game played on a special board by two people: the players have fifteen pieces each, which they move after throwing dice to get a number

bad·min·ton (bad′mint′ n *or* bad′mit′ n) *n.* a game like tennis, in which a cork with feathers in one end is batted back and forth across a high net by players using light rackets

bail (bāl) *n.* money left with a law court as a guarantee that an arrested person will appear for trial ◆*v.* to have an arrested person set free by giving bail

bail·iff (bāl if) *n.* **1** a sheriff's assistant **2** an officer who has charge of prisoners and jurors in a court

bank·rupt (baŋk′rupt) *adj.* not able to pay one's debts and freed by law from the need for doing so [Any property a *bankrupt* person may still have is usually divided among those to whom the person owes money.]

a	ask, fat
ā	ape, date
ä	car, lot
e	elf, ten
ē	even, meet
i	is, hit
ī	ice, fire
ō	open, go
ô	law, horn
oi	oil, point
oo	look, pull
ōō	ooze, tool
ou	out, crowd
u	up, cut
ʉ	fur, fern
ə	a in ago
	e in agent
	e in father
	i in unity
	o in collect
	u in focus
ch	chin, arch
ŋ	ring, singer
sh	she, dash
th	thin, truth
th	then, father
zh	s in pleasure

ban·quet (baŋ′kwət) *n.* a formal dinner or feast for many people: banquets, during which speeches are made, are often held to celebrate something or to raise money

bare·ly (ber′lē) *adv.* 1 only just; no more than; scarcely [It is *barely* a year old.] 2 in a bare way; meagerly [a *barely* furnished room, with only a bed in it].

be·lief (bē lēf′) *n.* 1 a believing or feeling that certain things are true or real; faith [You cannot destroy my *belief* in the honesty of most people.] 2 trust or confidence [I have *belief* in Pat's ability.] 3 anything believed or accepted as true; opinion [What are her political *beliefs*?]

be·lieve (bē lēv′) *v.* 1 to accept as true or real [Can we *believe* that story?] 2 to have trust or confidence [I know you will win; I *believe* in you.] —**be·lieved′, be·liev′ing** —**be·liev′a·ble** *adj.* —**be·liev′er** *n.*

bi·an·nu·al (bī an′yoo əl) *adj.* coming twice a year —**bi·an′nu·al·ly** *adv.*

bi·fo·cals (bī′fō kəlz) *pl. n.* eyeglasses in which each lens has two parts, one for reading and seeing nearby objects and the other for seeing things far away

bil·lion (bil′yən) *n., adj.* a thousand millions (1,000,000,000)

bin·oc·u·lars (bi näk′yə lərz) *pl. n.* a pair of small telescopes fastened together for use with both eyes [Field glasses are a kind of *binoculars*.]

bio. *abbreviation for* **biographical** *or* **biography**

bi·ol·o·gy (bī äl′ə jē) *n.* the science of plants and animals; the study of living things and the way they live and grow —**bi·ol′o·gist** *n.*

bi·plane (bī′plān) *n.* the earlier type of airplane with two main wings, one above the other

☆**bis·cuit** (bis′kit) *n.* a small bread roll made of dough quickly raised with baking powder

bi·sect (bī sekt′ *or* bī′sekt) *v.* 1 to cut into two parts [Budapest is *bisected* by the Danube River.] 2 to divide into two equal parts [A circle is *bisected* by its diameter.]

bit·ter (bit′ər) *adj.* 1 having a strong, often unpleasant taste [The seed in a peach pit is *bitter*.] 2 full of sorrow, pain, or discomfort [Poor people often suffer *bitter* hardships.] —**bit′ter·ness** *n.*

bi·week·ly (bī′wēk′lē) *adj., adv.* once every two weeks

bleak (blēk) *adj.* 1 open to wind and cold; not sheltered; bare [the *bleak* plains] 2 cold and cutting; harsh [a *bleak* wind] 3 not cheerful; gloomy [a *bleak* story] 4 not hopeful or promising [a *bleak* future]

blvd. *abbreviation for* **boulevard**

boil (boil) *v.* 1 to bubble up and become steam or vapor by being heated [Water *boils* at 100°C.] 2 to heat a liquid until it bubbles up in this way [to *boil* water] 3 to cook in a boiling liquid [to *boil* potatoes] —**boiled**

bor·ough (bur′ō) *n.* 1 in some States, a town that has a charter to govern itself 2 one of the five main divisions of New York City

bor·row (bär′ō *or* bôr′ō) *v.* 1 to get to use something for a while by agreeing to return it later [You can *borrow* that book from the library.] 2 to take another's word, idea, etc. and use it as one's own [The Romans *borrowed* many Greek myths.] —**bor′row·er** *n.*

bough (bou) *n.* a large branch of a tree

boul·der (bōl′dər) *n.* any large rock made round and smooth by weather and water

boun·ti·ful (boun′tə fəl) *adj.* 1 giving much gladly; generous [a *bountiful* patron] 2 more than enough; plentiful [a *bountiful* harvest] —**boun′ti·ful·ly** *adv.*

bowl·ing (bōl′iŋ) *n.* a game in which each player rolls a heavy ball along a wooden lane (bowling alley), trying to knock down ten wooden pins at the far end

brave (brāv) *adj.* willing to face danger, pain, or trouble; not afraid; full of courage —**brav′er, brav′est** ◆*v.* to face without fear; defy [We *braved* the storm.] —**braved, brav′ing** —**brave′ly** *adv.* —**brave′ness** *n.*

brawn·y (brôn′ē *or* brän′ē) *adj.* strong and muscular —**brawn′i·er, bran′i·est** —**brawn′i·ness** *n.*

break·a·ble (brāk′ə bəl) *adj.* that can be broken or that is likely to break

brief (brēf) *adj.* 1 not lasting very long; short in time [a *brief* visit] 2 using just a few words; not wordy; concise [a *brief* news report] —**brief′ly** *adv.* —**brief′ness** *n.*

bright (brīt) *adj.* 1 shining; giving light; full of light [a *bright* star; a *bright* day] 2 very strong or brilliant in color or sound [a *bright* red; the *bright* tones of a cornet] 3 lively; cheerful [a *bright* smile] 4 having a quick mind; clever [a *bright* child] —**bright′est** ◆*adv.* in a bright manner [stars shining *bright*] —**bright′ly** *adv.* —**bright′ness** *n.*

broc·co·li (bräk′ə lē) *n.* a vegetable whose tender shoots and loose heads of tiny green buds are cooked for eating

bro·chure (brō shoor′) *n.* a pamphlet, now especially one that advertises something

bruise (brooz) *v.* 1 to hurt a part of the body, as by a blow, without breaking the skin [Her *bruised* knee turned black-and-blue.] 2 to hurt the outside of [Some peaches fell and were *bruised*.] —**bruised, bruis′ing** ◆*n.* an injury to the outer part or flesh that does not break the skin but darkens it in color

budg·et (buj′ət) *n.* a careful plan for spending the money that is received in a certain period ◆*v.* 1 to plan the spending of money; make a budget 2 to plan in detail how to spend [I *budget* my time as well as my money.]

buf·fet (bə fā′ or boo fā′) *n.* platters of food on a buffet or table from which people serve themselves

build·ing (bil′diŋ) *n.* **1** anything that is built with walls and a roof; a structure, as a house, factory, or school **2** the act or work of one who builds

bun·ga·low (buŋ′gə lō) *n.* a small house with one story and an attic

Cc

cal·ci·um (kal′sē əm) *n.* a chemical element that is a soft, silver-white metal: it is found combined with other elements in the bones and teeth of animals and in limestone, marble, chalk, etc.

cal·cu·late (kal′kyoo lāt′) *v.* **1** to find out by using arithmetic; compute [*Calculate* the amount of cloth you will need for the skirt.] **2** to find out by reasoning; estimate [Try to *calculate* the effect of your decision.] —**cal′cu·lat·ed, cal′cu·lat·ing**

cal·cu·la·tion (kal′kyoo lā′ shən) *n.* **1** the act of calculating **2** the answer found by calculating **3** careful or shrewd thought or planning

cam·er·a (kam′ər ə) *n.* **1** a closed box for taking pictures: the light that enters when a lens or hole at one end is opened by a shutter forms an image on the film or plate at the other end **2** that part of a TV transmitter which picks up the picture to be sent and changes it to electrical signals

cam·paign (kam pān′) *n.* a series of planned actions for getting something done [a *campaign* to get someone elected] ◆*v.* to take part in a campaign —**cam·paign′er** *n.*

Ca·na·di·an (kə nā′dē ən) *adj.* of Canada or its people ◆*n.* a person born or living in Canada

can·ta·loupe or **can·ta·loup** (kan′tə lōp) *n.* a muskmelon, especially a kind that has a hard, rough skin and sweet, juicy, orange-colored flesh

can·vas (kan′vəs) *n.* **1** a strong, heavy cloth of hemp, cotton, or linen, used for tents, sails, oil paintings, etc. **2** an oil painting on canvas

ca·pac·i·ty (kə pas′i tē) *n.* **1** the amount of space that can be filled; room for holding [a jar with a *capacity* of 2 quarts] **2** the ability to be, learn, or become; skill or fitness [the *capacity* to be an actor] —*pl.* —**ca·pac′i·ties**

cap·i·tal (kap′it′l) *adj.* where the government is located [a *capital* city] *See also* **capital letter** ◆*n.* **1** *same as* **capital letter 2** a city or town where the government of a state or nation is located

capital letter the form of a letter that is used to begin a sentence or a name [THIS IS PRINTED IN *CAPITAL* LETTERS.]

Cap·i·tol (kap′it′l) the building in which the U.S. Congress meets, in Washington, D.C. ◆*n. usually* **capitol** the building in which a State legislature meets

car·bo·hy·drate (kär′ bō hī′drāt) *n.* any of a group of substances made up of carbon, hydrogen, and oxygen, including the sugars and starches: carbohydrates are an important part of our diet

car·bon (kär′bən) *n.* a chemical element that is not a metal, found in all plant and animal matter: diamonds and graphite are pure carbon, while coal and charcoal are forms of impure carbon

car·bu·ret·or (kär′bə rāt′ər) *n.* the part of a gasoline engine that mixes air with gasoline spray to make the mixture that explodes in the cylinders

care·ful (ker′fəl) *adj.* **1** taking care so as not to have mistakes or accidents; cautious [Be *careful* in crossing streets.] **2** done or made with care [*careful* work] —**care′ful·ly** *adv.* —**care′ful·ness** *n.*

car·i·ca·ture (kər′i kə chər) *n.* a picture or imitation of a person or thing in which certain features or parts are exaggerated in a joking or mocking way ◆*v.* to make or be a caricature of [Cartoonists often *caricature* the president.] —**car′i·ca·tured, car′i·ca·tur·ing** —**car′i·ca·tur·ist** *n.*

car·ni·val (kär′ni vəl) *n.* an entertainment that travels from place to place, with sideshows, amusement rides, refreshments, etc.

car·tridge (kär′trij) *n.* **1** the metal or cardboard tube that holds the gunpowder and the bullet or shot for use in a firearm. **2** a small container used in a larger device, as one holding ink for a pen **3** a roll of camera film in a case **4** a unit holding the needle for a phonograph

cas·tle (kas′əl) *n.* a large building or group of buildings that was the home of a king or noble in the Middle Ages: castles had thick walls, moats, etc. to protect them against attack

cas·u·al (kazh′oo əl) *adj.* **1** happening by chance; not planned [a *casual* visit] **2** not having any particular purpose [a *casual* glance; a *casual* remark] **3** for wear at times when dressy clothes are not needed [*casual* sports clothes] —**cas′u·al·ly** *adv.* —**cas′u·al·ness** *n.*

ca·ter (kā′tər) *v.* to provide food and service [Smith's business is *catering* for large parties.] —**ca′ter·er** *n.*

a	ask, fat
ä	ape, date
ã	car, lot
e	elf, ten
ē	even, meet
i	is, hit
ī	ice, fire
ō	open, go
ô	law, horn
oi	oil, point
oo	look, pull
oo	ooze, tool
ou	out, crowd
u	up, cut
u	fur, fern
ə	a in ago
	e in agent
	e in father
	i in unity
	o in collect
	u in focus
ch	chin, arch
ŋ	ring, singer
sh	she, dash
th	thin, truth
th	then, father
zh	s in pleasure

cau·li·flow·er (kôl′ə flou ər *or* käl′ə flou ər)
n. a kind of cabbage with a head of white,
fleshy flower clusters growing tightly
together

ceil·ing (sēl′iŋ) *n.* the inside top part of a
room, opposite the floor

cel·e·brate (sel′ə brāt) *v.* **1** to honor a
victory, the memory of something, etc. in
some special way [to *celebrate* a birthday
with a party; to *celebrate* the Fourth of July
with fireworks] **2** to have a good time:
used only in everyday talk [Let's *celebrate*
when we finish painting the garage.]
—**cel′e·brat·ed, cel′e·brat·ing**
—**cel′e·bra′tion** *n.*

cel·lo (chel′ō) *n.* a musical instrument like
a violin but larger and having a deeper tone:
its full name is **violoncello**
—*pl.* **cel′los** *or* **cel·li** (chel′ē)

cha·grin (shə grin′) *n.* a feeling of being
embarrassed and annoyed because one has
failed or has been disappointed ◆*v.* to
embarrass and annoy [Our hostess was
chagrined when the guest to be honored
failed to appear.]

chal·lenge (chal′ənj) *v.* **1** to question the
right or rightness of; refuse to believe unless
proof is given [to *challenge* a claim;
to *challenge* something said or the person
who says it] **2** to call to take part in a fight
or contest; dare [He *challenged* her to a
game of chess.] **3** to call for skill, effort,
or imagination [That puzzle will really
challenge you.] —**chal′lenged,
chal′leng·ing** ◆*n.* **1** the act of challenging
[I accepted his *challenge* to a race.]
2 something that calls for much effort;
hard task [Climbing Mt. Everest was
a real *challenge*.]

change·a·ble (chān′jə bəl) *adj.*
changing often or likely to change
[*changeable* weather]

check·ers (chek′ərz) *pl. n.* a game played
on a checkerboard by two players, each of
whom tries to capture all 12 pieces of the
other player: *used with a singular verb*

chem·is·try (kem′is trē) *n.* the science
in which substances are examined to find
out what they are made of, how they act
under different conditions, and how they
are combined or separated to form
other substances

chess (ches) *n.* a game played on a
chessboard by two players: each has
16 pieces (called **chess′men**) which are
moved in trying to capture the other's
pieces and checkmate the other's king

chis·el (chiz′əl) *n.* a tool having a strong
blade with a sharp edge for cutting or
shaping wood, stone, or metal ◆*v.* to cut
or shape with a chisel —**chis′eled** *or*
chis′elled, chis′el·ing *or* **chis′el·ling**
—**chis′el·er** *or* **chis′el·ler** *n.*

chives (chīvz) *pl. n.* a plant related to the
onion, having slender, hollow leaves that
are chopped up and used for flavoring

cho·les·ter·ol (kə les′tər ôl) *n.* a waxy
substance found in the body and in certain
foods: when there is much of it in the blood
it is thought to cause hardening of the arteries

cho·rus (kôr′əs) *n.* **1** a group of people
trained to speak or sing together [Ancient
Greek plays usually had a *chorus* which
explained what the actors were doing.]
2 singers and dancers who work together as
a group and not as soloists, as in a musical
show **3** the part of a song that is repeated
after each verse; refrain [The *chorus* of
"The Battle Hymn of the Republic" begins
"Glory, glory, hallelujah!"] ◆*v.* to speak
or sing together or at the same time
[The Senators *chorused* their approval.]

chrome (krōm) *n.* chromium, especially
when it is used to plate steel or other metal

chute (shoot) *n.* **1** a part of a river where
the water moves swiftly **2** a waterfall
3 a long tube or slide in which things are
dropped or slid down to a lower place
[a laundry *chute*]

cir·cuit (sur′kət) *n.* **1** the act of going
around something; course of journey in a
circle [The moon's *circuit* of Earth takes
about 28 days.] **2** the complete path of an
electric current; also, any hookup, wiring,
etc. that is connected into this path

cir·cu·la·tion (sur′kyə lā′shən) *n.*
1 free movement around from place to place
[The fan kept the air in *circulation*.]
2 the movement of blood through the veins
and arteries **3** the average number of copies
of a magazine or newspaper sent out or sold
in a certain period [Our school paper has a
weekly *circulation* of 630.]

cir·cum·fer·ence (sər kum′fər əns) *n.*
1 the line that bounds a circle or other
rounded figure or area **2** the length of
such a line [The *circumference* of the pool
is 70 feet.]

clause (klôz *or* kläz) *n.* a group of words
that includes a subject and a verb, but that
forms only part of a sentence [In the
sentence "She will visit us if she can,"
"She will visit us" is a *clause* that could be
a complete sentence, and "if she can" is a
clause that depends on the first *clause*.]

clean·ly (klen′lē) *adj.* always keeping clean
or kept clean —**clean′li·ness** *n.*

clev·er (klev′ər) *adj.* **1** quick in thinking
or learning; smart; intelligent **2** showing
skill or fine thinking [a *clever* move in
chess] —**clev′er·ly** *adv.* —**clev′er·ness** *n.*

close (klōz) *v.* **1** to make no longer open;
shut [*Close* the door.] **2** to bring or come
to a finish; end [to *close* a speech]
—**closed, clos′ing** ◆*n.* an end; finish

clothes (klōz *or* klōthz) *pl. n.* cloth or other
material made up in different shapes and
styles to wear on the body; dresses, suits,
hats, underwear, etc.; garments

Co. *or* **co.** *abbreviation for* **company, county**

coarse (kôrs) *adj.* **1** made up of rather large particles; not fine [*coarse* sand] **2** rough or harsh to the touch [*coarse* cloth] **3** not polite or refined; vulgar; crude [a *coarse* joke] —coars´est —coarse´ly *adv.* —coarse´ness *n.*

co·coa (kō′kō) *n.* **1** a powder made from roasted cacao seeds, used in making chocolate **2** a drink made from this powder by adding sugar and hot water or milk

cof·fee (kôf′ē *or* käf′ē) *n.* a dark-brown drink made by brewing the roasted and ground seeds of a tropical plant in boiling water

co·logne (kə lōn′) *n.* a sweet-smelling liquid like perfume, but not so strong

col·umn (käl′əm) *n.* **1** a long, generally round, upright support; pillar: columns usually stand in groups to hold up a roof or other part of a building, but they are sometimes used just for decoration **2** any long, upright thing like a column [a *column* of water; the spinal *column*] **3** any of the long sections of print lying side by side on a page and separated by a line or blank space [Each page of this book has two *columns*.]

com·bi·na·tion (käm′bi nā′shən) *n.* **1** the act of combining or joining [He succeeded by a *combination* of hard work and luck.] **2** the series of numbers or letters that must be turned to in the right order to open a kind of lock called a ☆**combination lock** [Most safes have a *combination lock*.]

com·bine (kəm bīn′) *v.* to come or bring together; join; unite [to *combine* work with pleasure; to *combine* chemical elements] —com·bined′, com·bin′ing

com·mo·tion (kə mō′shən) *n.* a noisy rushing about; confusion [There was a great *commotion* as the ship began to sink.]

com·mu·ni·cate (kə myōo′nə kāt′) *v.* to make known; give or exchange information [to *communicate* by telephone; to *communicate* ideas by the written word] —com·mu′ni·cat·ed, com·mu′ni·cat·ing

com·mu·ni·ca·tion (kə myōo′ni kā′shən) *n.* **1** the act of communicating [the *communication* of disease; the *communication* of news] **2** a way or means of communicating [The hurricane broke down all *communication* between the two cities.] **3** information, message, letter, etc. [They received the news in a *communication* from their lawyer.]

com·pact (kəm pakt′ *or* käm′pakt) *adj.* closely and firmly packed together [Tie the clothes in a neat, *compact* bundle.] ➔*n.* (käm′pakt) ☆a model of automobile smaller and cheaper than the standard model

com·pa·ny (kum′pə nē) *n.* a group of people; especially, a group joined together in some work or activity [a *company* of actors; a business *company*] —*pl.* **com′pa·nies**

com·pare (kəm per′) *v.* **1** to describe as being the same; liken [The sound of thunder can be *compared* to the roll of drums.] **2** to examine certain things in order to find out how they are alike or different [How do the two cars *compare* in size and price?] —com·pared′, com·par′ing

com·pel (kəm pel′) *v.* to make do something; force [Many men were *compelled* by the draft to serve in the armed forces.] —com·pelled′, com·pel′ling

com·pet·i·tor (kəm pet′i tər) *n.* a person who competes; rival [business *competitors*]

com·plaint (kəm plānt′) *n.* **1** the act of complaining or finding fault **2** something to complain about [The tenants gave a list of their *complaints* to the landlord.]

com·plete (kəm plēt′) *adj.* **1** having no parts missing; full; whole [a *complete* deck of cards] **2** finished; ended [No one's education is ever really *complete*.] **3** thorough; perfect [I have *complete* confidence in my doctor.] ➔*v.* to make complete; finish or make whole, full, perfect, etc. [When will the new road be *completed*?] —com·plet′ed, com·plet′ing —com·plete′ly *adv.*

com·po·si·tion (käm′pə zish′ən) *n.* **1** the act, work, or style of composing something **2** something composed, as a piece of writing or a musical work **3** the parts or materials of a thing and the way they are put together [We shall study the *composition* of this gas.]

com·po·sure (kəm pō′zhər) *n.* calmness of mind; self-control; serenity

com·pound (käm′pound) *n.* anything made up of two or more parts or materials; mixture ➔*adj.* made up of two or more parts ["Handbag" is a *compound* word.]

con·ceal (kən sēl′) *v.* to hide or keep secret; put or keep out of sight [I *concealed* my amusement. The thief *concealed* the stolen jewelry in a pocket.] —con·cealed′

con·ceit (kən sēt′) *n.* too high an opinion of oneself; vanity [His *conceit* shows when he talks about how bright he is.] —con·ceit′ed *adj.*

con·ces·sion·aire (kən sesh ə ner′) *n.* the owner or operator of a business, such as a refreshment stand

con·demn (kən dem′) *v.* **1** to say that a person or thing is wrong or bad [We *condemn* cruelty to animals.] **2** to declare to be guilty; convict [A jury tried and *condemned* them.] —con·dem·na·tion (kän′dem nā′shən) *n.*

con·fer·ence (kän′fər əns) *n.* a meeting of people to discuss something [A *conference* on education was held in Washington.]

con·fet·ti (kən fet′ē) *pl. n. used with a singular verb*: bits of colored paper thrown about at carnivals and parades [*Confetti* was all over the street.]

con·fir·ma·tion (kän fər mā′shən) *n.* **1** the act of confirming, or making sure **2** something that confirms or proves

a	ask, fat
ā	ape, date
ä	car, lot
e	elf, ten
ē	even, meet
i	is, hit
ī	ice, fire
ō	open, go
ô	law, horn
oi	oil, point
ōo	look, pull
ōo	ooze, tool
ou	out, crowd
u	up, cut
ʉ	fur, fern
ə	a in ago
	e in agent
	e in father
	i in unity
	o in collect
	u in focus
ch	chin, arch
ŋ	ring, singer
sh	she, dash
th	thin, truth
th	then, father
zh	s in pleasure

con·fuse (kən fyōōz´) **v.** **1** to mix up, especially in the mind; put into disorder; bewilder [You will *confuse* us with so many questions.] **2** to fail to see or remember the difference between; mistake [You are *confusing* me with my twin.] —**con·fused´, con·fus´ing** —**con·fus·ed·ly** (kən fyōōz´id lē) **adv.**

con·ju·gate (kän´jə gāt) **v.** to list the different forms of a verb in person, number, and tense [*Conjugate* "to be," beginning "I am, you are, he is."] —**con´ju·gat·ed, con´ju·gat·ing** —**con´ju·ga´tion n.**

con·science (kän´shəns) **n.** a sense of right and wrong; feeling that keeps one from doing bad things [My *conscience* bothers me after I tell a lie.]

con·scious (kän´shəs) **adj.** aware of one's own feelings or of things around one [*conscious* of a slight noise]

con·sum·er (kən sōōm´ər) **n.** a person or thing that consumes; especially, a person who buys goods for his own needs and not to sell to others or to use in making other goods for sale

con·tain·er (kən tān´ər) **n.** a thing for holding something; box, can, bottle, pot, etc.

con·trol (kən trōl´) **v.** **1** to have the power of ruling, guiding, or managing [A thermostat *controls* the heat.] **2** to hold back; curb [*Control* your temper!] —**con·trolled´, con·trol´ling** ▪**n.** **1** power to direct or manage [He's a poor coach, with little *control* over the team.] **2** a part or thing that controls a machine [the *controls* of an airplane] —**con·trol´la·ble adj.**

con·ven·tion (kən ven´shən) **n.** a meeting of members or delegates from various places, held every year or every few years [a political *convention*; a national *convention* of English teachers]

con·ver·sa·tion (kän´vər sā´shən) **n.** a talk or a talking together

con·vert·i·ble (kən vurt´ə bəl) **adj.** that can be converted [Matter is *convertible* into energy.] ▪**n.** ☆an automobile with a top that can be folded back

con·vey (kən vā´) **v.** **1** to take from one place to another; carry or transport [The cattle were *conveyed* in trucks to the market.] **2** to make known; give [Please *convey* my best wishes to them.] —**con·veyed´**

corps (kôr) **n.** **1** a section or a special branch of the armed forces [the Marine *Corps*] **2** a group of people who are joined together in some work or organization [a press *corps*]

cor·re·spond·ence (kôr´ə spän´ dens) **n.** **1** the writing and receiving of letters [to engage in *correspondence*] **2** the letters written or received [The *correspondence* concerning the new contract is in the file.]

coun·sel (koun´səl) **n.** **1** the act of talking together in order to exchange ideas or opinions; discussion [They took *counsel* before making the decision.] **2** the lawyer or lawyers who are handling a case ▪**v.** to give advice to; advise [a person who *counsels* students] —**coun´seled** or **coun´selled, coun´sel·ing** or **coun´sel·ling**

coun·se·lor or **coun·sel·lor** (koun´sə lər) **n.** **1** a person who advises; advisor **2** a lawyer **3** a person in charge of children at a camp

coun·ter·act (koun tər akt´) **v.** to act against; to stop or undo the effect of [The rains will help *counteract* the dry spell.]

coun·ter·at·tack (koun´tər ə tak) **n.** an attack made in return for another attack ▪**v.** to attack so as to answer the enemy's attack

coun·ter·bal·ance (koun´tər bal´ əns) **n.** a weight, power, or force that balances or acts against another

coun·ter·feit (koun´tər fit) **adj.** made in imitation of the real thing so as to fool or cheat people [*counterfeit* money] ▪**n.** a thing that is counterfeit ▪**v.** to make an imitation of in order to cheat [to *counterfeit* money] —**coun´ter·feit·er**

coun·ter·part (koun´tər pärt) **n.** **1** a person or thing that is very much like another [He is his father's *counterpart*.] **2** a thing that goes with another thing to form a set [This cup is the *counterpart* to that saucer.]

course (kôrs) **n.** **1** a going on from one point to the next; progress in space or time [the *course* of history; the *course* of a journey] **2** a way or path along which something moves; channel, track, etc. [a golf *course*; race*course*] **3** a part of a meal served at one time [The main *course* was roast beef.] **4** a complete series of studies [I took a business *course* in high school.] **5** any of these studies [a mathematics *course*] —**coursed, cours´ing**

cow·ard (kou´ərd) **n.** a person who is unable to control his fear and so shrinks from danger or trouble

cram (kram) **v.** **1** to pack full or too full [Her suitcase is *crammed* with clothes.] **2** to stuff or force [He *crammed* the papers into a drawer.] **3** to study many facts in a hurry, as for a test —**crammed, cram´ming**

cray·on (krā´ən *or* krā´än) **n.** a small stick of chalk, charcoal, or colored wax, used for drawing or writing ▪**v.** to draw with crayons

cra·zy (krā´zē) **adj.** **1** mentally ill; insane **2** very foolish or mad [a *crazy* idea] **3** very eager or enthusiastic: *used only in everyday talk* [I'm *crazy* about the movies.] —**cra´zi·er, cra´zi·est** —**cra´zi·ly adv.** —**cra´zi·ness n.**

cre·a·tion (krē ā'shən) *n.* **1** the act of creating **2** the whole world and everything in it; universe **3** anything created or brought into being

cre·a·tive (krē ā'tiv) *adj.* creating or able to create; inventive; having imagination and ability —**cre·a·tiv·i·ty** (krē'ā tiv'ə tē) *n.*

crepe or **crêpe** (krāp) *n.* **1** a thin, crinkled cloth **2** (krāp *or* krep) a very thin pancake, rolled up or folded with a filling: *usually* crêpe

cres·cent (kres'ənt) *n.* **1** the shape of the moon in its first or last quarter **2** anything shaped like this, as a curved bun or roll ◆*adj.* shaped like a crescent

croc·o·dile (kräk'ə dīl) *n.* a large lizard like the alligator, that lives in and near tropical rivers: it has a thick, tough skin, a long tail, large jaws, and pointed teeth

crois·sant (krə sänt') *n.* a rich, flaky bread roll made in the form of a crescent

cro·quet (krō kā') *n.* an outdoor game in which the players use mallets to drive a wooden ball through hoops in the ground

cru·el (krōō'əl) *adj.* **1** liking to make others suffer; having no mercy or pity [The *cruel* Pharaoh made slaves of the Israelites.] **2** causing pain and suffering [*cruel* insults; a *cruel* winter] —**cru·el·est** —**cru·el·ly** *adv.*

cruise (krōōz) *v.* **1** to sail or drive about from place to place, as for pleasure or in searching for something **2** to move smoothly at a speed that is not strained [The airplane *cruised* at 300 mile per hour.] —**cruised, cruis·ing** ◆*n.* a ship voyage from place to place for pleasure

crumb (krum) *n.* a tiny piece broken off, as of bread or cake

crutch (kruch) *n.* a support used under the arm by a lame person to help in walking —*pl.* **crutch·es**

crys·tal (kris'təl) *n.* **1** a clear, transparent quartz that looks like glass **2** a very clear, sparkling glass **3** something made of such glass, as a goblet or bowl **4** any of the regularly shaped pieces into which many substances are formed when they become solids: a crystal has a number of flat surfaces in an orderly arrangement [Salt, sugar, and snow are made up of *crystals*.] ◆*adj.* made of crystal

cul·ture (kul'chər) *n.* **1** improvement by study or training, especially of the mind, manners, and taste; refinement **2** the ideas, skills, arts, tools, and way of life of a certain people in a certain time; civilization [the *culture* of the Aztecs] —**cul'tur·al** *adj.* —**cul'tur·al·ly** *adv.*

cur·few (kʉr'fyōō) *n.* a time in the evening beyond which certain persons or all people must not be on the streets [Our town has a nine o'clock *curfew* for children.]

☆**cur·ren·cy** (kʉr'ən sē) *n.* the money in common use in any country; often, paper money —*pl.* **cur'ren·cies**

cus·tom (kus'təm) *n.* **1** a usual thing to do; habit [It is my *custom* to have tea after dinner.] **2** something that has been done for a long time and so has become the common or regular thing to do [the *custom* of eating turkey on Thanksgiving] **3 customs,** *pl.* taxes collected by a government on goods brought in from other countries; also, the government agency that collects these taxes ◆*adj.* made or done to order [*custom* shoes]

cym·bal (sim'bəl) *n.* a round brass plate, used in orchestras and bands, that makes a sharp, ringing sound when it is hit: cymbals can be used in pairs that are struck together

cy·press (sī'prəs) *n.* an evergreen tree with cones and dark leaves

damp (damp) *adj.* slightly wet; moist [*damp* clothes; *damp* weather] ◆*n.* a slight wetness; moisture [Rains caused *damp* in the basement.] —**damp'ly** *adv.* —**damp'ness** *n.*

dare (der) *v.* **1** to face bravely or boldly; defy [The hunter *dared* the dangers of the jungle.] **2** to call on someone to do a certain thing in order to show courage; challenge [She *dared* me to swim across the lake.] —**dared, dar'ing** ◆*n.* a challenge to prove that one is not afraid [I accepted her *dare* to swim across the lake.]

dar·ing (der'iŋ) *adj.* bold enough to take risks; fearless ◆*n.* bold courage

de·bate (dē bāt') *v.* **1** to give reasons for or against; argue about something, especially in a formal contest between two opposite sides [The Senate *debated* the question of foreign treaties.] **2** to consider reasons for and against [I *debated* the problem in my own mind.] —**de·bat·ed, de·bat'ing** ◆*n.* the act of debating something; discussion or formal argument —**de·bat'er** *n.*

de·brief (dē brēf') *v.* to question someone who has ended a mission, to get information [The astronaut was *debriefed* after the space flight.]

debt (det) *n.* **1** something that one owes to another [a *debt* of $25; a *debt* of gratitude] **2** the condition of owing [I am greatly in *debt* to you.]

de·cay (dē kā') *v.* **1** to become rotten by the action of bacteria [The fallen apples *decayed* on the ground.] **2** to fall into ruins; become no longer sound, powerful, rich, beautiful, etc. [Spain's power *decayed* after its fleet was destroyed.] —**de·cay'ing** ◆*n.* a rotting or falling into ruin

a	ask, fat
ā	ape, date
ä	car, lot
e	elf, ten
ē	even, meet
i	is, hit
ī	ice, fire
ō	open, go
ô	law, horn
oi	oil, point
ōō	look, pull
ōō	ooze, tool
ou	out, crowd
u	up, cut
ʉ	fur, fern
ə	a in ago
	e in agent
	e in father
	i in unity
	o in collect
	u in focus
ch	chin, arch
ŋ	ring, singer
sh	she, dash
th	thin, truth
th	then, father
zh	s in pleasure

de·cent (dē'sənt) *adj.* **1** proper and fitting; not to be ashamed of; respectable [*decent* manners; *decent* language] **2** fairly good; satisfactory [a *decent* wage] **3** kind; generous; fair [It was *decent* of you to lend me your car.] —**de'cent·ly** *adv.*

de·cep·tive (dē sep'tiv) *adj.* deceiving; not what it seems to be —**de·cep'tive·ly** *adv.*

dec·i·bel (des'ə bəl) *n.* a unit for measuring the relative loudness of sound

de·cline (dē klīn') *v.* **1** to bend or slope downward [The lawn *declines* to the sidewalk.] **2** to become less in health, power, or value; decay [A person's strength usually *declines* in old age.] **3** to refuse something, especially in a polite way [I am sorry I must *decline* your invitation.] ◆*n.* **1** the process or result of becoming less, smaller, or weaker; decay [a *decline* in prices] **2** the last part [the *decline* of life] **3** a downward slope [We slid down the *decline*.]

dec·o·ra·tion (dek'ə rā'shən) *n.* **1** anything used for decorating; ornament [*decorations* for the birthday party] **2** a medal, ribbon, etc. given as a sign of honor

de·crease (dē krēs' *or* dē'krēs) *v.* to make or become gradually less or smaller [She has *decreased* her weight by dieting. The pain is *decreasing*.] —**de·creased', de·creas'ing** ◆*n.* a decreasing or growing less [a *decrease* in profits]

ded·i·cate (ded'i kāt') *v.* **1** to set aside for a special purpose [The doctor has *dedicated* her life to cancer research.] **2** to say at the beginning of a book, etc. that it was written in honor of, or out of affection for, a certain person [He *dedicated* his novel to his wife.] —**ded'i·cat·ed, ded'i·cat·ing** —**ded'i·ca'tion** *n.*

de·fi·cien·cy (dē fish'ən sē) *n.* an amount short of what is needed; shortage [A *deficiency* of vitamin C causes scurvy.] —*pl.* **de·fi'cien·cies**

de·lete (dē lēt') *v.* to take out or cross out something printed or written [Her name has been *deleted* from the list of members.] —**de·let'ed, de·let'ing** —**de·le·tion** (di lē'shən) *n.*

de·liv·er·y (dē liv'ər ē) *n.* the act of delivering; a transferring or distributing [daily *deliveries* to customers; the *delivery* of a prisoner into custody] —*pl.* **de·liv'er·ies**

den·im (den'im) *n.* a coarse cotton cloth that will take hard wear and is used for work clothes or play clothes

de·pend (dē pend') *v.* **1** to be controlled or decided by [The attendance at the game *depends* on the weather.] **2** to put one's trust in; be sure of [You can't *depend* on the weather.] **3** to rely for help or support [They *depend* on their parents for money.] —**de·pend'ed**

de·pos·it (dē päz'it) *v.* **1** to place for safekeeping, as money in a bank **2** to give as part payment or as a pledge [They *deposited* $500 on a new car.] **3** to lay down [I *deposited* my books on the chair. The river *deposits* tons of mud at its mouth.] —**de·pos'it·ed** ◆*n.* **1** something placed for safekeeping, as money in a bank **2** something left lying, as sand, clay, or minerals deposited by the action of wind, water, or other forces of nature

dept. *abbreviation for* **department**

depth (depth) *n.* **1** the fact of being deep, or how deep a thing is; deepness [the *depth* of the ocean; a closet five feet in *depth*; the *depth* of a color; the great *depth* of their love] **2** the middle part [the *depth* of winter]

de·scend (dē send') *v.* **1** to move down to a lower place [to *descend* from a hilltop; to *descend* a staircase] **2** to become lesser or smaller [Prices have *descended* during the past month.] **3** to come from a certain source [They are *descended* from pioneers.] —**de·scend'ing**

des·ert (dez'ərt) *n.* a dry sandy region with little or no plant life ◆*adj.* **1** of or like a desert **2** wild and not lived in [a *desert* island]

de·serve (də zurv') *v.* to have a right to; be one that ought to get [This matter *deserves* thought. You *deserve* a scolding.] —**de·served', de·serv'ing** —**de·serv'ed·ly** *adv.*

de·serv·ing (də zur'viŋ) *adj.* that ought to get help or a reward [a *deserving* student]

de·sign·er (də zī'nər) *n.* a person who designs or makes original plans [a dress *designer*]

de·sir·a·ble (də zīr'ə bəl) *adj.* worth wanting or having; pleasing, excellent, beautiful, etc. —**de·sir'a·bil'i·ty** *n.* —**de·sir'a·bly** *adv.*

de·spair (də sper') *n.* a giving up or loss of hope [Sam is in *despair* of ever getting a vacation.] ◆*v.* to lose or give up hope [The prisoner *despaired* of ever being free again.]

☆**des·sert** (də zurt') *n.* something sweet served at the end of a meal, as fruit, pie, or cake

de·struc·tive (dē struk'tiv) *adj.* destroying or likely to destroy [a *destructive* windstorm]

de·vel·op (dē vel'əp) *v.* **1** to make or become larger, fuller, better, etc.; grow or expand [The seedling *developed* into a tree. Reading *develops* one's knowledge.] **2** to bring or come into being and work out gradually; evolve [Dr. Salk *developed* a vaccine for polio. Mold *developed* on the cheese.] **3** to treat an exposed photographic film or plate with chemicals, so as to show the picture

di·ag·o·nal (dī ag'ə nəl) *adj.* 1 slanting from one corner to the opposite corner, as of a square 2 going in a slanting direction [a tie with *diagonal* stripes] ➤*n.* a diagonal line, plane, course, or part —**di·ag'o·nal·ly** *adv.*

dic·tion·ar·y (dik'shə ner'ē) *n.* a book in which the words of a language, or of some special field, are listed in alphabetical order with their meanings, pronunciations, and other information [a school *dictionary*] —*pl.* **dic·tion·ar'ies**

die·sel (dē'zəl *or* dē'səl) *n.* *often* **Diesel** 1 a kind of internal-combustion engine that burns fuel oil by using heat produced by compressing air; *also called* **diesel engine** *or* **diesel motor** 2 a locomotive or motor vehicle with such an engine

dif·fer·ence (dif'ər əns *or* dif'rəns) *n.* 1 the state of being different or unlike [the *difference* between right and wrong] 2 a way in which people or things are unlike [a *difference* in size] 3 the amount by which one quantity is greater or less than another [The *difference* between 11 and 7 is 4.]

dif·fuse (di fyo͞os') *adj.* 1 spread out; not centered in one place [This lamp gives *diffuse* light.] 2 using more words than are needed; wordy [a *diffuse* style of writing] ➤*v.* (di fyo͞oz') 1 to spread out in every direction; scatter widely [to *diffuse* light] 2 to mix together [to *diffuse* gases or liquids]

di·gest (di jest' *or* dī jest') *v.* to change food in the stomach and intestines into a form that can be used by the body [Small babies cannot *digest* solid food.] —**di·gest'i·ble** *adj.*

di·no·saur (dī'nə sôr) *n.* any of a group of reptiles that lived millions of years ago: dinosaurs had four legs and a long, tapering tail, and some were almost 100 feet long

dis·ap·point (dis ə point') *v.* to fail to give or do what is wanted, expected, or promised; leave unsatisfied [I am *disappointed* in the weather. You promised to come, but *disappointed* us.]

dis·ap·point·ment (dis'ə point'mənt) *n.* 1 a disappointing or being disappointed [one's *disappointment* over not winning] 2 a person or thing that disappoints [The team is a *disappointment* to us.]

dis·ci·pline (dis'ə plin) *n.* 1 training that teaches one to obey rules and control one's behavior [the strict *discipline* of army life] 2 the result of such training; self-control; orderliness [The pupils showed perfect *discipline*.] ➤*v.* 1 to train in discipline [Regular chores help to *discipline* children.] 2 to punish —**dis'ci·plined, dis'ci·plin·ing**

dis·count (dis'kount) *n.* an amount taken off a price, bill, or debt [He got a 10% *discount* by paying cash, so the radio cost $90 instead of $100.] ➤*v.* (dis kount') 1 to take off a certain amount as a discount from a price, bill, etc. 2 to tend not to believe

dis·ease (di zēz') *n.* a condition of not being healthy; sickness; illness [Chicken pox is a common childhood *disease*. Some fungi cause *disease* in animals and plants.] —**dis·eased'** *adj.*

dis·guise (dis gīz') *v.* 1 to make seem so different as not to be recognized [to *disguise* oneself with a false beard; to *disguise* one's voice] 2 to hide so as to keep from being known [She *disguised* her dislike of him by being very polite.] —**dis·guised', dis·guis'ing** ➤*n.* any clothes, makeup, way of acting, etc. used to hide who or what one is

dis·may (dis mā') *v.* to fill with fear or dread so that one is not sure of what to do [We were *dismayed* at the sight of the destruction.] —**dis·mayed'** ➤*n.* loss of courage or confidence when faced with trouble or danger [The doctor's report filled her with *dismay*.]

dis·o·bey (dis'ō bā') *v.* to fail to obey or refuse to obey —**dis·o·beyed'**

dis·tort (di stôrt') *v.* 1 to twist out of its usual shape or look [The old mirror gave a *distorted* reflection.] 2 to change so as to give a false idea [The facts were *distorted*.] —**dis·tor'tion** *n.*

dis·turb·ance (di stur'bəns) *n.* 1 a disturbing or being disturbed 2 anything that disturbs 3 noisy confusion; uproar; disorder

di·vi·sor (də vī'zər) *n.* the number by which another number is divided [In 6 ÷ 3 = 2, the number 3 is the *divisor*.]

dom·i·no (däm'ə nō) *n.* a small, oblong piece of wood, plastic, etc. marked with dots on one side: a set of these pieces is used in playing the game called **dominoes**, in which the halves are matched —*pl.* **dom'i·noes** *or* **dom'i·nos**

doubt (dout) *v.* to think that something may not be true or right; be unsure of; question [I *doubt* that those are the correct facts. Never *doubt* my love.] ➤*n.* a doubting; being unsure of something [I have no *doubt* that you will win.] —**doubt'er** *n.*

dough·nut (dō'nut) *n.* a small, sweet cake fried in deep fat, usually shaped like a ring

down·stream (doun'strēm) *adv., adj.* in the direction in which a stream is flowing

draw·back (drô'bak *or* drä'bak) *n.* a condition that acts against one; hindrance; disadvantage

drought (drout) *or* **drouth** (drouth) *n.* a long period of dry weather, with little or no rain

drow·sy (drou'zē) *adj.* 1 sleepy or half asleep 2 making one feel sleepy [*drowsy* music] —**drow'si·er, drow'si·est** —**drow'si·ly** *adv.* —**drow'si·ness** *n.*

du·ti·ful (do͞ot'ə fəl *or* dyo͞ot'ə fəl) *adj.* doing or ready to do one's duty; having a proper sense of duty [a *dutiful* parent] —**du'ti·ful·ly** *adv.*

a	ask, fat
ā	ape, date
ä	car, lot
e	elf, ten
ē	even, meet
i	is, hit
ī	ice, fire
ō	open, go
ô	law, horn
oi	oil, point
o͝o	look, pull
o͞o	ooze, tool
ou	out, crowd
u	up, cut
ʉ	fur, fern
ə	a in ago
	e in agent
	e in father
	i in unity
	o in collect
	u in focus
ch	chin, arch
ŋ	ring, singer
sh	she, dash
th	thin, truth
th	then, father
zh	s in pleasure

ear·nest (ur´nəst) *adj.* not light or joking; serious or sincere [an *earnest* wish] —**ear´nest·ly** *adv.* —**ear´nest·ness** *n.*

earn (urn) *v.* 1 to get as pay for work done [She *earns* $10 an hour.] 2 to get or deserve because of something done [He *earned* a medal for swimming.] 3 to get as profit [Your savings *earn* 5% interest.] —**earn´ing** —**earn´ings** *pl. n.*

ear·ring (ir´riŋ) *n.* an ornament worn on or in the lobe of the ear

earth·en·ware (urth´ən wer) *n.* the coarser sort of dishes, vases, jars, etc. made of baked clay

ea·sel (ē´zəl) *n.* a standing frame for holding an artist's canvas, a chalkboard, etc.

east·ward (ēst´wərd) *adv., adj.* in the direction of the east [an *eastward* journey; to travel *eastward*]

ech·o (ek´ō) *n.* sound heard again when sound waves bounce back from a surface —*pl.* **ech´oes** ◆*v.* —**ech´oed, ech´o·ing**

e·clipse (e klips) *n.* a hiding of all or part of the sun by the moon when it passes between the sun and the earth (called a **solar eclipse**); also, a hiding of the moon by the earth's shadow (called a **lunar eclipse**) ◆*v.* to cause an eclipse of; darken —**e·clipsed´, e·clips´ing**

e·col·o·gy (ē käl´ə jē) *n.* the science that deals with the relations between all living things and the conditions that surround them —**e·col´o·gist** *n.*

ed. *abbreviation for:* 1 edition *or* editor —*pl.* **eds.** 2 education

ed·u·ca·tion (ej´ ə kā´shən) *n.* 1 the act or work of educating or training people; teaching [a career in *education*] 2 the things a person learns by being taught; schooling or training [a high-school *education*]

ef·fec·tive (ə fek´tiv) *adj.* 1 making a certain thing happen; especially, bringing about the result wanted [an *effective* remedy] 2 in force or operation; active [The law becomes *effective* Monday.] 3 making a strong impression on the mind; impressive [an *effective* speaker] —**ef·fec´tive·ly** *adv.*

ef·fi·cient (ə fish´ənt) *adj.* bringing about the result or effect wanted with the least waste of time, effort, or materials [an *efficient* method of production; an *efficient* manager] —**ef·fi´cien·cy** *n.*

E·gyp·tian (ē jip´shən) *adj.* of Egypt, its people, or their culture ◆*n.* 1 a person born or living in Egypt 2 the language of the ancient Egyptians: modern Egyptians speak Arabic

e·lec·tric·i·ty (ē lek´ tris´i tē) *n.* a form of energy that comes from the movement of electrons and protons: it can be produced by friction (as by rubbing wax with wool), by chemical action (as in a storage battery), or by induction (as in a dynamo or generator): electricity is used to produce light, heat, power, etc. electricity moving in a stream, as through a wire, is called **electric current**

em·bank·ment (im baŋk´mənt) *n.* a long mound or wall of earth, stone, etc. used to keep back water, hold up a roadway, etc.

em·bar·go (em bär´gō) *n.* a government order that forbids certain ships to leave or enter its ports —*pl.* **em·bar´goes** ◆*v.* to put an embargo upon —**em·bar´goed, em·bar´go·ing**

em·bat·tle (em bat´l) *v.* to prepare for battle —**em·bat´tled, em·bat´tling**

em·bel·lish (em bel´ish) *v.* to decorate or improve by adding something [to *embellish* a talk with details] —**em·bel´lish·ment** *n.*

em·bit·ter (em bit´ər) *v.* to make bitter; make feel angry or hurt [He was *embittered* by her remark.]

em·bla·zon (em blā´zən) *v.* 1 to decorate with bright colors or in a rich, showy way [The bandstand was *emblazoned* with bunting.] 2 to mark with an emblem [The shield was *emblazoned* with a golden lion.]

em·broi·der·y (em broi´dər ē) *n.* 1 the art or work of embroidering 2 an embroidered decoration —*pl.* **em·broi´der·ies**

em·pha·size (em´fə sīz) *v.* to give special force or attention to; stress [I want to *emphasize* the importance of honesty.] —**em´pha·sized, em´pha·siz·ing**

em·ploy·ment (e ploi´mənt) *n.* 1 the condition of being employed 2 one's work, trade, or profession

em·pow·er (em pou´ər) *v.* to give certain power or rights to; authorize [The warrant *empowered* the police to search the house.]

emp·ty (emp´tē) *adj.* having nothing or no one in it; not occupied; vacant [an *empty* jar; an *empty* house] —**emp´ti·er, emp´ti·est** ◆*v.* 1 to make or become empty [The auditorium was *emptied* in ten minutes.] 2 to take out or pour out [*Empty* the dirty water in the sink.] 3 to flow out; discharge [The Amazon *empties* into the Atlantic.] —**emp´tied, emp´ty·ing** —**emp´ti·ly** *adv.* —**emp´ti·ness** *n.* —*pl.* **emp´ties**

en·com·pass (en kum´pəs) *v.* 1 to surround on all sides; enclose or encircle [a lake *encompassed* by mountains] 2 to have in it; contain or include [A dictionary *encompasses* much information.]

en·cour·age (en kur´ij) *v.* 1 to give courage or hope to; make feel more confident [Praise *encouraged* her to try harder.] 2 to give help to; aid; promote [Rain *encourages* the growth of plants.] —**en·cour´aged, en·cour´ag·ing** —**en·cour´age·ment** *n.*

en·dan·ger (en dān′jər) *v.* to put in danger or peril [to *endanger* one's life]

en·dow (en dou′) *v.* **1** to provide with some quality or thing [a person *endowed* with musical talent; a land *endowed* with natural resources] **2** to provide a gift of money to a college, hospital, museum, etc., that will bring a regular income to help support it —**en·dow′ment** *n.*

en·gage (en gāj′) *v.* **1** to promise to marry [Harry is *engaged* to Grace.] **2** to promise or undertake to do something [She *engaged* to tutor the child after school.] **3** to draw into; involve [She *engaged* him in conversation.] —**en·gaged′, en·gag′ing**

Eng·lish (iŋ′glish) *adj.* of England, its people, language, etc. *n.* **1** the language spoken in England, the U.S., Canada, Australia, New Zealand, Liberia, etc. **2** a course in school for studying the English language or English literature

en·grave (en grāv′) *v.* **1** to carve or etch letters, designs, etc. on [a date *engraved* on a building] **2** to cut or etch a picture, lettering, etc. into a metal plate, wooden block, etc. to be used for printing; also, to print from such a plate, block, etc. [an *engraved* invitation] —**en·graved′, en·grav′ing** —**en·grav′er** *n.*

en·light·en (en līt′n) *v.* to get someone to have knowledge or know the truth; get rid of ignorance or false beliefs; inform —**en·light′en·ment** *n.*

en·list (en list′) *v.* **1** to join or get someone to join; especially, to join some branch of the armed forces [She *enlisted* in the navy. This office *enlisted* ten new recruits.] **2** to get the support of [Try to *enlist* your parents' help.] —**en·list′ment** *n.*

en·roll or **en·rol** (en rōl′) *v.* **1** to write one's name in a list, as in becoming a member; register [New students must *enroll* on Monday.] **2** to make someone a member [We want to *enroll* you in our swim club.] —**en·rolled′, en·roll′ing**

en·roll·ment or **en·rol·ment** (en rōl′mənt) *n.* **1** the act of enrolling **2** the number of people enrolled

en·sure (en shoor′) *v.* **1** to make sure or certain [Good weather will *ensure* a large attendance.] **2** to make safe; protect [Seat belts help to *ensure* you against injury in a car accident.] —**en·sured′, en·sur′ing**

e·qui·lat·er·al (ē′ kwi lat′ər əl) *adj.* having all sides equal in length

e·quip (ē kwip′) *v.* to provide with what is needed; outfit [The soldiers were *equipped* for battle. The car is *equipped* with power brakes.] —**e·quipped′, e·quip′ping**

☆**es·ca·la·tor** (es′kə lāt′ ər) *n.* a stairway whose steps are part of an endless moving belt, for carrying people up or down

es·cape (e skāp′) *v.* **1** to break loose; get free, as from prison **2** to keep from getting hurt, killed, etc.; keep safe from; avoid [Very few people *escaped* the plague.] —**es·caped′, es·cap′ing** *n.* **1** the act of escaping [The prisoners made their plans for an *escape*.] **2** a way of escaping [The fire closed in and there seemed to be no *escape*.]

Es·ki·mo (es′kə mō) *n.* **1** a member of a group of people who live mainly in the arctic regions of the Western Hemisphere —*pl.* **Es′ki·mos** or **Es′ki·mo** **2** the language of the Eskimos *adj.* of the Eskimos

es·say (es′ā) *n.* a short piece of writing on some subject, giving the writer's personal ideas

es·teem (e stēm′) *v.* to have a good opinion of; regard as valuable; respect [I *esteem* his praise above all other.] *n.* good opinion; high regard; respect [to hold someone in high *esteem*]

etc. *abbreviation for* et cetera

e·vap·o·rate (ē vap′ə rāt) *v.* **1** to change into vapor [Heat *evaporates* water. The perfume in the bottle has *evaporated*.] **2** to disappear like vapor; vanish [Our courage *evaporated* when we saw the lion.] **3** to make thicker by heating so as to take some of the water from [to *evaporate* milk] —**e·vap′o·rat·ed, e·vap′o·rat·ing** —**e·vap′o·ra′tion** *n.*

ex. *abbreviation for* example, extra

ex·cel·lence (ek′sə ləns) *n.* the fact of being better or greater; extra goodness [We all praised the *excellence* of their singing.]

ex·cept (ek sept′) *prep.* leaving out; other than; but [Everyone *except* you liked the movie.] *v.* to leave out; omit; exclude [Only a few of the students were *excepted* from her criticism.] *conj.* were it not that; only; *used only in everyday talk* [I'd go with you *except* I'm tired.]

ex·cit·ing (ek sīt′iŋ) *adj.* causing excitement; stirring; thrilling [an *exciting* story]

ex·haust (eg zôst′ *or* eg zäst′) *v.* **1** to use up completely [Our drinking water was soon *exhausted*.] **2** to let out the contents of; make completely empty [The leak soon *exhausted* the gas tank.] **3** to use up the strength of; tire out; weaken [They are *exhausted* from playing tennis.] —**ex·haust′ed** *n.* the used steam or gas that comes from the cylinders of an engine; especially, the fumes from the gasoline engine in an automobile

ex·hib·it (eg zib′it) *v.* to show or display to the public [to *exhibit* stamp collections] *n.* **1** something exhibited to the public [an art *exhibit*] **2** something shown as evidence in a court of law

ex·ist·ence (eg zis′təns) *n.* **1** the condition of being; an existing **2** life or a way of life [a happy *existence*] —**ex·ist′ent** *adj.*

a	ask, fat
ā	ape, date
ä	car, lot
e	elf, ten
ē	even, meet
i	is, hit
ī	ice, fire
ō	open, go
ô	law, horn
oi	oil, point
oo	look, pull
ōō	ooze, tool
ou	out, crowd
u	up, cut
ʉ	fur, fern
ə	a in ago
	e in agent
	e in father
	i in unity
	o in collect
	u in focus
ch	chin, arch
ŋ	ring, singer
sh	she, dash
th	thin, truth
th	then, father
zh	s in pleasure

ex·pe·ri·ence (ek spir′ē əns) *n.* **1** the fact of living through a happening or happenings [*Experience* teaches us many things.] **2** something that one has done or lived through [This trip was an *experience* that I'll never forget.] **3** skill that one gets by training, practice, and work [a lawyer with much *experience*] ◆*v.* to have the experience of [to *experience* success] —**ex·pe′ri·enced, ex·pe′ri·enc·ing**

ex·pla·na·tion (eks′ plə nā′shən) *n.* **1** the act of explaining [This plan needs an *explanation*.] **2** something that explains [This long nail is the *explanation* for the flat tire.] **3** a meaning given in explaining [different *explanations* of the same event]

ex·ploit (eks′ploit) *n.* a daring act or bold deed [the *exploits* of Robin Hood] ◆*v.* (ek sploit′) to use in a selfish way; take unfair advantage of [Children were *exploited* when they had to work in factories.] —**ex′ploi·ta′tion** *n.*

ex·plore (ek splôr′) *v.* **1** to travel in a region that is unknown or not well known, in order to find out more about it [to *explore* a wild jungle] **2** to look into or examine carefully [to *explore* a problem] —**ex·plored′, ex·plor′ing** —**ex′plo·ra′tion; ex·plor′er** *n.*

ex·po·sure (ek spō′zhər) *n.* **1** the fact of being exposed [tanned by *exposure* to the sun] **2** the time during which film in a camera is exposed to light; also, a section of film that can be made into one picture [Give this film a short *exposure*. There are twelve *exposures* on this film.]

ex·tra·ter·res·tri·al (eks′trə tər res′trē əl) *adj.* being, happening, or coming from a place not the earth [a science-fiction story about *extraterrestrial* beings]

ex·treme (ek strēm′) *adj.* **1** to the greatest degree; very great [*extreme* pain] **2** far from what is usual; also, very far from the center of opinion [She holds *extreme* political views.] ◆*n.* either of two things that are as different or as far from each other as possible [the *extremes* of laughter and tears] —**ex·treme′ly** *adv.*

eye·sight (ī′sīt) *n.* **1** the ability to see; sight; vision [keen *eyesight*] **2** the distance a person can see [Keep within *eyesight*!]

fab·ric (fab′rik) *n.* a material made from fibers or threads by weaving, knitting, etc., as any cloth, felt, lace, etc.

fa·cial (fā′shəl) *adj.* of or for the face ◆☆*n.* a treatment intended to make the skin of the face look better, as by massage and putting on creams and lotions

faith·ful (fāth′fəl) *adj.* **1** remaining loyal; constant [*faithful* friends] **2** showing a strong sense of duty or responsibility [*faithful* attendance] —**faith′ful·ly** *adv.* —**faith′ful·ness** *n.*

fal·low (fal′ō) *adj.* plowed but left unplanted during the growing season [Farmers let the land lie *fallow* at times to kill weeds, make the soil richer, etc.] ◆*n.* land that lies fallow

fan·ci·ful (fan′si fəl) *adj.* **1** full of fancy; having or showing a quick and playful imagination [*fanciful* costumes for the Halloween party] **2** not real; imaginary [a *fanciful* idea that horseshoes bring luck]

fas·ci·nate (fas′ə nāt) *v.* to hold the attention of by being interesting or delightful; charm [The puppet show *fascinated* the children.] —**fas′ci·nat·ed, fas′ci·nat·ing** —**fas′ci·na′tion** *n.*

fas·ten (fas′ən) *v.* **1** to join or become joined; attach [The collar is *fastened* to the shirt.] **2** to make stay closed or in place, as by locking or shutting [*Fasten* the door.] —**fas′ten·er** *n.*

fel·low·ship (fel′ō ship′) *n.* **1** friendship; companionship **2** a group of people having the same activities or interests **3** money given to a student at a university or college to help him or her study for a higher degree

fen·der (fen′dər) *n.* a metal piece over the wheel of a car, bicycle, etc. that protects against splashing water or mud

fes·ti·val (fes′tə vəl) *n.* **1** a day or time of feasting or celebrating; happy holiday [The Mardi Gras in New Orleans is a colorful *festival*.] **2** a time of special celebration or entertainment [Our town holds a maple sugar *festival* every spring.] ◆*adj.* of or for a festival [*festival* music]

fetch (fech) *v.* to go after and bring back; get [The dog *fetched* my slippers.] —**fetched**

fidg·et (fij′it) *v.* to move about restlessly [Children sometimes *fidget* if they have to sit still too long.]

fierce (firs) *adj.* **1** wild or cruel; violent; raging [a *fierce* dog; a *fierce* wind] **2** very strong or eager [a *fierce* effort] —**fierc′er, fierc′est** —**fierce′ly** *adv.* —**fierce′ness** *n.*

fif·teen (fif′tēn′) *n., adj.* five more than ten; the number 15

filth·y (fil′thē) *adj.* full of filth; disgusting **filth′i·er, filth′i·est**

firm (furm) *adj.* **1** that does not easily give way when pressed; solid [*firm* muscles] **2** that cannot be moved easily; fixed; stable [He stood as *firm* as a rock.] **3** that stays the same; not changing; constant [a *firm* friendship] —**firm´est** —**firm´ly** *adv.* —**firm´ness** *n.*

flash·bulb (flash´bulb) *n.* a lightbulb that gives a short, bright light for taking photographs

flo·rist (flôr´ist) *n.* a person whose business is selling flowers, house plants, etc.

flour·ish (flur´ish) *v.* to grow strongly and well; be successful or healthy; prosper [Daisies *flourish* in full sun.]

fo·li·age (fō´lē ij) *n.* the leaves of a tree or plant, or of many trees or plants

fol·ly (fä´lē) *n.* a lack of good sense; foolishness

fore·close (fôr klōz´) *v.* to end a mortgage and become the owner of the mortgaged property [A bank can *foreclose* a mortgage if payments on its loan are not made in time.] —**fore·closed´, fore·clos´ing** —**fore·clo´sure** *n.*

fore·ground (fôr´ground) *n.* the part of a scene or picture that is or seems to be nearest to the one looking at it

for·eign·er (fôr´in ər *or* fär´in ər) *n.* a person from another country, thought of as an outsider

fore·knowl·edge (fôr´nä´lij) *n.* knowledge of something before it happens

fore·most (fôr´mōst) *adj.* first in position or importance [the *foremost* writers of their time] ◄*adv.* before all else [to be first and *foremost* a dancer]

fore·sight (fôr´sīt) *n.* **1** a foreseeing **2** the power to foresee **3** a looking forward **4** a looking ahead and planning for the future

fore·warn (fôr wôrn´) *v.* to warn ahead of time [We were *forewarned* we wouldn't get tickets later.] —**fore·warn´ing** *n.*

foun·da·tion (foun dā´shən) *n.* **1** the part at the bottom that supports a wall, house, etc.; base **2** the basis on which an idea, belief, etc. rests

found·er (foun´dər) *n.* a person who founds, or establishes [the *founder* of a city]

fra·grant (frā´grənt) *adj.* having a sweet or pleasant smell

☆**frank·furt·er** (fraŋk´fər tər) *n.* a smoked sausage of beef or beef and pork; wiener

freight (frāt) *n.* a load of goods shipped by train, truck, ship, or airplane ◄*v.* to carry or send by freight [Cars are often *freighted* by trains or trucks to where they are sold.]

fre·quen·cy (frē´kwən sē) *n.* **1** the fact of being frequent, or happening often **2** the number of times something is repeated in a certain period [a *frequency* of 1,000 vibrations per second]: the frequency of radio waves is measured in hertz —*pl.* **fre´quen·cies**

fruit·ful (frōōt´fəl) *adj.* **1** bearing much fruit [a *fruitful* tree] **2** producing a great deal [Mozart was a *fruitful* composer.] —**fruit´ful·ly** *adv.* —**fruit´ful·ness** *n.*

Gg

gal·ax·y (gal´ək sē) ◄*n.* any vast group of stars —*pl.* **gal´ax·ies**

gal·ler·y (gal´ər ē) *n.* **1** a balcony, especially the highest balcony in a theater, with the cheapest seats **2** the people who sit in these seats **3** a place for showing or selling works of art —*pl.* **gal´ler·ies**

gawk (gôk *or* yäk) *v.* to stare in a stupid way [The crowd *gawked* at the overturned truck.]

gear (gir) *n.* **1** *often* **gears,** *pl.* a part of a machine consisting of two or more wheels having teeth that fit together so that when one wheel moves the others are made to move [The *gears* pass on the motion of the engine to the wheels of the car.] **2** tools and equipment needed for doing something [My *gear* for fishing consists of a rod, lines, and flies.] ◄*v.* to adjust or make fit [Our new cafeteria is *geared* to handle more students.]

gen·tle (jent´l) *adj.* **1** mild, soft, or easy; not rough [a *gentle* touch] **2** tame; easy to handle [a *gentle* horse] **3** gradual; not sudden [a *gentle* slope] **4** courteous, kindly, or patient [a *gentle* nature] —**gen´tler, gen´tlest**

gen·u·ine (jen´yōōin) *adj.* **1** really being what it seems to be; not false; true [a *genuine* diamond] **2** sincere or honest [*genuine* praise] —**gen´u·ine·ly** *adv.* —**gen´u·ine·ness** *n.*

ge·ol·o·gy (jē ä´lə jē) *n.* the study of the earth's crust and of the way in which its layers were formed: it includes the study of rocks and fossils —**ge·ol´o·gist** *n.*

gloom·y (glōōm´ē) *adj.* **1** dark or dim [a *gloomy* dungeon] **2** having or giving a feeling of deep sadness [a *gloomy* mood; a *gloomy* story] —**gloom´i·er, gloom´i·est** —**gloom´i·ly** *adv.* —**gloom´i·ness** *n.*

glo·ri·fy (glôr´ə fī) *v.* **1** to give glory to; cause to be famous and respected [Our town *glorified* the hero by building a statue.] **2** to praise in worship [to *glorify* God] **3** to make seem better than is really so [to *glorify* war] —**glo´ri·fied, glo´ri·fy·ing**

gnarled (närld) *adj.* full of gnarls or knobs; twisted and knotty [a *gnarled* tree; *gnarled* hands]

gnome (nōm) *n.* a dwarf in folk tales who lives inside the earth and guards the treasures there

govt. *or* **Govt.** *abbreviation for* **government**

a	ask, fat
ā	ape, date
ä	car, lot
e	elf, ten
ē	even, meet
i	is, hit
ī	ice, fire
ō	open, go
ô	law, horn
oi	oil, point
ŏŏ	look, pull
ōō	ooze, tool
ou	out, crowd
u	up, cut
ʉ	fur, fern
ə	a in ago
	e in agent
	e in father
	i in unity
	o in collect
	u in focus
ch	chin, arch
ŋ	ring, singer
sh	she, dash
th	thin, truth
th	then, father
zh	s in pleasure

gra·cious (grā′shəs) *adj.* **1** kind, polite, and charming [a *gracious* host and hostess] **2** full of grace, comfort, and luxury [*gracious* living]

grad·u·ate (grā′joŏət) *n.* a person who has finished a course of study at a school or college and has been given a diploma or degree ◆*v.* (grā′joŏ āt′) **1** to make or become a graduate of a school or college **2** to mark off with small lines for measuring [A thermometer is a tube *graduated* in degrees.] —**grad′u·at·ed, grad′u·at·ing** —**grad′u·a′tion** *n.*

greas·y (grē′sē *or* grē′zē) *adj.* **1** smeared with grease [*greasy* hands] **2** full of grease [*greasy* food] **3** like grease; oily [a *greasy* salve] —**greas′i·er, greas′i·est** —**greas′i·ly** *adv.* —**greas′i·ness** *n.*

greed·y (grēd′ē) *adj.* wanting or taking all that one can get with no thought of what others need [The *greedy* little boy ate all the cookies.] **greed′i·er, greed′i·est** —**greed′i·ly** *adv.* —**greed′i·ness** *n.*

greet·ing (grēt′iŋ) *n.* **1** the act or words of one who greets **2** *often* **greetings**, *pl.* a message of regards from someone not present

growth (grōth) *n.* **1** the act of growing; a becoming larger or a developing **2** the amount grown; increase [a *growth* of two inches over the summer] **3** something that grows or has grown [He shaved off the two weeks' *growth* of beard. A tumor is an abnormal *growth* in the body.]

guar·an·tee (′ger ən tē′ *or* ger′ən tē′) *n.* **1** a promise to replace something sold if it does not work or last as it should [a one-year *guarantee* on the clock] **2** a promise or assurance that something will be done [You have my *guarantee* that we'll be on time.] ◆*v.* **1** to give a guarantee or guaranty for **2** to promise or assure [I cannot *guarantee* that she will be there.] —**guar′·an·teed′, guar′·an·tee′ing**

guess (ges) *v.* **1** to judge or decide about something without having enough facts to know for certain [Can you *guess* how old he is?] **2** to judge correctly by doing this [She *guessed* the exact number of beans in the jar.] **3** to think or suppose [I *guess* you're right.] ◆*n.* a judgment formed by guessing; surmise [Your *guess* is as good as mine.] —**guess′er** *n.*

guilt·y (gil′tē) *adj.* **1** having done something wrong; being to blame for something [She is often *guilty* of telling lies.] **2** judged in court to be a wrongdoer [The jury found him *guilty* of robbery.] **3** caused by a feeling of guilt [a *guilty* look] —**guilt′i·er, guilt′i·est** —**guilt′i·ly** *adv.* —**guilt′i·ness** *n.*

gui·tar (gi tär′) *n.* a musical instrument with six strings: it is played by plucking the strings with the fingers or with a guitar pick. —**gui·tar′ist** *n.*

gym·na·si·um (jim nā′zē əm) *n.* a building or room with equipment for doing exercises and playing games

hand·ker·chief (haŋ′kər chif) *n.* a small piece of cloth for wiping the nose, eyes, or face, or worn as a decoration

hap·py (hap′ē) *adj.* **1** feeling or showing pleasure or joy; glad; contended [a *happy* child; a *happy* song] **2** lucky; fortunate [The story has a *happy* ending.] —**hap′pi·er, hap′pi·est** —**hap′pi·ly** *adv.* —**hap′pi·ness** *n.*

hatch·et (hach′ət) *n.* a small ax with a short handle

haz·ard·ous (haz′ər dəs) *adj.* dangerous; risky

head·ache (hed′āk) *n.* a pain in the head

health·y (hel′thē) *adj.* **1** having good health; well [a *healthy* child] **2** showing good health [a *healthy* appetite] **3** good for one's health; healthful [a *healthy* climate] —**health′i·er, health′i·est** —**health′i·ness** *n.*

height (hīt) *n.* **1** the distance from the bottom to the top; tallness [the *height* of a building; a child four feet in *height*] **2** the highest point or degree [to reach the *height* of fame]

hem·i·sphere (hem′i sfir′) *n.* **1** half of a sphere or globe [The dome of the church was in the shape of a *hemisphere*.] **2** any of the halves into which the earth's surface is divided in geography

he·ro (hir′ō *or* hēr′ō) *n.* **1** a person who is looked up to for having done something brave or noble [Washington was the *hero* of the American Revolution.] **2** the most important person in a novel, play, or movie, especially if the person is good or noble —*pl.* **he′roes**

hes·i·ta·tion (hez′i tā′shən) *n.* **1** the act of hesitating, as because of doubt, fear, etc.; unsure or unwilling feeling [I agreed without *hesitation*.] **2** a pausing for a moment [talk filled with *hesitations*]

hex·a·gon (hek′sə gän) *n.* a flat figure with six angles and six sides

hon·or·a·ble (än′ər ə bəl) *adj.* **1** worthy of being honored [an *honorable* trade] **2** honest, upright, and sincere [*honorable* intentions] **3** bringing honor [*honorable* mention] —**hon′or·a·bly** *adv.*

hor·i·zon·tal (hor′ə zänt′l) *adj.* parallel to the horizon; not vertical; level; flat [The top of a table is *horizontal*; its legs are vertical.] ◆*n.* a horizontal line, plane, etc. —**hor′i·zon′tal·ly** *adv.*

horse·rad·ish (hôrs′rad′ish) *n.* **1** a plant with a long, white root, that has a sharp, burning taste **2** a relish made by grating this root

house·hold (hous′hōld) *n.* **1** all the persons who live in one house, especially a family **2** the home and its affairs [to manage a *household*]

Hud·son (hud′sən) a river in eastern New York: its mouth is at New York City

hus·band (huz′bənd) *n.* the man to whom a woman is married

hwy. *abbreviation for* **highway**

hymn (him) *n.* **1** a song praising or honoring God **2** any song of praise

hy·phen·ate (hī′fən āt) *v.* to join or write with a hyphen —**hy′phen·at·ed, hy′phen·at·ing** —**hy′phen·a′tion** *n.*

hyp·no·tize (hip′nə tīz) *v.* to put someone into a state of hypnosis or a condition like it —**hyp′no·tized, hyp′no·tiz·ing** —**hyp′no·tist** *n.*

Ii

i·ci·cle (ī′sik əl) *n.* a hanging stick of ice formed by water freezing as it drips down

I·da·ho (ī′də hō) a state in the northwestern part of the U.S.: *abbreviated* **Ida., ID**

i·den·ti·fy (ī den′tə fī) *v.* **1** to think of or treat as the same [The Roman god Jupiter is *identified* with the Greek god Zeus.] **2** to show or prove to be a certain person or thing [She was *identified* by a scar on her chin.] —**i·den′ti·fied, i·den′ti·fy·ing**

ig·ni·tion (ig nish′ən) *n.* **1** the act of setting on fire or catching fire **2** the switch, spark plugs, etc. that set fire to the mixture of gases in the cylinders of a gasoline engine

il·le·gal (i lē′gəl) *adj.* not legal; not allowed by law; against the law —**il·le′gal·ly** *adv.*

il·leg·i·ble (il lej′ə bəl) *adj.* hard to read or impossible to read, as because badly written or printed —**il·leg′i·bly** *adv.*

Il·li·nois (il′ə noi′) a state in the north central part of the U.S.: *abbreviated* **Ill., IL**

il·lit·er·ate (il lit′ər ət) *adj.* **1** not educated; especially, not knowing how to read or write **2** showing a lack of education [an *illiterate* letter] *n.* a person who does not know how to read or write —**il·lit′er·a·cy**

il·log·i·cal (il läj′i kəl) *adj.* not logical; showing poor reasoning —**il·log′i·cal·ly** *adv.*

il·lu·mi·nate (il lōō′mə nāt′) *v.* **1** to give light to; light up [Candles *illuminated* the room.] **2** to make clear; explain [The teacher *illuminated* the meaning of the poem.] —**il·lu′mi·nat′ed, il·lu′mi·nat′ing**

im·ma·te·ri·al (im′ ə tir′ē əl) *adj.* **1** of no importance [The cost is *immaterial* if the quality is good.] **2** not made of matter; spiritual

im·ma·ture (im ə toor′ *or* im ə choor′) *adj.* not mature; not fully grown or developed [*immature* fruit; *immature* judgment] —**im′ma·tu′ri·ty** *n.*

☆**im·mi·grant** (im′ə grənt) *n.* a person who comes into a foreign country to make a new home

im·mor·tal (im môrt′l) *adj.* **1** never dying; living forever [The Greek gods were thought of as *immortal* beings.] **2** having fame that will last a long time [Shakespeare is an *immortal* poet.] *n.* a being that lasts forever —**im·mor·tal·i·ty** (i′môr tal′ə tē) —**im·mor′tal·ly** *adv.*

im·pair (im per′) *v.* to make worse, less, or weaker; damage [The disease *impaired* her hearing.]

im·pa·tient (im pā′shənt) *adj.* **1** not patient; not willing to put up with delay, annoyance, etc. [Some parents become *impatient* when their children cry.] **2** eager to do something or for something to happen [Rita is *impatient* to go swimming.] —**im·pa′tient·ly** *adv.*

im·per·fect (im pur′fikt) *adj.* not perfect; having some fault or flaw [an *imperfect* diamond]

im·po·lite (im pə līt′) *adj.* not polite; rude —**im·po·lite′ly** *adv.* —**im·po·lite′ness** *n.*

im·prac·ti·cal (im prak′ti kəl) *adj.* not practical; not useful, efficient, etc.

im·print (im print′) *v.* **1** to mark by pressing or stamping [The paper was *imprinted* with the state seal.] **2** to fix firmly [Her face is *imprinted* in my memory.] *n.* (im′print) a mark made by pressing; print [the *imprint* of a dirty hand on the wall]

im·prop·er (im präp′ər) *adj.* **1** not proper or suitable; unfit [Sandals are *improper* shoes for tennis.] **2** not true; wrong; incorrect [an *improper* street address] **3** not decent; in bad taste [*improper* jokes] —**im·prop′er·ly** *adv.*

in·a·bil·i·ty (in′ə bil′ə tē) *n.* the condition of being unable; lack of ability or power

inc. *abbreviation for* **included, income, incorporated, increase**

in·ca·pa·ble (in kā′pə bəl) *adj.* **1** not capable; not having the ability or power needed [*incapable* of helping] **2** not able to undergo; not open to [*incapable* of change] —**in·ca·pa·bil′i·ty** *n.*

in·cred·i·ble (in kred′ə bəl) *adj.* so great, unusual, etc. that it is hard or impossible to believe [an *incredible* story; *incredible* speed] —**in·cred′i·bly** *adv.*

in·def·i·nite (in def′ə nit) *adj.* **1** having no exact limits [an *indefinite* area] **2** not clear or exact in meaning; vague [*indefinite* instructions] **3** not sure or positive; uncertain [*indefinite* plans] —**in·def′i·nite·ly** *adv.*

a	ask, fat
ā	ape, date
ä	car, lot
e	elf, ten
ē	even, meet
i	is, hit
ī	ice, fire
ō	open, go
ô	law, horn
oi	oil, point
ơơ	look, pull
o͞o	ooze, tool
ou	out, crowd
u	up, cut
u	fur, fern
ə	a in ago
	e in agent
	e in father
	i in unity
	o in collect
	u in focus
ch	chin, arch
ŋ	ring, singer
sh	she, dash
th	thin, truth
th	then, father
zh	s in pleasure

in·di·rect (in′də rekt′) *adj.* **1** not direct or straight; by a longer way; roundabout [an *indirect* route] **2** not straight to the point [an *indirect* reply] —**in′di·rect′ly** *adv.*

in·dus·try (in′dəs trē) *n.* **1** any branch of business or manufacturing [the steel *industry*; the motion-picture *industry*] **2** all business and manufacturing [Leaders of *industry* met in Chicago.] —*pl.* **in′dus·tries**

in·flate (in flāt′) *v.* to cause to swell out by putting in air or gas; blow up [to *inflate* a balloon] —**in·flat′a·ble** *adj.*

in·for·ma·tion (in′fər mā′shən) *n.* **1** an informing or being informed [This is for your *information* only.] **2** something told or facts learned; news or knowledge; data [An encyclopedia gives *information* about many things.] **3** a person or service that answers certain questions [Ask *information* for the location of the shoe department.]

in·spec·tion (in spek′shən) *n.* **1** the act or process of looking at carefully **2** an official examination or review [The *inspection* of the troops was postponed.]

in·struc·tor (in struk′tər) *n.* **1** a teacher ☆**2** a college teacher ranking below an assistant professor

in·stru·ment (in′strə mənt) *n.* **1** a tool or other device for doing very exact work, for scientific purposes, etc. [surgical *instruments*] **2** a device used in making musical sound, as a flute, violin, piano, etc.

in·su·late (in′sə lāt) *v.* to separate or cover with a material that keeps electricity, heat, or sound from escaping [electric wire *insulated* with rubber; a furnace *insulated* with asbestos] —**in′su·lat·ed, in′su·lat·ing**

in·su·la·tor (in′sə lāt′ ər) *n.* anything that insulates; especially, a device of glass or porcelain, for insulating electric wires

in·sure (in shoor′) *v.* to get or give insurance on [We *insured* our car against theft. Will your company *insure* my house against storms?] —**in·sured′, in·sur′ing** —**in·sur′a·ble** *adj.*

in·tel·li·gent (in tel′ə jənt) *adj.* having or showing intelligence, especially high intelligence —**in·tel′li·gent·ly** *adv.*

in·tol·er·ant (in tä′lər ənt) *adj.* not tolerant; not willing to put up with ideas or beliefs that are different from one's own, or not willing to put up with people of other races or backgrounds —**in·tol′er·ance** *n.*

in·trude (in trood′) *v.* to force oneself or one's thoughts on others without being asked or wanted [I don't like to *intrude* when you are so busy.] —**in·trud′ed, in·trud′ing** —**in·tru′sion** *n.*

in·ven·tion (in ven′shən) *n.* **1** the act of inventing [the *invention* of television] **2** something invented [the many *inventions* of Edison] **3** the ability to invent [a novelist who shows great *invention* in telling a story]

in·ves·ti·gate (in ves′tə gāt′) *v.* to search into so as to learn the facts; examine in detail [to *investigate* an accident] —**in·ves′ti·gat·ed, in·ves′ti·gat·ing** —**in·ves′ti·ga′tion** *n.* —**In·ves′ti·ga′tor** *n.*

ir·ra·tion·al (ir rash′ən əl) *adj.* that does not make sense; not rational; absurd [an *irrational* fear of the dark] —**ir·ra′tion·al·ly** *adv.*

ir·reg·u·lar (ir reg′yə lər) *adj.* **1** not regular; not like the usual rule, way, or custom [an *irregular* diet] **2** not straight, even, or the same throughout [an *irregular* design] —**ir·reg′u·lar·ly** *adv.*

ir·rel·e·vant (ir rel′ə vənt) *adj.* having nothing to do with the subject; not to the point [That remark about the candidate's height was *irrelevant* to the issues of the campaign.]

ir·re·spon·si·ble (ir′ rē spän′sə bəl) *adj.* not responsible; not showing a sense of duty; doing as one pleases —**ir′re·spon′si·bly** *adv.*

is·sue (ish′ oo *or* ish′yoo) *n.* **1** a thing or group of things sent or given out [the July *issue* of a magazine] **2** a problem to be talked over [The candidates will debate the *issues*.] ◆*v.* **1** to put forth or send out [The city *issues* bonds. The general *issued* an order.] **2** to give or deal out; distribute [The teacher *issued* new books.] —**is′sued, is′su·ing**

i·vo·ry (ī′vər ē *or* ī′vrē) *n.* **1** the hard, white substance that forms the tusks of the elephant, walrus, etc. **2** any substance like ivory, as the white plastic used on piano keys **3** the color of ivory; creamy white —*pl.* **i′vo·ries** ◆*adj.* **1** made of or like ivory **2** having the color of ivory; creamy-white

☆**jack·knife** (jak′nīf) *n.* **1** a large pocketknife **2** a dive in which the diver touches the feet with the hands while in the air —*pl.* **jack′knives** ◆*v.* to bend at the middle as in a jackknife dive —**jack′knifed, jack′knif·ing**

Jef·fer·son (jef′ər sən), **Thomas** 1743–1826; the third president of the United States, from 1801 to 1809

jel·ly (jel′ē) *n.* **1** a soft, firm food that looks smooth and glassy, and is easily cut, spread, etc.: jelly is made from cooked fruit syrup, meat juice, or gelatin **2** any substance like this —*pl.* **jel′lies** ◆*v.* to become, or make into, jelly —**jel′lied, jel′ly·ing**

jew·el·er or **jew·el·ler** (joo′ə lər) *n.* a person who makes, sells, or repairs jewelry, watches, etc.

jock·ey (jäk′ē) *n.* a person whose work is riding horses in races

jour·nal·ism (jur'nəl iz əm) *n.* the work of gathering, writing, or editing the news for publication in newspapers or magazines or for broadcasting on radio or television

jour·nal·ist (jur'nəl ist) *n.* a person whose work is journalism, as a reporter, news editor, etc. —**jour'nal·is'tic** *adj.*

juic·y (jōō'sē) *adj.* full of juice [a *juicy* plum] —**juic'i·er, juic'i·est**

ju·ror (jōōr'ər *or* jur'ər) *n.* a member of a jury

ju·ven·ile (jōō'və nəl *or* jōō'və nīl) *adj.* 1 young or youthful 2 of, like, or for children or young people [*juvenile* ideas; *juvenile* books] ◆*n.* a child or young person

Kk

kan·ga·roo (kaŋ gə r ōō') *n.* an animal of Australia with short forelegs and strong, large hind legs, with which it makes long leaps: the female carries her young in a pouch in front —*pl.* **kan·ga·roos'**

Ken·ne·dy (ken'ə dē) **John F.** 1917–1963; the 35th president of the United States, from 1961 to 1963: he was assassinated

Ken·tuck·y (kən tuk'ē) a state in the eastern central part of the U.S.: *abbreviated* **Ky., KY**

key·board (kē'bôrd) *n.* the row or rows of keys of a piano, organ, typewriter, etc.

kin·dling (kind'liŋ) *n.* bits of dry wood or the like, for starting a fire

kitch·en (kich'ən) *n.* a room or place for preparing and cooking food

kneel (nēl) *v.* to rest on a knee or knees [Some people *kneel* when they pray.] —**knelt** or **kneeled, kneel'ing**

knelt (nelt) *a past tense and past participle of* **kneel**

☆**knick·ers** (nik'ərz) *pl. n.* short, loose trousers gathered in just below the knees

knot·hole (nät'hōl) *n.* a hole in a board or tree trunk where a knot has fallen out

knowl·edge (nä'lij) *n.* 1 the fact or condition of knowing [*Knowledge* of the murder spread through the town.] 2 what is known or learned, as through study or experience [a scientist of great *knowledge*] 3 all that is known by all people

knuck·le (nuk'əl) *n.* a joint of the finger, especially one connecting a finger to the rest of the hand

Ko·re·a (kô rē'ə) a country in eastern Asia, divided into two republics, North Korea and South Korea —**Ko·re'an** *adj., n.*

Ll

lan·guage (laŋ'gwij) *n.* 1 human speech or writing that stands for speech [People communicate by means of *language*.] 2 the speech of a particular nation, group, etc. [the Greek *language*; the Navaho *language*] 3 any means of passing on one's thoughts or feelings to others [sign *language*]

laugh·a·ble (laf'ə bəl) *adj.* causing laughter; funny; ridiculous [a *laughable* costume]

launch (lônch *or* länch) *v.* 1 to throw, hurl, or send off into space [to *launch* a rocket] 2 to cause to slide into the water; set afloat [to *launch* a new ship] —**launched** ◆*n.* the act of launching a ship, spacecraft, etc.

laun·dry (lôn'drē *or* län'drē) *n.* 1 a place where laundering is done 2 clothes, linens, etc. that have been, or are about to be, washed and ironed —*pl.* **laun'dries**

law-a·bid·ing (lô'ə bīd'in *or* lä'ə bīd'iŋ) *adj.* obeying the law [*law-abiding* citizens]

lb. *abbreviation for* **pound** —*pl.* **lbs.**

lec·ture (lek'chər) *n.* 1 a talk on some subject to an audience or class 2 a long or tiresome scolding ◆*v.* 1 to give a lecture 2 to scold —**lec'tured, lec'tur·ing** —**lec'tur·er** *n.*

leg·is·la·tion (lej' is lā'shən) *n.* 1 the act or process of making laws 2 the laws made

lei·sure·ly (lē'zhər lē *or* lezh'ər lē) *adj.* without hurrying; slow [a *leisurely* walk] ◆*adv.* in a slow, unhurried way [We talked *leisurely*.]

light·ning (līt'niŋ) *n.* a flash of light in the sky caused by the passing of electricity from one cloud to another or between a cloud and the earth

lik·a·ble or **like·a·ble** (līk'ə bəl) *adj.* easy to like because pleasing, friendly, etc.

lim·it·ed (lim'it əd) *adj.* 1 having a limit or limits; restricted in some way [This offer is good for a *limited* time only.] ☆2 making only a few stops [a *limited* bus]

lim·ou·sine (lim ə zēn' *or* lim'ə zēn) *n.* 1 a large automobile driven by a chauffeur, who is sometimes separated from the passengers by a glass window ☆2 a buslike sedan used to carry passengers to or from an airport

Lin·coln (liŋ'kən) **Abraham** 1809–1865; 16th president of the United States, from 1861 to 1865: he was assassinated

lis·ten (lis'ən) *v.* to pay attention in order to hear; try to hear [*Listen* to the rain. *Listen* when the counselor speaks.] —**lis'ten·ing** —**lis'ten·er** *n.*

live·li·hood (līv'lē hood') *n.* a means of living, or of supporting oneself [She earns her *livelihood* as a teacher.]

lock·smith (läk'smith) *n.* a person whose work is making or repairing locks and keys

a	ask, fat
ā	ape, date
ä	car, lot
e	elf, ten
ē	even, meet
i	is, hit
ī	ice, fire
ō	open, go
ô	law, horn
oi	oil, point
ōō	look, pull
ōō	ooze, tool
ou	out, crowd
u	up, cut
ʉ	fur, fern
ə	a in ago
	e in agent
	e in father
	i in unity
	o in collect
	u in focus
ch	chin, arch
ŋ	ring, singer
sh	she, dash
th	thin, truth
th	then, father
zh	s in pleasure

lounge (lounj) *v.* to move, sit, or lie in an easy or lazy way; loll —**lounged, loung´ing** ◆*n.* a room with comfortable furniture where people can lounge —**loung´er**

lunch·eon (lun´chən) *n.* a lunch; especially, a formal lunch with others

lus·cious (lush´əs) *adj.* 1 having a delicious taste or smell; full of flavor [a *luscious* steak] 2 very pleasing to see, hear, etc. [the *luscious* sound of violins] —**lus´cious·ly** *adv.*

lux·u·ry (luk´shər ē *or* lug´zhər ē) *n.* 1 the use and enjoyment of the best and most costly things that give one the most comfort and pleasure [a life of *luxury*] 2 anything that gives one such comfort, usually something one does not need for life or health [Jewels are *luxuries*.] —*pl.* **lux´u·ries**

ma·chin·e·ry (mə shēn´ər ē) *n.* 1 machines in general [the *machinery* of a factory] 2 the working parts of a machine [the *machinery* of a printing press] —*pl.* **ma·chin´er·ies**

ma·chin·ist (mə shēn´ist) *n.* 1 a person who is skilled in working with machine tools 2 a person who makes, repairs, or runs machinery

mag·i·cal (maj´i kəl) *adj.* of or like magic —**mag´i·cal·ly** *adv.*

mag·nif·i·cent (mag nif´ə sənt) *adj.* rich, fine, noble, beautiful, etc. in a grand way; splendid [a *magnificent* castle; a *magnificent* idea]

mag·ni·fy (mag´nə fī) *v.* to make look or seem larger or greater than is really so [This lens *magnifies* an object to ten times its size. He *magnified* the seriousness of his illness.] —**mag´ni·fied, mag´ni·fy·ing**

main·stay (mān´stā) *n.* 1 the line that runs forward from the upper part of the mainmast, helping to hold it in place 2 the main or chief support [She was the *mainstay* of her family.]

main·te·nance (mānt´ n əns) *n.* 1 a maintaining or being maintained; upkeep or support [Taxes pay for the *maintenance* of schools.] 2 a means of support; livelihood [a job that barely provides a *maintenance*]

mal·let (mal´ət) *n.* 1 a wooden hammer made with a short handle for use as a tool 2 a wooden hammer made with a long handle for playing croquet or with a long, flexible handle for playing polo

man·age·a·ble (man´ij ə bəl) *adj.* that can be managed, controlled, or done

man·u·fac·tur·er (man´yōō fak´chər ər) *n.* a person or company that manufactures; especially, a factory owner

mar·tial (mär´shəl) *adj.* 1 having to do with war or armies [*martial* music] 2 showing a readiness or eagerness to fight [*martial* spirit]

mas·ter·piece (mas´tər pes) *n.* 1 a thing made or done with very great skill; a great work of art 2 the best thing that a person has ever made or done ["The Divine Comedy" was Dante's *masterpiece*.]

match (mach) *n.* 1 any person or thing equal to or like another in some way [Joan met her *match* in chess when she played Joe.] 2 two or more people or things that go well together [That suit and tie are a good *match*.] 3 a game or contest between two persons or teams [a tennis *match*] ◆*v.* 1 to go well together [Do your shirt and tie *match*?] 2 to make or get something like or equal to [Can you *match* this cloth?] 3 to be equal to [I could never *match* that lawyer in an argument.]

may·on·naise (mā ə nāz´ *or* mā´ə nāz) *n.* a thick, creamy salad dressing made of egg yolks, olive oil, lemon juice or vinegar, and seasoning

mdse. *abbreviation for* **merchandise**

meas·ure (mezh´ər) *v.* 1 to find out the size, amount, or extent of, as by comparing with something else [*Measure* the child's height with a yardstick. How do you *measure* a person's worth?] 2 to set apart or mark off a certain amount or length of [*Measure* out three pounds of sugar.] —**meas´ured, meas´ur·ing** ◆*n.* 1 the size, amount, or extent of something, found out by measuring [The *measure* of the bucket is 15 liters.] 2 a system of measuring [Liquid *measure* is a system of measuring liquids.]

me·chan·ic (mə kan´ik) *n.* a worker skilled in using tools or in making, repairing, and using machinery [an automobile *mechanic*]

med·i·cine (med´ə sən) *n.* 1 any substance used in or on the body to treat disease, lessen pain, heal, etc. 2 the science of treating and preventing disease

mel·low (mel´ō) *adj.* 1 soft, sweet, and juicy from ripeness [a *mellow* apple] 2 having a good flavor from being aged; not bitter [a *mellow* wine] 3 rich, soft, and pure; not harsh [the *mellow* tone of a cello] 4 made gentle and kind by age or experience [a *mellow* teacher]

me·men·to (mə men´tō) *n.* an object kept to remind one of something; souvenir [This toy is a *memento* of my childhood.] —*pl.* **me·men´tos** *or* **me·men´toes**

☆**mem·o·rize** (mem´ər īz) *v.* to fix in one's memory exactly or word for word; learn by heart —**mem´o·rized, mem´o·riz·ing** —**mem´o·ri·za´tion** *n.*

Mex·i·can (mek′si kən) *adj.* of Mexico, its people, their dialect of Spanish, or their culture ➛*n.* a person born or living in Mexico

mgr. *abbreviation for* **manager**

mi·cro·phone (mī′krə fōn) *n.* a device for picking up sound that is to be made stronger, as in a theater, or sent over long distances, as in radio: microphones change sound into electric waves, which go into electron tubes and are changed back into sound by loudspeakers

mid·point (mid′point) *n.* a point in the middle or at the center

mid·sum·mer (mid′sum′ər) *n.* **1** the middle of summer **2** the period around June 21

Mid·west·ern (mid′wes′tərn) *adj.* of, in, or having to do with the Middle West

mil·dew (mil′dōō *or* mil′dyōō) *n.* a fungus that appears as a furry, white coating on plants or on damp, warm paper, cloth, etc. ➛*v.* to become coated with mildew

mil·lion·aire (mil yə ner′) *n.* a person who has at least a million dollars, pounds, etc.

mi·nor·i·ty (mī nôr′ə tē *or* mi nôr′ə tē) *n.* **1** the smaller part or number; less than half [A *minority* of the Senate voted for the law.] **2** a small group of people of a different race, religion, etc. from the main group of which it is a part —*pl.* **mi·nor′i·ties**

mis·cal·cu·late (mis kal′kyōō lāt′) *v.* to make a mistake in figuring or planning; misjudge [Our manager *miscalculated* the pitcher's strength and we lost the game.]

mis·cel·la·ne·ous (mis′ə lā′nē əs) *adj.* of many different kinds; mixed; varied [A *miscellaneous* collection of objects filled the shelf.]

mis·chief (mis′chif) *n.* **1** harm or damage [Gossip can cause great *mischief.*] **2** action that causes harm, damage, or trouble. **3** a playful trick; prank **4** playful, harmless spirits [a child full of *mischief*]

mis·chie·vous (mis′chə vəs) *adj.* **1** causing some slight harm or annoyance, often in fun; naughty [a *mischievous* act] **2** full of playful tricks; teasing [a *mischievous* child] **3** causing harm or damage; injurious [*mischievous* slander]

mis·pro·nounce (mis prə nouns′) *v.* to pronounce in a wrong way [Some people *mispronounce* "cavalry" as "calvary."] —**mis·pro·nounced′, mis·pro·nounc′ing** —**mis·pro·nun·ci·a·tion** (mis′prə nun′sē ā′shən) *n.*

mis·tle·toe (mis′əl tō) *n.* an evergreen plant with waxy white, poisonous berries, growing as a parasite on certain trees

mis·un·der·stand (mis′un dər stand′) *v.* to understand in a way that is wrong; give a wrong meaning to —**mis·un·der·stood** (mis′un der stōōd′), **mis′under·stand′ing**

mo. *abbreviation for* **month**

mo·bile (mō′bəl *or* mō′bīl *or* mō′bēl) *adj.* that can be moved quickly and easily [a *mobile* army] ➛*n.* (mō′bēl) a kind of sculpture made of flat pieces, rods, etc. that hang balanced from wires so as to move easily in air currents —**mo·bil·i·ty** (mō bil′ə tē)

mod·i·fy (mäd′ə fī) *v.* **1** to make a small or partial change in [Exploration has *modified* our maps of Antarctica.] **2** to make less harsh, strong, etc. [to *modify* a jail term] **3** to limit the meaning of; describe or qualify [In the phrase "old man" the adjective "old" *modifies* the noun "man."] —**mod′i·fied, mod′i·fy·ing** —**mod′i·fi·ca′tion, mod′i·fi′er** *n.*

mois·ten (mois′ən) *v.* to make or become moist

mon·o·gram (män′ə gram) *n.* initials, especially of a person's name, put together in a design and used on clothing, stationery, and so on

mon·o·rail (män′ə rāl′) *n.* **1** a railway having cars that run on a single rail, or track, and are hung from it or balanced on it **2** this track

mon·o·syl·la·ble (män′ō sil′ ə bəl) *n.* a word of one syllable, as "he" or "thought" —**mon·o·syl·lab·ic** (man′ e si lab′ik) *adj.*

mo·not·o·nous (mə nät′n əs) *adj.* **1** going on and on in the same tone [a *monotonous* voice] **2** having little or no change; boring or tiresome [a *monotonous* trip; *monotonous* work]

mon·soon (män sōōn′) *n.* **1** a wind of the Indian Ocean and southern Asia, blowing from the southwest from April to October, and from the northeast the rest of the year **2** the rainy season, when this wind blows from the southwest

mor·al (môr′əl) *adj.* **1** having to do with right and wrong in conduct [Cheating is a *moral* issue.] **2** good or right according to ideas of being decent and respectable [She was a *moral* woman all her life.] ➛*n.* **1** a lesson about what is right and wrong, taught by a story or event [the *moral* of a fable] **2 morals,** *pl.* standards of behavior having to do with right and wrong; ethics

mos·qui·to (mə skēt′ō) *n.* a small insect with two wings: the female bites animals to suck their blood: some mosquitoes spread diseases, as malaria —*pl.* **mos·qui′toes** *or* **mos·qui′tos**

mouth·ful (mouth′fool) *n.* **1** as much as the mouth can hold **2** as much as is usually put into the mouth at one time —*pl.* **mouth′fuls**

a	ask, fat
ā	ape, date
ä	car, lot
e	elf, ten
ē	even, meet
i	is, hit
ī	ice, fire
ō	open, go
ô	law, horn
oi	oil, point
͜oo	look, pull
͞oo	ooze, tool
ou	out, crowd
u	up, cut
ʉ	fur, fern
ə	a in ago
	e in agent
	e in father
	i in unity
	o in collect
	u in focus
ch	chin, arch
ŋ	ring, singer
sh	she, dash
th	thin, truth
th	then, father
zh	s in pleasure

mud·dy (mud′ē) *adj.* full of mud or smeared with mud [a *muddy* yard; *muddy* boots]
—**mud′di·er, mud′di·est** ◆*v.* to make or become muddy —**mud′died, mud′dy·ing**

mu·ral (myoor′əl) *n.* a picture or photograph, especially a large one, painted or put on a wall ◆*adj.* of or on a wall [a *mural* painting]

mus·cle (mus′əl) *n.* **1** the tissue in an animal's body that makes up the fleshy parts: muscle can be stretched or tightened to move the parts of the body **2** any single part or band of this tissue [The biceps is a *muscle* in the upper arm.] **3** strength that comes from muscles that are developed; brawn

my·thol·o·gy (mi thäl′ə jē) *n.* **1** myths as a group; especially, all the myths of a certain people [Roman *mythology*]
—*pl.* **my·thol′o·gies 2** the study of myths
—**myth·o·log·i·cal** (mith′ e läj′i kəl) *adj.*

nar·rate (ner′āt) *v.* to give the story of in writing or speech; tell what has happened [Our guest *narrated* her adventures.]
—**nar′rat·ed, nar′rat·ing** —**nar′ra·tor** *n.*

na·tion (nā′shən) *n.* **1** a group of people living together in a certain region under the same government; state; country [the Swiss *nation*] **2** a group of people sharing the same history, language, customs, etc. [the Iroquois *nation*]

nau·se·a (nô′zhə *or* nä′zhə *or* nô′zhē ə) *n.* a feeling of sickness in the stomach that makes a person want to vomit

ne·go·ti·ate (ni gō′shē āt′) *v.* to talk over a problem, business deal, dispute, etc. in the hope of reaching an agreement [to *negotiate* a contract] —**ne·go′ti·at·ed, ne·go′ti·at·ing** —**ne·go′ti·a′tion, ne·go′ti·a′tor** *n.*

neigh·bor·ly (nā′bər lē) *adj.* friendly, kind, helpful, etc. [It was very *neighborly* of you to shovel the snow from my walk.]
—**neigh′bor·li·ness** *n.*

niece (nēs) *n.* **1** the daughter of one's brother or sister **2** the daughter of one's brother-in-law or sister-in-law

No. *or* **no.** *abbreviation for* **number**

nois·y (noi′zē) *adj.* **1** making noise [a *noisy* bell] **2** full of noise [a *noisy* theater] —**nois′i·er, nois′i·est**
—**nois′i·ly** *adv.* —**nois′i·ness** *n.*

no·tice·a·ble (nōt′is ə bəl) *adj.* easily seen; likely to be noticed; remarkable [*noticeable* improvement] —**no′tice·a·bly** *adv.*

nour·ish (nur′ish) *v.* to feed; provide with the things needed for life and growth [Water and sunlight *nourished* the plants.]
—**nour′ish·ing** *adj.*

nui·sance (noo′səns *or* nyoo′səns) *n.* an act, thing, or person that causes trouble or bother [It's such a *nuisance* to put on boots just to go next door.]

numb (num) *adj.* not able to feel, or feeling very little [*numb* with cold] ◆*v.* to make numb [The cold *numbed* his toes.]

nu·tri·tion (noo trish′ən *or* nyoo trish′ən) *n.* **1** the process by which an animal or plant takes in food and uses it in living and growing **2** food; nourishment **3** the study of the foods people should eat for health and well-being —**nu·tri′tion·al** *adj.*

Oo

o·boe (ō′bō) *n.* a woodwind instrument whose mouthpiece has a double reed
—**o′bo·ist**

ob·serv·a·to·ry (äb zurv′ə tôr′ ē) *n.* a building with telescopes and other equipment in it for studying the stars, weather conditions, etc. —*pl.* **ob·serv′a·to·ries**

ob·serve (əb zurv′) *v.* **1** to see, watch, or notice [I *observed* that the child was smiling.] **2** to examine and study carefully [to *observe* an experiment] —**ob·served′, ob·serv′ing** —**ob·serv′er** *n.*

ob·vi·ous (äb′vē əs) *adj.* easy to see or understand; plain; clear [an *obvious* rust stain; an *obvious* danger] —**ob′vi·ous·ly** *adv.* —**ob′vi·ous·ness** *n.*

oc·ca·sion (ə kā′zhən) *n.* **1** a suitable time; good chance; opportunity [Did you have *occasion* to visit with them?] **2** a particular time [We've met on several *occasions*.] **3** a special time or happening [Independence Day is an *occasion* to celebrate.]

oc·cu·py (äk′yoo pī′) *v.* **1** to live in [to *occupy* a house] **2** to take up; fill [The store *occupies* the entire building.] **3** to keep busy; employ [Many activities *occupy* his time.] —**oc′cu·pied, oc′cu·py·ing**

oc·cur (ə kur′) *v.* **1** to come into one's mind [The idea never *occurred* to me.] **2** to happen; take place [That event *occurred* years ago.] —**oc·curred′, oc·cur′ring**

oc·ta·gon (äk′tə gän) *n.* a flat figure having eight angles and eight sides

of·fi·cer (ôf′i sər *or* äf′i sər) *n.* **1** a person holding some office, as in a business, club, or government **2** a member of a police force **3** a person who commands others in an army, navy, etc. [Generals and lieutenants are commissioned *officers*.]

of·fi·cial (ə fish′əl) *n.* **1** a person who holds an office, especially in government ☆**2** a person who sees to it that the rules are followed in a game, as a referee or umpire ►*adj.* **1** of or having to do with an office [an *official* record; *official* duties] **2** coming from a person who has authority [an *official* request] **3** fit for an important officer; formal [an *official* welcome] —**of·fi′cial·ly** *adv.*

oint·ment (oint′mənt) *n.* an oily cream rubbed on the skin to heal it or make it soft and smooth; salve

or·gan·ize (ôr′gə niz) *v.* to arrange or place according to a system [The library books are *organized* according to their subjects.] —**or′gan·ized, or′gan·iz·ing** —**or′gan·iz′er** *n.*

o·rig·i·nal·i·ty (ə rij′ə nal′ə tē) *n.* the quality or condition of being fresh, new, or creative

or·phan·age (ôr′fən ij) *n.* a home for taking care of a number of orphans

out·ra·geous (out rā′jəs) *adj.* **1** doing great injury or wrong [*outrageous* crimes] **2** so wrong or bad that it hurts or shocks [an *outrageous* lie] —**out·ra′geous·ly** *adv.*

o·ver·due (ō vər dōō′ *or* ō vər dyōō′) *adj.* delayed past the time set for payment, arrival, etc. [an *overdue* bill; a bus long *overdue*]

o·ver·e·mo·tion·al (ō′vər ē mō′shə nəl) *adj.* too full of emotion or strong feeling [an *overemotional* speech]

o·ver·flow (ō vər flō′) *v.* **1** to flow across; flood [Water *overflowed* the streets.] **2** to have its contents flowing over [The sink is *overflowing.*] ►*n.* (ō′vər flō) the act of overflowing

o·ver·grown (ō′vər grōn′) *adj.* **1** covered with foliage or weeds [a lawn that is badly *overgrown*] **2** having grown too large or too fast [an *overgrown* child]

o·ver·joyed (ō vər joid′) *adj.* filled with great joy

o·ver·pro·tect (ō′vər prə tekt′) *v.* to protect more than is necessary or helpful, especially by trying to keep someone from the normal hurts and disappointments of life

o·ver·sen·si·tive (ō′vər sn′sə tiv) *adj.* too quick to feel, notice, or respond to

o·ver·weight (ō′vər wāt′) *n.* more weight than is needed or allowed; extra weight ►*adj.* (ō vər wāt′) weighing more than is normal or proper; too heavy

oys·ter (ois′tər) *n.* a shellfish with a soft body enclosed in two rough shells hinged together: some are used as food, and pearls are formed inside others

oz. abbreviation for **ounce** —*pl.* **oz.** *or* **ozs.**

Pp

pain·ful (pān′fəl) *adj.* causing pain; hurting; unpleasant [a *painful* wound] —**pain′ful·ness** *n.*

pam·phlet (pam′flət) *n.* a thin booklet with a paper cover

pap·ri·ka (pə prē′kə) *n.* a red seasoning made by grinding certain peppers

par·a·chute (per′ə shōōt) *n.* a large cloth device that opens up like an umbrella and is used for slowing down a person or thing dropping from an airplane —**par′a·chut·ist** *n.* ►*v.* to jump with or drop by a parachute —**par′a·chut·ed, par′a·chut·ing**

par·al·lel·o·gram (par′ ə lel′ə gram) *n.* a figure having four sides, with the opposite sides parallel and of equal length

par·ent (per′ənt) *n.* **1** a father or mother **2** any animal or plant as it is related to its offspring —**par′ent·hood**

pa·ren·the·sis (pə ren′thə sis) *n.* **1** a word, phrase, etc. put into a complete sentence as an added note or explanation and set off, as between curved lines, from the rest of the sentence **2** either or both of the curved lines ( ) used to set off such a word, phrase, etc. —*pl.* **pa·ren·the·ses** (pə ren′thə sēz)

par·tial (pär′shəl) *adj.* **1** of or in only a part; not complete or total [a *partial* eclipse of the sun] **2** favoring one person or side more than another; biased [A judge should not be *partial.*] —**par′tial·ly** *adv.*

par·tic·i·pate (pär tis′ə pāt) *v.* to take part with others; have a share [Sue *participated* in the school play.] —**par·tic′i·pat·ed, par·tic′i·pat·ing** —**par·tic′i·pa′tion, par·tic′i·pa′tor** *n.*

pas·sive (pas′iv) *adj.* **1** not active, but acted upon [Spectators have a *passive* interest in sports.] **2** not resisting; yielding; submissive [The *passive* child did as he was told.] —**pas′sive·ly** *adv.*

pa·tience (pā′shəns) *n.* the fact of being patient or the ability to be patient

pa·tient (pā′shənt) *adj.* able to put up with pain, trouble, delay, boredom, etc. without complaining [The *patient* children waited in line for the theater to open.] ►*n.* a person under the care of a doctor —**pa′tient·ly** *adv.*

☆**pa·ti·o** (pat′ē ō *or* pät′ē ō) *n.* **1** in Spain and Spanish America, a courtyard around which a house is built **2** a paved area near a house, with chairs, tables, etc. for outdoor lounging, dining, etc. —*pl.* **pa′ti·os**

pa·trol (pə trōl′) *v.* to make regular trips around a place in order to guard it [The watchman *patrolled* the area all night.] —**pa·trolled′, pa·trol′ling** *n.* **1** the act of patrolling **2** a person or group that patrols

a	ask, fat
ā	ape, date
ä	car, lot
e	elf, ten
ē	even, meet
i	is, hit
ī	ice, fire
ō	open, go
ô	law, horn
oi	oil, point
ɷ	look, pull
ōō	ooze, tool
ou	out, crowd
u	up, cut
ʉ	fur, fern
ə	a in ago
	e in agent
	e in father
	i in unity
	o in collect
	u in focus
ch	chin, arch
ŋ	ring, singer
sh	she, dash
th	thin, truth
th	then, father
zh	s in pleasure

pause (pôz *or* päz) *n.* a short stop, as in speaking or working ◆*v.* to make a pause; stop for a short time [He *paused* to catch his breath.] —**paused, paus´ing**

pave (pāv) *v.* to cover the surface of a road, walk, etc., as with concrete or asphalt —**paved, pav´ing** —**pave the way,** to make the way ready for something; prepare

per·ceive (pər sēv´) *v.* **1** to become aware of through one of the senses, especially through seeing [to *perceive* the difference between two shades of red] **2** to take in through the mind [I quickly *perceived* the joke.] —**per·ceived´, per·ceiv´ing**

per·cep·tion (pər sep´shən) *n.* **1** the act of perceiving or the ability to perceive [Jan's *perception* of color is poor.] **2** knowledge or understanding got by perceiving [She has a clear *perception* of her duty.]

per·pen·dic·u·lar (pur´ pən dik´yoo lər) *adj.* **1** at right angles [The wall should be *perpendicular* to the floor.] **2** straight up and down; exactly upright [a *perpendicular* flagpole ◆*n.* a line that is at right angles to the horizon, or to another line or plane [The Leaning Tower of Pisa leans away from the *perpendicular.*]

per·son·al (pur´sə nəl) *adj.* of one's own; private; individual [a *personal* opinion; a *personal* secretary]

per·son·nel (pur´sə nel´) *n.* persons employed in any work, service, etc. [office *personnel*]

per·spec·tive (pər spek´tiv) *n.* **1** the way things look from a given point according to their size, shape, distance, etc. [*Perspective* makes things far away look small.] **2** the art of picturing things so that they seem close or far away, big or small, etc., just as they look to the eye when viewed from a given point **3** a certain point of view in understanding or judging things or happenings, especially one that shows them in their true relations to one another [Working in a factory will give you a new *perspective* on labor problems.]

pew·ter (pyoot´ər) *n.* **1** a grayish alloy of tin with lead, brass, or copper **2** things made of pewter, especially dishes, tableware, etc. ◆*adj.* made of pewter

phe·nom·e·non (fə näm´ə nän) *n.* **1** any fact, condition, or happening that can be seen, heard, and described in a scientific way, such as an eclipse **2** an unusual or remarkable event or thing [Rain is a *phenomenon* in the desert.] —*pl.* **phe·nom·e·na** (fə näm´ə nə) or (for sense 2 usually) **phe·nom·e·nons**

pho·to·graph (fōt´ə graf) *n.* a picture made with a camera ◆*v.* **1** to take a photograph of **2** to look a certain way in photographs [She *photographs* taller than she is.] —**pho·to·graphed**

phrase (frāz) *n.* a group of words that is not a complete sentence, but that gives a single idea, usually as a separate part of a sentence ["Drinking fresh milk," "with meals," and "to be healthy" are *phrases.*] ◆*v.* to say or write in a certain way [He *phrased* his answer carefully.] —**phrased, phras´ing**

phy·si·cian (fi zish´ən) *n.* a doctor of medicine, especially one who is not mainly a surgeon

pic·co·lo (pik´ə lō) *n.* a small flute that sounds notes an octave higher than an ordinary flute does —*pl.* **pic´co·los**

pierce (pirs) *v.* **1** to pass into or through; penetrate [The needle *pierced* her finger. A light *pierced* the darkness.] **2** to make a hole through; perforate; bore [to *pierce* one's ears for earrings] **3** to make a sharp sound through [A shriek *pierced* the air.] —**pierced, pierc´ing**

pig·ment (pig´mənt) *n.* **1** coloring matter, usually a powder, mixed with oil, water, etc. to make paints **2** the matter in the cells and tissues that gives color to plants and animals

pi·ta (pē´tə) *n.* a round, flat bread of the Middle East: it can be split open to form a pocket for a filling of meat, vegetables, etc.

☆**piz·za** (pēt´sə) *n.* an Italian dish made by baking a thin layer of dough covered with tomatoes, spices, cheese, etc.

pkg. *abbreviation for* **package** *or* **packages**

plain·tiff (plān´tif) *n.* the person who starts a suit against another in a court of law

plan·et (plan´ət) *n.* any of the large heavenly bodies that revolve around the sun and shine as they reflect the sun's light: the planets, in their order from the sun, are Mercury, Venus, Earth, Mars, Jupiter, Saturn, Uranus, Neptune, and Pluto —**plan·e·tar·y** (plan´ə ter´ē) *adj.*

plaque (plak) *n.* **1** a thin, flat piece of metal, wood, etc. with decoration or lettering on it **2** a thin film that forms on the teeth and hardens into tartar if not removed

play·wright (plā´rīt) *n.* a person who writes plays; dramatist

pledge (plej) *n.* **1** a promise or agreement [the *pledge* of allegiance to the flag] **2** something promised, especially money to be given as to a charity ◆*v.* **1** to promise to give [to *pledge* $100 to a building fund] **2** to bind by a promise [He is *pledged* to marry her.] —**pledged, pledg´ing**

plumb·er (plum´ər) *n.* a person whose work is putting in and repairing the pipes and fixtures of water and gas systems in a building

pol·y·gon (päl´i gän´) *n.* a flat, closed figure made up of straight lines, especially one having more than four angles and sides

pon·cho (pän´chō) *n.* a cloak like a blanket with a hole in the middle for the head: it is worn as a raincoat, etc., originally in South America —*pl.* **pon´chos**

por·trait (pôr′trit) *n.* a drawing, painting, or photograph of a person, especially of the face

por·tray (pôr trā′) *v.* 1 to make a picture of, as in a painting 2 to make a picture in words; describe [The writer *portrays* life in New York.] 3 to play the part of in a play, movie, etc. [The actress *portrayed* a scientist.] —**por·trayed′**

po·si·tion (pə zish′ən) *n.* 1 the way in which a person or thing is placed or arranged [a sitting *position*] 2 the place where a person or thing is; location [The ship radioed its *position*.] 3 a job or office; post [She has a *position* with the city government.] ◆*v.* to put in a certain position [They *positioned* themselves around the house.]

post·script (pōst′skript) *n.* a note added below the signature of a letter

post·war (pōst′wôr′) *adj.* after the war

po·ten·tial (po ten′shel) *adj.* that can be, but is not yet; possible [a *potential* leader; a *potential* source of trouble] ◆*n.* power or skill that may be developed [a baseball team with *potential*] —**po·ten′tial·ly** *adv.*

poul·try (pōl′trē) *n.* fowl raised for food; chickens, turkeys, ducks, geese, etc.

prac·ti·cal (prak′ti kəl) *adj.* 1 that can be put to use; useful and sensible [a *practical* idea; *practical* shoes] 2 dealing with things in a sensible and realistic way [Wouldn't it be more *practical* to paint it yourself than pay to have it painted?]

praise (prāz) *v.* 1 to say good things about; give a good opinion of [to *praise* someone's work] 2 to worship, as in song [to *praise* God] —**praised, prais′ing** ◆*n.* a praising or being praised; words that show approval

praise·wor·thy (prāz′wur′thē) *adj.* deserving praise; that should be admired

pre·cau·tion (prē kô′shən *or* prē kä′shən) *n.* care taken ahead of time, as against danger, failure, etc. [She took the *precaution* of locking the door before she left.] —**pre·cau′tion·ar′y** *adj.*

pre·cede (pre sed′) *v.* to go or come before in time, order, or rank [She *preceded* him into the room.]

pre·dict (prē dikt′) *v.* to tell what one thinks will happen in the future [I *predict* that you will win.] —**pre·dict′ed** —**pre·dict′a·ble** *adj.*

pre·fer (prē fur′) *v.* to like better; choose first [He *prefers* baseball to football] —**pre·ferred′, pre·fer′ring**

pre·lude (prel′yood *or* prā′lood) *n.* a part that comes before or leads up to what follows [The strong wind was a *prelude* to the thunderstorm.]

Pres. *abbreviation for* **President**

pre·scrip·tion (prē skrip′shən) *n.* 1 an order or direction 2 a doctor's written instructions telling how to prepare and use a medicine; also, a medicine made by following such instructions

pre·sume (prē zoom′ *or* prē zyoom′) *v.* 1 to be so bold as to; dare [I wouldn't *presume* to tell you what to do.] 2 to take for granted; suppose [I *presume* you know what you are doing.] —**pre·sumed′, pre·sum′ing**

☆**pret·zel** (pret′s'l) *n.* a slender roll of dough, usually twisted in a knot, sprinkled with salt, and baked until hard

pre·vent (prē vent′) *v.* 1 to stop or hinder [A storm *prevented* us from going.] 2 to keep from happening [Careful driving *prevents* accidents.] —**pre·vent′ed** —**pre·vent′a·ble** *or* **pre·vent′i·ble** *adj.*

pre·vi·ous (prē′vē əs) *adj.* happening before in time or order; earlier [at a *previous* meeting; on the *previous* page] —**pre′vi·ous·ly** *adv.*

prin·ci·pal (prin′sə pəl) *adj.* most important; chief; main [the *principal* crop of a State] ◆*n.* the head of a school

prin·ci·ple (prin′sə pəl) *n.* 1 a rule, truth, etc. upon which others are based [the basic *principles* of law] 2 a rule used in deciding how to behave [It is against her *principles* to lie.]

pro·ceed (prō sēd′) *v.* 1 to go on, especially after stopping for a while [After eating, we *proceeded* to the next town.] 2 to begin and go on doing something [I *proceeded* to build a fire.] 3 to move along or go on [Things *proceeded* smoothly.]

proc·ess (prä′ses) *n.* 1 a series of changes by which something develops [the *process* of growth in a plant] 2 a method of making or doing something, in which there are a number of steps [the refining *process* used in making gasoline from crude oil] 3 the act of doing something, or the time during which something is done [I was in the *process* of writing a report when you called.] ◆*v.* to prepare by a special process [to *process* cheese] —**proc′essed**

pro·duce (prə doos′ *or* prə dyoos′) *v.* 1 to bring forth; bear; yield [trees *producing* apples; a well that *produces* oil] 2 to make or manufacture [a company that *produces* bicycles] —**pro·duced′, pro·duc′ing** ◆*n.* (prō′doos) something that is produced, especially fruits and vegetables for marketing —**pro·duc′er**

pro·found (prō found′) *adj.* 1 showing great knowledge, or thought [the *profound* remarks of the judge] 2 deeply felt; intense [*profound* grief] 3 thorough [*profound* changes]

prog·ress (präg′res) *n.* 1 a moving forward [the boat's slow *progress* down the river] 2 a developing or improving [She shows *progress* in learning French.] ◆*v.* (prō gres′) 1 to move forward; go ahead 2 to develop or improve; advance [Science has helped us to *progress*.]

pro·jec·tor (prə jek′tər) *n.* a machine for projecting pictures or movies on a screen

a	ask, fat
ā	ape, date
ä	car, lot
e	elf, ten
ē	even, meet
i	is, hit
ī	ice, fire
ō	open, go
ô	law, horn
oi	oil, point
oo	look, pull
ōō	ooze, tool
ou	out, crowd
u	up, cut
ʉ	fur, fern
ə	a in ago
	e in agent
	e in father
	i in unity
	o in collect
	u in focus
ch	chin, arch
ŋ	ring, singer
sh	she, dash
th	thin, truth
th	then, father
zh	s in pleasure

prompt (prămpt) *adj.* **1** quick in doing what should be done; on time [He is *prompt* in paying his bills.] **2** done, spoken, etc. without waiting [We would like a *prompt* reply.] ►*v.* **1** to urge or stir into action [Tyranny *prompted* them to revolt.] **2** to remind of something that has been forgotten [to *prompt* an actor when a line has been forgotten] —**prompt′ly** *adv.* —**prompt′ness** *n.*

pro·noun (prō′noun) *n.* a word used in the place of a noun: *I, us, you, they, he, her, it* are some pronouns

pro·nounce (prə nouns′) *v.* **1** to say or make the sounds of [How do you *pronounce* "leisure"?] **2** to say or declare in an official or serious way [I now *pronounce* you husband and wife.] —**pro·nounced′, pro·nounc′ing**

pro·pel (prə pel′) *v.* to push or drive forward [Some rockets are *propelled* by liquid fuel.] —**pro·pelled′, pro·pel′ling**

pros·e·cute (präs′ə kyo͞ot) *v.* to put on trial in a court of law on charges of crime or wrongdoing —**pros′e·cut·ed, pros′e·cut·ing**

pros·e·cu·tor (präs′ə kyo͞ot′ər) *n.* a person who prosecutes; especially, a lawyer who works for the state in prosecuting persons charged with crime

pro·te·in (prō′tēn) *n.* a substance containing nitrogen and other elements, found in all living things and in such foods as cheese, meat, eggs, beans, etc.: it is a necessary part of an animal's diet

pro·vi·sion (prō vizh′ən) *n.* **1** a providing or supplying **2** something provided or arrangements made for the future [Her savings are a *provision* for her old age.] **3 provisions**, *pl.* a supply or stock of food

pro·voke (prō vōk′) *v.* **1** to excite to some action or feeling [to *provoke* a fight] **2** to annoy or make angry [It *provoked* me to see litter on the lawn.] **3** to stir up [to *provoke* interest]

pt. *abbreviation for* part, pint, point —*pl.* **pts.**

pur·pose (pur′pəs) *n.* **1** what one plans to get or do; aim; goal [I came for the *purpose* of speaking to you.] **2** the reason or use for something [a room with no *purpose*] —**pur′pose·ful, pur′pose·less** *adj.*

pur·sue (pər so͞o′ *or* pər syo͞o′) *v.* **1** to follow in order to catch or catch up to [to *pursue* a runaway horse] **2** to carry out or follow; go on with [She is *pursuing* a career in acting.] **3** to try to find; seek [to *pursue* knowledge] —**pur·sued′, pur·su′ing** —**pur·su′er** *n.*

Qq

qt. *abbreviation for* quart *or* quarts

quad·ri·lat·er·al (kwäd′rə lat′ər əl) *adj.* having four sides ►*n.* a flat figure with four sides and four angles

qual·i·fy (kwôl′ə fī *or* kwä′lə fī) *v.* to make or be fit or suitable, as for some work or activity [Your training *qualifies* you for the job. Does he *qualify* for the team?] —**qual′i·fied, qual′i·fy·ing**

qual·i·ty (kwôl′ə tē *or* kwä′lə tē) *n.* **1** any of the features that make a thing what it is; characteristic [Coldness is one *quality* of ice cream.] **2** degree of excellence [a poor quality of paper] —*pl.* **qual′i·ties**

quan·ti·ty (kwänt′ə tē) *n.* **1** an amount or portion [large *quantities* of food] **2** a large amount [The factory makes toys in *quantity*.] —*pl.* **quan′ti·ties**

ques·tion·naire (kwes chən ner′) *n.* a written or printed list of questions used in gathering information from people

quilt (kwilt) *n.* a covering for a bed, made of two layers of cloth filled with down, wool, etc. and stitched together in lines or patterns to keep the filling in place ►*v.* **1** to make in the form of a quilt [a *quilted* potholder] ☆**2** to make quilts —**quilt′ed**

quiz (kwiz) *n.* a short test given to find out how much one has learned —*pl.* **quiz′zes** ►*v.* **1** to ask questions of [The police *quizzed* the suspect.] **2** to test the knowledge of with a quiz [The teacher *quizzed* the class.] —**quizzed, quiz′zing**

quo·ta·tion (kwō tā′shən) *n.* **1** the act of quoting **2** the words or section quoted [Sermons often have *quotations* from the Bible.]

quo·tient (kwō′shənt) *n.* the number got by dividing one number into another [In $32 \div 8 = 4$, the number 4 is the *quotient*.]

Rr

ra·di·ance (rā′dē əns) *n.* the quality or condition of being radiant; brightness

re·al·ize (rē′ə līz) *v.* to understand fully [I *realize* that good marks depend upon careful work.] —**re′al·ized, re′al·iz·ing** —**re′al·i·za′tion** *n.*

reas·on·a·ble (rē′zən ə bəl) *adj.* **1** using or showing reason; sensible [a *reasonable* person; a *reasonable* decision] **2** not too high or too low; fair [a *reasonable* price; a *reasonable* salary] —**rea′son·a·bly** *adv.*

re·ceipt (rē sēt′) *n.* **1** the act of receiving [We are in *receipt* of your letter.] **2** a written or printed statement that something has been received [My landlord gave me a *receipt* when I paid my rent.]

re·cent (rē′sənt) *adj.* of a time just before now; made or happening a short time ago [*recent* news] —**re′cent·ly** *adv.*

rec·i·pe (res′ə pē) *n.* a list of ingredients and directions for making something to eat or drink [a *recipe* for cookies]

re·cruit (rē krōōt′) *n.* a person who has recently joined an organization, group, or, especially, the armed forces ➛*v.* **1** to enlist new members in [to *recruit* an army] **2** to get to join [Our nature club *recruited* six new members.]

re·fer (rē fur′) *v.* **1** to speak of or call attention; mention [You seldom *refer* to your injury.] **2** to go for facts, help, etc. [Columbus had no accurate maps to *refer* to.] **3** to tell to go to a certain person or place for help, service, information, etc. [Our neighbor *referred* me to a good doctor.] —**re·ferred′, re·fer′ring**

re·frig·er·a·tor (rē frij′ər āt′ ər) *n.* a box or room in which the air is kept cool to keep food, etc. from spoiling

reg·u·la·tion (reg yə lā′shən) *n.* **1** the act of regulating or the condition of being regulated [the *regulation* of the sale of alcohol] **2** a rule or law that regulates or controls [safety *regulations*]

re·hearse (rē hurs′) *v.* **1** to go through a play, speech, etc. for practice, before giving it in public **2** to repeat in detail [They *rehearsed* all their troubles to me.] —**re·hearsed′, re·hears′ing** —**re·hears′al** *n.*

reign (rān) *n.* the rule of a king, queen, emperor, etc.; also, the time of ruling [laws made during the *reign* of Victoria] ➛*v.* to rule as a king, queen, etc. [Henry VIII *reigned* for 38 years.] —**reigned**

rein·deer (rān′dir) *n.* a large deer found in northern regions, where it is tamed and used for work or as food: both the male and female have antlers —*pl.* **rein′deer**

re·joice (rē jois′) *v.* to be or make glad or happy [We *rejoiced* at the news.] **re·joiced′, re·joic′ing** —**re·joic′ing** *n.*

re·late (rē lāt′) *v.* **1** to tell about; give an account of [*Relate* to us what you did.] **2** to connect in thought or meaning; show a relation between [to *relate* one idea to another] —**re·lat′ed, re·lat′ing**

re·lease (rē lēs′) *v.* to set free or relieve [*Release* the bird from the cage.] ➛*n.* the act of setting someone or something free [a *release* from prison]

re·li·a·ble (rē lī′ə bəl) *adj.* that can be trusted; dependable [This barometer gives a *reliable* weather forecast.] —**re·li·a·bil·i·ty** (ri lī′ə bil′ə tē) *n.* —**re·li′a·bly** *adv.*

re·lieve (rē lēv′) *v.* **1** to free from pain, worry, etc. [We were *relieved* when the danger passed.] **2** to set free from duty or work by replacing [The guard is *relieved* every four hours.] —**re·lieved′, re·liev′ing**

re·main·der (rē mān′dər) *n.* the part, number, etc. left over [I sold some of my books and gave the *remainder* to the library. When 3 is subtracted from 10, the *remainder* is 7.]

re·mark·a·ble (rē märk′ə bəl) *adj.* worth noticing because it is very unusual [the *remarkable* strength of Hercules] —**re·mark′a·bly** *adv.*

rem·e·dy (rem′ə dē) *n.* **1** a medicine or treatment that cures, heals, or relieves [a *remedy* for sunburn] **2** anything that corrects a wrong or helps make things better [a *remedy* for poor education] —*pl.* **rem′e·dies** ➛*v.* to cure, correct, make better, etc. [Some money would *remedy* her situation.] —**rem′e·died, rem′e·dy·ing**

re·peat·ed (ri pēt′əd) *adj.* said, made, or done again or often [*repeated* warnings] —**re·peat′ed·ly** *adv.*

re·quire (rē kwīr′) *v.* **1** to be in need of [Most plants *require* sunlight.] **2** to order, command, or insist upon [He *required* us to leave.] —**re·quired′, re·quir′ing**

re·search (rē′surch′ *or* rē surch′) *n.* careful, patient study in order to find out facts and principles about some subject [to carry on *research* into the causes of cancer] ➛*v.* to do research

re·sem·ble (rē zem′bəl) *v.* to be or look like [Rabbits *resemble* hares but are smaller.] —**re·sem′bled, re·sem′bling**

re·sign (rē zīn′) *v.* to give up one's office, position, membership, etc. [We *resigned* from the club.] —**re·signed′**

re·sist·ance (rē zis′təns) *n.* **1** the act of resisting **2** the power to resist or withstand [Her *resistance* to colds is low.] **3** the opposing of one force or thing to another [the fabric's *resistance* to wear]

re·solve (rē zälv′ *or* rē zôlv′) *v.* **1** to decide; make up one's own mind [I *resolved* to help them.] **2** to make clear; solve or explain [to *resolve* a problem] ➛*n.* firm purpose or determination [her *resolve* to be successful]

re·sound (rē zound′) *v.* **1** to echo or be filled with sound [The hall *resounded* with music.] **2** to make a loud, echoing sound; to be echoed [His laughter *resounded* throughout the cave.] —**re·sound′ing**

re·trieve (rē trēv′) *v.* **1** to get back; recover [to *retrieve* a kite from a tree] **2** to find and bring back [The spaniel *retrieved* the wounded duck.] —**re·trieved′, re·triev′ing**

re·veal (rē vēl′) *v.* **1** to make known what was hidden or secret [The map *revealed* the spot where the treasure was buried.] **2** to show [She took off her hat, *revealing* her golden hair.] —**re·vealed′**

a	ask, fat
ā	ape, date
ä	car, lot
e	elf, ten
ē	even, meet
i	is, hit
ī	ice, fire
ō	open, go
ô	law, horn
oi	oil, point
oo	look, pull
ōō	ooze, tool
ou	out, crowd
u	up, cut
u	fur, fern
ə	a in ago
	e in agent
	e in father
	i in unity
	o in collect
	u in focus
ch	chin, arch
ŋ	ring, singer
sh	she, dash
th	thin, truth
th	then, father
zh	s in pleasure

rev·e·nue (rev′ə noo *or* rev′ə nyoo) *n.*
money got as rent, profit, etc.; income;
especially, the money a government gets
from taxes, duties, etc.

re·vers·i·ble (rē vur′sə bəl) *adj.* that can
be reversed; made so that either side can be
used as the outer side [a *reversible* coat]

☆**ro·de·o** (rō′dē ō) *n.* a contest or show in
which cowboys match their skill in riding
horses, roping and throwing cattle, etc.
—*pl.* **ro′de·os**

Roo·se·velt, Franklin D. (rō′zə velt)
1882–1945; 32d president of the United
States, from 1933 to 1945

Roo·se·velt, Theodore 1858–1919;
26th president of the United States, from
1901 to 1909

rough·en (ruf′ən) *v.* to make or become
rough [to *roughen* a smooth surface with
a coarse file]

row·boat (rō′bōt) *n.* a boat made to
be rowed

Ss

sauce·pan (sôs′pan *or* säs′pan) *n.*
a small metal pot with a long handle,
used for cooking

sax·o·phone (sak′sə fōn) *n.* a woodwind
musical instrument with a curved metal
body: its mouthpiece has a single reed

scald (skôld) *v.* **1** to burn with hot liquid or
steam **2** to use boiling liquid on, as to
kill germs **3** to heat until it almost boils
[to *scald* milk for a custard] —**scald′ing**
◆*n.* a burn caused by scalding

scam·per (skam′pər) *v.* to move quickly
or in a hurry [squirrels *scampering* through
the trees] —**scam′per·ing** ◆*n.* a quick
run or dash

scat·ter (skat′ər) *v.* **1** to throw here and
there; sprinkle [to *scatter* seed over a lawn]
2 to separate and send or go in many
directions; disperse [The wind *scattered* the
leaves. The crowd *scattered* after the game.]
—**scat′tered**

sce·ner·y (sēn′ər ē) *n.* **1** the way a certain
area looks; outdoor views [the *scenery*
along the shore] **2** painted screens,
hangings, etc. used on a stage for a play

sce·nic (sēn′ik) *adj.* **1** having to do with
scenery or landscapes [the *scenic* wonders
of the Rockies] **2** having beautiful scenery
[a *scenic* route along the river]
—**sce′ni·cal·ly** *adv.*

scent (sent) *n.* **1** a smell; odor [the *scent* of
apple blossoms] **2** the sense of smell [Lions
hunt partly by *scent*.] **3** a smell left by an
animal [The dogs lost the fox's *scent* at the
river.] ◆*v.* to smell [Our dog *scented* a cat.]
—**scent′ed**

sched·ule (skej′ool *or* ske′joo əl) *n.*
☆**1** a list of the times at which certain
things are to happen; timetable [a *schedule*
of the sailings of an ocean liner]
☆**2** a timed plan for a project [The work is
ahead of *schedule*.] ◆*v.* **1** to make a
schedule of [to *schedule* one's hours of
work] ☆**2** to plan for a certain time
[to *schedule* a game for 3:00 P.M.]
—**sched′uled, sched′ul·ing**

scheme (skēm) *n.* **1** a plan or system in
which things are carefully put together
[the color *scheme* of a painting] **2** a plan or
program, often a secret or dishonest one
[a *scheme* for getting rich quick] ◆*v.* to
make secret or dishonest plans; to plot
—**schemed, schem′ing**

schol·ar·ship (skä′lər ship) *n.* a gift of
money to help a student continue his
or her education

sci·en·tif·ic (sī′ən tif′ik) *adj.* **1** having to
do with, or used in, science [a *scientific*
study; *scientific* equipment] **2** using the
rules and methods of science [*scientific*
procedure] —**sci′en·tif′i·cal·ly** *adv.*

scis·sors (siz′ərz) *pl. n.* a tool for cutting,
with two blades that are joined so that they
slide over each other when their handles
are moved: *also used with a singular verb:
also called* **pair of scissors**

scour (skour) *v.* to clean by rubbing hard,
especially with something rough or gritty
[The cook *scoured* the greasy frying pan
with soap and steel wool.]

scowl (skoul) *v.* to lower the eyebrows and
the corners of the mouth in showing
displeasure; look angry or irritated
[She *scowled* upon hearing the bad news.]
◆*n.* a scowling look; an angry frown

scratch (skrach) *v.* **1** to mark or cut the
surface of slightly with something sharp
[Thorns *scratched* her legs. Our cat *scratched*
the chair with its claws.] **2** to rub or scrape,
as with the nails, to relieve itching [to
scratch a mosquito bite] **3** to cross out by
drawing lines through [She *scratched* out
what he had written.] —**scratched** ◆*n.*
1 a mark or cut made in a surface by
something sharp **2** a slight wound

scream (skrēm) *v.* **1** to give a loud, shrill
cry, as in fright or pain [They *screamed* as
the roller coaster hurtled downward.]
2 to make a noise like this [The sirens
screamed. We *screamed* with laughter.]
—**scream′ing** ◆*n.* a loud, shrill cry or
sound; shriek

scrimp (skrimp) *v.* to spend or use as little
as possible [to *scrimp* to save money]

sculp·ture (skulp′chər) *n.* **1** the art of
carving wood, chiseling stone, casting or
welding metal, modeling clay or wax, etc.
into statues, figures, or the like **2** a statue,
figure, etc. made in this way ◆*v.* to cut,
chisel, form, etc. in making sculptures
—**sculp′tured, sculp′tur·ing**
—**sculp′tur·al** *adj.*

seal (sēl) *n.* **1** a piece of paper, wax, etc. with a design pressed into it, fixed to an official document to show that it is genuine: such wax designs were once also used to seal letters **2** something that closes or fastens tightly ←*v.* to close or fasten tight [to *seal* cracks with putty; to *seal* a letter] —**seal′er** *n.*

search (surch) *v.* **1** to look over or through in order to find something [We *searched* the house. The police *searched* the thief for a gun.] **2** to try to find [to *search* for an answer] —**search′ing** —**search′er** *n.*

sea·son·al (sē′zən əl) *adj.* of or depending on a season or the seasons [*seasonal* rains; *seasonal* work] —**sea′son·al·ly** *adv.*

se·cu·ri·ty (si kyoor′ə tē) *n.* **1** the condition or feeling of being safe or sure; freedom from danger, fear, doubt, etc. **2** something that protects [Insurance is a *security* against loss.] **3** something given or pledged as a guarantee [A car may be used as *security* for a loan.] **4** securities, *pl.* stocks and bonds —*pl.* **se·cu′ri·ties**

Seine (sān *or* sen) a river in northern France: it flows through Paris into the English Channel

seize (sēz) *v.* to take hold of in a sudden, strong, or eager way; grasp [to *seize* a weapon and fight; to *seize* an opportunity] —**seized, seiz′ing**

se·lec·tion (sə lek′shən) *n.* **1** a selecting or being selected; choice **2** the thing or things chosen; also, things to choose from [a wide *selection* of colors]

sem·i·cir·cle (sem′i sur′kəl) *n.* a half circle —**sem·i·cir·cu·lar** (sem′i sur′kyə lər) *adj.*

sem·i·co·lon (sem′i kō′lən) *n.* a punctuation mark (;) used to show a pause that is shorter than the pause at the end of a sentence, but longer than the pause marked by the comma [The *semicolon* is often used to separate closely related clauses, especially when they contain commas.]

sem·i·fi·nal (sem′i fi′nəl) *n.* a round, match, etc. that comes just before the final one in a contest or tournament —**sem′i·fi′nal·ist**

sem·i·pre·cious (sem′i presh′əs) *adj.* describing gems that are of less value than the precious gems [The garnet is a *semiprecious* gem.]

ses·sion (sesh′ən) *n.* **1** the meeting of a court, legislature, class, etc. to do its work **2** the time during which such a meeting or series goes on **3** a school term or period of study, classes, etc.

sham·poo (sham poo′) *v.* to wash with foamy suds, as hair or a rug —**sham·pooed′, sham·poo′ing** ←*n.* **1** the act of shampooing **2** a special soap, or soaplike product, that makes suds

sharp (shärp) *adj.* **1** having a thin edge for cutting, or a fine point for piercing [a *sharp* knife; a *sharp* needle] **2** easily seen; distinct; clear [a *sharp* contrast] **3** very strong; intense; stinging [a *sharp* wind; *sharp* pain] —**sharp′ly** *adv.* —**sharp′ness** *n.*

sheaf (shēf) *n.* **1** a bunch of cut stalks of wheat, rye, or straw tied up together in a bundle **2** a bundle of things gathered together [a *sheaf* of papers] —*pl.* **sheaves**

shoul·der (shōl′dər) *n.* **1** the part of the body to which an arm or foreleg is connected **2** shoulders, the two shoulders and the part of the back between them

shuf·fle·board (shuf′əl bôrd) *n.* a game in which the players use long sticks to slide disks along a smooth lane, trying to get them on numbered sections

shut·ter (shut′ər) *n.* **1** a cover for a window, usually swinging on hinges **2** a part on a camera that opens and closes in front of the lens to control the light going in

siege (sēj) *n.* the act or an instance of surrounding a city, fort, etc. by an enemy army in an attempt to capture it

sight·see·ing (sīt′sē′iŋ) *n.* the act of going about to see places and things of interest —**sight′se′er**

sig·na·ture (sig′nə chər) *n.* **1** a person's name as he or she has written it **2** a sign in music placed at the beginning of a staff to give the key or the time

☆**sil·ver·ware** (sil′vər wer) *n.* things, especially tableware, made of or plated with silver

sim·mer (sim′ər) *v.* to keep at or just below the boiling point, usually forming tiny bubbles with a murmuring sound [*Simmer* the stew about two hours.]

sim·ple (sim′pəl) *adj.* **1** easy to do or understand [a *simple* task; *simple* directions] **2** without anything added; plain [the *simple* facts; a *simple* dress] —**sim′pler, sim′plest**

sketch (skech) *n.* **1** a simple, rough drawing or design, usually done quickly and with little detail **2** a short outline, giving the main points ←*v.* to make a sketch of; draw sketches —**sketch′ing**

☆**sleigh** (slā) *n.* a carriage with runners instead of wheels, for travel over snow or ice

slop·py (släp′ē) *adj.* not neat or careful; messy [*sloppy* clothes; a *sloppy* piece of work] —**slop′pi·er, slop′pi·est** —**slop′pi·ly** *adv.* —**slop′pi·ness** *n.*

smear (smir) *v.* **1** to cover with something greasy or sticky [to *smear* the actor's face with cold cream] **2** to rub or spread [*Smear* some grease on the axle.] **3** to make a mark or streak that is not wanted on something [He *smeared* the wet paint with his sleeve.] —**smeared** ←*n.* **1** a mark or streak made by smearing **2** the act of smearing or slandering someone

a	ask, fat
ā	ape, date
ä	car, lot
e	elf, ten
ē	even, meet
i	is, hit
ī	ice, fire
ō	open, go
ô	law, horn
oi	oil, point
oo	look, pull
o͞o	ooze, tool
ou	out, crowd
u	up, cut
u	fur, fern
ə	a in ago
	e in agent
	e in father
	i in unity
	o in collect
	u in focus
ch	chin, arch
ŋ	ring, singer
sh	she, dash
th	thin, truth
th	then, father
zh	s in pleasure

smooth (smo͞oth) *adj.* **1** having an even surface, with no bumps or rough spots [as *smooth* as marble; *smooth* water on the lake] **2** even or gentle in movement; not jerky or rough [a *smooth* airplane flight; a *smooth* ride; *smooth* sailing] **3** with no trouble or difficulty [*smooth* progress] —**smooth′er** ◆*v.* **1** to make smooth or even [*Smooth* the board with sandpaper.] **2** to make easy by taking away troubles, difficulties, etc. [She *smoothed* our way by introducing us to the other guests.] ◆*adv.* in a smooth way [The engine is running *smooth* now.] —**smooth′ly** *adv.*

so·cial (sō′shəl) *adj.* **1** of or having to do with human beings as they live together in a group or groups [*social* problems; *social* forces] **2** liking to be with others; sociable [A hermit is not a *social* person.] ◆*n.* a friendly gathering; party [a church *social*] —**so′cial·ly** *adv.*

so·di·um (sō′dē əm) *n.* a soft, silver-white metal that is a chemical element: it is found in nature only in compounds [Salt, baking soda, lye, etc. contain *sodium*]

sof·ten (sôf′ən *or* säf′ən) *v.* to make or become soft or softer —**sof′ten·er** *n.*

so·lar (sō′lər) *adj.* **1** of or having to do with the sun [a *solar* eclipse; *solar* energy] **2** depending on light or energy from the sun [*solar* heating]

sol·dier (sōl′jər) *n.* a person in an army, especially one who is not a commissioned officer ◆*v.* to serve as a soldier —**sol′dier·ly** *adj.*

sol·emn (säl′əm) *adj.* serious; grave; very earnest [a *solemn* face; a *solemn* oath] —**sol′emn·ly** *adv.*

so·lu·tion (sə lo͞o′shən) *n.* **1** the solving of a problem **2** an answer or explanation [to find the *solution* to a mystery]

soothe (so͞oth) *v.* **1** to make quiet or calm by being gentle or friendly [The clerk *soothed* the angry customer with helpful answers.] **2** to take away some of the pain or sorrow of; ease [I hope this lotion will *soothe* your sunburn.] —**soothed, sooth′ing** —**sooth′ing·ly** *adv.*

so·pra·no (sə pran′ō *or* sə prä′nō) *n.* **1** the highest kind of singing voice of women, girls, or young boys **2** a singer with such a voice or an instrument with a range like this —*pl.* **so·pra′nos**

spa·ghet·ti (spə get′ē) *n.* long, thin strings of dried flour paste, cooked by boiling or steaming and served with a sauce

spear·mint (spir′mint) *n.* a common plant of the mint family, used for flavoring

spe·cies (spē′shēz *or* spē′sēz) *n.* a group of plants or animals that are alike in certain ways [The lion and tiger are two different *species* of cat.] —*pl.* **spe′cies**

spec·ta·tor (spek′tāt ər) *n.* a person who watches something without taking part, onlooker [We were *spectators* at the last game of the World Series.]

sports·man (spôrts′mən) *n.* **1** a man who takes part in or is interested in sports **2** a person who plays fair and does not complain about losing or boast about winning —*pl.* **sports′men** —**sports′man·like** *adj.* —**sports′man·ship** *n.*

square (skwer) *n.* **1** a flat figure with four equal sides and four right angles **2** anything shaped like this [Arrange the chairs in a *square*.] ◆*adj.* **1** having the shape of a square **2** forming a right angle [a *square* corner] —**squar′er, squar′est** ◆*v.* to mark off in squares, as a checkerboard —**squared, squar′ing**

squawk (skwôk *or* skäwk) *n.* a loud, harsh cry such as a chicken or parrot makes ◆*v.* to let out a squawk —**squawk′ing** —**squawk′er** *n.*

squeeze (skwēz) *v.* **1** to press hard or force together [*Squeeze* the sponge to get rid of the water.] **2** to get by pressing or by force [to *squeeze* juice from an orange; to *squeeze* money from poor people] —**squeezed, squeez′ing** ◆*n.* a squeezing or being squeezed; hard press —**squeez′er**

stair·way (ster′wā) *or* **stair·case** (ster′kās) *n.* a flight of steps, usually with a handrail

sta·tion·ar·y (stā′shə ner′ē) *adj.* **1** staying in the same place; not moving; fixed [A *stationary* bicycle is pedaled for exercise, but does not move from its base.] **2** not changing in condition or value; not increasing or decreasing [*stationary* prices]

stead·y (sted′ē) *adj.* not changing or letting up; regular [a *steady* gaze; a *steady* worker] —**stead′i·er, stead′i·est** —**stead′ied, stead′y·ing** —**stead′i·ly** *adv.* —**stead′i·ness** *n.*

ster·e·o (ster′ē ō′) *n.* a stereophonic record player, radio, sound system, etc. —*pl.* **ster′e·os′**

stew·ard (sto͞o′ərd *or* styo͞o′ərd) *n.* a person, especially on a ship or airplane, whose work is to look after the passengers' comfort

stiff (stif) *adj.* **1** that does not bend easily; firm [*stiff* cardboard] **2** not able to move easily [*stiff* muscles] —**stiff′ly** *adv.* **stiff′ness** *n.*

stitch (stich) *n.* one complete movement of a needle and thread into and out of the material in sewing —*pl.* **stitch′es** ◆*v.* to sew or fasten with stitches [to *stitch* a seam] —**stitched**

stow·a·way (stō′ə wā) *n.* a person who hides aboard a ship, plane, etc. for a free or secret ride

strain·er (strān′ər) *n.* a thing used for straining, as a sieve, filter, etc.

stretch (strech) *v.* **1** to draw out to full length, to a greater size, to a certain distance, etc.; extend [She *stretched* out on the sofa. Will this material *stretch*? *Stretch* the rope between two trees. The road *stretches* for miles through the hills.] **2** to pull or draw tight; strain [to *stretch* a muscle] —**stretch'es** ➡ *n.* **1** a stretching or being stretched [a *stretch* of the arms] **2** an unbroken space, as of time or land; extent [a *stretch* of two years; a long *stretch* of beach]

strict (strikt) *adj.* **1** keeping to rules in a careful, exact way [a *strict* supervisor] **2** never changing; rigid [a *strict* rule] —**strict'est** —**strict'ly** *adv.* —**strict'ness** *n.*

sub·con·tract (sub'kän'trakt) *n.* a contract in which a company hires a second company to do part of a job that the first company has agreed to complete ➡ *v.* to make a subcontract [to *subcontract* for plumbing and electrical work]

subj. *abbreviation for* **subject, subjunctive**

sub·ma·rine (sub'mə rēn) *n.* a kind of warship that can travel under the surface of water ➡ *adj.* (sub mə rən') that lives, grows, happens, etc. under the surface of the sea [Sponges are *submarine* animals.]

sub·scrip·tion (səb skrip'shən) *n.* **1** the act of subscribing or something that is subscribed **2** an agreement to take and pay for a magazine, theater tickets, etc. for a particular period of time

sub·stan·tial (səb stan'shəl) *adj.* **1** of or having substance; material; real or true [Your fears turned out not to be *substantial*.] **2** strong; solid; firm [The bridge didn't look very *substantial*.] **3** more than average or usual; large [a *substantial* share; a *substantial* meal] **4** wealthy or well-to-do [a *substantial* farmer] —**sub·stan'tial·ly** *adv.*

sub·sti·tute (sub'stə tōōt *or* sub'stə tyōōt) *n.* a person or thing that takes the place of another [He is a *substitute* for the regular teacher.] ➡ *v.* to use as or be a substitute [to *substitute* vinegar for lemon juice; to *substitute* for an injured player] —**sub'sti·tut·ed, sub'sti·tut·ing** —**sub'sti·tu'tion** *n.*

suc·ceed (sək sēd') *v.* **1** to manage to do or be what was planned; do or go well [I *succeeded* in convincing them to come with us.] **2** to come next after; follow [Carter *succeeded* Ford as president.] —**suc·ceed'ed**

suc·cess·ful (sək ses'fəl) *adj.* **1** having success; turning out well [a *successful* meeting] **2** having become rich, famous, etc. [a *successful* architect] —**suc·cess'ful·ly** *adv.*

su·crose (sōō'krōs) *n.* a sugar found in sugarcane, sugar beets, etc.

suf·fi·cient (sə fish'ənt) *adj.* as much as is needed; enough [Do you have *sufficient* supplies to last through the week?] —**suf·fi'cient·ly** *adv.*

suit·a·ble (sōōt'ə bəl) *adj.* right for the purpose; fitting; proper [a *suitable* gift] —**suit'a·bil'i·ty** *n.* —**suit'a·bly** *adv.*

su·per·fi·cial (sōō'pər fish'əl) *adj.* of or on the surface; not deep [a *superficial* cut; a *superficial* likeness] —**su·per·fi·ci·al·i·ty** (sōō'pər fish'ē al'ə tē) *n.* —**su'per·fi'cial·ly** *adv.*

su·per·son·ic (sōō'pər sän'ik) *adj.* **1** of or moving at a speed greater than the speed of sound **2** *another word for* **ultrasonic**

su·per·vise (sōō'pər vīz) *v.* to direct or manage, as a group of workers; be in charge of —**su'per·vised, su'per·vis·ing**

sur·round (sər round') *v.* to form or arrange around on all or nearly all sides; enclose [The police *surrounded* the criminals. The house is *surrounded* with trees.] —**sur·round'ing**

sur·vey (sər vā') *v.* to measure the size, shape, boundaries, etc. of a piece of land by the use of special instruments [to *survey* a farm] ➡ *n.* (sur'vā) **1** a general study covering the main facts or points [The *survey* shows that we need more schools. This book is a *survey* of American poetry.] **2** the act of surveying a piece of land, or a record of this [He was hired to make a *survey* of the lake shore.] —*pl.* **sur'veys**

sur·vey·ing (sər vā'iŋ) *n.* the act, work, or science of one who surveys land

Swede (swēd) *n.* a person born or living in Sweden

Swiss (swis) *adj.* of Switzerland or its people. ➡ *n.* a person born or living in Switzerland —*pl.* **Swiss**

sym·me·try (sim'ə trē) *n.* **1** an arrangement in which the parts on opposite sides of a center line are alike in size, shape, and position [The human body has *symmetry*.] **2** balance or harmony that comes from such an arrangement

☆**syn·the·siz·er** (sin'thə sī zər) *n.* an electronic musical instrument that makes sounds that cannot be made by ordinary instruments

a	ask, fat
ā	ape, date
ä	car, lot
e	elf, ten
ē	even, meet
i	is, hit
ī	ice, fire
ō	open, go
ô	law, horn
oi	oil, point
͝oo	look, pull
͞oo	ooze, tool
ou	out, crowd
u	up, cut
ʉ	fur, fern
ə	a in ago
	e in agent
	e in father
	i in unity
	o in collect
	u in focus
ch	chin, arch
ŋ	ring, singer
sh	she, dash
th	thin, truth
th	then, father
zh	s in pleasure

tab·u·late (tab′yoo lāt′) **v.** to arrange in tables or columns [to *tabulate* numbers] —**tab′u·lat·ed, tab′u·lat·ing** —**tab′u·la′tion, tab′u·la′tor n.**

tam·bou·rine (tam bə rēn′) **n.** a small, shallow drum with only one head and with jingling metal disks in the rim: it is shaken, struck with the hand, etc.

tar·iff (ter′if) **n. 1** a list of taxes on goods imported or, sometimes, on goods exported **2** such a tax or its rate

taught (tôt *or* tät) *past tense and past participle of* **teach**

teach (tēch) **v. 1** to show or help to learn how to do something; train [She *taught* us to skate.] **2** to give lessons to or in [Who *teaches* your class? He *teaches* French.] **3** to make or help to know or understand [The accident *taught* her to be careful.] —**taught, teach′ing** —**teach′a·ble adj.**

tech·ni·cal (tek′ni kəl) **adj. 1** having to do with the useful or industrial arts or skills [A *technical* school has courses in mechanics, welding, etc.] **2** of or used in a particular science, art, profession, etc. [*technical* words; *technical* skill] —**tech′ni·cal·ly adv.**

tech·nique (tek nēk′) **n.** a way of using tools, materials, etc. and following rules in doing something artistic, in carrying out a scientific experiment, etc. [a violinist with good bowing *technique*]

tech·nol·o·gy (tek näl′ə jē) **n. 1** the study of the industrial arts or applied sciences, as engineering, mechanics, etc. **2** science as it is put to use in practical work [medical *technology*] **3** a method or process for dealing with a technical problem —**tech·no·log·i·cal** (tek′nə läj′i k′l) **adj.** —**tech′no·log′i·cal·ly adv.** —**tech·nol′o·gist n.**

tex·tile (teks′tīl *or* teks′təl) **n.** a fabric made by weaving; cloth ◆**adj. 1** having to do with weaving or woven fabrics [He works in the *textile* industry.] **2** woven [Linen is a *textile* fabric.]

tex·ture (teks′chər) **n. 1** the look and feel of a fabric as caused by the arrangement, size, and quality of its threads [Corduroy has a ribbed *texture*.] **2** the general look and feel of any other kind of material; structure; makeup [Stucco has a rough *texture*.] ◆**v.** to cause to have a particular texture —**tex′tured, tex′tur·ing**

the·ol·o·gy (thē äl′ə jē) **n. 1** the study of God and of religious beliefs **2** a system of religious beliefs —**pl.** (for sense **2** only) —**the·ol′o·gies**

the·o·ry (thē′ə rē *or* thir′ē) **n. 1** an explanation of how or why something happens, especially one based on scientific study and reasoning [Albert Einstein's *theory* of relativity] **2** the general principles on which an art or science is based [music *theory*] **3** an idea, opinion, guess, etc. [My *theory* is that the witness lied.] —**pl. the′o·ries**

the·sau·rus (thi sôr′əs *or* thi sī′əs) **n.** a book containing lists of synonyms or related words —**pl. the·sau·ri** (thi sôr′ī) or **the·sau′rus·es**

thick (thik) **adj. 1** great in width or depth from side to side; not thin [a *thick* board] **2** as measured from one side through to the other [a wall ten inches *thick*] —**thick′est** ◆**adv.** in a thick way —**thick′ly**

thief (thēf) **n.** a person who steals, especially secretly —**pl. thieves** (thēvz)

thirst·y (thʉrst′tē) **adj. 1** wanting to drink; feeling thirst [The spicy food made me *thirsty*.] **2** needing water; dry [*thirsty* fields] —**thirst′i·er, thirst′i·est** —**thirst′i·ly adv.** —**thirst′i·ness n.**

this·tle (this′el) **n.** a plant with prickly leaves and flower heads of purple, white, pink, or yellow

thor·ough (thʉr′ō) **adj. 1** complete in every way; with nothing left out, undone, etc. [a *thorough* search; a *thorough* knowledge of the subject] **2** very careful and exact [a *thorough* worker] —**thor′ough·ly adv.**

threw (thrōō) past tense of throw

through (thrōō) **prep. 1** in one side and out the other side of; from end to end of [The nail went *through* the board. We drove *through* the tunnel.] **2** from the beginning to the end of [We stayed in Maine *through* the summer.] ◆**adv. 1** from the beginning to the end [to see a job *through*] **2** in a complete and thorough way; entirely [We were soaked *through* by the rain.] ◆**adj.** finished [Are you *through* with your homework?]

through·out (thrōō out′) **prep.** all the way through; in every part of [The fire spread *throughout* the barn.] ◆**adv.** in every part; everywhere [The walls were painted white *throughout*.]

throw (thrō) **v. 1** to send through the air by a fast motion of the arm; hurl, toss, etc. [to *throw* a ball] **2** to make fall down; upset [to *throw* someone in wrestling] —**threw, thrown, throw′ing** ◆**n.** the act of throwing [The fast *throw* put the runner out at first base.]

tight (tīt) **adj. 1** put together firmly or closely [a *tight* knot] **2** fitting too closely [a *tight* shirt] —**tight′er** —**tight′ly adv.** —**tight′ness n.**

ti·ny (tī′nē) **adj.** very small; minute —**ti′ni·er, ti′ni·est**

tip·toe (tip′tō) **n.** the tip of a toe ◆**v.** to walk on one's tiptoes in a quiet or careful way —**tip′toed, tip′toe·ing**

ti·tle (tīt′l) *n.* **1** the name of a book, chapter, poem, picture, piece of music, etc. **2** a word showing the rank, occupation, etc. of a person ["Baron," Ms.," and "Dr." are *titles.*] **3** a claim or right; especially, a legal right to own something, or proof of such a right [The *title* to the car is in my name.] ◆*v.* to give a title to; name —**ti′tled, ti′tling**

tol·er·ate (täl′ə rāt) *v.* to let something be done or go on without trying to stop it [I won't *tolerate* such talk.] —**tol′er·at·ed, tol′er·at·ing**

tomb·stone (tōōm′stōn) *n.* a stone put on a tomb telling who is buried there; gravestone

tough·en (tuf′ən) *v.* to make or become tough or tougher

trans·ac·tion (tran zak′shən *or* tran sak′shən) *n.* **1** the act or an instance of transacting **2** something transacted [The *transaction* was completed when all parties signed the contract.]

trans·fer (trans fur′ *or* trans′fər) *v.* **1** to move, carry, send, or change from one person or place to another [He *transferred* his notes to another notebook. Jill has *transferred* to a new school.] **2** to move a picture, design, etc. from one surface to another, as by making wet and pressing —**trans·ferred′, trans·fer′ring** ◆*n.* (trans′fər) a thing or person that is transferred [They are *transfers* from another school.] —**trans·fer′a·ble** or **trans·fer′ra·ble** *adj.*

trans·form·er (trans fôr′mər) *n.* **1** a person or thing that transforms **2** a device that changes the voltage of an electric current

☆**tran·sis·tor** (tran zis′tər *or* tran sis′tər) *n.* an electronic device, made up of semiconductor material, that controls the flow of electric current: transistors are small and last a long time

trans·mis·sion (trans mish′ən *or* tranz mish′ən) *n.* **1** the act of transmitting or passing something along [the *transmission* of messages by telegraph]. **2** the part of a car that sends the power from the engine to the wheels

trans·par·ent (trans per′ənt) *adj.* so clear or so fine it can be seen through [*transparent* glass; a *transparent* veil]

trans·por·ta·tion (trans pər tā′shən) *n.* **1** the act of transporting **2** a system or business of transporting things

treas·ur·y (trezh′ər ē) *n.* **1** the money or funds of a country, company, club, etc. **2 Treasury**, the department of a government in charge of issuing money, collecting taxes, etc. **3** a place where money is kept —*pl.* **treas′ur·ies**

tri·an·gu·lar (trī aŋ′gyə lər) *adj.* of or shaped like a triangle; having three corners

tri·col·or (trī′kul′ər) *n.* a flag having three colors, especially the flag of France ◆*adj.* having three colors —**tri′col′ored**

tri·lin·gual (trī liŋ′gwəl) *adj.* **1** of or in three languages [a *trilingual* region] **2** using or able to use three languages, especially with equal or nearly equal ability [a *trilingual* child]

tril·o·gy (tril′ə jē) *n.* a set of three plays, novels, etc. which form a related group, although each is a complete work [Louisa May Alcott's *Little Women*, *Little Men*, and *Jo's Boys* make up a *trilogy.*] —*pl.* **tril′o·gies**

tri·ple (trip′əl) *adj.* **1** made up of three [A *triple* cone has three dips of ice cream.] **2** three times as much or as many ◆*n.* ☆a hit in baseball on which the batter gets to third base ◆*v.* to make or become three times as much or as many —**tri′pled, tri′pling**

trip·li·cate (trip′lə kət) *adj.* made in three copies exactly alike [a *triplicate* receipt]

tri·um·phant (trī um′fənt) *adj.* **1** having won victory or success; victorious [Our team was *triumphant.*] **2** happy or joyful over a victory [We could hear their *triumphant* laughter.] —**tri·um′phant·ly** *adv.*

☆**trol·ley** (trä′lē) *n.* **1** a device that sends electric current from a wire overhead to the motor of a streetcar, trolley bus, etc. **2** an electric streetcar: *also* **trolley car** —*pl.* **trol′leys**

trou·sers (trou′zərz) *pl. n.* an outer garment with two legs, especially for men and boys, reaching from the waist usually to the ankles; pants

Tru·man (trōō′mən) **Harry S.** 1884–1972; the 33d president of the United States, from 1945 to 1953

trust·wor·thy (trust′wur′thē) *adj.* deserving to be trusted; reliable —**trust′wor′thi·ness** *n.*

truth·ful (trōōth′fəl) *adj.* **1** telling the truth; honest [a *truthful* person] **2** that is the truth; accurate [to give a *truthful* report] —**truth′ful·ly** *adv.* —**truth′ful·ness** *n.*

tsp. *abbreviation for* **teaspoon** *or* **teaspoons**

tur·moil (tur′moil) *n.* a noisy or confused condition

☆**tux·e·do** (tuk sē′dō) *n.* **1** a man's jacket worn at formal dinners, dances, etc. It was often black, with satin lapels and no tails: now tuxedos have many patterns and colors **2** a suit with such a jacket, worn with a dark bow tie —*pl.* **tux·e′dos**

twitch (twich) *v.* to move or pull with a sudden jerk [A rabbit's nose *twitches* constantly.] ◆*n.* a sudden, quick motion or pull, often one that cannot be controlled [a *twitch* near one eye] —*pl.* **twitch′es**

ty·phoon (tī fōōn′) *n.* any violent tropical cyclone that starts in the western Pacific

typ·ist (tīp′ist) *n.* a person who uses a typewriter; especially, one whose work is typing

a	ask, fat
ā	ape, date
ä	car, lot
e	elf, ten
ē	even, meet
i	is, hit
ī	ice, fire
ō	open, go
ô	law, horn
oi	oil, point
㏇	look, pull
㏍	ooze, tool
ou	out, crowd
u	up, cut
u	fur, fern
ə	a in ago
	e in agent
	e in father
	i in unity
	o in collect
	u in focus
ch	chin, arch
ŋ	ring, singer
sh	she, dash
th	thin, truth
th	then, father
zh	s in pleasure

Uu

ul·tra·son·ic (ul′trə sän′ik) *adj.* describing or having to do with sounds too high for human beings to hear

ul·tra·vi·o·let (ul′trə vī′ə lət) *adj.* lying just beyond the violet end of the spectrum [*Ultraviolet* rays are invisible rays of light that help to form vitamin D in plants and animals and can kill certain germs.]

un- **1** *a prefix meaning* not *or* the opposite of [An *un*happy person is one who is not happy, but sad.] **2** *a prefix* meaning to reverse or undo the action of [To *un*tie a shoelace is to reverse the action of tying it.]

un·a·void·a·ble (unə void′ə bəl) *adj.* that cannot be avoided; inevitable [an *unavoidable* accident] —**un′a·void′a·bly** *adv.*

un·a·ware (un ə wer′) *adj.* not aware; not knowing or noticing [We were *unaware* of the danger in going there.]

un·be·liev·a·ble (unbə lēv′ə bəl) *adj.* that cannot be believed; astounding; incredible

un·con·di·tion·al (un′ kən dish′ən ′l) *adj.* not depending on any conditions; absolute [an *unconditional* guarantee] —**un′con·di′tion·al·ly** *adv.*

un·due (un dσο′ *or* un dyσο′) *adj.* more than is proper or right; too much [Don't give *undue* attention to your appearance.]

un·fair (un fer′) *adj.* not fair, just, or honest —**un·fair′ly** *adv.* —**un·fair′ness** *n.*

☆**u·ni·cy·cle** (yσο̄n′ə sī′kəl) *n.* a riding device that has only one wheel and pedals like a bicycle: it is used for trick riding, as in a circus

u·ni·form (yσο̄n′ə fôrm) *adj.* **1** always the same; never changing [Driving at a *uniform* speed saves gas.] **2** all alike; not different from one another [a row of *uniform* houses] ◆*n.* the special clothes worn by the members of a certain group [a nurse's *uniform*] —**u′ni·form′ly** *adv.*

un·i·lat·er·al (yσο̄n′ə lat′ər əl) *adj.* done by or involving only one of several nations, sides, or groups [a *unilateral* decision]

u·nique (yσο̄ nēk′) *adj.* **1** that is the only one; having nothing like it [Mercury is a *unique* metal in that it is liquid at ordinary temperatures.] **2** unusual; remarkable [It is a *unique* motion picture.]

u·ni·son (yσο̄n′ə sən) *n.* sameness of musical pitch, as of two or more voices or tones

u·ni·ver·sal (yσο̄n′ə vur′səl) *adj.* **1** of, for, or by all people; concerning everyone [a *universal* human need] **2** present everywhere [*universal* pollution of the air we breathe] —**u·ni·ver·sal·i·ty** (yσο̄′nə vər sal′ə tē) *n.*

u·ni·ver·si·ty (yσο̄n′ə vur′sə tē) *n.* a school of higher education, made up of a college or colleges and, usually, professional schools, as of law and medicine —*pl.* **u′ni·ver′si·ties**

un·matched (un machd′) *adj.* **1** not matching [These socks are *unmatched.*] **2** having no equal

un·paved (un pâvd′) *adj.* not paved; lacking a hard surface

u·su·al (yσο̄′zhσο əl) *adj.* such as is most often seen, heard, used, etc.; common; ordinary; normal —**u′su·al·ly** *adv.*

U·tah (yσο̄′tô *or* yσο̄′tä) a state in the southwestern part of the U.S.: abbreviated **Ut., UT**

Vv

veil (vāl) *n.* a piece of thin cloth, as net or gauze, worn especially by women over the face or head to hide the features, as a decoration, or as part of a uniform [a bride's *veil*; a nun's *veil*] ◆*v.* to cover, hide, etc. with or as if with a veil

ver·sion (vur′zhən) *n.* **1** something translated from the original language [an English *version* of the Bible] **2** a report or description from one person's point of view [Give us your *version* of the accident.] **3** a particular form of something [an abridged *version* of a novel; the movie *version* of a play]

ver·ti·cal (vur′ti kəl) *adj.* straight up and down; perpendicular to a horizontal line [The walls of a house are *vertical.*] ◆*n.* a vertical line, plane, etc. —**ver′ti·cal·ly** *adv.*

vi·bra·tion (vī brā′shən) *n.* rapid motion back and forth; quivering [The *vibration* of the motor shook the bolts loose.] —**vi·bra·to·ry** (vī′brə tôr′ē) *adj.*

vid·e·o (vid′ē ō′) *adj.* **1** having to do with television **2** having to do with the picture portion of a television broadcast **3** having to do with the display of data or graphics on a computer screen ◆*n.* **1** *the same as* **television** **2** *a short form of* **videocassette** **3** *a short form of* **videotape** **4** a program recorded on film or videotape for viewing on television or with a videocassette recorder

vid·e·o·tape (vid′ē ō tāp′) *n.* a thin magnetic tape on which both the sound and picture signals of a TV program can be recorded by electronics

vir·tu·ous (vʉr′chooͮwəs *or* vʉr′chyoōͮəs) *adj.* having virtue; good, moral, chaste, etc. —**vir′tu·ous·ly** *adv.*

vi·sion (vizh′ən) *n.* **1** the act or power of seeing; sight [She wears glasses to improve her *vision.*] **2** something seen in the mind, or in a dream, trance, etc. [“while *visions* of sugarplums danced in their heads”]

vis·u·al (vizh′ooͮwəl) *adj.* **1** having to do with sight or used in seeing [*visual* aids] **2** that can be seen; visible [*visual* proof] —**vis′u·al·ly** *adv.*

void (void) *adj.* **1** having nothing in it; empty; vacant [A vacuum is a *void* space.] **2** being without; lacking [a heart *void* of kindness] ►*n.* **1** an empty space **2** a feeling of loss or emptiness [His death left a great *void* in our hearts.]

vol. *abbreviation for* **volume** —*pl.* **vols.**

voy·age (voi′ij) *n.* **1** a journey by water [an ocean *voyage*] **2** a journey through the air or through outer space [a *voyage* by rocket] ►*v.* to make a voyage —**voy′aged, voy′ag·ing** —**voy′ag·er** *n.*

vs. *abbreviation for* **versus**

wait· (wāt) *v.* **1** to stay in a place or do nothing while expecting a certain thing to happen [*Wait* for the signal. I *waited* until six o'clock, but they never arrived.] **2** to remain undone for a time [Let it *wait* until next week.] **3** to serve food at a meal [He *waits* on tables. She *waits* on me.] ►*n.* the act or time of waiting [We had an hour's *wait* for the train.]

wan·der (wän′dər) *v.* **1** to go from place to place in an aimless way; ramble; roam [to *wander* about a city] **2** to go astray; drift [The ship *wandered* off course. The speaker *wandered* from the subject.] —**wan′der·er** *n.*

wash·a·ble (wôsh′ə bəl *or* wäsh′ə bəl) *adj.* that can be washed without being damaged

Washington (wôsh′iɳ tən *or* wäsh′iɳ tən), **George** (jorj) 1732–1799; first president of the United States, from 1789 to 1797: he was commander in chief of the American army in the Revolutionary War

wa·ter·way (wôt′ər wā) *n.* **1** a channel through which water runs **2** any body of water on which boats or ships can travel, as a canal or river

weath·er (weth′ər) *n.* the conditions outside at any particular time with regard to temperature, sunshine, rainfall, etc. [We have good *weather* today for a picnic.]

weight (wāt) *v.* **1** heaviness; the quality a thing has because of the pull of gravity on it **2** amount of heaviness [What is your *weight*?] **3** a piece of metal used in weighing [Put a two-ounce *weight* on the balance.] **4** any solid mass used for its heaviness [to lift *weights* for exercise; a paper *weight*]

weird (wird) *adj.* **1** strange or mysterious in a ghostly way [*Weird* sounds came from the cave.] **2** very odd, strange, etc. [What a *weird* hat! What *weird* behavior!] —**weird′ly** *adv.* —**weird′ness** *n.*

wel·fare (wel′fer) *n.* **1** health, happiness, and so on; well-being **2** aid by government agencies for the poor or those out of work

wheth·er (hweth′ər *or* weth′ər) *conj.* **1** if it is true or likely that [I don't know *whether* I can go.] **2** in either case that [It makes no difference *whether* he comes or not.]

whis·tle (hwis′l *or* wis′əl) *v.* **1** to make a high, shrill sound as by forcing breath through puckered lips or by sending steam through a small opening **2** to produce by whistling [to *whistle* a tune] —**whis′tled, whis′tling** ►*n.* **1** a device for making whistling sounds **2** the act or sound of whistling —**whis′tler**

with·draw·al (with drô′əl *or* with drô′əl) *n.* the act or fact of withdrawing, as money from the bank

wit·ness (wit′nəs) *n.* **1** a person who saw, or can give a firsthand account of, something that happened [A *witness* told the police how the fire started.] **2** a person who gives evidence in a law court ►*v.* to be present at; see [to *witness* a sports event]

woe·ful (wō′fəl) *adj.* full of woe; mournful; sad

wrath (rath) *n.* great anger; rage; fury

wreck·age (rek′ij) *n.* **1** the act of wrecking **2** the condition of being wrecked **3** the remains of something that has been wrecked

wrench (rench) *n.* **1** a sudden, sharp twist or pull [With one *wrench*, he loosened the lid.] **2** a tool for holding and turning nuts, bolts, or pipes ►*v.* to twist or pull sharply [She *wrenched* the keys from my grasp.]

wres·tle (res′əl) *v.* to struggle with, trying to throw or force to the ground without striking blows with the fists —**wres′tled, wres′tling** ►*n.* **1** the action or a bout of wrestling **2** a struggle or contest —**wres′tler**

wring (riɳ) *v.* **1** to squeeze and twist with force [to *wring* out the wet clothes] —**wrung, wring′ing**

wrist·watch (rist′wäch *or* rist′wôch) *n.* a watch worn on a strap or band that fits around the wrist

a	ask, fat
ā	ape, date
ä	car, lot
e	elf, ten
ē	even, meet
i	is, hit
ī	ice, fire
ō	open, go
ô	law, horn
oi	oil, point
oo	look, pull
ōō	ooze, tool
ou	out, crowd
u	up, cut
ʉ	fur, fern
ə	a in ago
	e in agent
	e in father
	i in unity
	o in collect
	u in focus
ch	chin, arch
ŋ	ring, singer
sh	she, dash
th	thin, truth
th	then, father
zh	s in pleasure

xy·lo·phone (zī'lə fōn) *n.* a musical instrument made up of a row of wooden bars of different sizes, that are struck with wooden hammers

yearn (yʉrn) *v.* to be filled with longing or desire [to *yearn* for fame]
yel·low (yel'ō) *adj.* having the color of ripe lemons, or of an egg yolk —**yel'low·ish**
◆*n.* a yellow color ◆*v.* to make or become yellow [linens *yellowed* with age]

yield (yēld) *v.* **1** to give up; surrender [to *yield* to a demand; to *yield* a city] **2** to give or grant [to *yield* the right of way; to *yield* a point] **3** to give way [The gate would not *yield* to our pushing.] **4** to bring forth or bring about; produce; give [The orchard *yielded* a good crop. The business *yielded* high profits.] ◆*n.* the amount yielded or produced

zo·ol·o·gy (zō äl'ə jē) *n.* the science that studies animals and animal life

Level F Student Record Chart

Name _____

			Pretest	Final Test
Lesson	1	Words with the Sound of **k**, **kw**, and **n**		
Lesson	2	Hard and Soft **c** and **g**; **dge**		
Lesson	3	Words with the Sound of **f**		
Lesson	4	Words with the Sound of **s**, **z**, and **zh**		
Lesson	5	Words with the Sound of **sh**		
Lesson	6	Lessons 1–5 • Review	███████	
Lesson	7	Words with **sc**		
Lesson	8	Words with **gn**, **wr**, and **tch**		
Lesson	9	Silent Consonants		
Lesson	10	Words with **ear**, **are**, and **air**		
Lesson	11	Words with the Sound of Long **e**		
Lesson	12	Lessons 7–11 • Review	███████	
Lesson	13	Words with the Sound of Long **o**		
Lesson	14	Vowel Digraphs **ei** and **ie** and Vowel Pair **ei**		
Lesson	15	Vowel Digraphs **au** and **aw**		
Lesson	16	Words with **oo**, **ew**, **ue**, and **ui**		
Lesson	17	Words with **ai**, **ay**, **oi**, and **oy**		
Lesson	18	Lessons 13–17 • Review	███████	
Lesson	19	Words with Diphthongs **ou** and **ow**		
Lesson	20	Prefixes **ir**, **in**, **il**, and **im**		
Lesson	21	Prefixes **de**, **pre**, **pro**, **con**, **com**, and **mis**		
Lesson	22	Prefixes **em**, **en**, **fore**, **post**, and **over**		
Lesson	23	Prefixes **anti**, **counter**, **super**, **sub**, **ultra**, **trans**, and **semi**		
Lesson	24	Lessons 19–23 • Review	███████	
Lesson	25	Prefixes **uni**, **mono**, **bi**, **tri**, and **mid**		
Lesson	26	Suffixes **or**, **er**, **ist**, **logy**, and **ology**		
Lesson	27	Suffixes **er**, **est**, and **ness**		
Lesson	28	Suffixes **able**, **ible**, **ful**, **hood**, **ship**, and **ment**		
Lesson	29	Suffixes **ion**, **ation**, **ition**, **ance**, **ence**, **ive**, and **ity**		
Lesson	30	Lessons 25–29 • Review	███████	
Lesson	31	Doubling Final Consonants; Adding Suffixes and Endings to Words Ending in **e**		
Lesson	32	Adding Suffixes and Endings to Words Ending in **y**		
Lesson	33	Plurals		
Lesson	34	Homonyms and Challenging Words		
Lesson	35	Abbreviations		
Lesson	36	Lessons 31–35 • Review	███████	

Lesson	6	12	18	24	30	36
Standardized Review Test						

Review Test
Answer Key

Lesson 6

1. b	11. c	21. d
2. c	12. b	22. b
3. a	13. a	23. d
4. c	14. c	24. c
5. d	15. b	25. c
6. b	16. a	
7. b	17. c	
8. a	18. a	
9. c	19. d	
10. d	20. a	

Lesson 12

1. a	11. c	21. b
2. d	12. c	22. c
3. b	13. d	23. a
4. a	14. a	24. d
5. b	15. d	25. a
6. c	16. a	
7. d	17. b	
8. c	18. a	
9. a	19. d	
10. c	20. a	

Lesson 18

1. d	11. a
2. b	12. a
3. c	13. d
4. c	14. d
5. a	15. c
6. b	
7. b	
8. a	
9. b	
10. d	

Lesson 24

1. d	11. a	21. a
2. c	12. c	22. b
3. a	13. d	23. d
4. a	14. b	24. a
5. b	15. b	25. b
6. c	16. d	
7. b	17. c	
8. d	18. a	
9. b	19. a	
10. d	20. c	

Lesson 30

1. a	11. b	21. a
2. c	12. a	22. b
3. a	13. d	23. b
4. b	14. d	24. d
5. c	15. a	25. a
6. d	16. c	
7. c	17. c	
8. d	18. a	
9. a	19. b	
10. d	20. c	

Lesson 36

1. b	11. c
2. b	12. a
3. d	13. b
4. b	14. c
5. c	15. d
6. c	
7. d	
8. d	
9. d	
10. b	

List Words

List Words

Word	Lesson	Word	Lesson	Word	Lesson	Word	Lesson
encourage	22	gloomy	16	investigator	26	mistletoe	13
endanger	22	gnarled	8	irrational	20	misunderstood	21
endow	19	govt.	35	irregular	20	modified	32
engaged	2	graduated	31	irresponsible	20	moisten	9
engrave	22	greasy	11	jackknives	33	monorail	25
enlighten	22	growth	13	jellies	32	monosyllable	25
enlistment	22	guarantee	11	jeweler	26	monotonous	25
enrollment	28	guesses	2	journalist	26	mosquitoes	33
equipped	31	guilty	16	juicy	16	mouthful	19
escalator	26	guitar	16	juror	26	muddiest	27
escape	7	gymnasium	4	kangaroos	33	muscles	7
Eskimos	33	handkerchiefs	33	keyboard	1	mythology	26
essays	17	happiness	27	kitchen	8	negotiate	5
esteem	11	hatchet	8	knelt	1	neighborly	14
evaporated	31	headache	1	knickers	9	nieces	11
ex.	35	healthier	27	knowledge	1	no.	35
excellence	29	height	14	language	2	noisiest	27
except	34	hemisphere	3	laughable	3	noticeable	28
exciting	31	hesitation	31	launched	15	nourish	5
exhausted	15	household	19	laundry	15	nuisance	16
existence	29	husband	4	lb.	35	oboe	13
experience	29	hymns	9	leisurely	4	occupied	32
explanation	29	hyphenate	3	lightning	9	occurred	31
exploit	17	icicles	2	likable	28	officer	3
exploration	5	identified	32	listening	9	official	5
extreme	11	illegal	20	locksmith	1	ointment	17
eyesight	9	illegible	20	lounge	19	organizing	31
facial	5	illiterate	20	luscious	7	outrageous	19
faithful	17	illogical	20	machinery	5	overdue	22
fallow	13	immaterial	20	machinist	26	overflow	22
fanciful	28	immature	20	magical	2	overprotect	22
fascinating	7	immigrant	20	magnificent	3	overweight	22
fasten	9	immortal	20	magnified	32	oysters	17
fetched	8	impolitely	20	maintenance	17	oz.	35
fiercely	14	impractical	20	manageable	28	pamphlet	3
fifteen	3	improperly	20	manufacturer	26	parachute	5
firmest	27	inc.	35	mayonnaise	17	parenthood	28
florist	26	incapable	20	mdse.	35	partial	5
foreground	22	incredible	20	measuring	4	passive	29
foreigner	8	indefinite	20	medicine	2	patience	34
foreknowledge	22	indirect	20	mementos	33	patients	34
foresight	22	industries	32	memorized	31	patios	33
forewarning	22	information	5	mgr.	35	paused	15
foundation	19	instructor	4	midsummer	25	perceived	14
fragrant	3	instruments	4	midwestern	25	personal	34
fruitful	16	insulator	26	mildew	16	personnel	34
galaxies	32	insure	5	millionaire	10	pewter	16
gears	10	intelligent	2	miscellaneous	7	photographed	3
genuine	2	intolerant	20	mischief	14	phrase	3
geologist	26	invention	5	mispronounced	21	physician	3

155

List Words

Word	Lesson	Word	Lesson	Word	Lesson	Word	Lesson
pierced	14	reigned	8	social	5	transferred	23
pkg.	35	reindeer	14	softener	9	transformer	26
playwright	9	rejoicing	17	solemn	9	transistor	23
pledges	2	relieved	14	soothing	16	transparent	23
plumber	9	remainder	17	spaghetti	33	treasury	4
ponchos	33	remarkable	1	species	33	triangular	25
portrayed	32	remedies	32	spectator	26	tricolor	25
position	4	repeated	11	sportsmanship	28	trilogy	25
postscript	22	required	1	squares	10	tripled	25
postwar	22	research	10	squawking	15	triplicate	25
potential	5	resemble	4	squeezed	11	triumphant	3
poultry	13	resigned	8	stairway	10	trolley	11
praised	17	resistance	29	steadily	32	trousers	4
precautions	15	resounding	19	stereos	33	turmoil	17
predicted	21	retrieve	14	stiffness	27	tuxedos	33
prefer	3	revealed	11	stowaway	13	typist	26
pres.	35	reversible	28	strainer	17	ultraviolet	23
prescription	21	rodeos	33	stretches	8	unavoidable	28
presume	21	rowboat	13	strictest	27	unaware	10
prevented	21	saucepan	15	subj.	35	unbelievable	14
previous	21	saxophone	3	submarine	23	unfairly	10
principal	34	scalding	7	subscription	23	unicycle	25
principle	34	scampered	7	substitution	23	uniform	25
proceed	11	scattered	7	succeeded	11	unique	1
processed	2	scenery	7	successful	28	unison	25
produced	31	scenic	7	sufficient	3	universal	25
progress	21	scented	7	suitable	16	university	25
projector	26	schedule	1	superficial	23	unmatched	8
promptness	27	scholarship	28	supersonic	23	unpaved	31
pronoun	19	scientific	7	supervise	23	usually	4
pronounced	19	scissors	7	surrounding	19	veil	14
propelling	21	scratched	8	surveying	32	version	4
protein	14	screaming	7	tariffs	33	visual	4
provision	21	sculpture	7	taught	15	vol.	35
pt.	35	sealing	34	technical	1	vs.	35
purpose	4	searching	10	technique	1	wait	34
pursued	16	seasonal	4	technology	26	waterways	32
qt.	35	seized	14	theories	32	weather	34
qualify	1	semicircle	23	thesaurus	15	weight	34
quantity	1	semicolon	23	thickest	27	weird	14
questionnaire	10	semifinal	23	thieves	33	whether	34
quilted	16	shampoo	16	thirstily	32	whistling	9
quotation	29	sharpness	27	thoroughly	13	withdrawal	15
quotient	5	shoulders	13	threw	34	wrath	8
realized	31	silverware	10	through	34	wreckage	8
reasonable	11	simplest	27	tighter	27	wrestling	8
recipe	2	sketching	8	tinier	27	wristwatch	8
referred	31	sleigh	14	tiptoed	13	yellow	13
refrigerator	2	sloppily	32	tombstone	9	yields	14
rehearsal	10	smoother	16	toughen	3		

Bonus Words

Word	Lesson
admitted	31
affection	3
ailment	28
antisocial	23
approach	13
ascend	7
attain	17
auction	15
bail	17
bifocals	25
bitterness	27
bleak	11
blvd.	35
borough	13
capacity	2
capitol	34
cauliflower	19
chagrin	5
challenged	31
chute	34
clause	15
coarsest	27
commotion	21
concessionaire	10
confetti	33
conscious	7
conveyed	32
corps	9
correspondence	29
counsel	19
counselor	26
counterbalance	23
debrief	14
decline	21
dictionaries	32
diffuse	4
digestible	28
eastward	11

Word	Lesson
empower	22
encompass	22
ensure	5
etc.	35
fellowship	28
fender	3
fidget	2
filthier	27
flourish	5
foliage	2
folly	11
foreclosure	4
foremost	22
founder	19
freight	14
gallery	2
gawk	15
gentler	27
glorified	32
gnomes	8
gracious	5
greedily	32
heroes	33
hwy.	35
hypnotist	26
illuminate	20
impair	10
imperfect	20
imprint	20
inability	20
inflatable	28
inspection	29
intrusion	4
irrelevant	20
jockey	32
kindling	1
knothole	1
knuckles	9

Word	Lesson
law-abiding	15
lecturer	26
legislation	29
livelihood	28
mainstay	17
martial	34
masterpiece	14
mechanic	1
mellow	13
midpoint	25
miscalculate	21
mischievous	14
mo.	35
monogram	25
monsoon	16
nausea	15
numb	9
originality	29
orphanage	3
overemotional	22
overgrown	13
overjoyed	17
oversensitive	22
painfulness	27
patrolling	31
phenomenon	3
plaque	1
precede	11
prelude	21
profound	19
provoke	21
quiz	1
radiance	29
receipt	14
recently	2
recruit	16
regulation	5
reign	34

Word	Lesson
relating	31
releases	4
resolve	4
roughen	3
scheme	7
scour	7
scowl	19
scrimp	7
semiprecious	23
sheaves	33
siege	11
smeared	10
soprano	33
stationary	34
steward	16
stitched	8
subcontract	23
theology	26
thistle	9
throughout	9
tolerated	31
transaction	23
trilingual	25
tsp.	35
twitch	8
typhoon	16
undue	16
unilateral	25
videos	33
void	17
welfare	10
woeful	13
wrench	8
wring	8
yearn	10
zoology	26

Spelling Enrichment

Bulletin Board Suggestion

Overcome the Hurdles Make large frame-like race barriers out of colored poster board and display them on a bulletin board. On separate strips of tagboard, write commonly misspelled words such as "receive" or "beautiful." Arrange these words on the bulletin board. Change the words periodically with other words students are finding difficult to spell. These words could come from other subject areas, such as science and social studies.

Encourage students to work with partners to test each other on these challenging spelling words. Extra credit might be given for these words when they are included at the end of regular tests.

Group Practice

Fill-In Write spelling words on the board. Omit some of the letters and replace them with dashes. Have the first student in Row One come to the board to fill in one of the missing letters in any of the words. Then, have the first student in Row Two continue the procedure. Continue having students in each row take turns coming up to the board to fill in letters until all the words are completed. Any student who is able to correctly fill in a word earns a point for his or her row. The row with the most points at the end of the game wins.

Erase Write list words on the board. Then, ask the class to put their heads down while you call on a student to come to the board and erase one of the words. This student then calls on a class member to identify the erased word. The identified word is then restored and the student who correctly identified the erasure can be the person who erases next.

Crossword Relay First draw a large grid on the board. Then, divide the class into several teams. Teams compete against each other to form separate crossword puzzles on the board. Individuals on each team take turns racing against members of the other teams to join list words until all possibilities have been exhausted. A list word may appear on each crossword puzzle only once. The winning team is the team whose crossword puzzle contains the greatest number of correctly spelled list words or the team who finishes first.

Scramble Prepare letter cards sufficient to spell all the list words. Distribute letter cards to all students. Some students may be given more than one letter card. The teacher then calls out a list word. Students holding the letters contained in the word race to the front of the class to form the word by standing in the appropriate sequence with their letter cards.

Proofreading Relay Write two columns of misspelled list words on the board. Although the errors can differ, be sure that each list has the same number of errors. Divide the class into two teams and assign each team to a different column. Teams then compete against each other to correct their assigned lists by team members taking turns erasing and replacing an appropriate letter. Each member may correct only one letter per turn. The team that corrects its entire word list first wins.

Detective Call on a student to be a detective. The detective must choose a spelling word from the list and think of a structural clue, definition, or synonym that will help classmates identify it. The detective then states the clue using the format, "I spy a word that…" Students are called on to guess and spell the mystery word. Whoever answers correctly gets to take a turn being the detective.

Spelling Tic-Tac-Toe Draw a tic-tac-toe square on the board. Divide the class into X and O teams. Take turns dictating spelling words to members of each team. If the word is spelled correctly, allow the team member to place an X or O on the square. The first team to place three X's or O's in a row wins.

Words of Fortune Have students put their heads down while you write a spelling word on the board in large letters. Then, cover each letter with a sheet of sturdy paper. The paper can be fastened to the board with magnets. Call on a student to guess any letter of the alphabet they think may be hidden. If that particular letter is hidden, then reveal the letter in every place where it appears in the word by removing the paper.

The student continues to guess letters until an incorrect guess is made or the word is revealed. In the event that an incorrect guess is made, a different student continues the game. Continue the game until every list word has been hidden and then revealed.

Dictionary Activities

Around the World Designate the first person in the first row to be the traveler. The traveler must stand next to the student seated behind him or her. Then, dictate any letter of the alphabet at random. Instruct the two

Spelling Enrichment

students to quickly name the letter of the alphabet that precedes the given letter. The student who is first to respond with the correct answer becomes the traveler while the other student sits at that desk. The traveler then moves to compete with the next person in the row. The game continues with the traveler moving up and down the rows as the teacher dictates various alphabet letters. See who can be the traveler who has moved the farthest around the classroom. For variety, you may want to require students to state the letter that follows the given letter. You may also want to dictate pairs of list words and have students name which word comes first.

Stand-Up While the teacher pronounces a word from the spelling dictionary, students look up the entry word and point to it. Tell students to stand up when they have located the entry. See who is the first student to stand up.

This game can be played using the following variations:

1. Have students stand when they have located the guide words for a given word.

2. Have students stand when they are able to tell on what page a given list word appears in the dictionary.

Guide Word Scramble Prepare tagboard cards with spelling words written on them in large letters. Distribute the cards to students. Call on two students to come to the front of the room to serve as guide words. Then, call one student at a time to hold their word card either in front of, in between, or behind the guide words so that the three words are in alphabetical order. You may want to vary the guide words occasionally.

Cut-Off Distribute a strip of paper to each student. Instruct students to write any four spelling words on the strip. All but one of the words should be in alphabetical order. Then, have students exchange their strip with a partner. Students use scissors to cut off the word that is not in alphabetical sequence and tape the remaining word strips together. If students find this activity too difficult, you might have them cut all four words off the strip and arrange them alphabetically on their desks.

Applied Spelling

Journal Allow time each day for students to write in a journal. A spiral bound notebook can be used for this purpose. Encourage students to express their feelings about events that are happening in their lives at home or at school. Or they could write about what their plans are for the day. To get them started, you may have to provide starter phrases. Allow them to use "invented" spelling for words they can't spell.

Collect the journals periodically to write comments that echo what the student has written. For example, a student's entry might read, "I'm hape I gt to plae bazball todae." The teacher's response could be "Baseball is my favorite game, too. I'd be happy to watch you play baseball today at recess." This method allows students to learn correct spelling and sentence structure without emphasizing their errors in a negative way.

Letter to the Teacher On a regular basis, invite students to write a note to you. At first you may have to suggest topics or provide a starter sentence. It may be possible to suggest a topic that includes words from the spelling list. Write a response at the bottom of each letter that provides the student with a model of any spelling or sentence structure that apparently needs improvement.

Daily Edit Each day, provide a brief writing sample on the board that contains errors in spelling, capitalization, or punctuation. Have students rewrite the sample correctly. Provide time later in the day to have the class correct the errors on the board. Discuss why the spelling is as it is while students self-correct their work.

Acrostic Poems Have students write a word from the spelling list vertically. Then, instruct them to join a word horizontally to each letter of the list word. The horizontal words must begin with the letters in the list word. They also should be words that describe or relate feelings about the list word. Encourage students to refer to a dictionary for help in finding appropriate words. Here is a sample acrostic poem:

Zebras
Otters
Ostriches

Words-in-a-Row Distribute strips of writing paper to each student. Ask students to write three spelling words in a row. Tell them to misspell two of the words. Then, have students take turns writing their row of words on the board. They can call on a classmate to identify and underline the correctly spelled word in the row. Continue until all students have had a chance to write their row of words.

Spelling Enrichment

Partner Spelling Assign spelling buddies. Allow partners to alternate dictating or writing sentences that contain words from the spelling list. The sentences can be provided by the teacher or generated by students. Have students check their own work as their partner provides the correct spelling for each sentence.

Scrap Words Provide each student with several sheets of tagboard, scraps of fabric or wallpaper, and some glue. Ask students to cut letters out of the scrap materials and glue them to the tagboard to form words from the spelling list. Display the colorful scrap words around the classroom.

Punch Words Set up a work center in the classroom with a supply of construction paper strips, a hole puncher, sheets of thin paper, and crayons. Demonstrate to students how the hole puncher can be used to create spelling words out of the construction paper. Permit students to take turns working at the center in their free time. Students may also enjoy placing a thin sheet of paper over the punch words and rubbing them with a crayon to make colorful word designs. You can then display their punch word and crayon creations.

Word Cut-Outs Distribute scissors, glue, a sheet of dark-colored construction paper, and a supply of old newspapers and magazines to the class. Have students look through the papers and magazines for list words. Tell them to cut out any list words they find and glue them on the sheet of construction paper. See who can find the most list words. This technique may also be used to have students construct sentences or cut out individual letters to form words.

Word Sorts Invite students to write each list word on a separate card. Then, ask them how many different ways the words can be organized (e.g., animate vs. inanimate, past-tense or vowel patterns, similarity or contrast in meaning). As students sort the words into each category, have them put words that don't belong in a category into an exception pile.

160

Spelling Notebook

Spelling Notebook

Definitions and Rules

The alphabet has two kinds of letters—**vowels** and **consonants**. The vowels are a, e, i, o, and u (and sometimes y). All the rest of the letters are consonants.

Each **syllable** in a word must have a vowel sound. If a word or syllable has only one vowel and it comes at the beginning or between two consonants, the vowel usually stands for a short-vowel sound.

> cat   sit   cup

A **long-vowel** sound usually has the same sound as its letter name.

When y comes at the end of a word with one syllable, the y at the end usually has the sound of long i, as in *dry* and *try*. When y comes at the end of a word with more than one syllable, it usually has the sound of long e, as in *city* and *funny*.

When two or more **consonants** come together in a word, their sounds may blend together. In a **consonant blend**, you can hear the sound of each letter.

> smile   slide   friend

A **consonant digraph** consists of two consonants that go together to make one sound.

> sharp   fourth   each

A **consonant cluster** is three consonants together in one syllable.

> thrills   patch   splash

A **vowel pair** consists of two vowels together where the first vowel stands for the long sound and the second vowel is silent.

> teacher   fail   soak

A **vowel digraph** consists of two vowels that together make a long-vowel sound, a short-vowel sound or a special sound of their own.

> bread   sooner   auto

A **diphthong** consists of two vowels that blend together to make one sound.

> boy   oil   cloud

A **base word** is a word to which a prefix or suffix may be added to change its meaning.

> unlawful   replace   shyness

A **root** is a word part to which a prefix or suffix may be added to change its meaning.

> induction   repel   conduct

An **ending** is a letter or group of letters added to the end of a base word to make the word singular or plural or to tell when an action happened.

> hats   foxes   runs   rained   helping

A **prefix** is a word part that is added to the beginning of a base word or a root. A prefix changes the meaning of the base word.

> unhappy   distrust   repel   conduct

A **suffix** is a word part that is added to the end of a base word or root to make a new word.

> cheerful   agreeable   diction   portable

When you write words in **alphabetical order**, use these rules:

1. If the *first letter* of two words is the same, use the second letter.
2. If the *first two letters* are the same, use the third letter.

There are two **guide words** at the top of each page in the dictionary. The word on the left tells you the first word on the page. The word on the right tells you the last word on the page. All the words in between are in alphabetical order.

The dictionary puts an **accent mark** (') *after* the syllable with the strong sound.

> pur'sən

There is a vowel sound that can be spelled by any of the vowels. It is often found in a syllable that is not accented, or stressed, in a word. This vowel sound has the sound-symbol /ə/. It is called the **schwa**.

The word *I* is always a **capital** letter.

A **contraction** is a short way of writing two words. It is formed by writing two words together and leaving out one or more letters. Use an **apostrophe** (') to show where something is left out.

> it is = it's   we will = we'll

A **compound word** is a word made by joining two or more words.

> cannot   anyway   maybe